"I've Seen It All!"

"I've Seen It All!"

LIVES OF OLDER PERSONS
WITH MENTAL RETARDATION
IN THE COMMUNITY

edited by

Robert B. Edgerton, Ph.D.   *Marcia A. Gaston, M.A.*
Associate Director   *Staff Research Associate*

Mental Retardation Research Center
University of California at Los Angeles

·P·A·U·L·H·
BROOKES
PUBLISHING CO

Baltimore • London • Toronto • Sydney

Paul H. Brookes Publishing Co.
P.O. Box 10624
Baltimore, Maryland 21285-0624

Typeset by Brushwood Graphics, Inc., Baltimore, Maryland.
Manufactured in the United States of America by
The Maple Press Company, York, Pennsylvania.

Library of Congress Cataloging-in-Publication Data
"I've seen it all!" : Lives of older persons with mental
    retardation in the community /   edited by Robert B.
Edgerton, Marcia A. Gaston.
        p.   cm.
    Includes bibliographical references and index.
    ISBN 1-55766-062-X :
    1. Mentally handicapped aged—United States—Case
studies. I. Edgerton, Robert B., 1931–   . II. Gaston,
Marcia A.
HV3006.A4I93   1990
362.3'084'6–dc20   90-2093
                                                                        CIP

Contents

About the Editors

Robert B. Edgerton, Ph.D., is Professor of Anthropology in the Departments of Anthropology and Psychiatry and Biobehavioral Sciences at UCLA. His research with people with mild mental retardation began in 1959. Since that time, his interests in this phenomenon have diversified, but his central concern continues to be the ethnographic study of people with mental retardation over the full range of their activities and the entire span of their lives.

Marcia A. Gaston, M.A., Staff Research Associate, has been part of the Socio-Behavioral Group in the Mental Retardation Research Center at UCLA for more than seven years, four of which she spent in field research for the project on which this book is based. She is currently involved in doing ethnographic research for, as well as helping to coordinate, the new phase of the Socio-Behavioral Group's ongoing research concerning the adaptation of older people with mental retardation in the community.

Also contributing to this volume:

Dana M. Baldwin, Ph.D., is currently a consultant for the Rand Corporation in Santa Monica, CA, on a project studying the course of homelessness. In addition to her ethnographic research on the people with developmental disabilities written about here while she was a Staff Research Associate for the Socio-Behavioral Group in the Mental Retardation Research Center, UCLA, she has worked on several research projects involving people with mental illness over the last 7 years, including her dissertation research on a community-based day treatment program serving individuals with long-term mental illnesses and her ethnographic work for the UCLA project, The Adaptation of the Homeless Mentally Ill.

Hilarie Kelly, M.A., is a doctoral candidate in the Department of Anthropology at UCLA. She has done over 4 years of field research in East Africa on topics that include gender differences, socialization, and local approaches to caring for people with developmental disabilities. She has worked for the last 5 years as a Staff Research Associate for the Socio-Behavioral Group in the Mental Retardation Research Center, UCLA, on the project written about here.

T. W. Ward, Ph.D., is a Staff Research Associate at UCLA who splits his time between The Community Adaptation of Mildly Retarded Persons project for the Socio-Behavioral Group in the Mental Retardation Research Center, UCLA, and The Adaptation of the Homeless Mentally Ill project under the auspices of the Neuropsychiatric Institute, UCLA.

Preface

For most of this century, research on mental retardation has concentrated on children or, more recently, young adults. Until the last few years, older people with mental retardation have been very largely ignored. It is only during the last 5 years or so that serious scholarly attention has turned to aging people with mental retardation. Much of this work, especially by scholars such as Janicki, MacEachron, Krauss, and Seltzer, is of high quality, and it serves notice that, as research on the life span extends to people in their 50s, 60s, and 70s, many of our long-held stereotypes about the premature decline in social and cognitive functioning among older persons with mental retardation have to be revised. Like the rest of us, people with mental retardation grow older in a variety of ways, and many find the happiness and self-respect in later life that they missed when they were younger.

The new research on aging in the study of mental retardation takes many perspectives (Seltzer & Krauss, 1987[1]), and all are welcome additions to knowledge. But the field is still very new and more basic information about the lives of aging people with mental retardation is badly needed. With this need in mind, the chapters in this book were chosen to document something of the variety that exists in the lives of older persons with mental retardation. The nine older persons whose lives are described here have some experiences in common, but the most striking thing about them may be the differences in their lives. Two of the men and one of the women have successfully lived by their wits in urban slums that have brutalized or defeated many more intelligent and resourceful people. The majority of these people have received no services from the mental retardation service network, although they have all been helped by other people. Most have lived remarkably independent lives, and paradoxically, the most independent of these people is probably the least intelligent, while two of the most intelligent people (their IQs are near 80) receive services as mentally retarded people and lead highly dependent lives. Some of these people are almost triumphant about their lives, but others are sad, anxious, and depressed. Some of their lives have changed dramatically over the years, but others have remained remarkably the same. It is these differences and similarities that this book documents.

---

[1]Seltzer, M. M., & Krauss, M. W. (1987). *Aging and mental retardation: Extending the continuum.* (American Association on Mental Retardation, Monograph No. 9). Washington, DC: American Association on Mental Retardation.

The research reported here has been in process for many years. Although 3 of the people described here have only been studied for a little over 4 years, the others have been contacted on and off for over 25 years. Much is known about all of these people, but it is quite clear that we cannot fully anticipate how their lives will change as they grow still older. This book, then, should be thought of not as a set of finished portraits, but as a report of older persons whose lives are in process. It must also be stressed that these lives are not meant to be representative of the full range of aging people with mental retardation. The lives of more severely retarded, physically handicapped aging people who live in restricted settings such as nursing homes are not described in detail here.

In Part I, we describe of the lives of some men and women who were released from Lanterman State Hospital (then Pacific State Hospital[2]) over 30 years ago. Like more than 100 other former "patients" who were released at that same time, for a while they were on probation and their lives were supervised by social workers. When their work performances were judged satisfactory and their lives thought to be reasonably trouble-free, they were discharged to live independently, or "on the outs" as they put it. When 48 of these individuals were studied intensively as part of *The Cloak of Competence* study soon after they were discharged (Edgerton, 1967[3]), it was found that their adaptation to life in the community was hampered by the stigma they experienced as a consequence of their years of enforced hospitalization, by a lack of knowledge of appropriate behavior, and by the absence of support when trouble occurred because very few had any friends or relatives they could count on. Eventually, most managed to avoid returning to the hospital because they were successful in finding one or more persons—I then called them benefactors—who were willing to give them the support they needed.

As the years passed, their sense of stigma lessened and so did their reliance on benefactors as they developed confidence in their ability to cope with life on their own. Over time, the original sample of 48 dwindled as some moved out of Los Angeles and others died. When 16 of the remaining sample members (mean age 61; mean IQ 62) were described in 1988, it was found that they were remarkably satisfied with their lives (Edgerton, 1988[4]). For the most part, they earned their own living, made friends, enjoyed life, and looked forward to the next day and the next year. Seen from the outside, the quality of their lives did not appear to be any worse than that of other older, low-income, poorly educated people who lived in the same neighborhoods. They said that they were happy and satisfied with their lives; direct observation suggested that what they said was true, at least most of the time. Of course, they had some concerns about the future such as ill health, loss of income, or the death of a loved one, but it was rare for anyone to dwell on these matters. These people were capable of looking into the future

[2]Formerly known as Pacific Colony.
[3]Edgerton, R. B. (1967). *The cloak of competence: Stigma in the lives of the mentally retarded.* Berkeley: University of California Press.
[4]Edgerton, R. B. (1988). Aging in the community—A matter of choice. *American Journal of Mental Deficiency, 92*(4), 331–335.

with realistic fears, but they enjoyed their lives in the present and faced the future with confidence.

In Part I of this book we describe the lives of three men and three women from this *Cloak of Competence* sample. We have not selected "success stories"; instead, we have tried to represent something of the range of life circumstances among these people. We have included accounts of some relatively independent and happy people, but we have also described the lives of others who are not so independent or happy, including the most unhappy person in the entire sample (Martha, Chapter 6). The lives of these relatively independent people contrast markedly with those of persons of similar age and IQ who live in more restricted residential settings. Such people are typically less independent and normalized in dress, speech, work activities, and recreational interests. Their lives are more regimented and supervised, and the result is often learned helplessness.

In Part II of this book we try to document some of these responses to dependency, not by presenting extreme examples of dependent and helpless people, but by examining the lives of people who were formerly highly dependent and who are struggling late in life with demands for greater independence. All three of the people whose lives are presented here began to live relatively independently quite late in life, after the death of one or both parents. The two women we discuss here had lived with their families until they were in their 50s; they are now roommates. The man spent 60 years of his life in a large institution in the East; he now lives in a retirement hotel for senior citizens. These three persons continue to receive services as mentally retarded persons. All three have worked in a sheltered workshop for people with developmental disabilities. They differ from the people described in Part I not only in the circumstances of their past dependency, but also because each has some physical limitations, although these are not so serious as to preclude most work or recreational activities. They are also different because they still have some concerned relatives, and they have higher IQs than most of the persons described in Part I.

All of the authors of the chapters in this book are anthropologists. Their research spanned long periods, relied on unobtrusive observation and conversation, not tests or interviews. As described elsewhere (Edgerton & Langness, 1978[5]), research of this kind requires close rapport, and rapport requires reciprocity and intimacy. As anyone who has engaged in participant-observation knows, complete objectivity is chimerical. We care about the people we study and to a degree we become involved in their lives. We would not have it otherwise. However, when we prepare reports such as those in this book, we make every effort to achieve objectivity, and with the help of our colleagues who sometimes challenge our interpretations, we believe that our descriptions are as accurate as care and understanding can make them. We also believe that in order to convey the truth of these lives, it is necessary to write about them at some length. Without the context and detail that more extended portraits can provide, the tex-

---

[5]Edgerton, R. B., & Langness, L. L. (1978). Observing mentally retarded persons in community settings: An anthropological perspective. In G. Sackett (Ed.), *Observing behavior: Vol. I. Theory and applications in mental retardation* (pp. 335–348). Baltimore: University Park Press.

ture and meaning of these lives with their moments of triumph and torment, like their routines of tedium, are lost.

When research with the *Cloak of Competence* sample began in 1959, each of the 48 sample members was contacted approximately every 2 weeks, a pattern that has been maintained in the 4 major restudies that took place over the ensuing 30 years. During the periods between major restudies, we have kept in touch with sample members by occasional visits, telephone calls, and sometimes correspondence.

The detailed stories in this volume are intended to present an immediate and vivid introduction to the lives and capabilities of these older people with mental retardation. For this reason, the present tense is often used, although the present is, in reality, the time of research contact.

It is impossible to disguise the fact that this research was conducted in Los Angeles, but the names of all individuals, institutions, and organizations have been altered.[6]

Robert B. Edgerton, Ph.D.

---

[6]There are two exceptions to this policy. Mr. Theodore Barrett, mentioned in the conclusion, requested that his real name be used, and Pacific State Hospital was written about previously in *The Cloak of Competence* and other publications using the correct name for the period, thus that name is also used here.

Acknowledgments

We gratefully acknowledge support from the National Institute of Child Health and Human Development, Grant No. HD 04612 to the Mental Retardation Research Center, UCLA, and Grant No. HD 11944-02, The Community Adaptation of Mildly Retarded Persons, to the Socio-Behavioral Group, UCLA. We are also grateful for the support given by the Mental Retardation Research Center at UCLA.

We would also like to express our gratitude to the many colleagues who helped in the preparation of this manuscript. Our thanks go to Linda Andron and Steven Stumpf, who provided research assistance during fieldwork with Hilda, Elaine, and Sam. We also thank those who spent their valuable time reading and commenting on various drafts of the manuscript—Lew Langness, Keith Kernan, Sandy Kaufman, and especially Sharon Sabsay, who graciously provided detailed editorial comment for which we were most grateful. A special thanks goes to all of the former members of the Socio-Behavioral Group whose research assistance and fieldnotes were of great help in the preparation of the life histories included in Part I of this book.

We would like to say a special thanks to those who helped in the physical production of the manuscript—Dana Stulberg, for editorial assistance; Esther Rose, for help in manuscript preparation and meeting deadlines; and Beverly Custard and Bill Smith in Reproduction Services at the Neuropsychiatric Institute, UCLA, for their willing help in reproducing various drafts of the manuscript, sometimes at the last minute when deadlines were approaching.

We wish to thank all of the friends, parents, and relatives who participated in our research and who were helpful in so many ways, as well as the concerned professionals from places like "Upward," Regional Center, and "the shop"—Andrea Davis, Harry Torres, Beth Helms, Marva Collins, and Katherine Masterson, the nurse's aide who is so helpful and kind to Sam.

Finally, it was not possible to include in this book all of the people who shared their lives with us, but we would like to take this opportunity to express our sincere thanks to all of them. Most of all, our deepest gratitude goes to the people whose lives appear here—whose friendship, patience, and teaching has made our research and this book possible.

Part I

The six people who are profiled in Part I have been chosen to represent a variety of life circumstances from among the 16 sample members of the *Cloak of Competence* study with whom we still have contact. They have all shared some experiences, particularly early in life—institutionalization at Pacific State Hospital as teenagers or young adults, forced surgical sterilization as a prerequisite for release from the hospital, (a requirement that was widespread at that time), mandatory vocational placement in order to remain outside the hospital, and heavy reliance on benefactors (defined as "someone whose assistance is necessary and not reciprocated [Edgerton, 1989, p. 333]"[1]) for successful community adaptation. They are all aware, to at least some degree, whether they admit it freely or not, that they were labeled "mentally retarded," and although their methods vary, they have all developed ways of dealing with that label and its stigma within their lives.

Unlike the people in Part II of this book, whose lives are closely entwined with one another, the six people in Part I, with two exceptions, do not interact with one another. Hal and Midge Nellin Arnaud (Chapters 1 and 2) met and married after both were released on industrial leave from the hospital; however, they no longer are in contact with each other. Richard Jarrett (Chapter 5) was friendly with Roberto Reyes (Chapter 3) at Pacific State, and he knew Hal Arnaud superficially at the hospital and saw him occasionally through the years on the streets of their mutual neighborhood. In general, the lives of these six people diverged after they left Pacific State and are now representative of several distinct lifestyles.

Ironically, it may have been the divergence of lifestyles that caused Hal and Midge Nellin Arnaud to separate after 7 years of marriage. Hal worked long hard hours, which left him tired when he came home, and he was quite content with a quiet homebody existence in his hours off

---

[1]Edgerton, R. B. (1989). Aging in the community—A matter of choice. *American Journal on Mental Retardation*, *92*(4), 331–335.

from work. To this day, Hal sees himself as the classic American working man, who worked hard at the same job for 30 years and is now "retired." Midge, on the other hand, wanted adventure and excitement. By far the most independent of the three women in Part I, Midge went on to lead an interesting and somewhat nomadic life, changing living quarters, jobs, and men often.

Roberto Reyes, the only known homosexual in our sample, also led a nomadic existence when he was younger, going so far as to "ride the rails" cross-country. Roberto, who is Latino, also faced discrimination at times in his life because of his minority status. Abandoned by his natural mother and orphaned by his adopted mother, Roberto was informally adopted as a young adult by a surrogate mother, who added him to the extended "family" who lived in her boarding house. By doing so, she gave Roberto a place he could always call home.

Myrtle Sheffield (Chapter 4) has spent the majority of her life since leaving Pacific State as a married woman and housewife. Her first marriage, to a man with physical handicaps who was fully aware of the fact that she had been labeled mentally retarded, left her a widow. Myrtle's second husband, who is nonretarded, believes that she was institutionalized as an epileptic, and he does not know about the label of mental retardation.

Richard Jarrett, III, who is now deceased, had by far the most severe health problems of the six people in Part I. Like Hal Arnaud, Richard worked at the same job for a long time, 31 years. Unlike Hal, Richard was a union member, and he made a better living, retiring with a good pension. However, when his health began to deteriorate seriously, Richard was unable to cope with the changes necessary to prolong his life.

Martha McDowell, in the final chapter, was by far the most dependent of these six people when she began her life outside Pacific State Hospital. Martha has never married, and in fact, she is the only one of these six people who has never had a romantic or sexual relationship with anyone, nor has she shown any desire whatsoever to do so. Although she is a lonely person, she has, through the years, made a remarkable transformation to an independent life.

Although these six people have lived widely varied lives and there are many differences among them, there are still similarities among them as well. As they have aged, their concern with the stigma of institutionalization and being labeled mentally retarded has greatly decreased. What is more, the heavy reliance on benefactors has virtually disappeared, and in fact, all of these people, either informally or through volunteer work, have spent considerable time taking care of others. With the exception of Martha, all have had at least one meaningful and long-term sexual relationship, although none have had children due to their forced sterilization. And again with the exception of Martha, all have had friends as well. None of the six has ever had a driver's license, and all have had to depend on other drivers or public transportation. There is also, in common, a growing concern with health and medical care, both for themselves and for those close to them.

Both these similarities and differences are what we are interested in documenting here. In order to portray the adaptation that has allowed these six people to lead the independent lives they now enjoy and the difficulty with which these lives have been achieved, we have chosen to present both a brief life history and a more detailed sketch of each person's life circumstances.

1

"That Was a Long Time Ago."

HAL ARNAUD

by Marcia A. Gaston

For most of his adult life, Hal Arnaud has lived in what is commonly known as the MacArthur Park area of Los Angeles. This area, once an affluent residential neighborhood bordering downtown, has degenerated through the years into a run-down transitional area between downtown and skid row on the east and the progressively more affluent neighborhoods to the west. The neighborhood is a mixture of old apartment buildings, a few remaining examples of what were once large homes now mostly broken up into apartments, SRO hotels, restaurants, and small businesses, most of which cater to neighborhood trade. The population is predominantly Hispanic, with a high percentage of illegal aliens, particularly from El Salvador and other Central American countries. Interestingly, although the population is largely Hispanic, business ownership is heavily Asian, particularly Korean, and "Koreatown" immediately to the west seems to be expanding into this area. The remaining population comprises mostly black people and elderly people. The population density in this area is already quite high, and according to the environmental impact report prepared for the Los Angeles MetroRail system:

> In absolute terms, the highest population density'[in Los Angeles] in the year 2000 will be in Westlake [the section of this area bordering MacArthur Park on the east and south], with 35,870 persons per square mile.[1]

Personal income in this area is overwhelmingly at poverty level or below, and the area is riddled with drugs, prostitution, and violent crime.

[1]U.S. Department of Transportation—Urban Mass Transportation Administration & Southern California Rapid Transit District. (1983). *Los Angeles rail rapid transit project: Metro Rail.* (Environmental Impact Statement/Environmental Impact Report, Draft). Los Angeles: Author.

Entering MacArthur Park itself is considered dangerous even in the day-time by those who are most vulnerable to crime, such as women or elderly people. After dark, to go there is quite literally to risk one's life. Homeless people, spilling over from downtown and skid row, are highly visible in this area, although somewhat less so since the city passed an ordinance making it illegal to sleep on the street. The general perception within the neighborhood is that police from the L.A.P.D.'s Rampart Division are making a concerted effort to crack down on criminals in the area and that there has been some recent improvement.

For all the problems this area endures, there is a distinct feeling of vitality and cohesiveness. Residents often refer to it as "the Neighborhood." There are many among the elderly people, such as Hal, who have lived in the neighborhood for long periods of time. Hal frequently reminisces about the way things used to be. He remembers when streetcars ran through the area and the park was still a field. One of Hal's friends, another ex-patient from Pacific State Hospital, often refers to the past when "this used to be a movie-star neighborhood," recalling the days when the affluent still lived here. (Hollywood still films in the area regularly, particularly for urban police shows.) According to Hal, the area did not begin to decline seriously until the 1970s, but the downhill slide has been rapid since then. Like many other old-time residents, Hal considers the rise in poverty and crime in the area to be a result of the tide of illegal aliens that has flowed into the neighborhood in recent years. However, unlike many of the others, Hal accepts this with a fatalistic shrug, blames it on the politicians, and seems to remain relatively unprejudiced toward minority groups in his day-to-day dealings.

The neighborhood is set to go through radical changes that were only just beginning when this research was carried out. One terminal on the city's MetroRail system will be located on the east side of MacArthur Park; construction had only recently begun. This project will likely bring some new businesses and revitalization to the neighborhood, as well as increased demands for the police to control crime. However, if the revitalization is widespread, it will also bring higher prices for housing and other necessities to an area that can little afford them. It remains to be seen how this will affect elderly people, such as Hal, and others in the neighborhood who live on fixed incomes. If dislocation occurs, the problem becomes where they will go, as most other areas of the city are already more expensive.

When one first meets Hal, his manner and appearance combine to present an impression of diffident, somewhat suspicious friendliness. He is small and wiry, and years of very hard manual labor have left him with somewhat overdeveloped musculature in his shoulders. Combined with his short torso and disproportionately long arms, and emphasized by encroaching age, this gives Hal the appearance of always hunching his shoulders, as if ready to duck an expected blow. Because of the severe circulatory problem in his legs, Hal walks with smallish steps and a slight shuffle. If he is walking quickly, he sometimes gives the appearance of "scurrying" along.

Hal's high-domed forehead is accentuated by his increasing baldness. The hair he has left on the top and the sides is thin and gray, going rapidly toward white. His blue eyes are rheumy, markedly so if he is not feeling well. However, they also sparkle with an ornery glint when he is teasing or telling one of his more outlandish stories. With his slightly leathery skin and wrinkles, his "long" lower lip, and his large ears that sport thick tufts of hair when he is in need of a trim, Hal looks like a watchful gnome. The other description that springs immediately to mind because of his penchant for western clothing, especially the western shirts he seems to have in endless supply, is that of a weathered ranch hand.

Hal has a low and moderately expressive voice, and his speech is clear and usually distinct, except for the occasional slurring caused by his dentures, which appear to be in good condition. Hal has a good basic vocabulary, and he obviously enjoys conversation, although he is quiet and a little shy. The one noticeably odd characteristic in Hal's communicative style is the unusually long lag in his response time, which occurs with some regularity. When Hal is spoken to, it sometimes appears that he has not heard what the person talking to him has said or that he is not going to respond. He will then unexpectedly continue on with the conversation. Hal himself seems to be unaware that this lag has occurred, although it is often quite noticeable. It does not appear that he is simply thinking things over and considering his response, although this is possible. Another possibility is that this slow response time is somehow connected to a severe hearing loss in Hal's left ear.

Hal is normally well groomed and clean shaven, with his hair trimmed and his clothing neat and clean. Although he has never had a weight problem, he watches that he does not gain too much. Hal sees his doctor regularly because of the medication (Coumadin) he takes for the circulatory problem in his legs, and he keeps a watchful eye on his general health. Other than the problem with his legs, Hal seems to be in good physical condition for his age. In fact, at age 65, Hal still does not need prescription glasses.

Hal's lifestyle is described in greater detail below, but in general he seems well adapted. He is entirely independent and manages to handle all of the business of living by himself, including dealing with the Social

Security and Medicare bureaucracy. His major complaint is loneliness, but he does get out of his apartment daily and interacts with others, although much of this interaction is of a fairly superficial nature.

By far the most striking aspect of Hal's social adaptation is his use of storytelling. His stories are many, highly detailed, and variable. In fact, over time it became apparent that most of Hal's stories fell into specific patterns or groups, which are described below. Hal's stories appear to fulfill two major functions in his life. One function is simply pleasure. During the telling of certain stories, often those which are the longest, most complicated, and fantastic, Hal will become noticeably more animated than usual. His eyes sparkle, he has a small smile around the corners of his mouth, and his voice has more expression.

The second function, and by far the more important of the two, falls into the realm of image management. Stephens (1976), in her work on SRO (single room occupancy) hotel dwellers, has given an excellent description of this phenomenon. (Hal was not living in an SRO hotel at the time of this study, but he has done so in the past.)

> These people are more than casually aware of the low repute in which their class is held. In addition, the group includes a sizable number who have had, at best, checkered careers, often involving petty crime, psychiatric treatment, indigence. In short, their personal biographies reflect their failure in varying degrees to fulfill cultural and social mandates. A consequence of this knowledge is the ubiquity of face-saving maneuvers. The most widely used technique for saving face is the remaking of personal history. . . . These people, in their need to conceal and refurbish, must jealously guard their own secrets, and yet be realistically cynical about the stories of others, who presumably are doing the same reconstructing of their pasts. Although this suspicion pervades many aspects of the ways they do (and do not) relate to one another, it is nowhere more manifest than in their routine assumption that everyone has something to hide and that, consequently, most explanations of background are false. As a core belief of the mystique, everyone is there for a "reason," and this "reason" probably is something reprehensible. Thus it is to be expected that if one is so imprudent as to inquire about backgrounds, fabrications will be in order. It is considered rude to inquire about another's past. When, on a rare occasion, an account is offered, the listener is expected to act as if he believes it.[2]

Stephens' reference to the tendency to be secretive and the expectation that others will accept the stories one tells points up a major difficulty in assessing the material gathered through fieldwork with Hal. Some of the stories Hal tells are more recognizable as such than others. The ones that involve famous people or, at best, highly improbable events

---

[2]Stephens, J. (1976). *Loners, losers, and lovers: Elderly tenants in a slum hotel.* Seattle: University of Washington Press.

fall into this category, as do the stories that are not at all consistent with known facts and the ones that blatantly change with each retelling. However, other stories involve people and events that are certainly within the realm of possibility, and some have remained basically consistent throughout the 3 years during which I maintained weekly research contact with Hal. The only two people who possibly could have verified any information concerning Hal's early life are his brother and sister. In the case of Hal's brother, there exists what Hal describes as great mutual dislike, and they have not spoken in many, many years, nor does Hal wish to re-establish contact. Hal does keep in sporadic touch with his sister, but when I requested to meet her and offered to take Hal to visit at her convenience, Hal effectively blocked me from doing so by stating that he had contacted her and she had requested that we not come to see her. There were a number of circumstances surrounding this refusal that at least cast doubt on the veracity of Hal's excuse. Perhaps it is more likely that Hal did not wish for his sister to contradict some of the past information he had provided and thereby disturb his self-description. The only records that exist are the hospital and court records available through Pacific State Hospital concerning Hal's past institutionalization. The hospital records themselves present problems because they are riddled with inconsistencies and gaps in information.

The only other source of information about Hal's past is Hal's wife, Midge (see Chapter 2), from whom he has been separated for almost 25 years. Midge was able to corroborate some information concerning at least the period they spent together, but her information often did not agree with Hal's, and it quickly became apparent that her information on Hal's early life was gleaned from stories Hal had told her.

As a result of these difficulties, it has been impossible in some important instances to know whether some reported events in Hal's life are factual or not. One of the most notable instances concerns Hal's report that his mother died when he was 8 years old, that he was unable to get along with his stepmother and her children, and that he and his brother and sister went to live with Hal's paternal grandmother. According to the hospital records, the woman listed as Hal's natural mother, complete with appropriate maiden name, was alive until approximately the time Hal was released on work leave from Pacific State Hospital after his second admission. (Hal would have been nearly 30 years old.) There is no mention of a stepmother or, indeed, of Hal's father remarrying. Hal has adamantly stuck to his version of events, even when confronted with the version provided in the hospital records. When asked directly about the discrepancy, Hal at first said that he did not know why they would say such a thing. However, the following week, Hal brought up the subject again. He said he had thought the matter over and had come up with an explanation. He then stated that the hospital must have been confused by the fact that both his mother and his stepmother had the same first name.

There are two additional pieces of information that cast doubt on Hal's version of these events. First, during a taped interview in 1972, when asked why he was committed to Pacific State Hospital, Hal responded:

> 'Cause I used to beat the heck out of my old man—my stepdad, I mean . . . my dad died when I was about 8 . . . my mother got married again . . . she died when I was 13 . . . and my stepmother said, "If you don't keep from beating up your old man, you're going to go someplace" . . . so anyway, my uncle was the chief of police then . . . and he told my stepmother, "You're not going to put him in there, the state hospital" . . . my stepmother's father was the judge . . . he put me in there. . . .

According to the tape, Hal also told his stepmother that if he ever got out, he would kill her, but she died before he got out.

The example above illustrates some of the difficulties in assessing the material gathered from someone who is actively engaged in storytelling as an image-management technique. Some of the stories are given below in the section on storytelling. When major discrepancies between Hal's version of his past and information from other sources occurs, the differences are noted. First, however, some material on Hal's life history and his current lifestyle will be given as a framework for understanding his stories and his use of storytelling.

LIFE HISTORY

The information on Hal's early life is sketchy and comes entirely from court and hospital records. He was born the second of three children to Anne and Robert Arnaud on October 31, 1921. The pregnancy and birth were unremarkable, and at 7½ pounds, Hal was considered "normal" at birth.

The family is described as Caucasian, low-income, and Baptist. Hal's father, Robert, had completed the fifth grade before his own father died and he quit school to support the family. He worked at various jobs and eventually became a brass moulder in a foundry. Anne, Hal's mother, quit school after the sixth grade and is described as not liking school. She eventually married Robert and became a housewife. Anne apparently had a series of rather serious physical problems that lasted through most, if not all of Hal's childhood. Between Hal's 3rd and 7th years, his mother had three miscarriages (one as late as 6 months) and a stillborn child. She eventually was found to have a tumor and had a hysterectomy. She had a great deal of trouble with her teeth, as did Hal, and by the time of Hal's first admission to Pacific State Hospital in 1937 at the age of 16 years, Anne was described as having been in poor mental and physical condition for "some years." She was noted as being confined to the house most of the time with a kidney ailment. (It is interesting to remember that Hal insists his mother died when he was 8 years old.)

According to the hospital records, the home conditions were "above average." The family lived in a rented five-room stucco house in a fairly good residential neighborhood, and the home was "decidedly clean and neat." There is almost no information on either of Hal's siblings. His sister, Lianne, graduated from high school and is described as feeling keenly the "disgrace of [Hal]" and not wanting to return to school. However, she is the family member who seems to have taken responsibility for the family through the years. When I asked Hal if his family used to visit him at Pacific State Hospital, he said that yes, his father and sister used to come regularly, and his sister used to send him cookies and candy. At one point during Hal's second admission to Pacific State Hospital (1946), Hal's father—who was ill—and brother were living with Lianne and her husband. She currently keeps in sporadic touch with Hal and has helped him when he has had financial difficulties.

Hal's younger brother, Robert Jr. (Bobby), was brought to court charged with burglary in 1936 at the age of 13, made a ward of the court, and sent to Juvenile Hall. Hal says he and Bobby were never close. According to Hal, after being in the Navy during World War II, Bobby ended up as president of his own company. Once when Hal was having financial difficulties, Hal's sister asked Bobby to help Hal out, and Bobby refused. Hal says it made him angry because he felt that Bobby could have afforded to help him.

The only references to Hal's early childhood consist of the statements that he was underweight until he was 12 years old, that his speech was indistinct, that he began speaking at 2 years of age, and that Hal's "mental deficit was first noticed at about 5 years." However, there is no description or substantiating evidence presented to support this last statement. (It should also be remembered that the hospital history was done at a time when Hal was being committed to that hospital as a "mental defective.")

Hal entered school at 6 years of age and continued his education until the last half of the 9th Grade. At that time, Hal was admitted to Pacific State Hospital and received no further schooling. The junior high school that Hal attended reported that his reading and writing were fair but his IQ was below normal. (No figures were given.) At the time Hal left school, his marks in English, math, science, and history were unsatisfactory, although his marks in shop and physical education were satisfactory. The school also reported that his behavior was good and that there was no record that he had "been in any trouble at school, such as molesting girls or committing any other breach of the school regulations."

Hal's companions were reported as desirable, and he got along with them well. They would have been welcome in the home, but he apparently never brought them there. There is no clue as to why.

Hal was also reported as well-behaved at home. "[He did not] resent correction, nor [was] he antagonistic toward those in authority. He [was] given to day dreaming; [was] restless and nervous, easily discouraged; like[d] to play alone; [was] industrious, honest, dependable, courteous."

As far as activities were concerned, Hal sold newspapers to earn his own money and was allowed to spend it as he liked, for things such as clothing, haircuts, and going to shows. He also liked to play cards, particularly poker. He went to the movies two or three times a week, liked to read, and played ball. He also played the harmonica, sang, and drew. Hal was reported to be "somewhat domestically inclined," and he helped with the dishes.

The picture that emerges is of a quiet, shy, well-behaved boy who perhaps was not doing too well in school but was passing grades, and who did not give anyone any trouble. He got along well with his peers, had his own money, and was pretty much allowed to do whatever he liked (perhaps also because, with his father at work and his mother in poor condition, no one was really around to give him much supervision). In 1937, at the age of 16, all of these *laissez-faire* child-rearing practices came to an abrupt end when Hal ended up in Juvenile Court on several charges based on sexual deviance:

> Boy first became known to the Juvenile Court on 8-25-37 at which time it was alleged that he went about the neighborhood peeping in windows to see women undressing and that on about 10 occasions he grabbed women on the street and embraced them. Boy admitted that for about 2½ years he had been in the habit of going to a boy friend's house and taking girls there whom he paid about 50 cents. [There are other references in the records that indicate that the money paid to the girls was for sexual favors.]

Hal's version of these events is considerably different and is covered in detail in the section below on storytelling. The final outcome of Hal's contact with the court system was his commitment to Pacific State Hospital, with the reason for commitment listed as: "A mentally deficient sexually delinquent boy who molests girls and women."

It is particularly notable that the 16-year-old Hal, who was described as having had no previous trouble at home, at school, or with the authorities, and who had had a paper route for several years and earned his own money to cover his own needs, was suddenly being described in the Supplemental Report to Juvenile Court from the Juvenile Hall Clinic as a sexually delinquent middle-grade "moron," with a mental age of 9 years. (This report is an evaluation apparently prepared for Juvenile Court as part of Hal's commitment proceedings.) Later records list Hal's measured IQ at that time as 60, but that information is not included in this report. In the psychological evaluation, Hal was rated within the lowest percentile group of 15-year-old boys. The report is quite negative, and it contains many references to his "unfortunate appearance."

> Patient has a disheveled, dirty and dull appearance. He has a rather silly smirk which he maintains throughout the examination. His mannerisms are repulsive. It appears that patient is very conscious of his inferiority in his appearance and in some degree of his inability. That he has accepted his condition through compensating in behaviorisms which will be consistent to his appearance and which will draw unfavorable attention [sic]. Practically, the only satisfaction he has been able to find has been through unacceptable behavior.

Another section of the report states: "He has the stigmata of mental deficiency." However, there is no further information as to what this statement refers. (At the present time, Hal exhibits no such "stigmata," nor does he have a particularly "unfortunate" appearance.) This report particularly stands out from all of the other records on Hal for its overall negativity. In other records, Hal is generally listed as pleasant and cooperative. One possible explanation for the poor impression that Hal made during the evaluation is that he was quite traumatized by the entire situation. He was 16 years old and being accused of rather severe sexual misconduct. He had to deal with the police, the court, and the Juvenile Hall examiners. All of this took place in 1937, when sexual "acting out" was even more stigmatized than it would be today. Whatever the reasons, the result of the examination was a recommendation:

> [Hal] undoubtedly should be placed in Pacific State Hospital or Sonoma without delay. This is the only hope—that by careful training and treatment (including sterilization) he may become a dependable member of the social group. . . . Patient needs a placement in a simplified environment, where conditions are adapted to his social and mental possibilities.

This recommendation was, in fact, followed, and Hal was committed to Pacific State Hospital in 1937.

There is almost no information in the records concerning Hal's stay at Pacific. He appears to have been cooperative and was apparently called "Frenchie." The only report of any trouble was a letter from the Board of Education stating that, according to the vice-principal of the junior high school Hal had attended, Hal was writing "objectionable" (this is not defined) letters to some of the girl students, and the school board requested that the letters be stopped.

Hal was granted home leave in early 1941, at age 19. He had trouble finding a job due to his lack of a high school diploma, and in February 1941, he was selling newspapers for $3 per week. In May of 1941, Hal again got into trouble, this time for theft of a bicycle. The judge suspended sentence on the condition that Hal return to Pacific State Hospital, and Hal spent another year at Pacific. On leave a year later, Hal was again selling newspapers, but this time he had three other boys working for him and was making $20 per week. By August of that year, the family had bought a home, Hal was still selling newspapers, and his mother was reportedly "quite pleased with his adjustment." Hal joined the Army in October of 1942, and subsequent information about this period came from contacts with his mother. As early as November, there was some question of the Army returning Hal to civilian life as "unfit for service" while he was still stationed locally. However, by December he was training in Arkansas and appeared to like Army life. He was subsequently shipped to Texas in the cavalry and then reassigned to the medical corps as an orderly in May of 1943. Hal's mother reported that he liked the work and would probably stay attached to the hospital there "for the duration." The next visit by the Pacific State Hospital social worker in September 1943 found Hal honorably discharged from the Army and back home in Los Angeles. Although the hospital records provide no information on why Hal was discharged from the Army, Hal has his own version of these events, which is discussed below in the section on storytelling. However, Hal finally disclosed the fact that there was a connection between his institutionalization at Pacific and his Army discharge. According to Hal, the problem was that he was still on extended leave from Pacific during that period. He was not completely discharged from his first admission until June of 1945. He says the Army had prohibitions against people with patient status carrying guns or being shipped overseas, and when they found out that he was still a patient at Pacific, they honorably discharged him. According to Hal, this chain of events was precipitated by a new chief of staff at Pacific who contacted the Army to "check" on Hal. (However, there is no mention of any of this in the records.)

The information on Hal's life from June 1942 to February 1944 is sketchy. All contacts by the hospital social worker were with Hal's parents, mostly his mother. Hal was always at work, in the Army, or sleeping because he worked nights. The information from Hal's parents is somewhat vague. They did not know, or perhaps would not tell, such rudimentary information as how much Hal earned. (This seems to have been a continuing problem. In a letter accompanying the application for readmission to Pacific State Hospital in 1946, an officer of the Psychopathic Probation Department stated that the officer's information on Hal's past was "somewhat sketchy" because Hal's parents "simply did not seem to be able to recall the simplest things.") During this period, Hal worked at several factory jobs, each for a few months, and eventually ended up as a cook's helper in a restaurant.

In 1945, Hal was again in trouble with the law, this time for a violation of the Vehicle Code. The records are insufficient to determine exactly what the charge was, but it was of a sufficiently serious nature to warrant a 9-month sentence plus probation. Hal apparently "left the road camp" where he was serving out his sentence, but ended up in court again in 1946, charged with vagrancy and car theft. (Hal insists that he was "set up" for this charge by a supposed friend, who actually took the car and then lied to the police about the circumstances.) The court decided that return to Pacific State Hospital was the most appropriate course of action. Hal readily agreed, and a second commitment proceeding was initiated.

As part of the commitment papers in March 1946, Hal's parents also signed a consent form for sterilization. Although there is no notation in the records regarding when the sterilization was performed, there is a note in June 1946 stating that Hal had been sterilized. (There is some confusion about the date because a note at the time of Hal's first discharge in 1945 also states that Hal had been sterilized, some 10 months before the date on the consent form. Hal himself says that the sterilization was performed during the second admission, and in fact, he claims that he fathered a child while he was out of the hospital between the first and second admissions.)

The psychological summary done by Pacific State Hospital in 1946 stands in striking contrast to the earlier summary done by Juvenile Hall in 1937:

> His is a picture of rather ordinary dull functioning which does not distinguish itself by any outstanding weaknesses. There is sufficient reason to establish the belief that his [past] delinquencies were not due to an emotional waywardness but to a failure on the part of his environment to provide information and direction when it was needed. . . . He is neither childish nor neurotic and should therefore be a good solid citizen of any community which does not expect too much of him.

The assessment of Hal's intellectual capacity had also changed dramatically. His IQ, previously rated at 60, was then measured at 82 on the Wechsler-Bellevue intelligence test (now superceded by the Wechsler Adult Intelligence Scale, or WAIS).

> His score on the Arithmetic test was among the highest on the Verbal Test [sic]. This fact alone would seem to be a contraindication of intellectual defectiveness. . . . He was mature in his general manner, grasped directions quickly and kept them well in mind, and was able to exercise self-criticism. He had little to say voluntarily, but when he spoke it was with assurance. He gave the impression of one who

"knows his way around" and who can take care of himself. If he is adjudged mentally defective, it should probably be on grounds other than intellectual.

(According to Hal, his IQ was tested at 98 when he was in the Army.)

Indeed, there seems to have been some question at Pacific State Hospital about Hal's diagnosis as mentally defective. In the July 1946 clinic notes, 4 months after he was readmitted, there seems to have been a consensus among four of the doctors that Hal was not mentally defective. However, the case was held for further consideration, and in the clinic notes one week later, with no explanation, it is stated that, "after further discussion, it was felt that this boy is suitably placed in the institution as a defective."

Again, there is virtually no information about Hal's stay at Pacific other than brief references to the facts that he had a good deal of dental trouble, including an infected mouth from a broken dental bridge, and that he worked with the mattress man at the hospital. The information resumes again some 3 years later, in 1950, when Hal's caseworker suggested that Hal be considered for work leave: "The attendant and cottage physician gave unqualified recommendations for this boy [Hal would have been nearly 30 at the time] as a good worker and as a stable individual who is probably brighter than his rated IQ."

It is noteworthy that, beginning with the resumption of the hospital information in 1950 when Hal's fieldworker began looking for a suitable industrial placement and was negotiating with Hal's sister concerning an indefinite home leave for Hal, Hal's mother is never mentioned again as she frequently was in all previous notes. The most likely explanation is that she died during the period between 1946, when her signature appears on the commitment papers, and 1950. Because Hal so staunchly maintains that his mother died when he was 8 years old, it is not possible to verify this information with Hal. The death of a parent at any age is traumatic, but the developmental difference between losing a parent at the age of 8 and losing one at 30 seems significant. Also, prior to the disappearance of the mother from the family, Hal was always able to return to the family home when he was released from the hospital. Beginning with his release in 1950, he was never again to live with his family. (However, interestingly enough, Hal was also never again institutionalized.) Although they remained vaguely supportive and somewhat interested in Hal, his sister said it was impossible for Hal to live at her house because their father and brother were already living there.

Many patients from that period at Pacific State Hospital went to jobs in sanitariums as their first industrial placements when they left the hospital on work leave, and Hal was no exception. The sanitarium was run by a Mrs. Wrigley, who had at one time been a nurse at Pacific State Hospital. Hal's beginning salary was $25 per month plus room and board. However, far more important to Hal than the money he earned was the fact that the Wrigleys treated him as a family member, including him in evening family activities and outings. Hal also had a girlfriend whom he had met when both were patients at Pacific, and who was working at a nearby sanitarium. All in all, Hal was very happy at Mrs. Wrigley's and got excellent reports on his work.

A notable incident from this period occurred in mid-1952. Hal was given 2 weeks vacation and, according to Mrs. Wrigley and the hospital fieldworker, he was thrown a little off balance by the unstructured time. During the 2 weeks, Hal returned to Mrs. Wrigley's saying that he had met a divorcee with two children and wanted to marry her. However, after Mrs. Wrigley discouraged him from doing so and finally told him that, because he was not entirely discharged from the hospital, he would have to go through the red tape of getting permission to marry, Hal gave up on the idea. This incident may be the basis for the story of what Hal insists was his first marriage, which is discussed below in the section on storytelling.

In total, Hal lived at Mrs. Wrigley's for 3½ years, until his final discharge from Pacific State in 1954. At the time of his discharge, Hal was still quite happy at Mrs. Wrigley's and getting excellent reports on himself and his work.

At this point, the official record on Hal comes to an end with the exception of a letter appended to the file concerning the fact that, within a year, Hal was working at another sanitarium, had married, and was in the process of trying to obtain a divorce. The marriage was an unfortunate affair almost from the beginning. While on a trip to San Diego, Hal met Hope, another former patient from Pacific State Hospital, and on impulse, the two decided to elope to Yuma, Arizona, and get married. However, when they returned to San Diego, Hope refused to leave her family and live with Hal, especially when Hal wanted to return to Los Angeles and his job. Hal also reports that her Hispanic family did not like the fact that Hope had married an Anglo.

Hal returned to Los Angeles alone and, in early 1955, went to work for Mr. Jacob Cohen in his foundry, Cohen Metal Company. Hal was in charge of stoking the furnace, which was used to melt metal. The work was extremely hot and strenuous, and Mr. Cohen had had difficulty keeping someone on the job. Hal was to stay nearly 30 years until he was laid off in 1981 when business declined. Although the pay was low and the physical conditions were difficult, Hal liked his job. He took a great deal of satisfaction in the fact that he was physically strong enough to do it and that he was able to continue on a job that most others gave up as too difficult. Also, Hal's employer took a personal interest in him through the years and made Hal feel like a valued employee. This job and his long continuous work record are one of the most significant elements of Hal's self-image. He is justifiably proud of the fact that he has always worked, and he has little respect for those who do not.

In the middle of 1955, Hal renewed his acquaintance with Midge Nellin (see Chapter 2), another former Pacific State Hospital patient, at a meeting of the Friendship Club (a social club for former Pacific patients). Hal and Midge began seeing one another, and a few months later they began planning to be married. Hal's relationship with Midge was to become by far the most significant female relationship that he has ever had. With the help of the hospital fieldworker, who coincidentally handled both Hal's and Midge's cases, Hal obtained a divorce from his first wife, Hope. In the meantime, Midge came to work as a domestic helper for Mrs. Cohen, the wife of Hal's employer and a regular employer of "girls" (Midge was in her 30s) from Pacific State Hospital who were on industrial leave awaiting discharge. The Cohens took great interest in Hal and Midge, providing help with their wedding among other things. Hal and Midge were finally married in December, 1956.

Hal and Midge lived in a shack provided by Mr. Cohen behind the foundry where Hal was employed. Midge got a job as a "companion/nurse" for an elderly paralyzed woman, as well as occasional cleaning jobs. Between the two of them, they earned about $75 per week, and they managed adequately. Their social world was small and consisted mostly of Pacific patients and former patients, although Hal had been out of Pacific State Hospital for several years. The Friendship Club was still their major social activity. They also occasionally went to the beach or to a ball game when Mr. Cohen gave Hal tickets. After 15 months of marriage and relative stability, Midge was discharged in 1958.

Midge's discharge marked the first time that Hal was without hospital contact, even though he had been completely discharged 4 years earlier. Because the same hospital fieldworker handled both Hal's and Midge's cases and had involved Hal in working with Midge from the time he started dating her, there was considerable continuity until the time of Midge's discharge, when Hal was 37 years old. Thus, except for brief periods, Hal was involved with the hospital in some capacity or other from the age of 15 to the age of 37, the entire period in which he grew to adulthood.

Although Hal and Midge no longer had the support of the hospital fieldworker, they did receive various kinds of help from two benefactors. Hal's employer, Mr. Cohen, had a strongly paternalistic relationship with Hal. In addition to providing living quarters and sometimes food, Hal describes how Mr. Cohen took him to baseball games and sometimes out to eat. Hal was very fond of the entire Cohen family. The woman who lived next door to Hal and Midge also helped the couple, particularly in domestic areas involving Midge, such as grocery shopping. She also kept a sharp eye out for anyone trying to take advantage of the couple.

Hal describes the first part of his married life as stable and relatively happy. Hal liked the fact that Midge cooked and cleaned for him, and according to Hal, Midge "kept a good house," although fieldnotes from that time describe Midge's housekeeping as considerably less than immaculate. Hal also said that Midge was a lot of fun and that he always had a good time with her. As time wore on, however, the couple moved into an apartment owned by Mr. Cohen when the shack at the metal company was condemned and then demolished. Midge went to work as a waitress at a nearby restaurant and began seeing other men. There is some indication in the fieldnotes that Hal may have been going out to bars occasionally and "chasing women," but he denies that he was ever unfaithful to Midge. Eventually, the couple began to fight over Midge's contact with other men. Midge claims that Hal hit her in the stomach during one of these fights, precipitating the ulcer she has trouble with today. Hal denies this incident just as vehemently as Midge insists that it happened, saying that he never hits women. Midge claims that she called the police, and when it was over, she left for good, after approximately 7 years of marriage. According to Hal, he came home from work one night and stopped to see Midge where she was working at the restaurant. He asked her if she was coming home later to cook dinner for him and she said yes. He went home and waited, and Midge just never showed up and never came home again except to pick up her belongings.

Even today when Hal talks about Midge, he sounds quite sad about their separation. His perception is that Midge left because she simply did not love him any longer. According to Hal, "She was young and beautiful, and all the guys wanted her," and he lost out to the others. (It should be noted that, although Hal always refers to Midge as being beautiful when he speaks of that period, he is the only one who refers to her as such. All other references describe her as "plain" at best.)

Hal and Midge were never formally divorced, and they are still legally married today, although they have not lived together since their separation in 1962. According to Hal, he never filed for divorce because there was never anyone else he really wanted to marry (his marital status may also have protected him from women in his life who wanted to marry *him*), and he "always thought Midge might come back."

Hal saw Midge two or three times in the intervening years, but she never returned to live with him. Through the years after his separation from Midge, Hal's life tended to be transient with the exception of his employment. He continued to work for the metal company until he was laid off in 1981, at the age of 59, when business declined and part of his job was automated. After nearly 30 years on the same job, Hal was left with no pension and no financial resources. His original employer, Mr. Cohen, had sold the business a few years earlier, and although Hal got on well with the new owner, he did not have the same strong paternalistic relationship with the new employer that he had enjoyed with Mr. Cohen. The new employer provided Hal with a letter praising his honesty and hard work, but at 59 years of age and unskilled, Hal found the letter to be of little help during a major national recession. While collecting unemployment, Hal tried to find a job, with no luck. He tried for a job as a security guard but was turned down due to his past record of institutionalization (according to Hal, ex-patients are not allowed to carry guns). By the time his unemployment ran out, a longtime circulatory problem in his legs had worsened and had reached the point of being disabling. Hal's doctor helped him to apply for and receive disability benefits, which carried him through until he was able to begin collecting his Social Security benefits when he turned 65 years old. In addition to the financial hardship, however, losing his job damaged Hal's self-image as a hard-working man who had *always* worked, starting with his first paper route at the age of 7. He also lost the social contacts that his job had provided. Although he did not socialize much with the other men outside of working hours, his employer, Mr. Cohen, did occasionally take a group of the men to breakfast or dinner.

From the time of his separation from Midge in 1962 and continuing into the present, Hal has lived in various apartment buildings and SRO hotels within the neighborhood where he now resides. (One of these hotels has a reputation as one of the roughest in an already violence-prone neighborhood.) He has lived through two major apartment building fires, one of which he escaped with only the pajamas he was wearing at the time. He lost everything else he owned in the fire. Hal currently lives in an old apartment building on a busy major thoroughfare in his neighborhood. The building is ostensibly for senior citizens, but a few younger tenants also live there. The building has a locked security entrance, and although the lobby is not very large, there are usually a few people congregated there, frequently including the manager. Hal reaches his fourth-floor apartment by means of an ancient wire-cage elevator. Like many old buildings in the area, Hal's building is slowly being renovated to bring it in line with the building codes for earthquake safety. In addition, a little over a year ago, the top floor where Hal is located flooded from a massive roof leak and repairs are still underway. Consequently, the fourth floor hallways have a dusty, barren, under-construction look. Hal lives in a "single" apartment with a "Murphy Bed" that folds down from the wall. There is a bathroom with a small walk-through dressing area and a good-sized kitchen. The apartment is old and in poor repair, and the furnishings are mismatched and somewhat shabby, but it is clean and neat, and has the definite air of someone's home. There are a few obviously decorative objects either sitting around on the tables or hanging on the wall, and Hal explained that some of them were given to him or had belonged to people he knew, for instance, a small framed picture of Christ that had belonged to Sally, one of the women with whom Hal has lived. The most obvious disrepair is in the bathroom, where the ceiling caved in when the fourth floor flooded and the window fell out and was replaced with plywood. However, even with such problems, Hal says he likes living where he does.

During the years since he lived with Midge, Hal has alternately lived alone or with one of a series of women who have passed through his life. Some of these women are discussed below in the section on storytelling, such as Sally and Marsha, Hal's pseudo-daughter. Others have included a Native American woman with whom Hal lived for quite some time, but who had a tendency to become violent when she was intoxicated. Hal finally left after the woman hit him in the head with a hammer, injuring him sufficiently for the paramedics to be called. Many of these women have been alcoholics or substance abusers or both. Hal does not like living alone because he gets lonely, and he misses a woman's presence around the apartment. When Marsha, his pseudo-daughter, moved out again a few months ago, he initially said he was glad to have his apartment back to himself, minus her messy ways and erratic hours. However, it was not long before he wistfully admitted that he was lonely living by himself. Shortly after that, he met a 47-year-old Mexican woman who moved in with him. For a while, Hal complained that she would sometimes "steal" money that he had around the apartment, but he then added that she would later return the money. He finally talked to her about the problem, and he now reports that it has stopped. Like several of the other women with whom Hal has lived, this woman is a drug user. She usually leaves over the weekends, and Hal speculates that she may go to visit her daughter and grandchild, but he does not know for sure. All in all, Hal seems relatively content with this arrangement.

The last few years since he was laid off from his job have been difficult for Hal in many ways. However, since he turned 65 years old in 1986, his circumstances have been more stable. Today, Hal draws a combination of Social Security and SSI (Supplemental Security Income) benefits for the aged, as well as a very small military pension, so his income is relatively secure. He has suffered some financial setbacks, including having his veteran's benefits reduced because the Veteran's Administration claims to have overpaid Hal in the past and has been deducting part of Hal's benefits to repay the overpayment.

Some of Hal's setbacks have been self-induced, however. For instance, shortly before he turned 65, Hal's monthly income was reduced when, according to Hal, the bank at which he maintains an account notified him that three checks that he had cashed for a "friend" had been returned to the bank because there were insufficient funds in the friend's account. (The friend, according to Hal, had moved out of town; however, there may have been more to this situation than Hal was willing to admit.) Over a period of 3 months, Hal's bank proceeded to deduct $1,025 from Hal's account, into which his benefit checks are automatically deposited. The deduction of such a large amount in such a short time from Hal's $553-per-month income left him devastated financially. (The bank allowed Hal $200 a month and kept the rest to pay back the check amounts.) During the same period of time, the office responsible for his SSI benefits contacted Hal and informed him that they had discovered that two of Sally's SSI checks had been cashed by Hal after her death. (Hal's name was also on Sally's checks so that he could cash them for her. He claims to have sent the posthumous checks back once, but when SSI returned them to him a second time, he went ahead and cashed them.) Hal contacted SSI and arranged to repay them by having $35 per month deducted from his benefits. Because of these financial blows, Hal was unable to pay his entire rent of $360. However, because he maintains a very cordial relationship with the manager of his apartment building, he was able to make arrangements to pay what he could and catch up over the following months. It took Hal about 4 months to recoup financially. At the same time, Hal was left with little or no food. By utilizing a church food bank and twice receiving food vouchers from the Salvation Army, Hal managed to get by. He was helped a little by money his sister sent him for Christmas and actually could have appealed to her for more, but he chose not to do so.

Hal did not seem to be terribly upset by this financial crisis. It was certainly very inconvenient, but he seemed to take it in stride and set about solving it as best he could. Hal says that except for paying rent he could survive for a while without money if it were necessary. In fact, Hal shows a pragmatic and astute ability to deal with an unwieldy and relatively unresponsive bureaucracy. He knows which offices to contact for specific problems and how to make arrangements to solve those problems. Although getting around is a slow and sometimes difficult process because of the problems with his legs, Hal prefers to use his bus pass and take care of his business in person rather than to use pay telephones. He will appeal to others for advice on these matters, but he usually accepts actual help only if he really has trouble solving a problem.

Hal occasionally tries to manipulate "the system" to his advantage, as in the case of Sally's checks. He seems to feel that he might get away with it, and if not, he will pay the price when the time comes without complaint. He also seems to take furtive glee in the attempt and accepts the consequences with wry humor. Hal also occasionally indulges in "scams" to supplement his income. After considerable fieldwork, Hal finally admitted that he sometimes sells the codeine-based painkillers (e.g., acetaminophen with codeine) his doctor prescribes for his arthritis to a friend. According to Stephens (1976), such schemes fall under the heading of "making it" and are both typical of and accepted by low-income SRO hotel dwellers.[3]

Hal's daily routine is somewhat limited these days by the circulatory problem in his legs that makes walking for any extended period of time tiring and painful. However, Hal does have a senior citizen bus pass, and there is a bus stop immediately in front of the main entrance of his apartment building. He utilizes the bus almost daily. Hal is a very early riser, sometimes rising as early as 4:00 A.M. He goes out quite early (6:30 A.M.) for coffee at one of the neighborhood restaurants that open for the breakfast trade.

Like many others in the neighborhood, Hal fondly reminisces about the local Denny's that used to be a social gathering place at all hours of the day and night. He was friendly with all of the waitresses, and when times got rough, he helped them out by doing small jobs, such as putting their food checks in numerical order, in return for free food. Denny's finally closed this location because of difficulty with crime and violence, especially late at night. Another local coffee shop, Hill's, which had for many years served as a social nexus for much of the neighborhood, especially older people like Hal, was closed when the property was bought by the city for construction of the MetroRail System. The loss of these two long-established meeting places has disturbed the social networks of the neighborhood, scattering people who used to come into daily contact. Recently, a new coffee shop has opened on the site of the old Denny's. People from the neighborhood are slowly beginning to frequent the new place, and with time it may develop into a new gathering place.

Almost daily, Hal spends an hour or two drinking coffee, smoking cigarettes, reading the morning newspaper, and quietly visiting with waitresses or customers he knows. Between the newspaper and television news shows, Hal is quite well informed on current events. He is especially interested in politics and is knowledgeable about politicians and political decisions that affect senior citizens and Social Security. Hal is a registered Democrat and votes regularly.

After morning coffee, Hal will sometimes make trips with his bus pass to take care of business matters, visit his doctor, or, very occasionally, visit a friend. Hal has a few friends who are people he met at school or knew at the hospital, and he occasionally visits a man he knew in the Army. However, most of Hal's acquaintances and most of his socializing

---

[3]Stephens, J. (1976). *Loners, losers, and lovers: Elderly tenants in a slum hotel.* Seattle: University of Washington Press.

consists of surface relationships with people such as his apartment manager, women who work at the bank where Hal does business, a favorite waitress, or people in small shops in the neighborhood whom he has met while walking. Even though he is shy, Hal will go out of his way to actively pursue these contacts and to maintain some sort of social activity for himself.

Hal does not like to go to the nearby downtown area because of the level of street crime. (During the time I have known Hal, he has been robbed twice, once on a downtown bus by a pickpocket and once at gunpoint at his own apartment door by a woman he knew.) Sometimes Hal returns home and naps or watches daytime television. (He prefers game shows, news, an occasional soap opera, and police and action shows.) He frequently goes out again in the late afternoon for coffee or to eat, depending on the condition of his finances. Hal is almost always home before dark to protect himself from street crime in his neighborhood, which is a very real threat. He watches some evening television and goes to bed early, usually by about 9:30 P.M.

HAL THE STORYTELLER

As mentioned above, several patterns emerged in Hal's stories over time. By looking at these patterns, it is possible to understand several important facets of the image of himself that Hal chooses to present to the outside world. The stories, of course, often contain elements from more than one pattern. Three major patterns and what they say about the image Hal wishes to project will be discussed here.

"I'm Kindhearted"

The first pattern presents Hal as a kind and caring person, particularly to those less fortunate than himself. Most of these stories involve family members, usually male (husbands, sons), but occasionally female (a mother), who insist that Hal take money for helping or caring for their loved ones (always female). The earliest time frame is at the "hospital" (Pacific State Hospital) when Hal was nice to a "crippled girl" and bought her candy and such with the money he made playing cards. Her mother came to visit and insisted on giving Hal money in return for being nice to her daughter. This same pattern appears in stories about the period when Hal was working at the "sanitarium" (Hal's first job when he went on work leave from the hospital):

> Hal talked a little about working in the sanitarium for the former nurse from Pacific State Hospital. A former female patient who worked there first, Maria, couldn't cook very well, so when Hal came to work there, he occasionally did the cooking. He was mostly doing outside work,

including putting up a "shack," complete with toilet, in the back yard for himself to live in. Hal says that the owner of the sanitarium finally approached him about helping with an older woman patient who for some reason didn't like Maria. The older woman wouldn't eat for Maria, so the owner asked Hal to try to feed her. [Hal says you just have to be patient when you are trying to feed someone like that.] The older woman took a liking to Hal, and he took over more and more of her care. They finally approached Hal about bathing her because she wouldn't let Maria bathe her. At first Hal refused [this is said with a shy, nervous laugh], but he finally gave in because they told him that if he didn't, the older woman would not get a bath. Hal says that one day her husband came to visit and asked his wife who was taking care of her. She said Hal, and the husband asked if she meant "everything," including bathing and dressing. The wife said yes, everything. The husband asked her if Hal ever "did anything wrong," and the wife told him no. The man then contacted Hal outside and told him that his wife had told him all about it, and the husband really appreciated that someone was taking good care of her. The husband told Hal that they were wealthy, and gave Hal a $100 bill. At first, Hal refused the money, but the husband surreptitiously slipped the money into Hal's pocket where Hal later discovered it. [The amounts of money given to Hal by grateful family members vary, but are usually $50 or $100.] It was clear during the telling that Hal was proud of the fact that he could take such good care of the wife when she wouldn't let Maria care for her. I asked Hal if it embarrassed him to bathe her, and he said no. Hal says that while he was at Pacific, he worked helping deliver bedding and mattresses to the wards, and he was on them all, including the women's ward. He says he saw "all that stuff" while he was doing his job, so he doesn't get embarrassed anymore. [Actually, I am not sure this is true, based on the way Hal says some things when he is telling stories—with a sort of shy laugh.][4]

The pattern of being rewarded with money for his kindness recurs in stories told of periods throughout Hal's life. He tells two separate stories that involve him receiving money from family members for caring for women who lived with him after he met them on the street and took them in. One was the teenage daughter of a police desk sergeant, and the other was a young woman whom Hal found wandering the streets and who had apparently run away from her family back east.

A more recent story concerns being given money by a neighbor's son for helping an older female neighbor, Shirley, by fixing her broken dining room table and one of the chairs:

According to Hal, one of Shirley's sons is on drugs and while visiting, broke the table and chair. To replace it would cost about $500 for the table alone. [Apparently, if you break any of the furniture, you must replace it, and Hal spoke as though this is a serious concern among the

---

[4]All directly quoted stories in this section, such as this one, are taken from the author's fieldnotes.

tenants. This is why he was willing to help Shirley out.] Shirley offered to pay him for fixing the breakage, but Hal says he told her no, that he knew she didn't have much money either, and he didn't mind helping. Sometime later, Hal came home and found an envelope slipped under his door with $100 in it. Somehow he knew that the money had something to do with Shirley's table, so he went to see her. It seems that her son [not the drug user] was there visiting and had put the money there to thank Hal for helping. Hal tried to give the money back and said he didn't want it. He and the son went back and forth about it, and finally the son, who was about 6'8" tall, picked Hal up and said, teasing, "Now do you want it?" So Hal said sure, he'd take it. The son said Hal deserved it, and it was far less than it would have cost to replace the table.

These stories not only present Hal as a kind and caring person, which indeed he is, but they also may have something to say about Hal's view that kindness and helpfulness should be at least acknowledged, and rewarded if resources are available to do so. (However, note that none of the rewards came from the person Hal was actually helping. He obviously perceived all of them as less fortunate than himself.) One of the stories that Hal related shows himself in a somewhat unflattering light, but it is instructive of his feelings when an appropriate reward is not forthcoming.

One morning when I met Hal for breakfast and his "daughter," Marsha, came along, they both informed me with some interest that the old woman whom Hal used to "wheel around" had died and that $80,000 had been found in her apartment. It seems that the woman was mostly confined to a wheelchair [although Hal says that she could get out of it when she wanted], and Hal used to help her by wheeling her to do her errands, such as visiting the bank. The woman had money, but Hal describes her as very "tight" with it. She grudgingly gave Hal quite small amounts of money in return for considerable work. One day when Hal was at her building, her building manager asked Hal to help her clean up her apartment, which was badly in need of cleaning. While Hal was cleaning the kitchen, he came across a woman's change purse which he dropped into his pocket, meaning to give it to the woman when he got done cleaning. However, he forgot about it until he got home and discovered it in his pocket. When he opened it, he found $50 in bills and some change. Hal says he decided to keep it. He had done a lot of hard work cleaning the apartment most of the day, and the woman had given him only $2 or $3 when she obviously could have afforded more. [This story was repeated at a later date, and the amounts of money had grown from one coin purse with $50 in it to 2 separate coin purses, one with $300 and the other with $100. In addition, Hal described himself in the second version as having intentionally taken them, instead of doing so by accident.]

Relationships with Women

The second story pattern concerns the ways in which Hal meets women. These stories fall into two distinct subgroups, the first of which bears some resemblance to the pattern discussed in the section above, in which Hal presents himself as taking care of those less fortunate than himself. Virtually all of the stories in which Hal makes the first approach to a woman fall into this category. The typical scenario is that Hal encounters a woman who is down on her luck, usually in need of a bath and clean clothes, and who is obviously close to, if not already, living on the street. He has mentioned these meetings in such settings as a restaurant, on the bus, or on the street. Hal begins talking to the woman, asks her what has happened to her, usually buys her a meal, and then asks if she would like to come back to his place and take a bath and clean herself up. He sometimes offers her clothes left from other women who have stayed with him and left things behind. (At the moment, Hal has a collection of clothes that belonged to Sally, who died a few months before I began fieldwork with Hal.) Hal usually describes these women as suspicious of coming home with a stranger, but Hal then reassures them that he is not going to "try anything," and they eventually accompany him. (Hal also assures me that he would not "try anything" with these women he is trying to befriend. In fact, Hal has frequently stated, when describing situations that could be misconstrued, that, "I didn't have sex with her or anything.") After the women that Hal befriended came back to his apartment and cleaned up, some of them asked if they could stay with him, or in some cases, Hal volunteered to let them stay overnight. The lengths of time they stayed varied from months or years to a few days in the case of the most recent story, which is fairly typical:

> According to Hal, he was exiting the front door of his apartment building when he ran into a "Spanish" woman in front of the building who was being accosted by a young "Mexican guy" who insisted upon offering her money for her favors. She was trying to get away from him, but he was being quite persistent. Hal spoke up and said, "You leave my sister alone." The young man pointed out that the woman couldn't be Hal's sister as Hal isn't Spanish, so Hal informed him that the woman was his adopted sister, and the young man finally left. The woman thanked Hal and they struck up a conversation. Hal discovered that the woman, June, had "been on the street" for about 3 days [Hal didn't know why], so Hal offered to buy her breakfast. He asked her if she would like to try on some of the deceased Sally's clothes, so she accompanied him back to his apartment. Unfortunately, Sally's clothes didn't fit. Hal also told June to take a bath. She said she couldn't do that; he might come in and look. He was incensed and said he wouldn't do that. She finally took a bath. He wanted to take her out to eat, but she said that he didn't need to do that, there was food in the refrigerator, and she would cook for him. She stayed for about 3 days and left to take her sister to a clinic, saying she would return, but by the time Hal told me this story a few days later, she still had not come back. She left a coat and a pair of stockings in Hal's apartment. Hal says she might have ended up in the hospital herself because she had a very bad

burn on her bottom, "some guy had burned her." Hal had the medicine which the doctor had given him when he burned his hand some time back, and he offered to put it on and bandage the wound. At first, June resisted, saying that Hal might "try something," but when he assured her that he wouldn't, she finally let him help her. A little later, Hal commented that he wouldn't have tried anything even if she had wanted him to because it would have hurt her burn. Hal also said at one point that she might be in jail because two "Spanish guys" tried to rape her, and she "kicked them where she shouldn't have." [I never got a clear answer as to why this should have put *her* in jail.] At any rate, Hal obviously wished that she would return.

One of the longer relationships that Hal has had with a woman falls into this subgroup as well. Hal has called her by various names (Caroline, Sarah) in different versions of this story. He "picked her up" on the street one day, down and out, dirty, and with nowhere to go. She came home with him and stayed for more than 3 years. According to Hal, she cooked and cleaned for him, and they did things together; he describes her as always very nice to him. At first, Hal denied having sex with her, saying that she was in her early 20s and he was in his late 30s at the time. However, when she was mentioned in conversation at a later time, he admitted that they had had sex. One day she simply disappeared. Hal later found out that she had decided to go back home to her family in the East. Hal says he got a letter from her mother offering him $1,500 for taking care of the young woman all that time.

The other two significant relationships with women (other than Midge, his wife) which have lasted for more than a short period of time are also both with women whom Hal was taking care of in some way. One was with Sally, mentioned above, who died a few months before I met Hal. When I first started seeing him, some of the other people in Hal's life were referring to Sally as Hal's wife. Hal told me that this was not so; not only was he still legally married to Midge, but Sally was his niece. However, during a later discussion, Hal said that Sally was his mother's sister's daughter, making her Hal's first cousin. Hal told me two completely different stories about how he and Sally came to live together. The first of these stories fits into the pattern described above:

> When I asked Hal what Sally was like, he told me that when she wasn't doing drugs, she was a "real nice girl." Hal then corrected himself and said, "woman, a real nice woman." I asked if she did street drugs, as well as her medicine for epilepsy, and Hal said yes. She was still doing street drugs up to the time of her death. I asked Hal how he met her and he said it was in Denny's. Hal says he was sitting there late at night tallying up checks for the waitresses when Sally walked up, sat down, and said, "Buy me something to eat." Hal says she was dirty and poorly dressed, and he handed her a comb and told her to go clean herself up and he would buy her dinner. She went into the ladies room and

combed her hair, washed up, and came back. Afterward, he took her to the Outlet [a local discount store] and bought her a new dress and some underwear. She told him he was nice and asked if he were "hooked up with anybody." He said no, and she asked if she could come and stay with him. At first he resisted and told her that he didn't really want anyone to live with him. However, she talked him into trying it for a week, and she said if he didn't like having her around, she'd leave. Hal finally agreed. They got along, so they stayed together. He says that when they went back to the hotel, Sally told the desk clerk that she was his niece, and that's how the story that they were related got started. I asked if she really was or not, because he had told me both at one time or another. Hal looked a little startled, but said, oh yes, they were actually related. However, he didn't know that when they started living together. His story of how he found out was a little confusing. Apparently, some other family member asked if he didn't have a woman named Sally living with him and then told him that they were actually related.

In the second story about how Hal met Sally, Hal told me that he met her when she worked as a waitress in a local restaurant about 10 years before she died. According to Hal, about 5 years later, Sally was hit in the back of the head with a gun during a robbery in the bar where she was working at the time. After that "she couldn't think straight." She was drawing SSI because of her epilepsy and having trouble handling her money. She went to the SSI office with a man she knew and had him listed as a co-payee on her checks so that he could cash her checks and control her money. The problem was that he also started taking about half of it. Hal finally told her that because she was his niece, they should have Hal's name put on her checks instead of the other man's name. From that time on, Hal helped her handle her money. Finally, about 2 years before she died of an epileptic seizure, Sally and Hal moved in together. During the time they lived together, Hal spent considerable time taking care of Sally. Not only did she have epilepsy, she also used drugs and was in occasional trouble with the police.

The second significant relationship, one that still continues intermittently, is with Marsha, a young woman approximately 35 years younger than Hal, with whom he has a father/daughter style relationship. Hal says that he dated Marsha's mother many years ago, and when the mother started having trouble controlling Marsha, who was about 17 years old then, she asked Hal if he would take care of her. When Hal first came into contact with Marsha, she was basically living on the street, sometimes spending the night in 24-hour restaurants or the bus station, so Hal took Marsha home to his apartment. At that time, Marsha was having frequent uncontrolled seizures, and Hal described having to take care of her, including cleaning her up after she was incontinent at the end of the seizures. Hal finally insisted that she see a doctor, who put her on medication, and she no longer has seizures. Marsha has lived with Hal off and on since that time, and she refers to him as her father. She often says that he is the only father she has ever really had. Marsha has worked sporadically through the years, but has frequently taken advantage of Hal to support her. Marsha was married for a time to an El Salvadoran, and she had a child. Both she and the baby eventually ended up living with Hal. This became a real problem because Marsha would leave the baby in Hal's care and then not come home in time for Hal to go to work. In fact, Marsha mentioned that she and Hal had been accused of beating her child when it was an infant, and they were taken to jail, according to Marsha, for 2 weeks, although she does not think any charges were ever filed. When Hal was asked about this story, he said that it was true, but it was for 5 days instead of 2 weeks. The only reason that they were there for that long was because the time fell over a long weekend.

> According to Hal's version, he was upstairs with the baby, [who] was lying on the bed. Marsha had gone downstairs to talk to an old man "who used to give her money." Hal went downstairs and told her to come back up and take care of her baby. Somehow, when they went upstairs, the father of the baby followed them "accidentally." The baby was lying on the floor, apparently having rolled off the bed, and she had a bruise on her cheek. Without asking the circumstances, the father of the baby accused Hal of having hit her and asked him why he did that. Hal told him that he didn't hit her, but the father wouldn't believe him. The father called the police, who came and took both Marsha and Hal away. Hal says that one of the policemen at the jail kept asking him, "Why did you hit that little baby?" Hal kept saying he didn't do it. They were eventually released without being charged or going to court.

Although there is no doubt that Marsha takes advantage of Hal, she also gives him intermittent affection and a sense of "family." Typically, she lives with Hal for a while and eventually either gets into a dispute with him or leaves to live with some new man in her life. In 1989, she went back to a small town to work at a waitressing job that she once held in the past. Her current boyfriend, a drug user whom Hal dislikes intensely, went with her. She keeps in touch by writing infrequently and seeing Hal when she comes to town once a month to get her seizure medication refilled.

In addition to the stories above concerning Hal's relationships with women, there is a second distinct subgroup. The typical format of the subgroup is as follows: Hal meets a woman, usually very attractive, who makes advances to him. She has a boyfriend or husband, usually big and tough, about whose reaction Hal is quite worried. (Hal always checks out whether or not these women are married almost immediately. They frequently are.) The woman flirts with Hal, often leading to her kissing him.

The boyfriend/husband finds out about it and asks Hal what is going on. Hal tells the truth, but earnestly assures the boyfriend/husband that it is all very innocent and he is not up to anything. The boyfriend/husband says everything is all right and becomes friendly with Hal, sometimes buying Hal a meal or otherwise helping him.

The one major variation on this format usually occurs when Hal is traveling (Las Vegas, Kansas City, Paris, etc.) and meets a woman who takes an interest in him. The woman is fairly aggressive about her attraction to him and offers to see him after work (she is usually a waitress). Hal asks the woman if she is married. She usually is, but assures Hal that it is all right. They have a brief fling, which Hal usually says involves hugging and kissing (except the woman in Kansas City, with whom he admitted having sex). Afterward, the woman longingly tells Hal that she is willing to see him again should he ever return. The following story is one of the more elaborate examples of this second subgroup. It actually contains both variations, as well as elements of another major story pattern, which will be discussed below.

In the midst of a conversation with me, Hal mentioned that he had been in many countries. He claims that one of the only countries he has never visited is Germany. He stated that he had been in France, Jamaica [which I had just mentioned that I had visited], Tahiti, and several others. I asked how he came to be in France, and Hal responded that after he had worked for Cohen Metal Company for about a year, he started being invited to occasionally travel with Mr. Cohen, the owner. Mrs. Cohen was a dress designer who designed dresses for movie stars. According to Hal, they "had money to burn," and traveled frequently. Mr. Cohen was going to France alone, and he invited Hal to go along. They went to Paris, and one night when they were out eating in a restaurant [Hal stipulated that it was just a "regular" restaurant, not a fancy one], the waitress came to their table and said, "Hi, Honey —What'll you have?" Hal simulated his shocked reaction to her American slang as he said, "What?!" He says that he was very surprised because in France, most waitresses speak French. However, this one spoke English and was quite friendly. Mr. Cohen told Hal that he should ask her out. Hal responded, "Who, me? Naaah!" He went on to explain that she might be married, and besides, he didn't have any money. At this point, Mr. Cohen gave Hal $100 and said to go ahead and ask her. Hal did so, and she said she wasn't married. Hal went on to ask her out. They arranged that Hal would meet her when she got off work at 4:00 p.m. Hal then took her out to dinner and a show. He says that he kissed her but "didn't have sex with her or anything." She told him that if he ever came back to France, he should look her up. One day, 2 or 3 years later, Hal and Mr. Cohen were in the Brown Derby restaurant when the waitress walked over and said, "Hi, Hal!" It turned out to be the woman Hal had taken out in France. Hal, of course, asked what she was doing in the United States, and she told him that she had accompanied her parents when they immigrated to

America. The waitress then asked Hal if he would like to go out again, but he told her that he had married since he saw her last. The waitress then said, "That's O.K.; my husband wouldn't like it either." As it turned out, the waitress was married to the "head cook, or head chef, or whatever you call it." She pointed out the husband, and he was about 6'2" and ruggedly built. Hal laughed and said, "No, thanks!" The husband then came out and asked Hal if he was the one who took his wife out on a date in France. Hal gingerly answered in the affirmative, but then went on to explain that he didn't know she was married; she told him she wasn't. As it turned out, she wasn't married at the time, just engaged. Hal then asked if the husband was going to beat him up, but the husband laughed and assured him that he wasn't going to do that. The husband also told Hal that if anyone ever "bothered" Hal, he should let the husband know and he "would take care of them."

Some time later, Hal was walking by the front of the Ambassador Hotel when a "colored guy" pulled a knife on him and started to rob him. As luck would have it, the French husband lived across the street and happened to be looking out the window. He saw what was going on with Hal and dashed across the street to help. The husband ran up and told the assailant that if he "put a knife in this guy [Hal], I'll kill you." Hal says the assailant dropped the knife and "ran like hell." However, a motorcycle cop who was just getting off of his motorcycle had seen the whole thing, and he came walking over and asked the Frenchman why he had dashed across the middle of the street. The French husband said he didn't want to see Hal get knifed. The police-man said O.K., but don't do it again. The assailant kept running down the street [at this point, Hal switched the ethnicity of his assailant— "You should have seen that Mexican guy run."], and he passed a parked patrol car about a block away. The policemen in the patrol car thought he looked suspicious because he was running. They searched him and found a large butcher knife in his boot. [Hal had already said that the assailant dropped the knife that he had used to threaten Hal.] The police took the man in for carrying a concealed weapon. By the time the event was over, the police had discovered that the "Mexican guy" had raped and killed a woman in the area and had stuffed her body in a trash can in an alley. Hal says that he hasn't seen the Mexican guy around the area since, so he must be in jail.

Saviors

As mentioned above, the story of the French husband also contains an-other major story pattern that reflects an element of Hal's self-image— namely, that there are those around who are bigger, meaner, and more powerful than usual, who like Hal, and who may show up at the last minute in a crisis to "save" him. In addition to the French husband de-scribed above, there have been several other examples. In one instance, Hal's savior was female, the sister of a longtime male friend of Sally's who had spent most of his adult life in and out of prison. According to Hal, the man came from a large family, the members of which were all tough and mean. The man liked Hal and told him that if anyone ever "bothered"

Hal, to let the man know and he would "take care of them." One day this man's sister was in one of the local doughnut shops when she saw someone trying to rob Hal on the street outside. She ran out and "beat the hell" out of the robber. Hal says she was just as tough as her brother.

There is a significant variation on this pattern of "savior" stories, in which Hal is harassed by some authority figure until he either gets unbearably angry and hits the person who has been harassing him, usually beating up that person, or is forced into doing something for which he would ordinarily get into trouble in order to defend himself. Hal is then saved by some equal or higher authority figure who was watching and saw the entire event or who investigates and finds out the truth, then testifies in Hal's behalf.

One of the best examples from this group concerns how Hal came to leave the Army:

> I asked Hal how long he was in the service, and he said a year and 8 months. I then asked him how he happened to end up out of the service. He says that he and some of the other guys were playing cards while they were off duty. The pot had gotten quite large, about $5,000. A captain came by and said they weren't supposed to be playing cards, but Hal told him that they were off duty so they could do what they wanted. Hal went on to win the pot, but the captain stepped in, took the money, and said he would give it to their commanding officer. Hal confronted the captain (at about this point, one of the other men, a friend of Hal's, went running for the commanding officer), and told him that he had no right to take Hal's money. The captain said there was nothing that Hal could do about it, so Hal hit him. Hal says that he broke the captain's nose, broke his teeth, and blackened his eye. About this time, Hal's commanding officer showed up. According to Hal, there was some disagreement about what to do with Hal. General MacArthur and General Eisenhower wanted to court-martial him, but General Doolittle [Hal's ultimate commander] and Admiral Hershey said the captain shouldn't have taken the money away. "Some brigadier general" said let's compromise and give him an honorable discharge, but get him out of the service, so they did.

It should be noted here that, according to the hospital records, Hal was in the Army for about 9 months. Also, so far as I was able to determine, he never left the United States. In fact, at one time Hal said he was all set to be shipped overseas when the fact of his previous institutionalization turned up, and the Army would not let him go overseas. There probably was not a court-martial involved with Hal's leaving the Army because, according to the hospital social worker's notes, there was some question for the first few weeks after Hal got home from the Army as to whether or not he was going to go back to the service. When I asked Hal about this, he said yes, the Army wanted him back, but he was working by then and earning good money, so he decided not to go back. Hal told me other improbable stories about his service time, including that he was at Pearl Harbor the day after the attack and saw all the damage (he also maintains that his brother was below decks on the Arizona when it sank, but managed to get out alive), and that Hal's plane (he was the bombardier) was shot down over Tokyo on a mission with General Jimmy Doolittle. All five men aboard the plane stole separate Japanese planes and flew them to the Phillipines, where they ran out of gas. Hal was incredibly lucky. He did not know how to land the plane, but his co-pilot talked him down in a swampy area, so he got out with only minor scratches. Hal also told another fieldworker that he saved a girl's life on Guadalcanal.

There is no question that Hal's veteran status is very important to him. He collects a small veteran's pension, and he frequently mentions his time in the Army. He has remade history to give himself a more acceptable record of what most likely was a very traumatic experience (being unwillingly discharged from the Army during wartime).

The story above also contains another element that is important to Hal's self-image and that recurs in other stories—that Hal is physically able to take care of himself and to defend himself or others in his life when necessary. In stories in which he actually has fights, Hal is always the winner, usually without a scratch, and the men he hits usually end up with severe damage—broken noses, broken teeth, and lost consciousness. Some of these fights are in defense of himself, such as the one above, and some are in defense of others, such as the story he told me concerning why one of the local waitresses calls him "Bang Bang" as a nickname.

> I asked Hal why Terri calls him "Bang Bang." [When I had called the restaurant tying to get in touch with Hal, Terri had been confused about who I meant, but when she understood, she said, "Oh! You mean Bang Bang."] Hal says that there used to be another cafe in the area where he used to eat sometimes. There was a cute blonde waitress with whom Hal was friends, and one day, a man was giving her a hard time. When Hal told him to stop, he didn't and got belligerent with Hal. The man swung on Hal, and Hal hit him twice with short hard punches—bang bang. According to Hal, this is how he got the nickname.

At another time, an older man who obviously knew Hal, spoke to him as we were having breakfast in the same restaurant where Terri works. The older man called Hal "Shotgun." When I asked Hal later where the nickname "Shotgun" originated, Hal said he had known the man in the Army and the nickname must have come from there. The possibility also exists that both "Bang Bang" and "Shotgun" are related to the fact that Hal consistently wears western-style shirts.

This particular element is the only area of Hal's storytelling in which there seems to be a distinct change in the last few years. As recently as 3 years ago, Hal was telling a fieldworker who was seeing him at that time stories containing fighting sequences that were much more immediate in time (within 3 or 4 years of the telling). One of these stories involved Hal's beating up two young Hispanic would-be robbers so badly that they both died. The stories that Hal told me during the most current fieldwork cycle all took place much further in the past. In fact, Hal commented several times that he was quite strong when he was young. The stories he tells about recent times usually have Hal being "saved" by someone else. The explanation for this change is probably tied in with Hal's perception of himself as aging. He frequently mentions his age, and compares himself with the way he was when he was younger.

Famous People

In addition to the stories in which someone more powerful comes to save Hal from a bad situation, there is a group of stories in which famous people take notice of Hal and do something nice for him, such as treat him to dinner.

> Hal asked me if I knew who Dick Butkus was, and I said that I did. Hal says that one day he was at a football game sitting in seats which his boss had arranged for him on the 50-yard line. It seems that during one of the plays, Butkus tackled another player who then came piling into the crowd at the sidelines and into Hal. Hal says that Dick Butkus stopped to see if Hal was hurt, and when Hal said he was all right, Butkus told him to come down to the locker room after the game. When Hal did, Butkus talked to him and offered to take Hal out for a steak. He told Hal to wait in the parking lot for him, and then took Hal to the Pantry, bought him a steak, and was really a nice guy.

> The story about Dick Butkus led into a story that Hal had told before about "Glorious George," the wrestler [I think Hal means Gorgeous George because he describes him as a huge wrestler with long blond curls who was quite a dandy]. It seems that when Hal was working as a cook downtown in a restaurant next door to the local burlesque house, one of the girls gave him passes to the show, and Gorgeous George was in the audience because he was dating one of the girls, K.K. Hal met George because one of the girls introduced them, and George insisted on taking everyone out to eat, including Hal. When they got to the restaurant, Hal said he wasn't very hungry, but George insisted that he order a steak anyway. While they were eating, Hal was distracted talking to one of the girls, and he felt someone pat his shirt pocket. Hal says he assumed that George had reached over and taken a cigarette out of Hal's pack and he didn't think anything about it. However, the next day, Hal found a $100 bill in his pocket. When Hal saw George at a later time, George said, "Well, how'd you like your birthday present?" Hal says he told him it wasn't his birthday, but George just laughed.

The first version of this story that Hal told me was somewhat different, although most of the same characters were involved:

Hal was telling me about the girls he used to know at the Follies on Main Street. They were strippers, and he knew the head stripper, Jenny Lynn. She gave him a pass one night to sit down front by the runway. One of the girls, K.K., was dating "Glorious George," the wrestler. One night, K.K. asked if Hal wanted to kiss her. Hal thought George would beat him up. As it turned out, George said it was O.K., and even tried to tip Hal for cooking him a good steak. [That's how Hal knew the girls; he was a cook in the restaurant next door.] Hal says George pulled out a $500 bill and tried to give it to him, but Hal says he couldn't take that much.

Many of Hal's stories vary from telling to telling like the one above. This is especially true of smaller stories that are more for entertainment than to convey serious information about his past.

In addition to actual story patterns, there are stories that fall into groupings around particular subjects and that are reflective of the image Hal wishes to create of his life. The most important of these subjects are discussed below. My criteria for choosing those that seem most important to Hal are the frequency with which stories about these subjects arise and how elaborate the stories are.

Work

Perhaps the single most important element to Hal in his self-image is his identity as a worker. He is very proud of the fact that he has worked hard all of his life, starting with a paper route at the age of 7. Throughout my fieldwork with Hal, our conversations have been sprinkled with stories and comments referring to various jobs he has held. In fact, even when Hal refers to his periods of institutionalization at Pacific State Hospital, it is usually either about, or in the context of, whatever job he held at the time.

The majority of Hal's stories about work revolve around the period when he worked for Cohen Metal Company (which is not so unusual considering that this was by far the longest period of his work history). The stories have ranged from what Hal actually did on the job (such as working very long hours or overtime when they needed him, and working extra hard to make special production quotas), to traveling with the owner, Mr. Cohen (such as in the story above about the trip to Paris). There are also stories about being taken out with the other men from work for breakfast or dinner with the owner.

Hal also claims that at one time he drove a truck to places all over the United States, making deliveries for the company. In some of these stories, he was with other people, such as the owner's brother, and in others, Hal was alone. Some of these stories involved meeting women, such as the one in Kansas City mentioned above, and others involved things that happened with the truck, such as breakdowns or near-misses in accidents.

It is difficult to separate fact from fiction in these stories, although the trips to Europe and Hawaii seem highly unlikely at best. As far as I was able to determine, Hal has never actually had a driver's license, which makes over-the-road truck driving unlikely. (One interesting note is that Hal's wife Midge left him initially for a local truck driver, and then eventually was involved with an over-the-road driver. However, this possible connection is speculation.)

Family Life

Interestingly, the stories that Hal tells about this area of his life do not concern his two marriages, the first one to Hope and the second to Midge. Hal has told me virtually no stories concerning his life with either of these women. We have talked about them, and he answered my questions, but our discussions were more strictly informational, with few anecdotes or stories volunteered by Hal. Especially in the case of Midge, whom I also interviewed, this may have been partially because I was also visiting her (as had other fieldworkers in the past) and therefore had a way of trying to verify the stories if Hal had told them to me.

Hal has talked repeatedly, however, about what he claims was his first marriage, before Hope. There is no mention in the hospital records of this marriage, which is especially unlikely because a hospital social worker was making regular contact with Hal and his family during the time that this marriage supposedly took place. The woman Hal says he married had two children from a previous marriage. According to Hal, this marriage took place just before he went into the Army. The name of his first wife has changed in different discussions—Dorothy, Georgia, or Sarah. (Midge, Hal's wife, mentioned this first wife when talking about the past and called her Georgia, but I later discovered that Hal had told Midge about her.) The first time Hal mentioned this wife, the story was in abbreviated form:

> Hal says that he got married for the first time while he was in the service. They were both 18. [However, he later said she had three children, indicating that he meant before she met him.] I asked what happened to her, and he said she was killed in a car wreck. I asked what had happened to the children, and he said he didn't know. He then said they were in the car with her, but they "were strapped in the back seat" so they didn't get hurt in the wreck.

Over time, Hal elaborated on this basic story. In one discussion, he explained that the fatal accident happened while they were living in Hawaii when Hal was in the Army. However, in all of the other versions, Georgia was killed in Los Angeles. He later claimed that Georgia had two children when they got married, but that the third child was his. Hal says he had bought them a house and sent money home from the Army so that Georgia and the children would be provided for. Hal was in Texas at the time the accident happened, and the Army tried to send him a telegram, but by the time it got there, Hal had been shipped to Arkansas. By the time the telegram followed him to Arkansas, Hal had been shipped back to Texas. He claims that it was almost a year before he finally got the telegram. He went home to try to find his children, but no one knew what had happened to them. By asking questions of the police and people who lived near the accident location, Hal found out that a man and a woman had stopped at the accident, and seeing that Hal's wife was dead and no one was taking care of the children, they took the children and left with them. In one version of the story, Hal found out that the man let the woman and the children off at a bus stop. They took a bus to the Greyhound bus terminal and got on a bus to West Virginia. Hal was all set to drive to West Virginia looking for them, but the bus company checked and found that no one fitting that description got off of the bus at the other end, so Hal finally gave up.

At another time, Hal said that he eventually ran into his daughter, Janet, in Las Vegas where she was working as a waitress. When I asked how he recognized her after all those years, he said that he had had all of the children's names tattooed on their upper arms ("I don't know why; I just did."), and he recognized the tattoo. He told her who he was, showed her her birth certificate, and found out that a nice family had adopted her from an orphanage when she was very small. She did not know what happened to the other children. Because she had a nice family who had raised her, he decided to leave her there. She kept in touch with him for a while, but he has not heard from her in a long time.

In another version, Hal said his daughter's name was Sarah, and she had eventually met and married Ted Williams, the baseball player, and moved to Boston. In this version, he still hears from her occasionally.

When assessing this type of story, it is important to remember that Hal has never successfully arranged a real family life for himself. He has married twice, but his first wife, Hope, refused to leave her home town of San Diego and never actually lived with Hal. His second wife, Midge, lived with him for a few years and then left him for another man. Since that time, he has lived with a series of women for relatively short periods of time. Because he was sterilized as a patient at Pacific State Hospital, he was unable to have children. When asked about his feelings concerning the sterilization, Hal said that he wishes it had not been done, and that he would have liked to have had children. In the story above, Hal has created a more acceptable reality for himself. His wife, although not around at the present time, died as opposed to leaving him, thereby implying no rejection. His children, especially the natural daughter, were taken from him through no fault of his own, but still exist somewhere in the world. Hal has, in fact, carried on a pseudo–father/daughter relationship with Marsha through the years, but this is as close to a traditional family life as Hal has been able to come.

Institutionalization

The final cluster of stories to be covered here involves Hal's explanations of how he came to be institutionalized at Pacific State Hospital. One such story from a previous fieldwork period was related earlier in this chapter. The following story is indicative of the kinds of stories Hal told me:

> Hal says that when he was 13 years old, he had a doctored driver's license that said he was 16. He took his father's car without permission, and went with his girlfriend to park at the beach. He says that kids used to have fun going to the beach in those days. They were in the car kissing, when two policemen came by and shined their lights on them. They told them to get out of the car, and one of the policemen started pushing Hal around. The second one told him to quit pushing the kid around; Hal might get mad. The first policeman said, "Oh to hell with him," and pushed Hal again. Hal says he got mad and hit the policeman. According to Hal, he broke the policeman's nose and cracked his teeth. When he was brought to court, the first policeman [as a courtesy to Hal's father, who Hal claims was on the L.A.P.D. at the time] told the judge that Hal hit him "accidentally." However, the second policeman told the truth. Hal says that at first they were going to send him to "Norwalk," which Hal says is for the criminally insane, but instead they sent him to Pacific. He says that they sent him there because he was a violent kid who got into trouble all of the time, and they didn't want to send him to Juvenile Hall.

All of the stories Hal told me were either versions of the story above or similar stories in which he got into trouble with the police and ended up in Pacific.

After working with Hal for a considerable length of time, I finally broached the subject of the differences between his version of events and those contained in the hospital records and the court records of his commitment (i.e., that he had grabbed unknown women on the street and hugged them, that he frequented a house with other young people where sexual activity took place, that he had molested two young girls in a movie theater, and that he had been accused of being involved in a rape, although the records were very unclear on this last). Hal calmly addressed each charge. He said that he had never grabbed strangers on the street. Twice on his way home from the movies, he had walked by women who tripped (one tripped over her shoe lace, the other over the curb) and were about to fall down. Hal reached out to catch them, and he says perhaps someone saw this. Hal went on to say that, although he did frequent the house in question, he was not having sex there. There was some kissing and "fooling around" going on. Some adults showed up and caught some of the kids who were having sex and insisted that everyone was involved. No one would believe those who were not involved. Concerning the incident in which Hal was accused of molestation, he said he was sitting with friends at the movies, and two girls who were sitting in front of them kept standing up so that he and his friends could not see the movie. Hal finally put his hand on the head of the girl directly in front of him and pushed her down into her seat. The two girls complained to the manager, and it was the manager who insisted that Hal was "molesting" the girls and called the police. Hal said that all of his friends tried to stand up for him, but the adults did not believe them. As for the rape incident, Hal was not sure what this referred to. The only thing he could think of was an incident that happened one night as he was coming home from the movies. He was crossing a vacant lot when he saw something white on the ground on the other side of the lot. When he went to investigate, he found a woman who had just been raped and dumped in the lot. Hal took off his coat and covered her. About that time, the police showed up. (Hal speculated that someone in the neighborhood must have called them.) The police accused him of the rape, but the woman finally cleared him. We talked about these things briefly, and then Hal drew back and said quietly, but firmly, "That was a long time ago." He then deliberately changed the subject.

It is not difficult to understand why Hal might wish to recreate this period of time. For a 16-year-old boy to have been accused of such sexual misconduct in the 1930s, forced to deal with the police, taken to court, and then institutionalized must have been extremely traumatic. As in the stories involving women discussed above, Hal is still quite sensitive to the idea that people will misunderstand his sexual intentions.

Whatever the reasons behind Hal's storytelling, the fact remains that the stories, and particularly the quickness and consistency with which Hal can answer questions about them, show a highly developed imagination. Rather than adopt the label and lifestyle of being "mentally deficient," Hal has chosen to remake his personal history. In more than two years of regular contact with Hal, I had never heard him make any sort of reference to himself as mentally retarded, mentally deficient, or even disabled (except for the SSI-connected disability status based on the physical problem Hal has with his legs). I finally asked Hal if he was aware that he had been diagnosed as mentally retarded when he was at Pacific State Hospital. Hal did not seem surprised by my question, and although his answers were delivered in a tone of serious conversation, he did not seem upset by being asked. He explained that yes, he was aware of the diagnosis. He was also aware that his later test scores were significantly higher for his second admission, and he proceeded to tell me what those two test scores had been, 60 and 82. He then explained that he had tested still higher, 98, when he was in the Army. When asked how he felt about this diagnosis having been made when he was young, he shrugged and said it did not bother him because he knew it was wrong.

The reasons Hal gives for both periods of institutionalization in his life are based on trouble with the law and the avoidance of Juvenile Hall in the first instance, and jail in the second. These reasons are based on partial fact and are obviously more acceptable to Hal as a self-description. He told several stories about why he was in trouble that also blanked out references to unacceptable sexual activity, and when confronted with the version of events from the official records available, he carefully gave alternative explanations for each accusation. Some of these alternative explanations were quite plausible and may, in fact, have been true. It appears that Hal has adapted his personal history in such a way that he can live comfortably with unpleasant events without denying that they occurred.

The pleasure and amusement that Hal also derives from his storytelling should not be underestimated. The stories he weaves are a source of entertainment, in addition to their function as a method of image management, and they provide an opportunity for Hal to exercise his obviously fertile imagination. Hal's life and his environment do not provide many such opportunities, and he uses his storytelling as an outlet for his creativity.

CONCLUSION

Hal's life as he enters old age is reflective of many older retired men in America. He misses the purposefulness and routine of working life, as well as the sense of identity that being a "working man" gave him. He also misses the social interaction of work. When asked whether he considered himself better or worse off today as opposed to 10 years ago, he answered that things were definitely better 10 years ago when he was working.

Objectively speaking, however, Hal is certainly better off today than he was 5 years ago, when he had already been laid off from his job but was not yet collecting Social Security, and when the problem with his legs had worsened but was not yet medically controlled as it is today. His finances are more stable now than they have been at any time since he was working. Hal recently managed, through great persistence, to qualify himself for a subsidized housing program that pays a substantial portion of his rent, and the extra money he receives each month has been a great help. Although Hal preferred his old working life, he has adapted to his non-working lifestyle, and he says that he enjoys his life.

Hal's major complaint today is loneliness, as it is with many older single Americans. He is indeed somewhat socially isolated, but even though he is shy, he actively pursues social interaction for himself by getting out and around the neighborhood. He continues to search for the permanent relationship with a woman that has so far eluded him.

The major threat to Hal's continued well-being is, without doubt, the possibility that something will happen to his health. In general, Hal's medical care ranges from adequate to good. He has managed by trial and error, as well as through recommendations from other people, to find a doctor who seems to take good care of him. Hal has a standing monthly appointment with his doctor, so he is well monitored. Hal is fortunate that he is now old enough to have both Medicare and Medi-Cal, because his doctor, like increasing numbers of doctors in the area, does not accept Medi-Cal alone any longer. However, a major problem with Hal's medical care is that he frequently does not understand what is going on or what is going to be done to him. The example that follows occurred recently:

> Hal called me at the office to tell me that "they" were going to operate on him the following day for his "ulcers." (He had told me previously that his doctor was having him tested for ulcers.) I was quite surprised at the speed with which all this had arisen. When I questioned Hal about the details, he did not know the answers to most of my questions. He did not know exactly what they were going to do or how long he would be in the hospital. He only knew that he was to be operated on at 2:00 P.M. the following day. He then said with nervous embarassment, that they were going to "operate on [his] ass." By this time, I was quite confused as well. I volunteered to call his doctor's office for some information and Hal agreed. I talked to one of the nurses in the doctor's office, who remembered speaking to me before when I called to check out the possibility of bringing another member of the study to see the doctor. The nurse was quite willing to give me information about Hal. She gave me a complete rundown on him, including things that were not directly involved with the issue of surgery. The nurse said that Hal had been complaining of soreness in his rectal area, so they examined him and did a sigmoidoscopy. They found "huge" hemorrhoids that are quite severe, and the nurse was sure that he must have been in great discomfort for quite some time. However, she said that his complaints to them had just started recently. The doctor referred Hal to a surgeon who specializes in treating such conditions with cryosurgery (which is far less invasive than the old-style operation). However, she said that Hal's appointment with the surgeon was not scheduled for several days. She had no idea how Hal got the idea that they were going to operate on him the following day, unless he got confused about when his appointment with the surgeon was scheduled and went early. It is conceivable that if he did, the surgeon might have had an opening and scheduled Hal for surgery right away. The nurse said that if this had occurred, Hal's doctor had not been notified yet. As far

as the nurse was aware, they had never checked Hal for ulcers, nor had he complained of any symptoms that would lead them to suspect ulcers. It is probable that Hal had somehow confused ulcers with hemorrhoids, or else was embarrassed about the hemorrhoids. The nurse said that Hal's prostate is also quite enlarged. They ran an ultrasound test on him, and she said that there is no sign of malignancy. They think it looks like a cyst. She said that Hal insisted that it was not bothering him, so they decided to clear up the painful hemorrhoid problem first. They obviously really like him in the office. The nurse said several times that if there was anything at all they could do or explain for him to please call. She also commented on what a "sweet" man he is. She told me not to hesitate to call her if I needed more information in the future. She did make the comment that Hal always seemed to not want to bother them and therefore they sometimes did not know if he needed something or when he did not understand something. I contacted Hal and gave him the information from the nurse, and he agreed to call the surgeon's office to double-check his appointment. The result was that Hal eventually had the first of three treatments for his hemorrhoids approximately 2 weeks later.

Hal is fortunate to have found a good doctor and an office staff who like him and are interested in his welfare. Not all of it is luck, however; Hal can be very persistent until he gets what he wants, and this includes his medical care. However, like many, if not most, of the people in the general population, Hal has some trouble understanding what he is told about his medical conditions and care. What he really needs is an advocate ("translator") to help explain things to him and to know what questions to ask medical professionals so that he gets appropriate information. Hal is quite capable of making his own decisions, once he is given enough understandable information to do so. When he does not have such information, he simply does the best he can and trusts that things will work out. However, if he has more serious health problems as he gets older, particularly if those problems involve more difficult-to-understand treatments or complex at-home care, Hal's lack of understanding may pose greater difficulty.

Hal's life is relatively stable at the current time (1990). But for someone like Hal, who is alone and who does not have much in the way of a personal support system in the event of a crisis, that hold on stability can be tenuous. Hal possesses, however, two qualities that have helped him endure crises and periods of instability in the past. One is his persistence, and the other is a quiet faith in himself and his ability to handle events and obstacles in his life. In fact, rather than merely trying to hang on to stability, Hal is actively involved in trying to improve his life, as witnessed by the long and tedious bureaucratic process he recently went through to qualify for subsidized housing. With even a little luck, Hal may remain independent, compctent, and actively involved with the world around him for some time to come.

2

"I'll Manage These Things as They Come Up."
MIDGE NELLIN ARNAUD

by Marcia A. Gaston

Although the description springs more from her appearance and manner than from actual behavior, Midge Arnaud looks as though she were born to play the role of neighborhood busybody. With her brusque approach, forthright friendliness, and aggressive physical movement, she seems to have "no nonsense" written all over her. Midge has gained weight in the last few years, but she gives the impression of strength and stockiness rather than obesity. She rarely, if ever, wears dresses, but instead favors various pants outfits that, combined with her bustling walk, contribute to the impression of an active, competent person engaged in various errands and activities. Her style of dress may, in fact, contribute to the impression that she is younger than her 65 years. Midge enjoys thinking and talking about what she calls her "outfits," and she obviously puts a good deal of thought into planning her wardrobe. She is always appropriately dressed, and her clothing is neat and clean. The overall image she projects is one of being middle-aged and middle-class. In terms of appearance, Midge's two most individual characteristics are the curler caps in various colors that she always wears over her graying hair and the large and heavy shopping bag that she habitually carries with her, filled with all the things she thinks she might need while she is away from home, such as extra clothes, snacks, and her purse, as well as purchases she makes and odds and ends that she simply likes to carry with her, such as photos and word puzzle books. Because she flushes easily from heat or exertion, Midge's round face is frequently a bit red from bustling about. (She insists that she has always flushed this way and that she has never had any trouble with either her blood pressure or her heart.)

LIFE TODAY

Midge lives with her brother in a small city to the east of Los Angeles. The house they live in was jointly owned by her brother and their mother, and all three had been living there together before the mother's death in 1986. Crammed with a collection of items accumulated by the family through the years, the house is in an ethnically mixed, lower middle-class neighborhood that Midge says has deteriorated through the last few years. The house itself would be rather attractive except for the fact that the yard is mostly bare dirt. Midge says that, several years ago before her mother died, someone who had been hired to mow the grass cut it too close, the grass died, and they have never had enough money to have the yard replanted.

According to Midge, crime is a problem in the area because of drugs and the people who deal them, particularly those in one of the houses across the street from her home. She says that one of the young black men who lives in that house, along with some of his friends, was "busted" for drugs not long ago, and that these young men now have "a revenge thing" against Midge and her brother because this group thinks that Midge and her brother turned them in to the police. Midge claims that although she and her brother have seen "limousines drive up to the house and people with bags of dope," they were not the ones who contacted the police; it was other neighbors. She describes a rather constant police presence within the area, including both uniformed and plain-clothes patrols and helicopter patrols at night. Midge and her brother, like many older people, do not go out after dark, and they usually do not both leave the house at the same time, thus avoiding the risk of leaving it unattended. According to Midge, she and her brother also sleep in their clothes so as not to be taken by surprise, and she keeps a length of pipe by her bed for protection. However, although there is no doubt that Midge takes the situation seriously and is careful about protecting herself, she also tells of the police activity in her neighborhood with a certain sense of relish and excitement. Midge seems to have very positive feelings about the police. She says that she and her brother wave at the police helicopters when they fly over the house and that the pilots "dip" at them. She also says that they received condolences from both the police and the sheriff's department when her mother died, because "everyone" knew her mother.

Midge's relationship with her brother, who has been supporting her financially since her mother died, seems to be a good one. When she moved back into the home in 1982, there was an initially stormy period of adjustment, during which her brother attempted to dominate her and to tell her what to do. Midge, who has been stubborn and independent all of her life, did not take kindly to the attempt. As Midge puts it: "Some people I can get along [sic]. But some people like to push you and I don't like to be pushed. 'Cuz when I lose my temper, you better watch out." However, after the intercession of both their mother and an older brother, a workable relationship was built between the two. Midge says that her brother has come to accept that Midge is an adult with her own life and that he should not try to run it for her. He has also come to value the help she has provided in caring for her mother before she died and, subsequently, for him as well. On her part, Midge speaks of her brother with real affection and worries about his well-being and his multiple health problems. He has an impairment in one leg from an accident for which he draws a railroad pension, and he has heart problems. He also has skin problems that Midge says are brought on by "nerves." Midge even worries over the fact that he has no girlfriend and wishes that she could find "some nice woman" for him. She tells tales of practical jokes they play on one another, and she indicates that he shares her well-developed sense of humor. With the two parakeets they keep and an occasional stray cat, home is anything but a dull place.

However, although Midge speaks very positively of her relationship with her brother, she still becomes agitated when she feels she has made a mistake, in her words "screwed up," and she worries about what he will say. An example occurred when she did not adequately carry out the at-home instructions for a test she was to undergo at a local hospital. (She drank the several glasses of water as instructed, but she urinated although instructed not to do so before coming to the hospital.) After being spoken to in a rude and highly critical manner by the technician at the hospital and told that she would have to reschedule the test and come back at another time, Midge spent considerable time worrying about what her brother would say if he found out. She finally stated:

> I'm not going to say anything to my brother about it. He gets me upset every time. And he can't learn to keep his mouth shut. He did it this morning. I was in the bathroom this morning and, uh, I got dressed and everything and I came out. I didn't see any ants on the, uh, floor. So when he went in there he seen some ants on the floor. And he jumped on my mother too, my mother and I both. Why we didn't come, uh, go in the kitchen and get the spray can and go in there and spray it. Then later on he finally apologized.

Midge sometimes simply keeps her activities secret from her brother when she thinks they will displease him. When I first began fieldwork with Midge, she requested that we meet at a public place away from her home. She said that her brother did not approve of her visiting with our fieldworkers, saying that we were "too nosey," but that she enjoyed the visits. Her attitude seemed to be that, although she felt that she had a right to do as she pleased, she did not want him to know about it. During a later visit, Midge said that she finally had told her brother that she was meeting with me and that he did not mind as long as I did not come to the house. (This attitude is in marked contrast to that of Midge's mother who welcomed a previous fieldworker to the home and talked with her during one of the visits with Midge.)

It should be noted, however, that Midge is concerned in general with other people knowing about her business, and based on descriptions of her behavior recorded by past fieldworkers, her secretiveness seems to have increased over the past few years. In the past, Midge allowed fieldworkers to tape-record their conversations with her, although she requested at one point that the tape recorder not be in plain sight on a restaurant table. Recently, she has refused any tape recording at all in public, which effectively cut off all taping because Midge's brother did not want fieldworkers at the home. "You never know who might be listening," she explained, "and they might use it against me. This is a small town you know." Midge often has mentioned, "I don't like everybody to know my business." She is noticeably concerned about being overheard in public, and when discussing something she considers sensitive, she usually lowers her voice and acts mildly conspiratorial.

In the evenings, Midge and her brother watch television or play cards. Midge likes word puzzle books and usually carries one tucked away in her shopping bag. Her brother likes jigsaw puzzles and frequently has one in progress. Midge has always been interested in current events and is usually quite well informed on the current news, both local and national. She is a staunch Democrat, but she says that since her mother, the only other Democrat in the family, died, she feels surrounded by Republicans. Midge is a registered voter and sees voting as her absolute obligation. She is a loyal supporter of the female mayor of her city, and she carries a newspaper photograph of the woman in her wallet. Midge is also quite familiar with the geographical layout of her city and its landmarks. Even though she does not drive, Midge can usually give succinct and clear directions, using a combination of streets and landmarks.

With the exception of recurring problems with a bleeding ulcer, Midge says that she is generally in good health. She has minor trouble with arthritis, but not enough to worry her. Midge was diagnosed as diabetic in the past, and at one time, she was working with a nutritionist to control her diabetes through proper diet. She no longer mentions diabetes as a health problem. However, Midge's diet seems to be very high in sugar. She continually buys cookies, candy, and other sweets to take home for herself and her brother to eat while they are watching television, so the diabetes may become more of a problem again in the future.

Midge's daily routine is centered around keeping house for herself and her brother and running errands for both of them. She takes the bus downtown to pay bills as they come due and to buy groceries and other items that they need at home. If she has a large load of groceries or packages, she usually takes a cab home. Along her route, Midge knows many people by sight and frequently by name as well. These include bus drivers, cab drivers, police officers, salespeople, and the occasional regular customer like herself. Midge greets them all with a wave and a hello, and sometimes a teasing comment or two. These interactions are usually quite superficial, but they are obviously important to Midge, and she uses them to help her feel connected to her community. However, Midge does seem lonely at times, despite the fact that she covers it with her busy demeanor, her friendliness, and her future plans. In the past, Midge has talked of friends with whom she socialized and boyfriends whom she dated, but since she returned to live in her mother's home, she makes no such references. Other than the superficial interactions mentioned above, Midge's activities seem to be confined to things she does by herself or with her brother. She does sometimes seem hungry for company, although she *never* gives the impression of feeling sorry for herself. When asked whether she had investigated any of the senior centers in her area concerning their trips and social activities, Midge answered that she could not be gone that long from checking on her brother. She says that he has pains in his chest from his heart condition and sometimes passes out, so she is never gone from home more than a few hours.

In general, Midge seems content with her life although she continues to make optimistic plans for changes in the future—winning enough money in one of her mail-order contests to buy a nicer house in a better neighborhood for herself and her brother, or possibly finding "some nice woman" as a potential wife for her bachelor brother. After decades of struggle against what might have proved insurmountable circumstances for many people, Midge remains independent and optimistic. A brief sketch of Midge's life is presented below in order to document just how hard-won Midge's belief in herself has been.

THE PAST

Midge's family background is lower middle-class, white, Baptist, and a hodgepodge of British and Scandinavian ancestries. Her father, a naturalized U.S. citizen, was born in England and immigrated to the U.S. at the age of 24. Within 3 years, he had settled in California and was working for the railroad from which he would eventually retire as a car inspector. At the age of 33, he married Midge's mother, who was originally from the midwest and who was 19 years old at the time of her marriage in

1916. Both of Midge's parents had eighth-grade educations. The first of seven children (two sons, Midge, another son, and three younger daughters, in descending birth order) was born the following year. The births of the seven children were widely spaced (1917, 1919, 1922, 1925, 1933, 1938, 1941) over an unusually long period of 24 years.

Midge was a full-term baby, born after a normal labor (3 hours). Although her birth weight was low (4 lbs.), she was considered "normal" at birth. On the admission application for Pacific State Hospital, Midge is listed as developing normally physically, but not mentally. However, on the same form, she is listed as beginning to talk by about 1 year of age, but not beginning to walk until the age of 3. (It is possible that whoever was filling out the application made an error.) Her parents stated that her mental "defect" was first noted "by her school reports." They also replied "do not know" when asked what they considered to be the cause of her "mental deficiency." Midge had the standard childhood diseases of the time: measles, chickenpox, mumps, and whooping cough. When asked to pick traits from a prepared list, her parents chose "cheerful, changeable, emotional, dull, truthful, [and] affectionate." When asked what they expected of Pacific State Hospital, Midge's parents stated: "to find out what is wrong with her [and] treat her, so when she is cured, [she] will be able to take care of herself."

According to Midge's oldest brother, who came forward to provide information when Midge was admitted, Midge's home life was not a happy one. The parents had "never gotten along well together," and Midge's mother constantly scolded and criticized her. He said that Midge was unwanted and their mother told her so repeatedly. The mother also picked on her and would not let her go out as she did the other children. According to Midge's brother, the mother's behavior became more abusive as she got older and reached menopause; in conjunction, Midge became more difficult to handle as she, in turn, grew up. Midge finally reached the 11th grade by the time she was 20 years old, and although her reading and writing were listed as good and fair respectively, her attitude toward school was poor. She was being teased by the other students, her behavior was disruptive, and she would not study, so her parents finally took her out of school and kept her at home.

Institutional Life

By the time of her commitment to Pacific State Hospital 5 years later, Midge was described as fairly efficient at helping her mother with the housework, but quite unreliable in that she could not be left alone in public, and when left at home with the other children, she sometimes disappeared. This last factor had become crucial because Midge had begun to brag about her relationships with men and that she had had intercourse. The parents had kept quite a strict watch on Midge, and they did not think the stories of intercourse were true, although such a possibility existed. The parents thought it more likely that the stories were made up to get attention, after Midge overheard other girls discuss sex. However, Midge's father felt that some of the young men she knew were "no good," and he was worried about his daughter. Pacific State Hospital agreed to admit Midge and to sterilize her as soon as possible so that she would not "get into difficulty."

Midge was nearly 26 years old when she was admitted. Although her IQ was measured at 65 at the time of admission, the results of her psychological tests at the time (Rorschach Test, Thematic Apperception Test, Minnesota Multiphasic Personality Inventory) indicated that her potential intelligence may have been somewhat higher than measured. However, the psychological tests also found considerable indication of emotional disturbance ("schizophrenic personality structure," "autistic thinking," "evidence of paranoid personality elements") that may have confounded the intelligence test scores. The summation of information at the time suggested:

> Poor social adjustment in a setting of no more than mediocre intelligence with considerable tendency to ignore reality and to condemn in others faults which she does not admit in herself. This may amount not so much to active pathology as to a schizoid trend associated with limited intelligence.

Midge was admitted to Pacific State Hospital in April 1948 and was sterilized in February 1949. She attended one more year of school at Pacific from 1949 to 1950 and was assessed at approximately 5th-grade level overall. Her reading, writing, and spelling were listed as 6th-grade level, and she apparently wrote the school news. However, her performance assessment in arithmetic was slightly under 4th-grade level. There was evidence of what seems to be an intense lifelong interest in current events, and she was familiar with important dates and happenings in American history. She was also praised for her homemaking skills. In the sheltered atmosphere of school at Pacific State Hospital, Midge was described as sociable, courteous, thoughtful, trustworthy, and dependable. The only criticism was that, although she would accept correction, she had a tendency to work without waiting for the direction she needed and therefore made many errors and became impatient.

Although her father repeatedly asked that she receive training in some sort of trade so that she could be self-supporting, it was decided at Pacific that work training for Midge would center around her homemaking skills. From the time of her admission, Midge had stated that she wished to work in a beauty shop. However, when she was placed in the beauty shop at Pacific on a trial basis, she proved to be very slow and to require a great deal of supervision. It was decided by the staff that the work was beyond her capabilities and that the family's plans for Midge to learn a trade were "evidently above the patient's mental level." Consequently, Midge spent the 7 months following her year of school in homemaking class, with the ultimate goal being industrial parole and placement as a domestic worker in a private home or sanitarium. Midge's family seemed willing to go along with any reasonable plan that included removing the burden of Midge's support from their already overtaxed resources. (Midge's father had only his $100-per-month railroad pension and still had small children in the home, and her older brother was having difficulty supporting his own family.)

The remarks on Midge's progress in homemaking class were somewhat at variance with the more lenient assessment in school, and they give evidence of problems that continued on her work leave placements:

> Quite friendly when in a social group, but rather aloff [sic] in the classroom. Has quite a few sly mannerisms which suggest selfishness more than deceit. She does not enjoy close personal relations and would rather work alone. She is quite firm in her beliefs to the point where she thinks she is always right. Her appearance is always neat, but she is vain and conscious of boys. . . . Quiet and orderly, becomes upset when she makes an error, but is respectful when reprimanded even though she does not agree. . . . She resents being directed in any of her work routines and has a "know it all" attitude. She feels far more superior than she really is, will begin a task without directions and makes quite a few errors. . . . Midge has the ability to do excellent work. She is quite alert, catches on quickly and with clear directions needs little supervision. . . . Midge can become a good helper, and emotionally, she is quite mature. She is slow and does need directions. Her work habits need improving. She needs a placement where she can be supervised.

There are also brief mentions in the hospital notes of difficulty with poor behavior on the ward, extending, at one point, to Midge allegedly giving another female patient a black eye.

Work Leave

In 1950, Midge was given work leave and placed in a private home as a domestic helper. Returning Midge to the family home was not considered, due to the opinions of both the hospital caseworker and Midge's brother that the mother's treatment of Midge was quite destructive. (In fact, the woman who was Midge's second employer happened to be visiting in the small town where Midge's parents lived and paid them a visit, hoping to interest them in Midge. She concluded, after her visit, that "the mother's feelings were so deep-seated that very little could be accomplished to help her to feel differently towards [Midge].") The feeling of the staff at Pacific State Hospital was that perhaps an alternative family situation could be created for Midge by placing her in a private home and creating a stable situation. However, Midge's history over the next 5 years was anything but stable.

Midge had nine placements over the 5 years. Each typically began with great enthusiasm on the part of her employers, who welcomed her into their homes, and then rapidly degenerated to the point at which they asked that she be removed. Part of the problem lay in Midge's personality. She could be quite stubborn, intransigent, and argumentative when confronted with criticism. The major objective problems seemed to be that, although her work was generally good, Midge tended to be very slow and would sometimes try to get out of work; that she was not able to assume responsibility or to handle work without close supervision; and that she was overly interested in pursuing her relationships with men and sometimes behaved inappropriately in this respect.

Midge's first placement lasted only one week before her new employer requested that Midge be removed because she had become too friendly with a man who lived in the apartment building. Midge's caseworker from Pacific State Hospital felt that the employer had over-reacted to the situation and that, under the circumstances, it was just as well that Midge's placement was being changed.

The second placement, which occurred as a result of the transfer, began with a great deal of interest and understanding on the part of Midge's employer. This is, in fact, the same employer who visited Midge's family, and she was very understanding of the fact that some of Midge's problems probably stemmed from her rejection by her mother. The employer also seemed to understand Midge's above average interest in almost any man with whom she came into contact. Midge, for the most part, just wanted these men to notice her and speak to her, and she openly admitted this to her employer. The hope was that as Midge felt more secure and wanted in this placement, some of her problems would lessen. Midge remained in this placement for approximately 1½ years, but during the last year, it became apparent that the employer wanted Midge removed from her home. She stated that Midge needed a change and to make new friends, and indeed Midge's only complaint was that she was lonely there. However, the new Pacific caseworker assigned to Midge stated that it was quite obvious that the employer was not happy with Midge's work, particularly because Midge was not fast enough to please her. The caseworker suggested a sanitarium placement, and Midge was very enthusiastic. However, when the search for such a placement stretched out over several months, the employer finally insisted that Midge be removed even if it meant returning her to the hospital. The employer stated that she was going on a short vacation and then into the hospital for surgery and wanted Midge settled before she left. The case-worker managed an emergency transfer to a sanitarium the following day.

Unfortunately, through no fault of her own, Midge found herself caught in the crossfire of personnel disputes and "office politics" at the sanitarium in a very short time. The head nurse accused Midge of being a "sex problem." The owner of the sanitarium found Midge's behavior no more than ordinary and told Midge's caseworker that the head nurse was "mentally ill," that Midge's sexual problem was mostly in the head nurse's mind, and that the owner was asking the head nurse to resign. However, it came to light, through the caseworker for another Pacific patient working at the sanitarium, that the head nurse had been one of the informants who complained to the Social Welfare Department and other authorities that the owner was not properly feeding the patients from Pacific who worked at the sanitarium and was making them work long hours. The owner was therefore angry at the head nurse. Both Pacific caseworkers became involved in investigating the allegations, and after a misunderstanding with the owner brought about by false gossip spread by the second Pacific patient, Midge's caseworker decided that Midge was being properly and fairly treated.

By this time, however, the owner was considering asking for Midge's removal because she was not a good worker. Midge had fallen under the influence of one of the young nurses and a young boy who had been hired to do the yard work. She was very slow at her work of making beds and preparing ambulatory patients for getting up and going to bed, and her attitude had become poor. Midge's caseworker counseled her on these problems and discovered that Midge thought that she would be discharged entirely from Pacific, which she wanted, simply by remaining outside the hospital for 3 years. Her caseworker informed her that this was not the case and that her final discharge was entirely dependent on her ability to hold on to a job, to plan for herself, and to make "an adequate adjustment in the community." In response, Midge's work improved, helped along by the owner's firing of the young nurse and the yard boy, ostensibly because they were a bad influence on Midge. Through the next few months, the quality of Midge's work and the owner's feelings about keeping her on the job fluctuated in tandem, helped at times by such changes as having Midge see a social worker and the hiring of a new head nurse who took a great deal of interest in Midge.

The general consensus was that, with someone to take an interest in her and to provide close supervision, Midge was capable of doing her job. Through monthly contacts with both Midge and her employer, the Pacific caseworker managed to keep Midge on the job at the sanitarium for a year. However, no matter what the caseworker said or how many times she said it, Midge held to her belief that she would indeed be discharged from Pacific at the end of her 3 years outside the hospital (which coincided with the end of a year at the sanitarium) and that the sanitarium job was only temporary. According to the caseworker, Midge continued to make vague and unrealistic plans to find work in a factory when her discharge came through. When it was pointed out that she would have to pay her own room and board if she worked at a factory, Midge's response was that she would "manage these things as they come up." The caseworker stated: "Patient apparently has no recognition of her own limitations. Her judgment appears to be very poor and she has no sense of reality about living in the community." The caseworker was also quite concerned about the fact that Midge had very little supervision in her hours off from work at the sanitarium, and she felt that Midge showed the same poor judgment in her social life. Midge was apparently quite unrealistic about her relationships with men, continually speaking of marriage to men she had only just met under very casual circumstances.

At the end of Midge's 3 years on work leave, her discharge, predictably, did not come through. However, she was insistent on leaving the sanitarium as she had planned. She was told by her caseworker that she could leave only if she had a definite job and living arrangements confirmed first. During the first week after her 3-year anniversary, Midge found a job in the paper, interviewed for it, had the new employers contact her caseworker, and went to work in a private home again as a helper with the home and children. Her caseworker had reservations about the job because the children in the family were very young and because she felt that the employer would expect too much of Midge. However, Midge and the employer were both very enthusiastic, and the caseworker agreed to the move. As it turned out, the caseworker was right. In a little over 2 months, the employer was asking that Midge be replaced.

Midge proceeded to find another position, again as a "mother's helper," but this time the two children were older. When the caseworker pointed out that the $25-per-month (instead of the usual $40-per-month) pay offered by the job was not enough to cover her personal needs, Midge reluctantly but successfully negotiated with the new employers to raise the amount to $40. Midge got along relatively well in this position for about 7 months. Although her work continued to be slow, her employer felt that Midge tried hard to do a good job, and she got along quite well with the family.

Midge's caseworker continued to view her as "unrealistic about the adequacy of her work and her relationship to the employer," and "unaccepting of her own limitations." However, the caseworker's focus seems to have shifted to the problem of Midge's social relationships with men. Midge's employer had, in fact, commented on what she considered to be

Midge's poor social adaptation and the friends that Midge brought to the house. Midge continued to speak of men who were, in reality, "one-night-stands" or whom she had met briefly in bars, as loving her and wanting to marry her. According to her own statements, she sometimes accompanied men she had briefly met to motels; however, she seemed to see her activities as expressions of love and affection.

It is not difficult to see Midge as trying to capture the love and acceptance and freedom she so craved through her liaisons, no matter how brief, with men. These incidents must have been among the few times when there was no one around to watch and judge and report on what she did. Midge had always gotten along far better with her father than with her mother, and it is likely that she associated what warmth and affection she had known mostly with men. From Midge's experiences with her mother, her employers, and her caseworkers, it was usually women who had criticized, judged, and placed limitations on her. Midge's caseworker saw a return to Pacific State Hospital as the only way to limit Midge's activities with men, and she stated that she hesitated to do this because of Midge's competence in many other areas.

The decision to move on to her next position actually came from Midge rather than her employer or her caseworker. A couple who had met Midge more than a year before while she was working at the sanitarium had become close friends with Midge. She spent holidays at their home and was well liked by the couple and their five sons, one of whom was in juvenile hall. The couple had been requesting for some time that Midge be allowed to live and work in their home. They seemed to have a sincere interest in Midge, and identified with her because they had come from the same poor background and because Midge resembled the wife's own sister. They were realistic about Midge's problems, but felt that they could handle them. The caseworker had some misgivings about the move because the home showed some problems and was, she said, "not the type of home we would usually choose for our patients," but because of the warm relationship that already existed and the possibility of "more of a real home" for Midge, the caseworker gave her agreement. Also, because she wanted so much to make the move, Midge was losing interest in her current position and having difficulty concentrating on her work. Midge was, in fact, quite willing to move in with the couple and work without pay, which only strengthened her caseworker's opinion that Midge had no realistic awareness of money. The caseworker insisted that Midge must be paid Pacific's minimum wage for its patients, and the couple readily agreed.

Midge was very happy in the couple's home and was considered a part of the family. However, during the caseworker's second monthly visit, Midge was describing how well she was doing in the home when she happened to mention going out with the couple, Midge with the husband and the wife with a boyfriend. When the caseworker questioned her further, Midge spoke unself-consciously of having an ongoing intimate relationship with the husband. She "seemed unable to understand" why the caseworker felt that Midge should not be living with the couple. The wife denied Midge's allegations, spoke of Midge's tendency to misinterpret and her overactive imagination, and said she did not want Midge removed from the home. The caseworker was unable to contact the husband because of his work schedule during the week. The stalemate continued for some time, with the family and Midge firmly resisting her removal, until the caseworker pointed out to the wife "that the situation jeopardized both her children and her family," at which point the wife finally agreed to Midge's removal. Midge also finally agreed, although the caseworker stated that neither Midge nor the couple "fully accepted it but were merely doing it because of patient's status with the Agency and if patient is discharged she will return to their home."

The question of whether or not Midge was telling the truth was never resolved. Even the caseworker was unsure. On one hand, Midge had been quite explicit during her meetings with the caseworker about the situation. On the other, the couple denied that the story was true and said that Midge was misinterpreting. Midge did, in fact, have a history of misinterpreting relationships, particularly with men. The decision was made to place Midge at a sanitarium in an entirely different part of the city, not only to remove her from the vicinity of the couple's home, but also because she had worked in the same area for a number of years and both her caseworker and the wife of the couple felt that she was known in the neighborhood bars as an easy pick-up. Once Midge accepted the idea, she apparently looked forward to the move as a chance to make new friends. However, Midge remained at the sanitarium for only a month. She was very unhappy and said that the work was too difficult. She also had trouble getting along with other Pacific patients working there and wanted to work in a private home.

Unfortunately for Midge, she was moved into a home in which other Pacific patients had already had difficulty. The reasoning seems to have been that there were no small children in the home, and therefore the workload would not be excessive. Also, the employer was known for not being too strict, and Midge would have as much independence as possible. Things went well at first, but within a month, the situation began to deteriorate seriously. The new employer had no tolerance or understanding of Midge's need to exaggerate, and she began to argue with Midge and question any story she told. Things finally came to the point where Midge and the employer were shouting at each other constantly, and Midge was removed at the end of the second month. All involved, except the employer, came to the conclusion that the employer seemed to be hysterical and disturbed.

Midge's removal and subsequent placement were negotiated by a new caseworker to whom Midge's case had been transferred. The new caseworker seriously considered returning Midge to the hospital due to her poor record of adjustment. Prior to transferring Midge to the next placement, the caseworker talked extensively with the new employer, giving her a very realistic report on Midge's problems and negative history. The new employer, however, was still willing to give Midge a chance.

The new placement went smoothly for nearly a year. The employer was quite satisfied with Midge's work, and even though the employer was gone from home frequently, Midge seemed to handle the house and the children with ease. She settled into a very warm relationship with the family, who took a personal interest in Midge and her life. Both the employer and her husband were outgoing, casual people, and neither they nor Midge's new caseworker seemed put off by Midge's attitude and behavior toward men. They accepted Midge's lifestyle with considerable understanding and without making moral judgments. Because Midge continually expressed her desire for marriage, both the employer and her husband tried to counsel Midge on better ways to go about it, including exercising restraint with men as a basis for building more lasting relationships. The employer helped Midge with the selection of more attractive clothing and included such items in holiday gifts to Midge.

Midge's caseworker felt that, even though Midge's casual affairs never led to the marriage she wished, she still derived a great deal of satisfaction from them. The caseworker saw Midge as a cheerful person who had no trouble making friends. Midge also seemed to be maturing somewhat about her social relationships. After several months of wishing to return to the couple's home that she had been forced to leave, Midge had finally disassociated herself from them after coming to the disillusioning conclusion that the wife wanted her in the home mostly as a source of cheap labor. Midge had also become involved with the Friendship Club that Pacific State Hospital had organized for ex-patients and patients on leave, and she had been elected to serve as one of the club officers, which delighted her. However, she did not socialize with these other patients outside of the club. Midge had also ceased pushing so hard for her final discharge from the hospital. Perhaps because of her happiness with her environment and the good relationship she had with her caseworker, Midge seems to have seen her relationship with the hospital as more supportive than she had previously.

After nearly a year on this placement, Midge herself created an unfortunate and quite unpleasant incident. Because things had been going so well, Midge's caseworker was quite surprised when Midge called to ask permission to go on a job interview. Although Midge was initially evasive, she finally told the caseworker that the job was doing maid's work at a hotel in Hollywood for $75 per week plus a room. After buying food, this would have left her with less money than she was already making. The caseworker asked why Midge wished to change jobs, and Midge came up with a series of reasons, each of which was rationally countered by the caseworker. When none of her reasons worked, Midge finally accused her employer's husband of making advances to her, beginning some 4 months earlier. When the caseworker asked why Midge had waited so long to report this, Midge said that he had warned her not to discuss it with anyone. Needless to say, everyone involved was very upset. However, the following day, Midge came forward on her own and admitted that the accusation was not true and that she had made it up on the spur of the moment so that she would be allowed to leave the job. Through further questioning, her caseworker discovered that the entire situation had sprung from an idle suggestion from Midge's boyfriend, whom Midge fantasized marrying, that she get a job closer to him. According to Midge's employer, the young man took Midge out on dates occasionally but had no real interest in her and had actually spoken quite derisively about Midge in conversations with her employer, stating that he would never take her seriously. Through a great deal of discussion involving all parties, it was decided that Midge, who was devastated by what she had done, actually wished to remain on the job and that the family understood what had happened and wished for her to remain as well. It was strongly suggested to Midge that she quit seeing the boyfriend who had been such a bad influence. Midge and the caseworker, along with the employer and her husband, worked out some reasonable limits for Midge's time off and the friends that she brought to the house. The caseworker also volunteered to start seeing Midge on a weekly basis to give her further support in making some positive changes in her social life.

Things took a definite turn for the better within the next few days when Midge became reacquainted with Hal, another ex-patient from Pacific State Hospital (see Chapter 1), at a meeting of the Friendship Club, and they began dating. For the first time, Midge had a man in her life who not only continued to see her on a more than casual basis, but who wanted to marry her.

Midge continued on her job for about 2½ months, and initially things went smoothly. However, during that time, Midge's employer went to work outside the home, leaving responsibility for the household with Midge. When Midge was unable to take over the entire responsibility, her employer became critical, and Midge lost her temper and became abusive. As a matter of mutual consent, it was agreed that Midge should move to another placement.

Midge's caseworker, who was by chance responsible for both Hal and Midge, arranged a placement for Midge with Mrs. Cohen, the wife of Hal's employer. There seem to have been two reasons for choosing this placement. Mrs. Cohen was considered one of the best employers of the female patients from Pacific. She was generous and kind, and she was sincerely interested in her employees. There were no children in the home because the Cohens' daughters were grown. Also, the relationship between Hal and Midge was deepening, and everyone concerned seemed to hope this relationship would finally be the one that worked out for both of them. Hal, as well as Midge, genuinely wanted to find someone to marry.

Midge's adjustment in the Cohen home was assessed as only fair. She was still very slow about her work, particularly when Mrs. Cohen was gone, and she was "fairly insolent at times." Even Midge's caseworker stated that she was frequently irresponsible and inefficient on the job.

Marriage

During the 14 months that Midge lived at the Cohens', she and Hal started planning to get married when his divorce from his first wife was final. Hal was genuinely devoted to Midge and was looking forward to the marriage. According to their mutual hospital caseworker, Hal showed considerable understanding of Midge's problems and an ability to deal with them. The caseworker stated that Midge had gotten along better with Hal than she had with any other single person. For the first time, Midge sustained her interest in one man, rather than running to one after another. On her day off, Midge cooked, cleaned, and washed clothes for Hal.

Even when working with Midge was difficult at times, Mrs. Cohen was determined to struggle through, due in part to the high regard she and Mr. Cohen had for Hal. Midge was more irritable and explosive than usual, but there was a feeling on the part of all concerned that this was due to a mixture of impatience and anxiety about her upcoming marriage to Hal. Because Midge had still not been completely discharged from Pacific State Hospital, it was necessary for her to gain permission from the hospital to marry. Everyone tried to pull together to keep Midge on her job so that she would receive that permission. As the time for the marriage drew closer, Midge's behavior deteriorated even further with everyone but Hal, and finally reached the breaking point about a week before the wedding when Mrs. Cohen caught Midge trying to leave the house with several cashmere sweaters and some other household items. When confronted, Midge became "quite antagonistic and threatening," according to her caseworker. She finally walked out and went to her mother's house to stay until the marriage.

The wedding took place at the end of 1956, a little more than 6 years after Midge was paroled on work leave. Hal and Midge moved into a "shack" located behind the foundry where Hal worked, which was provided for them by the Cohens. They got along well, although Midge's housekeeping was described as "slovenly" by her caseworker. Within a few months, she found a job as a "companion-nurse" for an elderly, paralyzed woman, working from 2:30 P.M. to 1:00 A.M. for $25 per week. With the $50 per week that Hal earned, the couple managed to get by. In about 6 months, Midge began asking about her final discharge from the hospital. Although things seemed stable with the couple, Midge's caseworker advised that she wait a little longer, in view of Midge's history of poor adjustment. However, when the couple had been married 15 months and the stability continued, Midge at last received her final discharge from Pacific State Hospital.

Hal and Midge, both of whom had seen marriage as a goal for many years, managed to keep their marriage intact for nearly 7 years. Especially for Midge, married life may have been somewhat less exciting than she had hoped. Hal worked long and very strenuous hours, and he was tired when he arrived home. Although Midge loved to do things, including roller skating, movies, and going to the beach, she usually had to do them alone or not at all because Hal was too tired to accompany her. Midge's greatest interest was baseball, particularly the Los Angeles Dodgers. She knew the players' names and a wealth of statistics about both the players and the team. Occasionally, she and Hal would go to a game, particularly when Hal's employer gave him tickets, but most often Midge had to go alone and in fact usually listened to the games on the radio instead. Both Hal and Midge enjoyed watching television together, and occasionally on weekends they still attended the Friendship Club to dance and socialize.

For approximately the first 4 years of their marriage, Hal and Midge lived in the quarters provided by Mr. Cohen. Although the living space was rent-free, it was described by a fieldworker who contacted the couple at that time as rather dismal:

> This residence appears to have been an office for an auto wrecking company or something similar. There were two large rooms with a kitchen off the back room, a hall across the back with a room I did not see. The walls appeared to be heavy cardboard, papered quite some long time ago, now mostly faded dark brown. The floors were wood, imbedded with grease. Although scrubbed, they were still quite black appearing. They were clean at this time, but had no finish or wax, etc. A tattered rug covered part of the room. The front room had a bedspread across the window, and the opening between rooms had plastic

curtains that showed some age. The back window had neither shade nor curtain. Another side window was boarded up. The only light was at the end of a wire dropped from the ceiling. The room had a couch that was opened into a bed and was made up with sheets and blankets. There were a few chairs, straight-backed, and some from a dinette set, metal tubing with plastic seats. There was one chest of drawers. There were other items of furniture, perhaps tables, or more like benches. These were piled quite high with cardboard boxes, stacks of papers, and a tremendous amount of miscellaneous items appearing not to have been used for quite some time. There were a few pictures on the walls—a hammered copper dog, an art calendar, and a "Home Sweet Home" plaque made with glitter on a black background. A small puppy was present, also a bird and cage. The kitchen was quite dark. The sink was cast iron in fair condition. The drainboards were wood and quite black from moisture around the sink. There was a gas stove in fair condition, and an 8 or 9 cu. ft. refrigerator. A fairly recent table model radio was on the kitchen table which went with the chairs in the living room. The outside was completely wild—no grounds care at all —and there were some junk cars around. One out in front was [Hal's], but it was no longer running.

Although others had always described Midge's housekeeping as marginal without supervision, when Hal was asked many years later just what it was that he liked so much about Midge, one of his responses was that she "kept a good house."

When Midge was finally discharged from Pacific State Hospital, the couple lost one element of their support network. However, they still received help from other benefactors. In addition to the rent-free living space, Mr. Cohen and his wife also provided periodic packages of food and the knowledge that there was someone to turn to if some crisis should occur. Also, the woman who lived next door to Hal and Midge took an interest in them and helped by taking Midge to the grocery store once a week and assisting her with both food selection and handling her money. This neighbor also kept a watchful eye out for strangers or anyone who might try to take advantage of the couple.

According to both Hal and Midge, there was some trouble with members of her family, particularly with Midge's older brother, over her marriage to Hal. Even many years later, neither of them seems to know just why he took such an outright dislike to Hal, but both tell stories of quite outspoken unpleasantness on his part. For instance, after Hal and Midge had been married about 3 years, Midge's youngest sister was killed in an automobile accident. This loss was keenly felt by Midge, who considered this sister the baby of the family and her favorite sibling. Plans were made for both Hal and Midge to attend the funeral, but the eldest brother created bitter dissension when he announced that Hal could not attend because the brother did not want him there. According to Hal, he went anyway because Midge wanted him to go, but the entire affair was quite unpleasant. Luckily, Hal got on reasonably well with both Midge's mother (Midge's father had died in 1952) and at least one of the other brothers. The couple took the bus periodically to the small city where Midge's mother lived, and they spent some holidays there.

Separation

After living in the place that Mr. Cohen had provided for approximately 4 years, the couple was forced to move when the building, which had been condemned by the city some time earlier, was scheduled for demolition. They moved to an apartment in a building also owned by Mr. Cohen in a nicer part of town. However, the change, rather than improving their lives, actually seems to have helped create the situation that eventually caused their separation. Hal continued to work for Mr. Cohen, taking as many as four buses to reach the relocated company. Midge went to work as a waitress in a cafe a few doors from where they lived. She began to meet other men, and according to Hal, she eventually began going out with them.

It should be noted here that Hal and Midge disagree vehemently about the circumstances of their breakup. Midge maintains that Hal hit her in the stomach during a fight they were having, thus precipitating the bleeding ulcer that still plagues her today. Her version of events is as follows:

> When he hit me, it knocked the wind out of me. Went staggering down the back steps. Asked my neighbors to use their phone. [You called the police?] Sure. [Why did he hit you?] Fight. You know he liked to watch T.V., you know, how these guys, you know, throw everybody around and with their fists and everything? [You mean when they're fighting on T.V.?] Yeah. I told him to relax, you know. Don't get all excited like that. So that's when he hit me right in the stomach.

With just as much conviction, Hal maintains that he never hit Midge, nor any other woman for that matter. According to Hal, he was willing to accept Midge's seeing other men because he did not want her to leave, but she eventually met another man who promised to marry her (although he never did), and she simply never returned home again, except to pick up her things.

Midge's claim that her bleeding ulcer was caused by Hal hitting her in the stomach is a good example of the way in which Midge sometimes adapts available information to fit the way she wishes to believe things occurred. In a later conversation, she finally admitted that she consulted a doctor at the county hospital after the incident, and he told her he could find nothing wrong with her. Later, while consulting another doctor, she told him about the incident with Hal, and the second doctor told her that being hit *might* have had something to do with her ulcer. Midge has translated all of this information into her flat statement that Hal caused her ulcer by hitting her.

During a conversation with a fieldworker in 1982, however, Midge indicated that she still held fast to her version of events and also that this was not an isolated incident in her life. (Bill, who is mentioned in the conversation below, is a man Midge lived with several years after separating from Hal. He is discussed later.)

> I don't want him [Hal] down here. I got a special reason why I don't want him to know where I'm livin'. [Are you afraid he'll hurt you?] Yeah! He might hit me again. Course I can call the law on him. They was waitin' for him to come out so's they could get him. See, he has a police record. [pause] He just better not hit me again, 'cause he'd be in serious trouble. . . . He's over there where he's at, and I'm over here, and that way it's peace and quiet. No, 'cause when I was with Bill, he used to beat me up too. [Oh, he did?] Yeah. He did it on, uh, there at 1010 Rosemont. Lived in, uh, North Hollywood, uh—no, not North Hollywood—San Fernando he'd do it. I told him, "You keep your hands off me, I'm gonna turn you in." I wanted him to, you know, to keep his hands off. I said, "You've got no right to hit me!" and he said, "Yes I do. You're my woman. You do what I tell you to do." And I told him, "I'm not your woman. I'm not married to you!" Him and I went up to Oregon. We went to see this friend up there that he knew. And we's stayin' up there and, by golly, he hit me. Got me on the side of the nose there and hurt this finger here. He was *drunk*, and his buddy was "Oops! Oops! Oops!" [Seems like you're almost better off without these men, huh?] Yup! I can find a decent guy that don't hit me, but those kind, they think they hit women, they think it's smart and it's not!

Although she may have faced physical abuse in her relationships, as this story suggests, Midge saw herself as independent enough to protest such treatment and to leave if necessary.

On Her Own

After Hal and Midge separated in 1963, Midge adapted well to her new and independent lifestyle. Although her life was not particularly stable, she described herself to fieldworkers in 1972 as content with her life and happier than she had been 10 years earlier when she was married to Hal. She had moved frequently in both her jobs and living quarters, but in 1972, she had a studio apartment of her own and was collecting disability benefits due to back and stomach problems. However, she saw this as a temporary state of affairs and spoke of returning to work in the future after a proposed move to be closer to her boyfriend. She had worked intermittently in the intervening years, mostly doing the same kinds of institutional or private domestic work that she had done before she married Hal.

Midge had a good working knowledge of the city bus system and was thus highly mobile. Although she no longer attended the Friendship Club after her breakup with Hal, Midge led an active social life. She had a number of friends in her neighborhood, and she went with them to the local "clubs" (beer bars), where she enjoyed playing the bowling games, and also occasionally to the movies or the Roller Derby. Midge had always had an active interest in politics, and she went so far as to work in the June primary campaign of a man running for city office. She also took the bus to visit her mother almost every Sunday. In addition, Midge saw her boyfriend on a regular basis, although he apparently did not accompany her to any of the above activities. According to Midge, he often stopped by on his lunch break and sometimes came by to visit or to take her out to dinner after work or on weekends. She had met her boyfriend several years before, right after her separation from Hal, and they dated for about a year at that time. Midge then met a divorced man with three children whom she "went with" for nearly 5 years. When they broke up, a chance encounter brought Midge back into contact with the first boyfriend, and they had been seeing each other since then. Midge was planning to move to the area where he lived, which was some distance away, as well as to marry him eventually, although she was still not divorced from Hal. According to Midge, she had tried filing for divorce twice, but both times neither Hal nor her witness had showed up, so the divorce had not gone through.

Midge had become much more independent through the years. She had no known benefactors and seemed able to cope with life quite well on her own. She handled the bureaucratic social welfare system in order to arrange for her disability benefits, and she handled her own money, including using the food stamps that she got as part of her disability benefits. She was game to try new activities and life experiences, and she described herself as "strong, smart, friendly, having personality, and athletic."

When she was next contacted some 10 years later, in 1982, the circumstances of Midge's life had changed considerably. She had recently come to visit her mother and ended up staying to live with her mother and her brother, who was collecting his railroad pension and sharing the house with their mother after being injured in an accident.

In the 10-year period between contacts, Midge had continued to move and change circumstances frequently. When asked about her peripatetic existence, Midge laughed and said, "Just like a boomerang, movin' around. Don't like one place; move to another place. It's hard though. Sometimes she [Midge's mother] can't keep up with me either." Midge had mostly relied on sporadic part-time employment, goods and services provided by the government, and support from the man she lived with much of that time. The boyfriend she had hoped to marry turned out to be homosexual, and Midge broke up with him when he brought a male lover over to stay. According to Midge, her boyfriend had gone so far as to suggest sex change operations for both Midge and himself. Although Midge tells of this incident in an off-handed, gossipy manner, a conversation that occurred with a fieldworker indicates that she has unpleasant memories of the episode. Midge was showing the fieldworker pictures of people she had known in the past that she carries in her wallet, and the fieldworker asked if Midge had any pictures of her old boyfriends. Midge said, "No. We took pictures there at that apartment building, the Worthington. Kenny took 'em. The Polaroid kind. I took 'em and tore 'em up. Didn't want to be bringing any memories back. Just wanted to forget about it."

Midge eventually met another man, Bill, with whom she lived for about 5 years. This relationship was apparently based on friendship as much as love, and Midge still speaks of him warmly although she has not seen him for several years. At the end of the 5 years, Bill told Midge that he wanted to find a younger woman and start a family. Midge seems to have accepted this with little difficulty; when he eventually decided to marry a mutual acquaintance of theirs, Midge says, "I told him if he wanted a younger woman to go ahead. She was my friend, so why should I be jealous." Midge even provided a dress for the bride, who did not have one of her own. The married couple then moved to a rural area outside the city. However, according to Midge, "They come and got me and moved me out there," and the three of them lived together for about a year. At that point, Midge says, "They wanted to be by themselves. They didn't want to be bothered with me anymore, so let 'em go on their way." A second couple who lived in a nearby town, friends of Bill and his wife, came periodically to visit. On one of these visits, Bill and his wife asked if Midge could move to an apartment building owned by the second couple. Midge moved into one of the apartments and worked off part of her rent by cleaning the public areas of the building. Midge left this job when the second couple's daughter invited Midge to come and work with her in a nearby mountain vacation area, cleaning houses that were rented to vacationers. While on this job, Midge spent 2 weeks visiting her mother. During this visit, the woman she had been working with called Midge, saying that there was not enough work and Midge was no longer needed.

Midge, who was nearly 60 years old at this time, was left without a place to live and no source of income. According to Midge, her disability benefits had been discontinued a few years before when the office in charge of her case discovered her sporadic part-time employment. Worse yet, she claimed that this same office had told her that she owed $16,000 in overpayment because of this and could not have her benefits reinstated until this amount was repaid.[1] Due to her precarious financial condition, Midge stayed on with her mother and brother. However, at that time, she was still optimistic about the future and hoped to once again be independent and have a place of her own.

It is interesting to note that, when Midge was last contacted in 1987, her story concerning how she came to be living at her mother's house had changed considerably. In Midge's 1987 version, she had voluntarily returned to her mother's home to help care for her mother when she became ill with cancer and needed live-in care. She said that her brother, in addition to his impaired leg, had developed heart trouble and could no longer care for their mother alone. Midge cared for her mother until the mother's death in 1986, and, according to Midge, before her mother died she told Midge that she was sorry for what she had done to Midge, that Midge came to take care of her when the other daughters would not, and that she was sorry she had sent Midge away to be institutionalized. Understandably, this interchange was extremely important to Midge. She speaks of it with a sense of pride and gratitude.

CONCLUSION

After many years of leading a quite independent life, sometimes living with a man, sometimes on her own, sometimes working, sometimes collecting SSI on the basis of either physical or psychiatric disability (certified by a psychiatrist and, according to Midge, unrelated to her institutionalization), Midge now leads the most stable life she has ever known. She seems to see the mobile, independent, sexually active life she previously led as a period that she enjoyed, but that is now in the past. She busies herself with caring for her brother, and she sees herself as important to him, as she indeed is.

Midge is a complex combination of strengths and weaknesses, and assessing her general level of competence is a difficult task. There is absolutely no doubt that Midge sees herself as a fully competent and independent person, but it is also obvious from the material above that there have been numerous people throughout Midge's life who have not seen her in the same light. However, it is very important not to underestimate Midge. Through a combination of stubbornness, persistence, and sometimes outright guile, Midge has managed to accomplish many of the things that

---

[1]When Midge, who turned 65 years old in 1987, went to file for Social Security/SSI benefits, the records claimed that she owed a little more than $14,000 in back overpayment. However, although the information was sketchy because the records were so old, the reason seems to have had something to do with confusion over her marital status rather than her work record. Rather than trying to fight their claim, which would have required answering innumerable questions about her past, Midge chose to allow them to deduct 10% of her Social Security/SSI benefits each month until the debt is repaid.

were really important to her. She wanted to be discharged from the hospital, and although it took her far longer than she anticipated, she managed it. She wanted to be married, and although it did not last, she managed that as well, and to a man who still speaks of her wistfully after 30 years. Even after so many years of separation, Midge's status as a "married woman" is still very important to her. When Midge became truly independent after her separation from her husband, she managed to remain so for nearly 20 years before circumstances forced her to return to her family. The life she lived was certainly unstable, including a series of diverse and unconventional living situations, but Midge looks back and talks about many parts of this period with obvious relish and enjoyment. Many years ago, when Midge's Pacific State Hospital caseworker found Midge to be very unrealistic about taking care of herself if she were to be completely discharged, Midge told her simply, "I'll manage these things as they come up," and that is exactly what she has done.

Managing has certainly not been easy for her, but it is very difficult to get Midge to speak directly about the unpleasant parts of her experience because strong denial has been one of her chief mechanisms for coping with the hurts and failures of her life. She would far rather tell stories than answer questions concerning how she feels about things. Midge can be very effective in cutting off communication when faced with a subject she does not wish to discuss. She uses a rather distant, flat tone of voice and monosyllabic answers, and at the first seemingly unobtrusive opportunity, she changes the subject. She also does not show deep negative feelings, such as hurt and anger, at all easily. She gets very still and quiet, the struggle to control her feelings obvious only from her sudden stillness, and she then completely changes the subject. Midge's determined optimism through the years, sometimes in the face of what others perceived to be reality, may have been a major factor in accomplishing as much as she has. If Midge had focused on the negative aspects of her life, or if she had been willing to believe the people who thought she was not capable of taking care of herself, it is doubtful that she would have established her independent lifestyle. It is Midge's very optimism that sometimes causes her to appear unrealistic. She seems to see no reason not to believe that the good things she wishes for herself and others will come to pass, such as winning one of her mail-order contests, and she sometimes speaks of these things as virtual realities. However, she does not seem to be unduly upset if they do not happen. She expresses some regret and proceeds to make new plans.

Competence is a significant issue for Midge. In the past, things have not always gone smoothly, and Midge has sometimes gotten herself into difficulty, such as losing her SSI benefits in 1978. Midge will become embarrassed if she feels that she appears less than competent in a given situation, and she sometimes gets upset and anxious when confronted with new or confusing situations. When this occurs, Midge usually responds in one of two ways; she either becomes very quiet and tries to avoid the situation, or paradoxically, considering her penchant for secrecy, she deluges the person with whom she is interacting with a blizzard of explanatory information, much of it tangential or irrelevant. But most of all, Midge simply keeps going until she has somehow worked out the situation. She never just gives up and asks to be taken care of. Midge does not seem to see competence as a matter of intelligence, but rather as a matter of determination and "getting used to it"; in other words, anyone can do anything "if they get used to it."

It is tempting to see Midge's life with her brother as stable and satisfactory and to wonder how she would be able to get along if he should die before her, a distinct possibility because of his poor health. Although it would certainly be an emotional blow because Midge is very fond of her brother, she did not seem particularly upset when asked what she would do if anything happened to him. Her answers were vague, and she said that she had not thought about it very much. Midge says that the house would be left to her and that her brother has insurance as part of his railroad pension, although she does not know whether or not she is the beneficiary. Since turning 65, Midge has received a monthly check of her own, a combination of Social Security and SSI, but this might be affected if ownership of the house passes to her at her brother's death. She says she does not know whether the rest of her family would be willing to help her, but she worries that her "bossy" older brother "might be a problem." Midge has made it quite clear that she sees herself as independent from her family. In the past, when discussing the effect of her family's opinions on decisions that she makes, Midge has stated emphatically that it is her life, not theirs, and that she will do what she wants. She says that as far as she is concerned, "They don't have anything to say about it." If Midge outlives her brother, her life will probably become less stable, but it may also become less socially isolated when she is no longer as tied to the house by caring for him. Age may also be a factor; at the age of 65 or 70, it would not be as easy to lead the peripatetic life Midge lived in the past. However, Midge's attitude toward aging can be summed up pretty well by her statement: "I'm not going to stay home and feel sorry for myself 'cause I'm getting up in years like a lot of them do." Midge also has a true survivor's determination and sense of humor. She is indeed aggressive and eccentric, but she seems generally happy and involved with life, and likely to remain so even in the face of future obstacles.

3

"I've Seen It All! . . .
Well, Just About All."
ROBERTO REYES

*by T.W. Ward*_____

In January 1962, Roberto Reyes, working as kitchen helper in a sanitarium in Los Angeles, decided he did not have enough excitement in his life. Leaving without a word, he hopped on the next freight train out of town. Discussing it later, Roberto said:

> I was bored. I had to get away. I wanted some excitement, so I hopped on a train to San Francisco. It's dangerous riding the train. I mean, you don't know what's going to happen to you. Because sometimes you meet bums in the cars, and they're drunk and you gotta be careful what you say to these people. But I took a chance, I had nowhere to go. Unfortunately, I got on the wrong train and ended up in Portland, Oregon.

Adding the proverbial insult to injury, Roberto was arrested by the police for vagrancy and thrown into jail.

This story is indicative of Roberto's wilder, more turbulent days when he was a young man. "I've had a good life," he once said, summing up his career, "But I've made it hell for myself." Although Roberto blames himself for his difficulties, many of his problems have not been self-inflicted. Roberto has confronted numerous obstacles, including a broken family, poverty, racial discrimination, mild mental retardation, and the stigma attached to being a deinstitutionalized inmate of a state hospital and a homosexual Latino. Despite these obstacles, Roberto has adapted well to his changing circumstances, and little of what he has suffered in previous years shows today. His carefree (if not careless) attitude, which translated into trouble in his earlier years, has become a general feeling of contentment at the age of 62. Today, Roberto feels good about himself, and he likes his present state of affairs. None of his friends knows or even suspects that Roberto was committed to a state hospital as a "mental defective" and that he spent, in his own words, "8 miserable years there." The fact that he was classified as mildly mentally retarded is a secret that Roberto has kept to himself for over 30 years. His friends are quite familiar, however, with the years during which Roberto bounced about from job to job as a kitchen helper or truck loader, rode the trains, and fought alcoholism, much of his time spent in and out of jails. Roberto has settled down in his later years; he has traded the excitement of his early years for some stability in old age.

THE EARLY YEARS

Roberto Reyes was born on June 2, 1926. Adopted when he was 2 years old by a young Mexican-American couple, Sara and Mauricio Reyes, Roberto remembers "meeting" his biological mother only once in what was for him a tragic experience at the age of 4. Tears still appear in Roberto's eyes as he tells of his single encounter with his mother.

> I just met my real mother one time. That was a long time ago. I was about four years old. I remember it but not too clear. She came by to see me, but my adopted mother told her she didn't want her around me. 'Cuz, you know, I would... I don't know, just... something about her, she didn't want her around me that's all. I just remember she came to see me one time in the restaurant up there. And my mother told her not to come no more. She passed away a long time ago, in the thirties sometime. I never knew her name. She was from Mexico. All I remember was that she was short and dark, and she had black hair. I don't remember her too well.

Roberto's mother, who moved to the U.S. from Mexico, reportedly gave him up because she was an alcoholic and could not properly care for him. The idea that he was given up for adoption by his alcoholic mother has stayed with him over the years. Roberto felt abandoned by his mother, whose name he did not know until recently, when hospital records were released to him for the first time. When Roberto was told her name was Maria, he repeated it over and over to himself, as if he were afraid he might forget it.

In spite of this painful experience, Roberto looks back on this time with his adoptive parents as good years, years without worry. "My mother was a business woman," he said. "She had five or six beer joints. My father was an alcoholic. But anyway, I had a good life, I didn't have to worry about a place to sleep or eat."[1] In contrast to his adult years, that was a time of stability. Although she was often not at home, Roberto had a good relationship with his adoptive mother, Sara. "She gave me prac-

---

[1]Roberto refers to his adoptive mother as "my mother," but he refers to his adoptive father alternately as "my father" and "my stepfather," which reflects his ambivalence toward the latter.

tically everything I needed," he said. "My mother was strict as hell, but she was good to me."

Roberto remembers this period as pleasant but brief. In 1933, after 5 years together, Sara divorced her husband because of his heavy drinking, and she was awarded sole custody of Roberto. At this time, Roberto was doing poorly in school because he had great difficulty learning to read and write. As a result of his poor performance, Roberto was sent to what he calls "a dumb school for slow learners." In 1936, he was transferred to yet another school and repeated the fourth grade. Despite his difficulties in school, Roberto still feels those were the best years of his life. Sara was a successful businesswoman, and they lived comfortably. Their home was a large market converted into a house in what was then a Latino neighborhood. Roberto felt very close to Sara even though he did not get to see her as much as he would have liked. Her work kept her away from home most of the time, and a maid took care of most of Roberto's needs (but notably not the need for his mother). His mother bought a 1929 convertible Duesenberg sedan, in which they took Sunday drives. Roberto's only memento from that period of his life is a newspaper photo of a Duesenberg on his wall.

In 1937, when Roberto was 11 years old, Sara died giving birth to twin boys, who also died a week later. Her death was the beginning of hard times for Roberto. "I had it good until I was 11 years old," he said. "And then she died and everything went down the drain." Roberto's subsequent years were marked by impermanence, most of it self-induced because he refused to stay in one place for long. After his mother died, Roberto moved to Watts, where he lived with his godparents for 2 years. During this time he attended two schools—one of them for remedial reading skills—and learned virtually nothing at either. After the second year, bored with his situation, Roberto ran away from his godparents' home. He said he wanted to live in the house his mother had left him. His adoptive mother's lawyer arranged for Roberto to live in this house with people who had been friends of Sara's; they received free rent in return for his board and care. "They were a Spanish-speaking family and had three boys and one girl who were already grown up when I lived with them," Roberto said. "They owned a small market in town. I helped out at the store on Friday afternoons and Saturdays, and they gave me 25 cents to see a movie on Sundays. I lived in the back, in the guest-house, but ate my meals with the rest of the family." Roberto said he liked living there because "they treated me like one of the family," but he stayed only 4 months. At the time, he thought he had lost his house to the tax collector and therefore had to move out. "In November of 1939," he said, "the house was sold because my mother's lawyer hadn't paid any taxes on it." In fact, his adoptive mother had left the house to support Roberto, but after the estate was settled, it was found that there were no remaining assets, and the house had to be sold. Roberto also remembers that he was restless at the time and was glad to return to live with his godparents in Watts.

Roberto's years without worry had become years without roots. In January 1940, at the age of 13, he returned to his godparents' house, but left again after only 4 months. In April, Roberto contacted his adoptive father, Mauricio, and asked permission to move in with him. This experiment lasted 7 months, during which time Roberto moved to another school and repeated the fifth grade. Mauricio was working as a cook on a ranch in Van Nuys, but he was fired for drunken behavior. He and Roberto moved to downtown Los Angeles, where they rented a cheap hotel room. Soon after, Mauricio was arrested for drunken and disorderly conduct and sentenced to 6 months in jail. Roberto went to Skid Row in downtown Los Angeles and lived on the streets for 3 or 4 months. There he ran into one of Mauricio's drinking pals and stayed with him until Mauricio was released from jail. Initially, Roberto was glad to move back in with his adoptive father, but their living together soon proved to be too much of a strain. Mauricio was usually drunk or not at home and thus did not supervise Roberto, who skipped school often, frustrated by his inability to learn. When he was drunk, Mauricio shouted and swore at Roberto. "He was drinking too much and I was too young for it," Roberto said. Tensions between them reached a peak when Mauricio discovered Roberto's homosexuality. He became furious when he found out that Roberto was gay. "I was staying out late and running around," Roberto said. "My father didn't like it, but I didn't care." Mauricio kicked Roberto out of the house. "I was not close to my father but he was the only father I had. He didn't really like me too much when he found out I was gay. That was the main problem. He never cared for me or anything like that and he never bothered to look for me again."

For 2 months Roberto, who was by now 14 years old, hung out on Skid Row, but on New Year's Day 1941, he decided to go see his adoptive mother's former cook. She could not put him up so, Roberto said, "She called the detectives because I had no place to stay." The police took Roberto to Juvenile Hall, and a week later he was transferred to a boarding home in East Los Angeles. While there, Roberto attended a sixth grade class, only, as he said, "Because I was getting too old [to repeat fifth grade a third time]." In September 1942, after less than 2 years there, Roberto ran away from home to look for Mauricio on Skid Row. Roberto took what he now refers to as "a 3-day vacation" because he felt the rules at the boarding house were too confining. "The lady there was kinda strict. You had to go by rules, you know. We had to stay there 7 days a week. We weren't allowed to go out Sundays, and we had to go to church. I didn't like it there." This was not Roberto's first "vacation." In her progress report, his social worker recounted:

> For the first year and a half in the boarding home of Mrs. Fonseca, Roberto exhibited no particular behavior problem other than the usual lethargy. However, in the latter months of his stay, he absented himself from the home during the long summer vacation days and apparently was able to obtain money in fairly large amounts for a boy his age. He refused to give any accounting of the money and spent it as he pleased. He would explain the source of the money as being a gift from either his godfather, or that he had seen his stepfather in Metropolitan Los Angeles and had been given the money by him. Roberto began to desire to go into Los Angeles frequently and haunt the Main Street restaurants where he believed he could locate his father. The boarding mother attempted to dissuade him from this habit without success.

After the third or fourth time he ran away, Roberto was transferred to a downtown Boy's Club, where he lived for 6 months. He liked this arrangement, despite his continuing frustration with school. "The manager [of the club] got me a part-time job doing yardwork and housecleaning in Beverly Hills. I went to a school for special education, but I didn't make it there either." Roberto skipped school often and stayed out past curfew, sometimes not returning to the Boy's Club until the next day. Roberto said he was punished for this by being transferred to Pacific State Hospital in 1943 at the age of 16. According to the records from Juvenile Court that are part of Roberto's file from Pacific State Hospital, Roberto was admitted to the hospital because he had no one in his life to "exert parental control" over him. The clinical examination that was part of the admission procedure assigned Roberto a chronological age of approximately 8 years and an IQ of 67. Pacific State Hospital then admitted him as "feebleminded." His years of rootlessness and impermanence thus ended with the "security" of confinement in a state institution for the mentally deficient.

LIFE IN AN INSTITUTION

Roberto vividly remembers arriving at the state hospital at one o'clock in the afternoon, for the beginning of what he called "8 miserable years there." Roberto blames himself for being locked up. "It was my fault for being sent to [Pacific State Hospital] because I was running around and staying out late." He compares the hospital to a big jail surrounded by gates, but with one important difference. For him, the experience of being there was worse than jail:

> Being there years in a place like that, it gets anybody down. It's not like being in jail. In jail, you go to jail and you know when you're gonna get out, but being in an institution you don't know when you're going to

get out. I wanted to get out . . . and the only way I could get out of there was by getting sterilized.

Nevertheless, Roberto obstinately refused to be sterilized. "They didn't tell me they were going to sterilize me until I got to the hospital," he said.

> For the first year I worked only on the ward, sweeping, mopping, helping in the kitchen, and stuff like that. Because, you couldn't leave the ward until you were sterilized. I could have gotten out earlier but I wouldn't sign the papers to be sterilized, and they couldn't find my father to get him to sign. I made them wait a whole year before I would sign.

After he finally agreed to be sterilized, Roberto was allowed to work in the main kitchen, and later in the butcher shop and the bakery. A nurse who knew Roberto from his days at the hospital said he was a very good worker:

> Bobby was one of the best orderlies in the hospital. All the nurses fought over him. He was a real good worker and he always dressed real nice: white pressed pants, white shirt with his name on the pocket, and polished black shoes.

In spite of his good work record, Roberto got into trouble several times while in the hospital.

> I blew it four times there. The first time was when I ran away. That was in 1944, right after I was sterilized. I ran away with a little boy who was crippled. His name was John and he worked in the shoe shop. We hid behind the kitchen, and then ran across the tracks. But they caught us fast because John was paralyzed in one leg. We only got as far as the highway.

Both were confined to the punishment ward for 30 days. The second incident cost Roberto an early parole.

> I got in a fight with a tenant. I hit him because he wouldn't let me go to work. I was trying to leave and he told me to stay in my room. He wouldn't let me out the door so I hit him. The reason he wanted me to stay there was because the doctor was coming to check me out because I was getting out on parole.

Roberto felt unjustly punished and deprived of his parole. "I didn't know that [I was getting out], and he didn't tell me. I found out later and [still] got 6 months for hitting him." Roberto does not consider his next fight one of the four incidents in which he "blew it" because first, he felt justified in acting to protect his honor, and second, he was not punished for the fight. "I hit a tenant who called me gay and so his friends were going to beat me up." For his own safety, Roberto was moved to another ward, but soon after he got into trouble a third time by having sexual relations in the laundry room with a man he knew. "They caught us because we both got the clap," Roberto said. "And they were going to send me to Chino [State Prison], but the cooks said I was a damn good worker, so they let me stay and work in the kitchen instead. They said I was their best-ever worker." Meanwhile, Roberto was treated for gonorrhea and confined at night to the punishment ward for 6 months. Things went along smoothly after this, and eventually he was paroled from the institution in 1946 at the age of 19, but he "blew it" a fourth time and was returned to the state hospital.

> I went to work in a sanitarium in Whittier, where I was a kitchen helper. I cleaned the kitchen and set up the trays. To set up the trays I had to memorize all the symbols for the food: C for coffee, W for water, M for milk, and they wrote letters on the cups or trays and I had to put the right food on them. It took me quite a while to learn. It was going all right until I got into a fight with the cook. She was an Italian lady. I would take my time and she got mad. I didn't want to do some of the things and my boss got tired of it. When I got into a fight with the cook, he sent me back to [Pacific State Hospital]. That was August, 1947.

An interoffice memorandum from the hospital stated simply: "Mr. Mac-Donald returned Roberto Reyes to [Pacific State Hospital] after phone call that Roberto had incited several riots in their kitchen." After being transferred back, Roberto was assigned to work for Dr. Tarjan, the director of the hospital.

> I worked for Dr. Tarjan from 1947 to 1950. I was his houseboy and did yardwork. When the Tarjans had a baby boy they named him after me. I took care of him until he was 2 years and a half. They didn't want me to go [on parole] because I was a good worker.

In July 1951, Roberto, now age 25, got his second parole and returned to work at the sanitarium in Whittier. According to a report from Pacific State Hospital, this took "a bit of working out" because of the employer's previous difficulties with Roberto. He got into two arguments while he was there but was not punished for either. In her progress report for May 1952, his social worker reported that Roberto had "blown his top."

> Apparently Roberto had gotten upset at some situation in the kitchen and had cursed a new assistant cook in the most highly colorful language. Had this been with the staff of the sanitarium alone present Mr. MacDonald would not have minded but since there was a visiting physician it was rather an embarrassing situation.

Roberto also got into a fight with his roommate about which television program they would watch. When his roommate objected to his choice, Roberto vaingloriously claims he "punched the guy out." The underlying motive for this fight was a history of abuse of their friendship by Roberto's roommate, John. Roberto had developed an attachment to John, who did not reciprocate his feelings but did use them to his own advantage. "John had used him, taken his money, spent it for his own needs and had actually gotten Roberto to use his entire salary to entertain him," his social worker reported. She also wrote that, because of the "violent fight," Roberto was "acutely distressed . . . [that] I would be returning him to the hospital and was so fearful he could hardly speak with me." This threat of return to the hospital hung over Roberto like an ax and was used by his employer, Mr. MacDonald, with varying degrees of effectiveness to keep him in line. When Mr. MacDonald found out that Roberto was in fact the victim and not the perpetrator, he asked that John be moved instead of Roberto. Although Roberto's social worker felt that they should stick to the original plan, Roberto was transferred to another sanitarium, and 5 months later, he received word of his discharge.

> Around Christmas, 1952, I got my discharge papers. My social worker called me over the phone on Christmas Eve and she says, "I got a Christmas present for you, Bobby." And I says, "What is it?" And she said, "Well, you just got discharged."

OUT OF THE HOSPITAL, IN AND OUT OF JAILS

Roberto said he was excited to be free at last. After discharge he worked at a number of different sanitariums, but he quickly lost interest in the work and quit. At 26 years old, Roberto was still young, sometimes uncooperative, and always restless. When he grew bored, he either left or behaved in such a way as to ensure his dismissal. For his first job after parole, Roberto chose the security of returning to work at Mr. MacDonald's sanitarium in Whittier. Mr. MacDonald welcomed him back because he did not blame Roberto for his earlier troubles there and because he considered Roberto to be a good worker. However, Roberto lasted only 7 months before he was fired for insubordination. "I went downtown one day and stayed overnight and didn't show up for work the next day until nine in the morning. I was supposed to be there at 5:30 a.m., and my boss told me, 'If you want to quit, quit.' So I quit." Roberto's second job was in a sanitarium in Culver City; he quit after 5 months. His third job lasted almost 2 years, but eventually he got bored there too. He quit to take a trip and get some excitement into his life. "I wanted to see San Francisco and I had never been in a boxcar so I just got me one," he said. Finding himself on the wrong train, Roberto took the next train back. His "vacation" over, Roberto returned to Los Angeles and his sanitarium job. But he was still not satisfied.

Roberto finally found contentment and stability in November 1956, in a relationship with Ben, a man he met on the street in downtown Los

Angeles. This was to be not only the first, but the longest and most important of three major intimate and caring homosexual relationships in Roberto's life.

> We took the bus together to his place in Highland Park and then he gave me a ride on his motorcycle back to my apartment at the sanitarium in Culver City. He still came to see me every weekend. We became good friends. I got to be a good friend to Ben's mother and grandmother too. He asked me if I'd like to come and work for him. I moved in with him and lived with him from '56 to '60. I cooked breakfast and kept the place clean. He bought me a dog, a little brown one, and I named him "Poncho." I would take the dog for a walk, and then might go to the beach or shopping in El Monte. Ben worked as a machinist.

This was an idyllic time for Roberto. A good friend of Roberto's remarked that he and Ben were like a married couple and that they were very romantic, citing a candlelight dinner they prepared for her as an example. Initially, Roberto said that he moved out because he wanted to get a job and that he was bored staying in the house all day, but later he admitted that this was only part of the story. He confessed, with tears in his eyes, that the relationship had deteriorated because his drinking had steadily increased over the years, and at 33 years old, he was becoming an alcoholic. Ben began to protest Roberto's drinking; a recovering alcoholic himself, Ben said he did not want to see Roberto drink himself to death. Although Roberto wanted to quit, he says he "lacked the will power," and Ben finally asked him to move out: "The last time I saw Ben was in 1960, not long after I moved out. He was at the bus station, taking a trip to Tijuana with a friend. We just said hello but didn't talk."

Roberto moved back to downtown Los Angeles. He met a man on the streets, and together they rented a room in a seedy hotel on Skid Row. "The rent was cheap," Roberto said. "I paid half, which was $7 a week. I was a paperboy; I sold newspapers. It's a good job if you have enough regular customers. I had only two regular customers." Roberto knew little about his roommate except that he was Mexican, went by the name "Green Eyes," and spoke no English but had a "green card" or work permit. Green Eyes was a day laborer, cleaning bricks from wrecked buildings to be resold. Their friendship ended abruptly when Roberto got arrested.

> In April of 1960, I got drunk and was put in jail. I remember it was April because some church people came to the jail and gave us candy and sang songs at Easter time. I was transferred to another jail later, 90 days in all. This was a farm jail for alcoholics. There were cottages there and a big cafeteria. We just walked around and tried to pass the time. Bedtime was at 10 P.M. They showed a movie every Friday. One of the officers brought a rattlesnake in a box and told the men that if you want to run away, go ahead, but that these snakes were in the hills. After that, no one wanted to run away.

On July 21, 1960, Roberto was released from jail and his social worker found him a job with Mrs. Caldwell, who owned a sanitarium in Highland Park. "She asked me my name and then asked if I drank. I said, 'Only after work and on my days off.' So she hired me." Roberto worked 5 years for her, doing yardwork and cleaning, and then was given the added responsibility of babysitting two of Mrs. Caldwell's children. He enjoyed Mrs. Caldwell's large house and equally large family; she adopted five children after having four children of her own. Roberto lived with them for 25 years, and unofficially but recognized by all, he became another adopted member of her family. He still calls her "Grandma." Roberto left Mrs. Caldwell's place several times to "get away from it all," but like a prodigal son, he was always welcomed back.

The first time Roberto left Mrs. Caldwell's was in 1962, 2 years after he started working for her. This trip, described at the beginning of this chapter, began with his hopping a train for San Francisco, and ended with his arrest in Portland, Oregon.

> I got 30 days for vagrancy and vandalism. When I was arrested, I didn't have any money in my pocket. Me and this other guy went to a building where there was a candy machine. I went in there just to get water. But the other guy broke into the machine to get money. Somebody saw him and called the police, and by the time we got to the boxcar, we were both arrested. They took us down to the station and questioned us separately. The other guy said that I hadn't done anything, but we both got 30 days anyway. But I made good there. I worked for the policemen, sweeping up streets and washing the trucks on Saturday when the guys were off. Everybody liked me there.

After getting out of jail, Roberto stayed in Portland at a home for members of Alcoholics Anonymous. "A man from AA came each week to see the inmates to try and help us. So when I got out I went to the AA house. I stayed there 3 weeks and a half." Roberto got a job in a restaurant, cleaning the kitchen and bathrooms, but was released after only 2 days. "They wanted to hire me but I couldn't remember my Social Security number," he said. "I had lost my Social Security card, so I decided to go back to L.A. and Grandma's." On his way to Los Angeles, Roberto stopped in Fresno and stayed at the Salvation Army for 2 weeks. "I worked as the dining-room boy," he said. "I made coffee in the morning, clean [sic] up the floor, wax and polish, and clean my tables and set them up for breakfast, lunch, and dinner." Roberto soon tired of this place and returned home to work at Mrs. Caldwell's sanitarium.

About this time Roberto learned third-hand of his adoptive father's death. Roberto was wandering the downtown streets of Los Angeles and met an acquaintance who told him that he had heard that Mauricio had died of cirrhosis of the liver. "In 1962, a friend I met on the street told me he passed on, you know. I liked the man and everything, but I didn't know him that well. He was just trouble to me. We just couldn't get along, that's all." In spite of Mauricio's rejection of him, Roberto loved his adoptive father and lamented the fact that he could not attend his funeral. "I don't know where he's buried. I felt sad when I found out [he died], but I have to keep on going, you know. You can't think about it all the time."

In 1963, Roberto began his second significant sexual relationship when he met a man named Jim during another brief stay in jail. After their release from jail, they lived together for 4 months. The name "Sandy" is tattooed on Roberto's left arm, a gift from Jim. "It was my nickname, and he wanted the tattoo. At the hospital they put that on my record for identification purposes in case something happens to me." But Roberto said their relationship did not work out because Jim took drugs and "drank like a fish." He decided to end their friendship after the two of them took a train trip to visit Jim's stepfather in St. Louis. They hitchhiked and rode the trains, staying in the Salvation Army one night and the police station the next. "They let you stay there overnight in jail," he said. "We got out of jail that morning, and we got a ride as far as Silver City [New Mexico]. We went around to the bakeries and ask them for bread, like 2 days old." Roberto and Jim continued on a boxcar to Denver, Colorado, where they stayed in a mission for 2 days, then hitchhiked to St. Louis. Jim returned by himself to Los Angeles, and Roberto stayed on, working the Salvation Army trucks for 3 weeks picking up furniture.

> And then I got bored. So I decided to get a boxcar. It took me about four days to get from that place to L.A. I went down to the mission on Main Street and I washed up and shaved and had dinner. And the next day I called Mrs. Caldwell up and her son come and pick me up. I went back to work for her.

Because Roberto considered Jim a "wino" and a bad influence, he decided not to look him up again.

At the age of 46, Roberto "retired" from work. He marks 1972, the year he started receiving SSI, as the year he officially stopped "working" for Mrs. Caldwell and started paying rent instead. The 13-year period from 1972 to 1985 was uneventful for Roberto. He continued to receive his monthly "paycheck," as he called it, and except for occasional stints "away from home," he continued to live at Mrs. Caldwell's house. Although he continued to clean the house and do yardwork, Roberto now had a permanent source of income and the security that went with it. This sense of security helped him make an important move toward even greater independence.

In September 1985, Roberto made a significant change. After 25 years of living on and off with Mrs. Caldwell, he decided to rent his own apartment. He felt that he had been with Mrs. Caldwell for too long and that he needed a change of pace. "I don't usually stay in one place so long," he said. "I moved because I wanted something different. I wanted to be by myself for a while. I wanted a quieter place." But Roberto has not severed ties with her completely.

> Grandma asks me to come over and arrange her room and make her bed, and sometimes I do the laundry or fix a meal. I am also welcome to stay the night whenever I want. I like to do things for Grandma because she has always been good to me. When I came home drunk I would sleep on the floor beside her bed.

Roberto still toys with the idea of moving back to Mrs. Caldwell's place, but it is unlikely because "too much has changed there," and he does not want to work. At 62, Roberto is content to spend his leisure hours alone and he does not want to give up his newfound independence.

"RETIREMENT" AT 62

Now that Roberto is "retired," his days are his own to do what he wants. But with so much time on his hands, his retirement is sometimes as much a wealth of boredom as a wealth of leisure. Roberto says he does not go out much.

> I don't have money because I'm paying off my debts. I don't socialize. I go to the theater [alone], or to the beach, or out to dinner. I don't go downtown [Los Angeles] too much because of the robbery and killing. And I don't go out that much at night because I get scared. I've been robbed before.

When Roberto was younger he used to go swimming at the beach once a week; now he rarely goes. Rare also are the days when he invites a friend to the movies. Because he usually does not have money for the movies, Roberto spends most evenings at home watching old movies on television, especially horror films and Westerns. To satisfy this craving, he has two televisions in his room, a 19-inch color television with a built-in videocassette recorder and a portable black-and-white television that he keeps on his bed. On Sundays, he takes the "old lady downstairs" to the Episcopal Church, which is across the street from their apartment building, because "it is good for her to get out."

Another of Roberto's favorite pastimes is traveling.

> I like to ride the bus. When I get a pass I ride it every day, and go from one end of the line to the other. I haven't had a bus pass for a long time because I'm still paying off my debts. When I get that pass, whew, I'm gone. I never stay home. I go everywhere. You see a lot of interesting people and different places, kind of like riding the boxcars. I like to

look at the people and where I'm going and buildings and cars and everything. I may get off somewhere and walk for a little while and then get another bus and go somewhere else. If I get lost I have to ask which bus to take. I can't read and spell too good so I have to ask.

Many of Roberto's bus trips end up at a shopping mall or thrift store. He enjoys window shopping or browsing about for a good deal on another decoration for his already cluttered apartment.

Roberto does not frequent the bars as much as he used to because he is trying to quit drinking alcohol. However, Roberto said that if he were very lonely he might seek company there, and on occasion, his visits with his friends will end up in one of the local bars. However, generally speaking, Roberto occupies his time in other ways now. For example, about once or twice a week Roberto takes the bus to downtown Los Angeles to eat at one of the missions. He hangs out with the other diners and sometimes makes new friends. "I get dressed up to go down there," he said.

> These people think I'm rich, which I guess I am compared to them. One guy asked me, "You sure you're not a movie star?" I just laughed and said, "No, I'm hungry, man." Mrs. Caldwell couldn't believe I actually go down there, but I'm not ashamed. It's not bad food."

Roberto also told of a man, who, after waiting 25 minutes, got out of the food line and said, "I'll never eat here again." Roberto laughed, "I told my friend in line [a woman Roberto had just met], 'Hell, he'll eat here when his stomach gets hungry; he'll be the first in line!' They all laughed at that one."

DESCRIBING ROBERTO: MORE THAN A "DEINSTITUTIONALIZED, MILDLY MENTALLY RETARDED, HOMOSEXUAL, REFORMED ALCOHOLIC, ELDERLY MEXICAN-AMERICAN MAN"

With only these labels to categorize Roberto, one would know little of Roberto's character or spirit. Each of these terms captures one of the multiple social roles he plays, but taken together, they do not form a complete picture of Roberto. A "depersonalized" description of Roberto would include the assessment of the psychologist, who in 1941 and 1942 tested Roberto's IQ scores at 69, 54, and 59, and that of the psychiatrist in 1973 whose diagnosis of Roberto consisted of "depression, anxiety, and homosexuality." A more detailed description was provided by a researcher who also interviewed Roberto in 1973:

> Roberto has a quite "pulled together" appearance. He was well groomed and well dressed in sports clothes and polished shoes. A small, brown man of moderate good looks, he in no way gives the impression of being "down and out," an alcoholic or "wino," or an

"MR." He does speak with a lisp, however; this and certain stereotypic intonations in his speech indicate that he is a homosexual. His general manner is one of deference and reserve.

As the researcher comments, there is nothing about Roberto that would indicate that he is a recovering alcoholic or that he is mildly retarded. His limited ability in reading and writing are the only indications of his mental retardation, but these are interpreted by his friends as lack of formal education. His age is also well hidden. The only signs of his 62 years are a few streaks of gray through his jet-black hair, which he wears combed straight back. Some strangers have mistaken him for as young as 45, but most think he looks about 50 years old, as indicated by his difficulty in convincing movie cashiers and waitresses that he qualifies for a senior citizen discount. Roberto is proud of the fact that he has "kept [his] shape." At 5 feet 5 inches tall, he is concerned about gaining weight and usually eats only one meal a day—for economic as well as aesthetic reasons. He blames being sterilized at the state hospital for putting pounds on him. "Before I was sterilized I was real skinny," he said. Roberto is also self-conscious about his crooked nose and damaged eye, the result of a fist fight in his early 30s. At times he wears dark glasses to hide his crooked left eye, and he presents only his right profile for photographs. His stocky muscularity and his rugged face, which is always clean-shaven, remind one of a retired boxer. "If I don't shave then I feel like hell the rest of the day," he once said. "Even when I was out on the street I would go to the Salvation Army to shower and shave." Roberto likes to wear brightly colored Hawaiian flower-print shirts, polyester slacks, and polished white loafers. Although the colors of his shirt and pants do not always match, his clothes are always very clean, another source of pride for Roberto.

Roberto is also proud of the fact that he keeps his room clean. "I learned that from working in the hospital at [Pacific State Hospital]," he said. "I had to get on my knees to scrub and wax floors. Whenever they took a patient to surgery, I had to clean the bed, take it out on the porch and water it down and clean it and fix it up nice." Roberto's one-bedroom apartment is a study in contrasts; it is spotlessly clean, but completely cluttered with things. The tiny room, without a speck of dust, is burgeoning with little knickknacks that cover every available counter space: on his bedside table is a large fish tank full of plaster statues decorated with Christmas tree lights and plastic bead jewelry; on his bed sits a huge plastic frog on a lime-green shag floormat; on his couch rests a toy airplane on the matching lime-green toilet-lid cover; his coffee table, refrigerator, and stove are covered with plastic kittens and tigers with plastic beads strewn about them; and on the walls are pinned cat- and dog-food advertisements torn from magazines, a bright blue and white polar-bear blanket, and a large faded poster of Elvis Presley.

Among strangers, Roberto is quiet and deferential, and he speaks softly in a mildly effeminate manner; with friends he is somewhat more talkative, but he rarely dominates conversations. When talking, Roberto sometimes has a nervous habit of stroking the small blanket on his bed in circular motions. Roberto's good sense of humor and his ability to laugh about his own mistakes endear him to his friends. Although he is usually quiet and friendly, he has a short, sometimes violent temper, exacerbated by his defensiveness. His inability to control his outbursts has often caused him problems in the past. "Bobby has trouble holding a job because his temper gets away from him," Mrs. Caldwell has commented. "He gets mad if he thinks someone's picking on him. If somebody says something and he thinks they're talking about him, it bothers him and he just walks off or hits them." Roberto prefers to work alone because he gets angry or frustrated if he feels he is being "bossed around." "I really should control myself," he said. "To relieve myself—it all builds up—so I gotta get away." Roberto's short temper has often landed him in fist-fights, in which he usually takes a beating because of his small stature. Roberto says his fighting days are over. "I had quite a temper then. Well, I still have a temper, but I guess I'm too old for that now. I don't want to be bothered." Although he still flares up easily, Roberto's anger dissipates rapidly, and he does not hold a grudge.

SELF-DESCRIPTION: MEXICAN-AMERICAN HOMOSEXUAL

Roberto does not consider himself mildly mentally retarded, but instead sees himself as a "slow learner" who did not get enough schooling. The fact that he can read a little is sufficient proof for himself that he is not "dumb."

> I don't tell people about my stay in the hospital because of what they might think. I wasn't sent out there because I was dumb or anything like that. I just got into some trouble and there was no where else for them to send me.

In contrast, Roberto has long recognized his homosexuality. "I first knew I was gay when I was about 14 or 15 years old," he said. "I started hanging around with gay people and I had more fun with them. At first it was just to have friends. Then later I started drinking and hanging out in gay bars."

Although many of Roberto's homosexual relations have been short-term and sometimes volatile—he was once given a black eye by a man with whom he refused to go home—he has also shared intimate and caring relationships with other men, such as those discussed in this chapter. Today, Roberto does not go out with anyone unless he knows him well, and he refuses to be "picked up." "No, I don't like it. I come by myself, go by myself . . . . There's too many things can happen, man. Like murder, like robbery, all that. Some of those men are mean." Reflecting today's somewhat less judgmental attitude toward homosexuals, Roberto is now more comfortable with his homosexuality. "I used to hide it from the public, and it bothered my conscience. Then I said, 'Forget it, it don't bother me anymore. Fuck it, I'm too old for that.' " Although he tried to hide his homosexuality from most people, Roberto never saw being gay as a problem in terms of the people who mattered most to him. "Mrs. Caldwell and her kids never made fun of me. I guess they knew but they never said anything to me about it."

Roberto believes, ironically, that his homosexuality brought him security during the years he was in and out of jails.

> The first time I was thrown in jail was in 1955 in Van Nuys. I got drunk one night and they arrested me. I was so nervous, I thought they'd throw away the key. I didn't know what could happen to me. But it was okay because they put me in the gay side. They can just tell by the way you act and talk. When they see that, they separate you to protect you from the other men. Gay men are like women, they need to be separated from the men. It's much safer in the gay section.

Roberto identifies with historical figures whom he has been told were homosexual, such as King Louis XIII and Queen Elizabeth I, and he is fascinated by the fact that, as he said, "Rome had a lot of gays." Given the appearance of the tights worn by men of the 16th Century, Roberto remarked, "They all must have been gay too." He is impressed by muscular men; he once said, referring to body builders who are security guards, "They are built like gorillas. You know, good-looking men." Maintaining his sense of humor, Roberto is able to joke about his homosexuality. During a visit to a local shopping mall, he once remarked, "Did you see that woman? She was *beauuutiful!* It's too bad I'm gay!" On another occasion, he extolled the virtues of an organ player at a local bar, saying, "Man, that guy used to burn that organ up." "Really, he was good?" a fieldworker asked. "No," Roberto joked, "He was straight."

Although Roberto is perpetually short of money and often must eat his meals at the skid-row missions, he does not consider himself poor. On the contrary, he sees himself as very fortunate, especially in comparison to the homeless people he sees on skid row in downtown Los Angeles. "You see a lot of people in the street, I'm not lying—God strike me dead. Children in boxes, sleeping in rags. It's terrible." After a moment's pause he added, "Boy, I thank God I got a bed upstairs. It might be small, but it's a bed."

Roberto also does not consider himself either an alcoholic, or a recovering alcoholic. He acknowledges that he drank heavily for 15 years and spent time in jail because of it, but when he compares himself to others he knew, including his stepfather who died from alcohol, Roberto says that he was never "that far gone." In fact, Roberto still drinks on occasion—sometimes to excess—but he says he does not feel he needs to drink, a claim his landlord and friends have substantiated.

Roberto regards his Mexican-American identity with ambivalence. Sometimes he shows pride in his Mexican heritage, as illustrated in his room by his prominently displayed large red sombrero with gold embroidery. But at other times, Roberto downplays his ancestry. He considers it more prestigious to be from Italy, and he fancies that he is often mistaken for an Italian. "You should have seen me in that doctor's office. I walked in there and everyone looked at me, and I could tell they thought I was Italian. It makes me feel good when people think I'm Italian," he said. Roberto feels that being Mexican is less exotic, and he is not unaware of the discrimination that results from this minority status. After a bitter argument with a friend, he remarked: "Maybe he doesn't like Mexican people. I don't care what others think. I am a Mexican-American, and I am homosexual, but we're all the same. He's no better than me and I'm no better than him. We're all just human beings." Roberto said he rarely uses his fluent Spanish because if he does not speak English, Anglos will think he is ignorant. However, his ability to speak Spanish was helpful in his work at the Salvation Army stores, where he translated for many of the Spanish-speaking clientele and communicated with non-English-speaking workers. His minority identity also gives Roberto a more tolerant view of others. "Some people make fun of foreigners who can't speak English, but they shouldn't," he said. "When we go over there we can't speak their language."

FINANCES AND HEALTH

Except for his bout with alcoholism, one could characterize Roberto's health and finances as, in his words, being "in good shape but without money." It is no exaggeration to say that money burns holes in Roberto's pockets. By his own admission, he cannot save a dime. Although he knows the value of money and how to make change, Roberto has never kept track of his money, and he complains about how fast it disappears. Although he has never had much money, when he does have some, Roberto is generous in buying gifts and giving loans to friends. His income was modest when he worked in sanitariums doing cleaning, kitchen work, and yardwork, but this was offset by free room and board.

Because he was a hard worker, Roberto had no trouble finding a job, but because of his inability to save, he was always without money.

During the 1960s, Roberto worked off and on for the Salvation Army loading trucks before he seriously hurt his back. Those temporary jobs provided Roberto with a little money, a place to stay, and a feeling of independence. Having been, in his own words, "locked up" for 8 years in a state institution, he attached great importance to this feeling of independence. However, in the late 1960s, Roberto hurt his back helping Mrs. Caldwell move a bed. "We were moving a bed from one room to another, and afterward my back hurt and was sore. Then someone touched me and I screamed. They had to take me to General Hospital immediately. I had to sleep on the floor for a month." Because he could not work, Roberto attempted to get welfare benefits.

> But all I could get was a meal ticket and a room. I never did get the room because there were so many people waiting ahead of me, but I did get three meals a day. The welfare hotels are filled and they send you from one to the other. I would stay with Mrs. Caldwell and then go out and eat on the ticket. Sometimes I would use what little change I had to spend the night in an all night show.

For 5 years, Roberto gave blood once or twice a week to make extra money. "I got $5 a pint," he said. "It was the only way I could get money because I couldn't lift things after I hurt my back. But I stopped selling my blood because I got too weak. I'd lost about 35 pounds."

His financial trials and tribulations—if not his spending sprees— ended for the most part in 1972, when a researcher helped him get disability benefits. One might suspect that Roberto did not receive such benefits earlier because he was unable to fill out the application by himself, but he has been resourceful in the past in soliciting help from friends for these tasks. What primarily stood in Roberto's way was a fear that, if he complained to the welfare office, he might be sent back to the state hospital. When he started receiving benefits, he no longer felt the need to work full-time, and he went into "retirement," although he continued to do odd jobs to earn extra money.

Roberto now spends approximately half his monthly income on rent, and much of the rest goes toward paying off debts accumulated to friends. He used to spend a lot of money on clothes, but stopped because of his current debts. For years he bought clothes at the same store, and he was allowed to charge up to $100 worth of clothing, which he paid back over several months. He sometimes lends money to friends, but more frequently he borrows from them after his monthly check is spent, which is usually the first week after he gets it. His money is spent either eating out or on his "decorations." He especially likes things made of glass (dolls, cats, and dogs) and plastic (beads and figurines). His penchant for these decorations led him to buy on credit from his new landlady, Alice. Although the value of these items is minimal (a few ceramic figures, some glass bowls, stuffed dolls, and plastic beads), the debt Roberto incurred seems interminable. To date he has paid $75 a month for over 2 years, and he continues to pay. "I'm almost done paying it," he said, "But I don't know how much I still owe her." Roberto has asked Alice how much he owes her on a couple of different occasions, and she has said she would tell him later, but she has not yet done so. "I don't mind paying; if it's $300 or $400, okay. I can pay it, but I want to know. Don't get me wrong, Alice is good people, but I just want to know how much I have to pay." The same was true for the trinkets Roberto bought from Mrs. Caldwell. "Grandma took out the rent and some for what I owed her and gave me a certain amount out of the check each month," he said, but he does not know how much she charged him for these things.

Because his borrowing and spending often leave him short of funds, Roberto looks for new ways to make extra money, such as cleaning friends' apartments. He spent one month collecting aluminum cans for recycling. "Every little bit of change helps," he said. "They pay 20 cents per pound." Roberto sometimes dreams about what he would do if he could learn to save money: a trip to Catalina Island or San Francisco, or a motorcycle and maybe a car. He knows that these dreams are not realistic, given his inability to save and the fact that he does not drive, but he said it is fun to think about anyway. He is also aware that his financial schemes will hardly make him rich, but that will not keep him from enjoying life. "Money isn't everything," Roberto said. "People spend too much time worrying about money. I like money but I'm not that damn crazy."

For the most part, Roberto also does not worry about his health. At 62, he is in good physical condition; he does not overeat, and he gets a lot of exercise. Roberto likes to get out of his apartment, and because he does not drive, he walks to wherever he is going, sometimes walking as much as 10 miles in a day. He likes to walk because "you get to see things that you wouldn't otherwise." Roberto used to smoke two packs of cigarettes a week, but he seldom smokes now. He catches colds perhaps two or three times a year, and when he does, he makes visits to the doctor for penicillin shots. Roberto still has back problems from the injury he sustained in the 1960s, and he takes pain medication for it. "It's very painful when it happens. If I didn't go to the doctor I would walk like this," he said, imitating the Hunchback of Notre Dame.

In his early 30s, Roberto nearly lost an eye when he was punched by a boarder at Mrs. Caldwell's. When drunk, he often dared people to hit him to show how tough he was, possibly in an attempt to counteract his effeminate manner. To Roberto's dismay, a man at the boarding house took him up on his dare and punched him in the face. Roberto was rushed to the nearest hospital where quick attention by a doctor saved the eye, but it is visibly different from the other. He briefly wore prescription glasses, but gave them up because he did not like the way he looked in them. At first he missed the curbs when crossing streets, but he quickly adjusted. He said his boxer's broken nose got bent from several falls on his face when he was drunk.

Roberto does not know how he managed to give up his heavy alcohol intake or why he finally decided to do so, but the early deaths from alcohol of his biological mother and his adoptive father may have had some effect on his decision. It was not easy, however. During his 15 years of heavy drinking, Roberto would use almost any excuse. "I drank when I was happy or when I felt sorry for myself. I drank a lot because I was just lonely. Maybe sometimes I would drink because I wanted to drink. Everybody gets lonely in this world, you know what I mean?" His drinking habits wreaked havoc on his social relations, destroying his relationship with his lover, Ben, and souring a number of other friendships. As Mrs. Caldwell explained:

> I used to really get aggravated at Bobby when he drank. When he would come home from a drunk he would come in and sleep on the floor next to my bed as if serving penance. He was trying to get back into my good graces. In 1978, Bobby came home real drunk and sat on the edge of my bed to talk, like he usually did. When my son came into the room, Bobby leapt up and tried to hit him in the face several times. My son started to hit Bobby back but then decided against it. Bobby's small compared to my son. Some of the other men pulled Bobby away. He was very distraught about this incident and kept trying to apologize to my son. My son eventually forgave him, but it had a lasting impact on Bobby and he hasn't drunk much after that.

However, it was his friendships that made it difficult for Roberto to quit drinking. This is best illustrated recently by his friendship with Sam, a man he met at Mrs. Caldwell's house. Sam had just left his wife and daughter after 20 years of marriage, telling his wife he was gay and could no longer live with her. Sam became the unofficial manager of Mrs. Caldwell's place, and he received free room and board in return. It was not long before Sam moved into Roberto's room so that Roberto could take care of him. Roberto said:

> Sam needs someone to take care of him. Sometimes he has epileptic fits during his sleep. He will make gasping sounds and kick his arms and legs and try to get up. He might bite his tongue off, so I have to hold him down and put something in his mouth so he can breathe.

Sam was an alcoholic who encouraged Roberto to drink with him. Both became argumentative when they drank, and they often fought. Finally, after one of these fights, Roberto moved from Mrs. Caldwell's house. He said Sam was bossing him around too much. "We got in an argument and he told me to get out," Roberto said. Mrs. Caldwell cried when Roberto left, but he ignored her entreaties and refused to reconsider because he felt that she favored Sam over him. True to character, however, Roberto did not hold a grudge. Two months later, he and Sam were friends again. Roberto considered inviting Sam to live with him but decided against it because he was drinking too much, up to three six-packs of beer a day according to Roberto. Roberto correctly predicted that Sam would never give up drinking. Three months later, Sam died of an overdose of drugs and alcohol.

The last time Roberto was arrested for drunken behavior was in 1977. "I just stopped," Roberto said. "I don't want to drink no more. You get tired of it. I got tired of going to jail, I really did." Despite these remarks, Roberto's transition to sobriety was neither smooth nor complete. The greatest temptations for Roberto are still drinking with friends and going to bars in search of company. The morning after, Roberto swears off drinking again and might even attend an Alcoholics Anonymous (AA) meeting. (He laughs at the fact that the meeting place for the AA chapter he attends is right next-door to a gay bar.) Roberto also credits age for causing him to reduce his alcohol intake. "Mrs. Caldwell used to always get after me. She told me, 'You know, Bobby, you gonna get old and it's gonna come all back to you.' And she's right, it does. I can't do that no more like I used to, ten, twenty years ago. I'm too old for that."

SOCIAL RELATIONS

Most of Roberto's relationships have been temporary to varying degrees, with the exception of his second adopted family. Roberto was informally adopted a second time when he was 34 years old by Mrs. Caldwell, who provided him with a job and large family surroundings. This second, informal adoption of Roberto lasted 25 years and gave him some stability during that time. According to Roberto, Mrs. Caldwell was always there when he needed help, and he says that she was "like a mother" to him. "If I was in jail, she would send her son to come bail me out," he explained. Mrs. Caldwell acknowledges her fondness for Roberto and her willingness to help. "I told him, 'As long as you're hungry I'll always feed you,' " Mrs. Caldwell said. "He usually ended up by calling me about one o'clock at night, and then I got my son up out of bed to go pick him up so Bobby didn't have to sleep out in the street." Roberto became her charge, and she accepted responsibility for him despite his irresponsible behavior. Mrs. Caldwell also said that she and her family feel that Roberto is part of the family and that if she and her husband were no longer around another member of her family would help Roberto. Roberto also feels close to Mrs. Caldwell's children. He has visited her son, Henry, in Portland three times, with each visit lasting about a month. The first time he went to visit, Roberto traveled by plane, but he got air-sick on the flight, so Henry had to drive Roberto back to Los Angeles in the car. For the next two visits, Henry drove from Portland to Los Angeles to get Roberto and then drove him home again at the end of his visit. Roberto also feels emotionally close to Henry because he was the one who frequently bailed Roberto out of jail.

Some people in Roberto's life have questioned whether he has been exploited by Mrs. Caldwell. One social worker thought Mrs. Caldwell might have frightened Roberto into thinking he might be sent back to the state hospital in order to keep him under her control. (This strategy was also used by Mr. MacDonald, Roberto's employer at the sanitarium while Roberto was on parole from Pacific State Hospital.) Roberto's friend Joanne also thinks Mrs. Caldwell exploited his fear of being sent back.

> Mrs. Caldwell has robbed Bobby blind. When Bobby first went on SSI, she took his $600 check and gave him $30, and the rest she gave to her son Henry, who used it on a down payment for a new car. Henry gets all the money from her place. He doesn't work, and yet he gets a new car every year.

Roberto did agree that, "Grandma's smart, she'll take you to your last dollar." But he is ambivalent about his treatment from Mrs. Caldwell, because she has also helped him out for so many years.

> Well, I guess she took advantage at first, but I don't—I don't—It doesn't bother me. She's never slapped her door in my face; she's always welcoming me. Grandma told me that if I ever was hungry I could come over there. She's good people. I don't have anyone else. I have friends but not that would take an interest if something happened to me, if I got hurt or died.

To Roberto, money for which he has not had to work seems small compensation for all the years during which Grandma provided him with love and shelter.

Mrs. Caldwell would like Roberto to move back into her house, but he would rather stay in his apartment, where he can relax and enjoy himself. He also points out that there have been many changes at Mrs. Caldwell's house and that the situation has degenerated since he left. The house is now a shambles, whereas before it was quite neat. At 87, Mrs. Caldwell's health is failing, and she has given up trying to control activities in the house. She has been to the hospital several times recently, suffering from pneumonia and respiratory problems that are compounded by her extreme obesity. As Joanne said, "Mrs. Caldwell is too old and she can't control the people there. It is drunken parties all the time now." Despite his feelings for her, Roberto does not want to live at her place any more. "Things have changed too much there," Bobby said. "I want to remember it as it was before."

Roberto's friendships have tended to be temporary, and at times Roberto is not sanguine about his friends. "I really don't have many friends," he said. "I do have friends when I have money in my pocket, but I haven't had money in my pocket for a long time." Most of the time, however, Roberto acknowledges that he does have a number of good friends. During his early years of instability when he was moving about frequently, he was helped by many of these friends. He stayed with his adoptive mother's friends after she died, and later his godparents in Watts welcomed Roberto into their home. His adoptive mother's former cook helped Roberto find a place to stay, and her daughter, Angie, became a friend to Roberto. He once stayed with her for 2 weeks when he had no place to sleep.

Roberto has lost track of most of his old friends, but he is gregarious and makes new friends easily. Over the many years at Mrs. Caldwell's house, he has made innumerable friends among the boarders who have come and gone, and he has tried to maintain contact with a few of them after they have moved out. Annie is one such friend with whom Roberto has kept in contact. She has a car and they sometimes take trips to Griffith Observatory or to the shopping center. Annie, like many of the boarders at Mrs. Caldwell's, is an alcoholic. She was arrested recently, and her 9-year-old daughter was placed in the custody of her aunt. In the past, Roberto accompanied Annie and her daughter on several outings to the park and the zoo. He said that she must go to AA meetings for a month in order to get her daughter back and he hopes that she complies.

Three of Roberto's closest friends live in an apartment downstairs from him: Joanne, Matt, and "the old lady," as he calls her (he doesn't know her name). Joanne said that the old lady likes Roberto, although "she is 80 years old and rarely talks . . . . But she comes out to the living room when he visits. She was a bag lady when I got ahold of her. She was not bathing and was a wreck. I took her in and cleaned her up." Roberto met Joanne in 1960 at Mrs. Caldwell's sanitarium, where she was working as a nurse's helper. He said he "couldn't stand" Joanne when he first met her. "We used to get into arguments all the time." Like Mrs. Caldwell, Joanne is very overweight and has trouble getting around. According to Roberto, she does not get around much in the apartment, much less go outside. She spends most of the day in her easy chair watching television or talking with the old lady, Matt, or Roberto. If he is not eating microwaved frozen dinners in his apartment, Roberto eats his meals downstairs at Joanne's. "I do a little work for her: clean her bedroom, make her bed, clean the bathroom, and wash her dishes in return for meals, and sometimes she pays me."

Roberto also met Matt at Mrs. Caldwell's house in 1979. Matt takes care of Joanne and the old lady and does the grocery shopping, and Joanne and the old lady each pay half of the rent. Matt sometimes helps out with the food costs, and he takes Joanne to the hospital for emergencies when she has trouble breathing. Roberto thinks that Matt is mentally retarded. He said, "When you talk to him you can tell, 'cuz he's kinda slow." However, Roberto added that Matt is smart, "He can spell and write and is real good at arithmetic. Matt helped me with my bank account." They usually get along well, but they have also gotten into heated arguments. One fight, which occurred after they had had a few beers, ended abruptly when Matt picked up Roberto and threw him out of the apartment. Roberto thinks jealousy was the real reason for the fight.

> I have known Joanne a lot longer than Matt. He is jealous of me and afraid that I will take his job away, taking care of Joanne. But since he and Joanne aren't married he shouldn't be jealous. Matt is the manager of the apartments, but he doesn't do anything; he sleeps half the day and then gets up and does nothing. I've given Matt money for cigarettes and Matt never does anything for me. Some people thought that he and I were lovers, but we are just friends.

Despite this and many other arguments, Roberto and Matt have remained good friends.

Roberto thinks another of his friends, his new landlady, Alice, has treated him admirably. When he wanted to move back to his apartment, Roberto said, "My landlady didn't have to take me back. She knows I drink—I get all plastered. But she took me back." Roberto met Alice through his friend Joanne, who also lives in Alice's apartment building. Alice takes Roberto to flea markets and sometimes loans him money to buy his many trinkets. However, as mentioned previously, he has been paying her back for these trinkets for quite a long time without being able to ascertain how much he actually owes her. Alice is also a friend of Mrs. Caldwell.

Mrs. Caldwell is the keystone for most of Roberto's diverse network of friends. "I met Jackie through Grandma in 1963," said Roberto. Jackie is approximately 70 years old, married, and has three sons. She takes Roberto to yard sales, and he does cleaning jobs for her from time to time for extra cash. "Sometimes I don't see her for a long time. One time I didn't see her for 2 whole years." Dan was another good friend of Roberto's from Mrs. Caldwell's house. They often went to the gay bar together, after Roberto made the surprising discovery that Dan was gay.

When I found out Dan was gay I said, "But I thought you were married!" He told me, "That doesn't mean shit." Dan also drank a lot but not as much as Sam. He was killed in 1981. He was drunk and jaywalking in the street and was hit by a car and killed instantly.

Most of Roberto's friends from Mrs. Caldwell's house are problem drinkers, a good reason for him to stay away. "Every damn one of them is an alcoholic. They all drink like a fish," Roberto said. When he is there, the temptation to drink is overwhelming. Because of this, he prefers not to visit now. This has one disadvantage, however. Although he likes his privacy and independence, Roberto sometimes misses all of the activity at Mrs. Caldwell's house. He said, "Sometimes I get tired of living by myself. Damn lot of privacy."

THE TWO ROBERTOS: PUBLIC AND PRIVATE

The social facts of Roberto's life and the public persona that he projects convey little of the emotional, psychological, or spiritual side of the private person called "Bobby" by his friends. Bobby, Roberto's private side—vulnerable, abandoned, and lonely—is hidden behind the rough exterior that Roberto tries to maintain. In time, one begins to see behind the public tough-guy image to the private, soft-spoken, sensitive individual. For all his knowledge of the world and varied experiences in it (like Tiresias, the blind prophet of T. S. Eliot's poem *The Wasteland*, Roberto often says "I've seen it all"), he is at times unexpectedly innocent and vulnerable. How does one reconcile the train hopping, jail sitting, and fist fighting with the doll collecting, baby-sitting, and window shopping?

Roberto has survived adoption and the death of his adoptive family, life as a transient on skid row, and being an alcoholic, an inmate of a state hospital, a rover/tramp, and a tough Mexican-American who frequently gets into fights and lands in jail. The tough-guy shell can be seen as something he wears to protect himself from exploitation and discrimination. Roberto's secrets, that he spent 8 years in a state hospital where he was tested as a "high moron" (the term used at that time) and that he is homosexual, are certainly soft spots in the armor of adaptability. That these secrets have, for the most part, remained hidden attests to Roberto's ability to pass. He has managed his limited ability to read and write by soliciting help from friends and crediting this deficit to lack of education, and although not unknown to others, Roberto does not flaunt his homosexuality but keeps it to himself and minds his own business. ("They don't mind what I am as long as they don't bother me and I don't bother them.")

Roberto knows that he has a low IQ score. But he does not know, nor if he were told would he admit, that he was committed to Pacific State

Hospital as "feebleminded," as it reads in the record. In his eyes, he was punished for being a bad boy rather than for being stupid. Of all the labels he carries, mental retardation is the only one he does not accept. When applied to Roberto, the term "mentally retarded" seems to lose meaning with time and in the absence of the role. That no one, including his closest friends and his "Grandma," suspects that he is mentally retarded is proof enough for Roberto that he is not. He has proved that he is able (and usually willing) to work. He recently said, betraying some insecurity about the future, that if he got cut off from Social Security and SSI benefits he would find a job. "If I had to go to work I'd go to work," Roberto said. "I'm not too lazy to go to work."

While Roberto's tough-guy side is willing and able to work at age 62, his vulnerable and soft-spoken side is unwilling and unable to control his money. He is generous with his friends and with himself, and his spending sprees consume most of his expendable income. Had he managed his finances differently, Roberto said he might have saved quite a bundle of money over the years, but instead, he is usually in debt for buying things on credit. It could be argued that some of his friends have taken advantage of his generosity, but as he has said, "What are friends for if not to make happy?" Such was the case in Bobby's relationship with his roommate John at the sanitarium in Whittier. John was jealous of Bobby's popularity with the cooks and the other boarders, and he exploited Bobby by pretending to be his friend while spending his money. Bobby's emotional attachment to John was romantic and innocent (Bobby is passive and never made advances). In the words of Roberto's social worker:

> Roberto went on to explain his affection for John in language that was quite simple and rather dignified. Roberto admitted that he "liked" John, that he still cared for him more than he cared for anyone else despite the fact that he knew that John had used him to his own end. Roberto realized that John had tolerated a homosexual relationship with him only so that he could take many of the possessions Bobby had accumulated. However, patient expressed no bitterness for John and told me that he felt that this was half his fault, that he had wanted to give things to John since "when you like someone you want to give them things to make them happy."

Roberto conceals his private side when interacting with all but his closest friends, but this side of him is readily visible in his concern for children. Bobby loves children more than most men his age, more than most people at any age. He adores babies, and he took care of them for three different families over a period of more than 10 years. Because he is "retired," he does not baby-sit as much as he used to, but he still takes a proprietary concern in the children who live in the apartment down the hall. "My baby upstairs had the flu the other day. 104. And she [the baby's mother] wanted to give him a shower. I says, 'Why, girl, are you crazy? That's bad. Just give him alcohol,' " Bobby said (meaning an alcohol rub). Excluding his 9 years with his adoptive mother, Bobby's fondest memories are of baby-sitting for Mrs. Caldwell's children when he was her family's only boarder in the early 1960s: "My favorite time was when Jimbo and Debbie were small. I really love kids; I would have liked to have my own. But I've had enough problems, how could I take care of a kid?"

His enjoyment of baby-sitting is definitely characteristic of his private side; the public Roberto would never admit to changing diapers and warming bottles of milk. His empathy with children is evidence of his sensitivity, and he shares their psychological if not material vulnerability.

The passive vulnerable side is as much present in him as is the active culprit side, as the story that opened this chapter illustrates. The active culprit quit his job (because he was "bored") and hopped a train to San Francisco in search of adventure ("I wanted some excitement") and danger ("You don't know what's going to happen to you," and "I took a chance") because he was independent ("I had nowhere to go"). But the vulnerable Bobby made a mistake ("Unfortunately I got on the wrong train and ended up in Portland, Oregon.") and got arrested for vagrancy (not having money or a place to live—a charge also leveled against the homeless) and vandalism, a crime he did not commit. As Roberto points out, "The other guy broke into the machine to get money," and "The other guy said that I hadn't done anything." Nevertheless, Roberto was unjustly convicted and spent time in jail. While he illegally hopped on the train without fear, he got lost and never quite made it to San Francisco no matter how many times he tried. While he boldly got into drunken brawls and slept out on the street, he also made friends with the homeless on Skid Row. And while he got into trouble for staying out past curfew, he also ran away from the hospital with a boy with an impaired leg, knowing he had little chance of success.

CONCLUSION

Roberto has faced a number of crises over time that have contributed to his unstable life. The most dramatic change he faced, what for him was the major turning point in his life, was the death of his adoptive mother when he was quite young. He often says that things were great until his "mother" died. And although one might suspect an over-romanticization of his early childhood experience, Roberto's history subsequent to his adoptive mother's death bears out the fact that, indeed, this was the beginning of many years of instability for him. Despite this lack of stability, Roberto seems to have survived these obstacles admirably well.

Triumphs

Having dealt with the adversities of a lost family (twice), institutionalization, alcoholism, and discrimination, Roberto rightly assesses his past as a triumph, and sees himself as a survivor. He attributes much of his success to luck and to help from friends along the way. His attempts to make connections with these significant others and places from his past have been continually frustrated. In 1946, Roberto went out to visit the family with whom he lived in his adoptive mother's house, but they had moved and sold the store they owned. "I should have stayed with them," he lamented. "I could have owned that store right now." In 1971, Roberto again went back to see this house, and found it demolished and a new one built in its place. Later he visited his former home to find that "the place where I lived with my mother is now a Chinese seafood market." Finally, one could be pardoned for finding symbolism in Roberto's last trip to rediscover the past. On his long trip out to Whittier, to visit the sanitarium where he had worked on his first parole, he found that it had been sold to the cemetery next door. "The sanitarium sold out," he said, "They torn [sic] the place down. It's being turned into a graveyard. When I go [die], Highland Park will change completely too. They'll change it around. I'll get up and say, 'You fool, what are you doing to my town!' "

Today his closest tie to the past is Mrs. Caldwell, who moved 5 months ago because she was unable to make payments on her large house (too few paying boarders, as Roberto had predicted). Roberto has yet to pay her a visit in her new, smaller house because he does not want to be put to work. But this also indicates that he does not always attempt to cling to the past. It is not always worth clinging to. Mrs. Caldwell's previous house, like its owner at the age of 87, had gone into a state of general decline. (Mrs. Caldwell now weighs over 250 pounds and spends most of her time in bed.) The carpets reeked of dog urine and beer, containers of food stood open on the kitchen counter, and dirty dishes lay in the sink. Dogs roamed the hallways, littered with beer cans, and loud rock music boomed from behind closed doors.

Seeing the physical decline of friends has strengthened Roberto's resolve to stay in good physical shape. He has watched his friends Joanne and Mrs. Caldwell grow more obese as they grow older, and he does not want to share their fate. Recently, through the efforts of a fieldworker, he was reunited, after 30 years, with one of his best friends from the state hospital. During this time, his friend Richie (see Chapter 5) had grown enormous around the waist, and Roberto was shocked by the change. "I can't believe it," he said. "He didn't have that fat belly and he was damn good-looking . . . thin and blond and handsome." Roberto was so convinced that this large man before him was not his former friend that he refused to get out of the car to talk with him. Later, Roberto commented, "He sounds like Richie and he's still got that same smile, but I can't believe he changed so much. I wanted to see him just like the last time." Roberto added, "I hope I never look like that."

Roberto admits that age has caught up with him, and he cannot do the things he used to do. He claims that alcohol aged him faster than usual and that he finally reached "burn out" and is now too old to drink. "You get tired of seeing the problems. I was going downhill. . . . I got tired of going to jail, I really did." Roberto says he is also too old to ride the trains.

> It was kind of exciting when I first rode a boxcar. It made me feel good. It made me feel like I wanted do it again and again, you know. When you don't have a job or place to stay, hell, there's no difference in staying in one town and staying in another town. You just want to travel and do things, see different things.

But at 62, Roberto said that, for him, the adventure has gone out of that lifestyle. "I'm too old for that kind of thing."

But, for Roberto, old is relative; some days he feels old and worn out by his wilder youth, and other days he is quite chipper and comments on how young he feels. There are times when Roberto doubts he will last much longer. On seeing an old woman on the street corner, edging a shopping cart out into the traffic against the red light, Roberto commented: "I hope I never get that old. I don't think I'll make it that long. I'm too wild. I get tired sometimes, not my mind but my body." However, he usually considers the future with optimism. "I'll be all right in old age as long as I have three meals a day, TV to watch, and a bed to sleep in," he said. "I don't want to be a bother to nobody. I just want to go to a sanitarium and let them take care of me." He estimates that he has "twenty more good years to live." Whatever he thinks about the future, Roberto is clearly content with his present circumstances, and he is proud of the fact that he has survived. "I'm having a good life right now. 'Cuz I've seen it all, you know," Roberto said. And then after a slight pause, he added, "Well, practically . . . just about all."

4

"Two Is Enough."
MYRTLE SHEFFIELD

by Dana M. Baldwin

Myrtle is a small, plain, moderately overweight 58-year-old woman who shows no visible signs of retardation but who looks a few years older than her age. With her dark hair going to gray, her plump body, and her taste in clothes running to printed tops and polyester slacks, she projects a matronly image. Myrtle's strong-boned face is softened by the attractive, large-lensed glasses that she wears, especially when she smiles one of her rare smiles; however, most of the time her affect is extremely flat, often making it difficult for others to know what she is thinking or feeling. In manner, she is quiet, even withdrawn on occasion, although when she is around people with whom she feels comfortable, her rather impish sense of humor sometimes shines through. For the most part, however, the word *taciturn* might have been coined to describe Myrtle, and in any situation other than one-on-one, she is far more comfortable staying to the side and observing than entering into the interaction. Myrtle's second husband, Lennie Sheffield, is a tall self-described "Okie" with an enormous paunch and an appetite for cigarettes and conversation that never seems to be satisfied. Lennie seems to feel as comfortable monopolizing a conversation as Myrtle does listening to it. Their life together is typical of many conservative, working-class people in Los Angeles, particularly the large number with Midwestern backgrounds who came here as part of the mass migration that occurred during the 1930s and 1940s.

Myrtle and Lennie live in a small, inexpensive two-bedroom house, built as one of many just like it, in a lower-middle income neighborhood about 25 miles south of Los Angeles. Myrtle and her paraplegic first husband bought the house when it was new 25 years ago, and Myrtle has lived there throughout her first marriage, her widowhood, and her remarriage. "Don't like to move," Myrtle likes to explain with a mischievous smile. According to Myrtle, the composition of the neighborhood has changed dramatically since she first moved there. In 1962, when she and her first husband bought the house, the neighborhood consisted primarily of "Dutchmen" who owned or worked in the many dairies that still existed in the area at that time. Now most of the dairies are gone and the neighborhood is predominantly Latino, or, as Myrtle and Lennie sometimes disparagingly remark, "full of wetbacks."

Until last year, the house was as run-down and unkempt as most of the other houses in the neighborhood. Many of the houses on the block look all of their 25 years, because they have not been substantially altered or renovated since they were built. Some of the yards are badly tended, with overgrown lawns or no lawns at all, and many of the houses are in need of a new coat of paint. In the first few months of 1987, Lennie received a large windfall of back pay, money that he and Myrtle decided to put toward refurbishing their home. (This decision was prompted by the fact that their Social Security officer told them the money had to be spent within a set period of time or they would lose their disability benefits.) They painted the house inside and out, did a minor remodeling job on the kitchen, and filled almost the entire house with new furniture. In repainting the exterior of the house, they turned it from a faded and peeling salmon color to a smooth coffee color. However, the most dramatic change was inside the house. Before Myrtle and Lennie redecorated, an old brown Naugahyde couch and recliner took up one wall of the living room, while a television and VCR were featured prominently on the opposite wall. An area known as "Myrtle's corner" was placed along a third wall; it included an old moth-eaten chair in which she sat to talk on her Citizen's Band radio (one of her favorite diversions), her CB radio itself, and an old television that had long since been gutted of its workings in order to serve as a display for assorted dusty old knickknacks. As part of the refurbishment process, the Naugahyde furniture was sold and "Myrtle's corner" was exiled to the spare bedroom, a room that still serves as a repository for whatever junk Myrtle and Lennie cannot figure out where else to store. To refurnish the living room, as well as their bedroom and kitchen, they bought a number of inexpensive and cheaply made pieces of furniture, among them a new bedroom set, a kitchen table, a hutch, a new sofa, side tables, and lamps. Outside, the house is surrounded by a sporadically cared-for yard; Lennie's garage workshop is stuffed with tools, car parts, and the assorted paraphernalia often accumulated by mechanical-minded men; and their covered boat stands next to the house in the driveway.

Lennie and Myrtle's main source of income is a combination of Social Security and SSI, although Lennie, who is a retired auto mechanic, keeps busy and brings in some extra cash by doing odd jobs for family and friends. Although their combined monthly income is certainly not excessive, they seem to have everything they need, as well as some luxury items. They shop mostly at discount stores, but the number of expensive consumer goods Myrtle and Lennie own is notable; they count among their possessions a truck and camper, a 12-year-old Ford sedan, a van, a 14-foot motorboat, a large color television set, a videocassette recorder, and an expensive videocassette camera.

Myrtle and Lennie have not always been so financially secure. Several years ago, they were faced with serious financial trouble because Lennie's disability benefits were cut and Myrtle was receiving no government support. Their only income came from the rental of a second house they had bought together several years before. Their financial difficulties were finally resolved when Lennie sorted out his problems with Social Security by selling the second house, and Myrtle was referred to a Regional Center and deemed eligible to receive SSI.

A previous researcher, who contacted Myrtle in 1982, was partly responsible for referring Myrtle to the Regional Center where steps were taken to see that she received SSI benefits. Myrtle and Lennie are apparently now of the understanding that it is Myrtle's epilepsy, not a mental deficiency, that is the handicap that qualifies her for SSI and as a Regional Center client. In fact, this is largely, though not completely, true; it was her mild mental retardation combined with her seizure disorder that rendered her eligible for SSI. Although Myrtle was originally tested at Pacific State Hospital as having an IQ of 56, that figure may be low given that Myrtle's current Regional Center social worker considers her to be in at least the top 10 percent of his clients, both cognitively and adaptively.

When contacted in 1982, Myrtle admitted to the researcher that she had never told Lennie about her hospitalization at Pacific State Hospital. Because Myrtle felt called upon to explain the researcher's presence, she told Lennie that she had been hospitalized years ago for seizures. Lennie seemed to accept this explanation readily enough.

"Two is enough. No more headaches," Myrtle said when asked if she would ever marry again should anything happen to Lennie. Although Myrtle may say this with conviction born of a sometimes difficult second marriage, it is also the case that for the last 29 years she has found the shelter and security of marriage to be her primary means of adapting to the demands of the world. Her second marriage has proven to be more turbulent and insecure than her first; yet, perhaps for this very reason, she has grown within it. Myrtle has not only become more independent and assertive, but she has also significantly expanded her social contacts. In her first marriage, Myrtle relied heavily on her paraplegic husband to mediate between her and the outside world, a task he readily accepted. The degree to which she has made strides towards acting independently of her husband in her second marriage is impressive. Myrtle probably has more, as well as more varied, social contacts now than at any other time in her life. This chapter examines Myrtle's life as it is today, including her own perspective, and attempts to trace how this evolution has occurred by considering the impact of her second marriage and the adjustments she has made to it.

MYRTLE'S EARLY LIFE AND MARRIAGES

Myrtle was born in Iowa in 1929 and moved with her family to a small agricultural community on the outskirts of Los Angeles when she was 7 years old. One of six children, she was singled out as different at an early age. Myrtle recalls, "They didn't treat me like they did the others . . . 'cause anything went wrong I was the one that got blamed for it. . . . They thought I was dumb I guess or something. I don't know. I had a rough life." Myrtle blames many of her problems on partial complex seizures that started when she was a child. In Myrtle's view, the seizures are why she had trouble learning in school, why she was put in the state hospital, why she is not able to drive, and why she cannot do certain kinds of work. Myrtle managed to complete the eighth grade and, at the age of 17, was committed by her parents to Pacific State Hospital. While in the hospital, she was sterilized, something about which she subsequently expressed no strong regrets. Of the 9 years she spent in the hospital, all Myrtle admits to remembering is that she took care of children and had several bouts of a severe physical illness. Myrtle claims, rather defensively, to have no other memories and to not remember how long she was there.

Myrtle's home life did not improve when she returned on home leave. Her parents were willing to keep her only as long as she could pay her own way; when she was out of work, her life at home was marked by verbal abuse and threats of reinstitutionalization. Myrtle made several attempts at living independently of her parents during this period but had to return home each time out of financial necessity. Fortunately Myrtle had met Peter, who used a wheelchair after being paralyzed from polio, at a club for people with handicaps shortly after her return on home leave. He provided emotional support and, as time went by, help with finances and everyday problems as well. When Myrtle's parents unsuccessfully tried to recommit her to Pacific State Hospital and then threatened to commit her to a local mental hospital, Peter intervened with a social worker and got her a job at a sanitarium known for employing former patients. This job did not last long, however, because Peter felt that Myrtle was being exploited. He "told off" her employer and secured work for her as a phone solicitor at a rehabilitation agency. Peter married Myrtle not long after this, despite his initial reluctance to do so because he felt he was being pressured into the marriage by her family. A month after the wedding, Myrtle quit the phone solicitor job to take care of the house; Peter felt he could adequately support her on the income he earned working at an electronics company. Other than short periods of employment working for a rehabilitation agency and a convalescent hospital, Myrtle henceforth devoted herself to housekeeping and occasional outside work as a house cleaner and baby-sitter.

Myrtle had known Peter for 5 years when she married him in 1958; she was 29 years old. This relationship provided the security and stability that Myrtle needed, and apparently it fulfilled Peter's needs as well. The marriage seemed to be, in Peter's mother's words, a "good arrangement." Although there was no verbal expression of "love," each certainly had concern for the other's welfare. The researcher who contacted Myrtle and Peter in 1960 noted the way in which Myrtle quietly accepted Peter's almost complete domination of the interview situation. Myrtle relied heavily on Peter for almost everything. She stayed at home alone during the day, did not socialize with the neighbors, and relied on Peter for transportation. Moreover, other than occasional visits with one of her sisters, Myrtle and Peter did not see anyone socially on a regular basis. Peter had quit their one regular social activity, the club for people with disabilities, because of pressure he felt to assume a more active leadership role.

Myrtle never spoke explicitly to researchers about her feelings concerning her life. In addition to her notably flat affect, Myrtle seemed to experience a certain degree of discomfort in expressing herself verbally when asked about these things. Then, as now, it was sometimes difficult to tell what Myrtle was feeling. Nevertheless, Myrtle seemed quite content to let Peter manage and direct her life.

According to Myrtle, Peter suffered from high blood pressure so severe as to cause bleeding from his ears. Although he was on medication, he died suddenly at home of a stroke on New Year's Day, 1975. Myrtle was alone in the house with Peter when he died, and she describes the experience as so frightening that she panicked and still does not remember what happened afterward.

Three months later, she married Lennie, an alcoholic whom she and Peter had met through a square-dancing club. When I asked why she married Lennie, her only response was to shrug and say, "I don't know," as if the marriage was a totally capricious event. Lennie never discussed why he married Myrtle, although he did admit that he had lived alone in an apartment for 8 years after his divorce from his first wife. He noted how difficult it was to live alone, how "the walls close in around you." It is probable, then, that Lennie married Myrtle because he was sick, lonely, and wanted stable companionship; the fact that Myrtle also owned her own home undoubtedly added to her attractiveness.

When visited by a researcher in 1982, Myrtle was very depressed and felt that her life was worse than 10 years before. She said, "I'm really tired a lot. . . . I've been tired all my life. I think I was born tired. I don't know. I still don't understand why I'm walking around really." In part, this statement stemmed from the fact that she was suffering from daily seizures, a back problem, and a painful cyst on the back of her leg. But Myrtle was also extremely depressed about Peter's death and her marriage to Lennie. "I don't know why I'm still living for," she remarked at the time, "Why couldn't it be me instead of him? . . . Always take the good ones and leave the drunks around." From an objective vantage point, Myrtle's life did not look so bad. Lennie had quit drinking in 1979, she owned her own home, she and Lennie had bought another house together, and she had recently gotten reinvolved with the club for people with handicaps. Emotionally, however, she had not finished grieving for Peter and could not help comparing her first marriage to her second. Lennie did not meet her standards of what a husband should be like: he did whatever he liked whether or not she approved, he did not work every day, and he did not save money. Myrtle found the latter particularly irksome, because Lennie's Social Security benefits had been discontinued.

Myrtle's social life was far more constricted in 1982 than it would be when she was recontacted in 1986. Of Myrtle's four living siblings, she stayed in touch with only one, a brother who lived about 20 miles away, by means of an occasional phone call. She still did not associate with her neighbors and the only regular activity that got her out of the house was the bimonthly club meeting.

By 1986, Myrtle seemed to have weathered the worst of her depression. Although her improved health and financial situation at that time undoubtedly contributed to this change, there was also the fact that she seemed to have quit grieving for Peter and to have accepted the fact that she was married to Lennie. When I asked her if she ever thinks about Peter, she replied very concretely, and in a flat and unemotional way, that she thinks of him only when she passes by the cemetery.

It is notable that Myrtle's social milieu is probably richer and more varied now (1986–1987) than at any other time in her life. Several members of Lennie's family, particularly two of his grown children, are regular visitors to the house. Lennie's daughter, Mollie, along with her live-in boyfriend and her daughter, moved from Seattle in 1985 and settled into a house several doors down from Myrtle and Lennie. Almost every day Lennie and Myrtle have a visitor from that house, even if it is just Lennie's granddaughter coming over to share dessert with him. Lennie's unemployed son lives further away, but he also visits frequently.

Myrtle has numerous extended family members who live in the area, people whom she knows but with whom she does not usually socialize. Special occasions or circumstances, such as an aunt and uncle's 50th wedding anniversary or the admission of a relative to the hospital where she volunteers, occasionally bring her into contact with these relatives. Myrtle also stays in touch with one member of her immediate family, a brother with whom her contact has increased from an occasional phone call to occasional visits. In the first five months of 1987, she had seen this brother, Manny, three times. Two of these visits occurred when Manny solicited Lennie's help in repairing his car, and the third occurred when he stopped by briefly to bring Myrtle a gift on the day of her housewarming party.

Not only is Myrtle surrounded by a fairly "normal" family life, but Lennie is much less dependent on her than Peter had been. Myrtle has, in turn, become correspondingly more independent, as witnessed by the fact that her extrafamilial social contacts have increased significantly. Her involvement in the club for people with handicaps has increased, partly because Lennie joined and became one of the directors. Even with Lennie's involvement, however, Myrtle and Lennie maintain some independence from each other. One weekend, for instance, Myrtle went to a convention for people with handicaps with another club member while Lennie stayed home, and the next day Lennie went to the racetrack while Myrtle stayed home. Myrtle's social contacts have also been expanded by volunteer work. In early 1984, her Regional Center social worker, concerned about her inactivity, secured volunteer work for her at a local hospital, where she has become one of the most active volunteers, working 2 or 3 days a week. In addition to the club and her volunteer work, Myrtle also goes to bingo every Wednesday night. These activities not only structure her week by getting her out of the house and facilitating interaction with other people, but they also provide her with regular opportunities to go on excursions to local tourist spots, such as Las Vegas. Finally, Myrtle's increased independence and ease in social situations is reflected by the fact that she took the initiative in organizing several parties at her house: a Tupperware party, her own birthday party, and a housewarming party. These parties were attended almost exclusively by family members, however, and mostly by members of Lennie's family. Myrtle rarely socializes with her acquaintances from work or the club outside of organized activities.

Although Myrtle and Lennie are acquainted with all of their immediate neighbors, they are not on close terms with any of them. They have the most contact with the next-door neighbors who share their driveway. Frequent interaction with these neighbors is almost unavoidable, because most foot traffic comes and goes through their respective kitchen entrances, which open onto the common driveway. Despite their relatively frequent interaction, however, Myrtle maintains her distance.

When left alone in the house, she shuts the door (which is otherwise left open except in cold weather), not out of concern for her safety but because she does not want to deal with the neighbors. Myrtle justifies her aloofness on the grounds that her neighbors are "dopeheads." She also accuses one of the women who lives there of being "two-faced" and is very critical of the fact that she married a "wetback" (as Myrtle tends to call all Latinos). As Myrtle tells the story, this woman married a "wetback" against her mother's fervent wishes. When the mother died, the woman and her husband inherited the house and moved in. Both Myrtle and Lennie are fond of saying that the old woman would "turn over in her grave" if she only knew what had happened.

Myrtle's talk of "wetbacks" is an indication of her and Lennie's general negative attitude toward non–Anglo peoples. Much to their consternation, increasing numbers of minorities have moved into their community. The Indian community in particular has become increasingly visible, given the number of restaurants, markets, and clothing stores catering to these immigrants. Myrtle's reaction to this change is typical of her reactions to the presence of other ethnic groups. In her view, "They should go back to where they come from if they can't speak American." In a similar way, Lennie's bigotry was revealed when he showed me a picture of one his sons-in-law and asked me what "nationality" I thought he was. When I observed that he looks black, Lennie explained that he's Hawaiian, but since he is the blackest one of his family he is the "black sheep." Lennie added that, "He doesn't talk like a nigger or anything, but she's the one that has to wake up and look at those white eyeballs in the morning."

Myrtle and Lennie both have multiple health problems. Although Myrtle likes to talk about her ailments, they currently appear to be chronic but relatively minor. She has about one seizure a day of short duration, which does not seem to bother her very much. In addition, she suffers from arthritis and occasionally has problems with her back, stomach, and leg. Myrtle is conscientious about making and keeping doctor's appointments. Lennie is another matter altogether. Although both he and Myrtle smoke, Lennie chain smokes and suffers from emphysema. When his doctor at the Veterans Administration took away his medication several years ago and told him to quit smoking, Lennie just quit seeing the doctor. In addition to his chain smoking, Lennie is often fatigued and appears to be quite depressed; he mentioned, for instance, how he just sits and stares at his work, thinking about what needs to be done. Myrtle often complains that Lennie is always tired, that he falls asleep suddenly at any time of the day. Although she may protest that she does not care, she obviously does. One day when Myrtle exploded in frustration, "You're going to die before you go see a doctor!" Lennie coolly replied, "So what if I die?" In spite of Lennie's avowed indifference to his own health and refusal to visit a doctor, however, he was forced to do so because of severe leg pain caused by a sciatic nerve shortly before I ended my weekly visits in 1988. This condition effectively rendered Lennie housebound, and Myrtle had to curtail some of her outside activities temporarily in order to stay home and take care of him.

MYRTLE'S PRESENT MARRIAGE AND SOCIAL SUPPORTS

Although Myrtle and Lennie seem genuinely to care for each other, their relationship is characterized by teasing, bickering, and occasional outbursts of real anger. Each is fond of teasing the other, and generally this is done in a playful manner. However, there is sometimes an undercurrent of hostility, particularly when Lennie teases Myrtle. Whether by teasing or bickering, both Myrtle and Lennie know how to diffuse tensions that threaten to get out of hand. For instance, when Lennie and Myrtle argued over exactly when to go to the doctor and Lennie saw that Myrtle was not going to back down, he made her laugh by calling her a "crabby old lady." Occasionally the irritation each feels toward the other flares into full-blown anger. When Myrtle vents her anger at Lennie verbally, Lennie challenges her and communicates in one way or another that he will not be spoken to in that way. Myrtle copes with Lennie's anger in a manner that is characteristically her own—she turns her back on the outburst and withdraws.

Myrtle's main complaints about Lennie are that he refuses to help out around the house, that he does not offer much companionship, and that he does exactly what he wants, whether or not she approves. As she puts it, he is "all take and no give." Myrtle complains that he is not much company because he is either asleep or not at home. "I may as well talk to myself," she once grumbled. Myrtle also frequently feels slighted by Lennie; she alleges that he never stands up for her in front of other people, and that he helps other people immediately if they ask him for help while he makes her wait indefinitely. Another source of irritation for Myrtle is the fact that Lennie doles out small amounts of money to her and then buys things for himself that she considers frivolous. For instance, Lennie spent $400 on a gun, a purchase that Myrtle believed Lennie needed "like a hole in the head." This purchase was the source of an ongoing argument for more than a week. During one of my visits with Myrtle, Lennie asked me whether or not I had seen the gun, knowing perfectly well that he was goading Myrtle and that he could expect a hostile reaction. Myrtle became sullen, and Lennie called her on it, declaring that he was going to keep the gun and that she was just going to have to live with it. When she defiantly asked, "What if I throw it away?" he threatened her with some sort of undefined retribution.

Lennie, for his part, regularly expresses impatience with Myrtle. In the area of finances, for instance, Lennie accuses Myrtle of being the "tightest" woman he has ever known. He became particularly irritated on one occasion when he gave Myrtle $200 to take to Las Vegas. The problem arose when they got to Las Vegas and he found out that she had taken along only $25; she had hidden the rest of the money at home. Much of Lennie's impatience can be traced to his reactions to Myrtle's incompetence. He becomes impatient, for instance, over her difficulty in getting facts right, her inability to follow his reasoning, and her occasional lapses into confusion. His response to Myrtle's statement that one of her brothers lives in Alaska was typical. Lennie boomed out, "Woman, where's your head screwed on?!" as he corrected her and told me that her brother lives in Africa. Similarly, it is not unusual for Lennie to mistakenly lash out at Myrtle for some alleged oversight or wrongdoing simply because he assumes that she must be culpable, much as Myrtle describes her parents doing when she was young. Lennie became very angry, for example, when Myrtle was unable to find a tape measure in the disorderly garage that is jammed with his tools and automobile engines. He declared with great irritation as he stormed out of the room to find the tape measure, "Oh, you're the most. . . ." Lennie did not finish the sentence, but it does not take much imagination to guess how he might have done so.

The biggest source of tension between Myrtle and Lennie is her jealousy of other women and his family. This tension is not always obvious, as when Lennie and Myrtle good-naturedly joke about their respective "girlfriends" and "boyfriends." For instance, when Lennie made a typical joke about "getting a motel room and taking along a 'baby,' " Myrtle took it in stride and cheerfully offered that he has three "babies"— herself and her two parakeets. Myrtle sometimes even counters such joking with talk of her own "boyfriends," namely her doctor and a fellow who runs a dairy stand down the street. At other times, however, Myrtle genuinely perceives other women as a threat. Myrtle is extremely jealous of a young woman who lives next door. At various times, she described her to me as "stupid," a "dopehead," and a "two-bit whore" who follows Lennie around "like a dog in heat."

More serious in terms of their everyday lives is Myrtle's resentment of Lennie's relationship with his grown children and other relatives. When confronted with members of Lennie's family and friends, particularly if there are several of them present, Myrtle tends to sit in a corner, speak only if spoken to, and occasionally withdraw into another room.

Myrtle feels as though she is being rejected in these situations, because everyone talks about family affairs and no one talks to her. Lennie has no sympathy for Myrtle's position; all he sees is that she does not make an effort to talk to anyone and hides in another room when she is feeling uncomfortable. The tension this causes between them became very clear in the following incident. Lennie had already driven Myrtle to a Wednesday-night bingo game when his son called to suggest that they get together for a barbecue. Lennie thought this was a fine idea, mainly because it would give him a chance to see his visiting grandson, a teenager whom he had not seen since the boy was a young child. When I arrived to visit Myrtle the next morning, she was sulking about this family get-together. She seemed to have mixed feelings about it. She felt slighted for not having been invited, even though Lennie made a point of explaining that the decision to have the barbecue was made after he had driven her to bingo. Myrtle seemed to compensate for her feelings of being left out by saying that she did not care, that she did not want to be there anyway. She mentioned several times, "If I'd known they was there, I wouldn't have come home," and went on to complain that when she is present at family gatherings, everyone talks about Lennie's ex-wife and no one speaks to her. Lennie finally got furious at her—he threw a pencil on the floor so hard that it broke—and yelled, "Why don't you ever want to get involved?! When they are here, you sit there, don't say anything, and then go hide in your room. . . . You knew I had kids when you married me!" Myrtle responded to this outburst by turning her back on him and indicating to me that it was time to leave. Myrtle's jealousy of Lennie's ex-wife in particular was revealed on another occasion, when she threatened to destroy any of the ex-wife's mail that came to the house.

Myrtle acknowledges that her tendency towards withdrawal sometimes causes problems with other people. She mentioned, for instance, that Lennie's family members have made critical comments about her being so uncommunicative. Although Myrtle now refuses to say much at all about her time in Pacific State Hospital, 15 years ago she blamed the hospital for causing these problems. "They harmed me," she said at the time. "Anybody'd come over, I just go under the table and hide or in the bathroom. I didn't want to see nobody or talk to nobody. . . . It took years and years to get over that."

Lennie and his family are not simply a source of stress for Myrtle, of course; they are also a significant source of support. Lennie not only provides companionship, but also handles their financial affairs and drives Myrtle almost everywhere she wants to go. Lennie's daughter, Mollie, is especially helpful to Myrtle, regularly stepping in to offer assistance with such matters as transportation and errands. Myrtle dismisses the importance of this help, however. One day, when she was complaining that she needed to move some boxes and Lennie would do nothing to help, I asked if Mollie could help. Myrtle dismissed this idea with a wave of her hand and said, "Forgit her!" Myrtle expects Mollie to help her, and she becomes critical when Mollie does not help to the degree that Myrtle wants.

The fact that Myrtle cannot drive considerably limits what she can do for herself and others, a fact that Myrtle recognizes. The importance of being able to drive can be seen in Myrtle's claim that she would never have gotten married—either to Peter or to Lennie—if she had known how to drive. Given the importance that transportation has for her, I asked Myrtle why she did not learn to drive when she was younger. She replied only, "I couldn't," and would not elaborate, even when urged to do so. As is always the case, Myrtle said nothing about being unable to learn to drive because of either epilepsy or mental retardation.

Although Myrtle relies on other people for help more than they rely on her, she does have ways of making her own contributions to the welfare of others. Her main contributions are cooking, taking care of the house, and offering support and companionship to Lennie. Her volunteer work at the hospital, of which she is justly proud, also offers her an opportunity to give to others. Myrtle enjoys being needed and wanted, and it is perhaps easier for her to think of herself as being so when she is caring for those she perceives as weaker or more vulnerable. For instance, she seemed very pleased when one of her fellow volunteers, who was recovering from a "nervous breakdown," asked Myrtle to "re-teach" her because she had "forgotten." Myrtle is also very protective and doting over her two parakeets, her "babies" as she calls them. Myrtle has named her two female parakeets "Pretty Boy." These are two in a series of birds she has owned over the years, birds that have all been called "Pretty Boy." Although she does not seem to differentiate between these birds, the numerous photographs she has taken of them bears testament to her attachment.

It is also notable that two emotionally charged memories having to do with dependents stand out in Myrtle's very sketchy and generally unemotional recollection of her past. Because Myrtle's expressions of emotion are usually blunted, it is not easy at first to discern what is and is not significant to her. After numerous visits, however, and the frequent mention of her "baby sister" who died 42 years ago, I came to realize that this is a focal event in Myrtle's life. Part of the impact of her sister's death seems to stem from the fact that this was someone who was smaller, weaker, and more vulnerable than she, someone whom she took care of and who accepted her completely—and who then died. A similar dynamic seems to be at work in Myrtle's recollection of the death of a young child whom she cared for while at Pacific State Hospital. Myrtle's face disclosed as much emotion as I ever saw from her when she said, "I had this one kid that call me 'mama' all the time. Nobody would come and see her and I was sitting on the bed, she was in the bed, got hold of my hand, says 'mama' and died. That killed me."

There is another possible interpretation of the importance Myrtle attaches to the last two incidents, both of which involve children whom Myrtle has described herself as "taking care of." Although Myrtle has exhibited little feeling or regret concerning her sterilization, there are comments through the years that at least call this lack of feeling into question. When Myrtle was contacted in 1960, her first husband totally dominated the interview, so there is no first-hand information from Myrtle concerning the issue of their childlessness. Her husband, Peter, told the interviewer that he thought there might have been some merit to the idea of sterilizing Myrtle for genetic reasons, although they would have liked to have had a child. He also said that they would have been willing to adopt, but he felt they would not be successful because of their combined disabilities. Myrtle told a somewhat different story when she was interviewed alone in 1972. When interviewers asked Myrtle if she had ever wanted children, she replied, "These days I don't think so, kids are too ornery these days," but she explained that at one time she had discussed adopting children with her husband, Peter, and "he told me I was crazy." In a taped interview in 1982, Myrtle said, "I don't know, I did like kids, and I found out I couldn't have one, I thought well, maybe it was better if I didn't. I mean I didn't want to hurt 'em or do something to 'em, drop 'em. . . ." Myrtle now says she could no longer handle having children because they make her "nervous." The possibility exists that Myrtle has greater conflict about her sterilization than is apparent from her lack of expressed feelings. She is generally very unforthcoming and inarticulate about her feelings, but the scattered comments above, coupled with the intense significance to Myrtle of the deaths of the two children under her care, suggest that she may have had ambivalent feelings about children and her ability to care for them, and by extension, about her sterilization as well.

AREAS OF COMPETENCE

Myrtle explains that she is so quiet because her parents told her "not to say something when someone else was talking, so I don't." Indeed, Myrtle does seem to find it difficult to intrude on a conversation, something that is not made any easier in her home by the fact that Lennie seldom stops talking. In addition, Myrtle has a hard time expressing herself verbally. Not only does she tend to mumble, forcing the listener to ask her to repeat herself, but she frequently speaks ungrammatically and experiences difficulty finding the right word. For instance, speaking of how she and Lennie stayed home for New Year's Eve, Myrtle commented, "Not too much noises around here. They have different places where they can go." She also uses malapropisms, such as "invitation" for "installation," as in installation of officers at the club for people with handicaps. Her difficulty in finding the right word is illustrated by the way she spoke of treating a scrape on her elbow: "I put a little green bottle on it." However, she then could not think of the word for elbow either—she had to point to it. This is not unusual; Myrtle will often point to an object or point in a certain direction rather than use a word that is commonly known. At other times, she will fend off a question that calls for a lengthy answer by smiling and saying "dunno" or "forgit it." Rather than thinking that she does not have the requisite verbal skills, the casual observer is likely to think that she is just a slightly cranky and stubborn old lady. Her advancing age obviously facilitates this impression. Her difficulty in expressing herself verbally causes problems, however, as when members of Lennie's family wonder why she does not talk to them, or when Lennie gets angry because she does not speak up to tell him something he should know. For instance, Lennie once yelled at Myrtle because she did not interrupt a long story with which he was regaling me to tell him to pick up his granddaughter from school. Myrtle is likely to go unheard even when she does speak up, because her voice is faint and she mumbles.

In addition to problems with verbal skills, Myrtle experiences difficulty with reading, writing, counting, and dealing with time. Myrtle can read simple words although she frequently makes mistakes, for instance, when she reads "Azusa" as "Arizona," or "Alpha Beta" as "Albertsons." It is probably for this reason that she usually does not even make the effort to read. When a letter came for her from a relative in Iowa, Myrtle looked at the letter for awhile, as though reading it. When Lennie asked if she had read it, she admitted that she had not because, she said, "The words are too close to the paper." Lennie then read the letter out loud to her. Myrtle takes a similar stance when trying to read a menu. She usually gazes at the menu for a while and then orders the same thing as her companion or asks the waitress for the special. As for writing, Myrtle can sign her own name and scrawl a few half-legible words, but for the most part, Lennie does all the writing for both of them. Counting and handling money also pose problems for her. She has difficulty adding numbers larger than five. When she goes shopping, Lennie gives her bills of large denominations so that all she has to do is give the money to the cashier and collect the change. It was probably luck (and my presence) more than anything else that accounts for the fact that Myrtle was never short-changed when we were shopping. Finally, Myrtle seems to have as fuzzy a sense of time as she does of higher numbers. For instance, she thought that an upcoming club convention was the coming weekend when in fact it was the weekend afterward. She had been looking forward to this event, so her confusion over its scheduled time is notable. Myrtle made a similar mistake when she estimated that Lennie had bought a new van 3 or 4 months earlier, when he actually had bought it only the previous month.

In spite of Myrtle's difficulties in these areas, she exhibits remarkable self-confidence under certain circumstances. For instance, Myrtle's self-confidence shines through in one-to-one interactions with casual acquaintances, such as other club members, fellow volunteers, and distant relatives. She appears very comfortable in these situations, even though she seems to expect people to be friendly and engage her, and to feel rejected if they do not.

Myrtle has enough confidence in her abilities to believe that she could be a "caller" at the Wednesday night bingo game she often attends. Because she had already had some experience "calling" bingo at the club for people with handicaps, she saw no reason to believe that she could not do the same in a different context. Myrtle's confidence in her abilities was not borne out, however. The contrast between Myrtle and the official caller, a man who did this for a living, was pronounced given her slurred ungrammatical speech, lack of animation, and inability to improvise small talk. A problem arose during the first game when someone called out "bingo" and Myrtle failed to hear it. The audience was intolerant of such lapses, and several people yelled at her that bingo had been called. As for the second game, it was unfortunately one of the most difficult kinds of bingo games to call, because it entailed recognizing and calling even numbers. Not only did Myrtle not explain to the group the rules of this particular game (something the caller is supposed to do), but she was unable to recognize even numbers, and the official caller had to take the game over from her. Myrtle's only comment about her performance after the game was that she called out the numbers too quickly. When asked about her difficulty with the second game, Myrtle did not act particularly disturbed about it and pronounced the game "dumb."

Although Myrtle has a strong desire to be treated as special and enjoys whatever attention she receives, the following incident suggests that her expectations in this regard are not high. Myrtle organized her own birthday party, knowing that if she did not do it, no one else would. She went to the trouble of inviting her brother, members of Lennie's immediate family, as well as one of Lennie's friends and myself. Myrtle also recruited Mollie's help by asking her to make the birthday cake. In the end, Myrtle only partially realized her wish of having a special day dedicated to herself. Although most of her guests showed up and she served cake and ice cream, what she did *not* get was equally significant. Myrtle received very few cards and gifts, and she cut and served her own birthday cake, without candles or accompanying "Happy Birthdays." Myrtle did not act particularly unhappy about how the party turned out, even though her guests showed little enthusiasm for celebrating her birthday.

MYRTLE'S PERSONALITY

Myrtle calls herself "ornery" and clearly relishes the self-image of being somewhat contrary or stubborn. Her stubbornness shows itself in different ways. Sometimes she refuses to believe that she is wrong about something as, for example, when she argued with Lennie and Mollie over the location of a certain store. Myrtle finally realized that she was wrong, but not before insisting that she was correct, even in the face of Lennie's and Mollie's growing irritation. Myrtle's stubbornness also manifested itself, although somewhat differently, when she was suffering from diarrhea and was under doctor's orders to eat a select diet. She deliberately ignored her doctor's advice and ordered what she wanted when she went out to eat.

Myrtle can be quite assertive in certain situations, although close examination shows that she generally exhibits this assertiveness in connection with initiation of an action but not necessarily with its follow-through. For example, although some of her interactions with salespeople could be smoother, Myrtle exhibits unalloyed confidence when asking salespeople where she can find a particular piece of merchandise. It is only when it comes to actually finding the item that Myrtle relies on her companion(s). There were many times on our numerous shopping expeditions when Myrtle left it up to me to find an item for which she was looking. When it came time to make a purchase decision, however, Myrtle made it quickly, although I sometimes had to explain the different options to her.

This pattern of initiating but not following through is most evident in more complex undertakings. After Myrtle and Lennie finished redecorating their house, I suggested that they have a housewarming party. Myrtle thought this was a good idea but seemed rather reluctant to organize it. When she asked me to contact Mollie to discuss arrangements, I demurred and insisted that she do it herself. Myrtle successfully rose to the occasion; she set the date, invited the guests, and told Mollie and me what to bring. For all the initiative this showed, however, when the day of the party came, Myrtle did not fulfill her role as hostess; she let the guests get their own drinks and left others to set out and serve the cake. None of the guests seemed particularly disturbed by Myrtle's behavior and Myrtle, for her part, seemed only too happy to abdicate her hostess duties. Although Myrtle enjoys attention and can be assertive under certain circumstances, she also has a strong desire to withdraw or become dependent at times, particularly when she is in the presence of Lennie and his family.

Myrtle's self-confidence falters most noticeably around Lennie. He has the ability to fluster and confuse her, especially when he is in an impatient or fault-finding mood. For example, when Lennie played an old videotape of Myrtle, in which Myrtle explained that she has lived in California since 1936, Lennie looked at her skeptically and asked pointedly, "How old are you now?" Myrtle became noticeably flustered and replied, "56 . . . 54 . . . I don't know. I can't keep count." There is no question that under less pressure Myrtle would have been able to recall that she is 58 years old.

Myrtle enjoys teasing and being teased, and it is notable that a good deal of her humor speaks to issues of competence. For instance, if someone cannot remember something, she will tease them, "Where's your memory gone to?" or if someone does not notice something she is pointing out, she will say, "I'm going to get you a pair of glasses." Myrtle does not hesitate to joke about her own competence as well. When her throw of the dice during a game of Yahtzee did not turn out as she wished, she called herself an "idiot"—but then she also called the dice "idiots." On another occasion, when she referred to a street by the wrong name, she made light of the fact that sometimes she gets "confused." "Sometimes my mind just goes blank," she said. "Sometimes things just fly out of my head." Similarly, when she answered a question by nodding into the audiotape recorder and I told her to speak up, she chuckled as she remarked, "It don't hear my head rattle."

Although Myrtle may joke about her own inadequacies, she is not always so tolerant of the inadequacies of others. Myrtle's conversation is peppered not only with complaints about Lennie but also with criticisms of other people. As with Myrtle's teasing, her criticisms often involve the issue of competence in some way. For example, Mollie's boyfriend, whom both Myrtle and Lennie dislike, is a "beetle-brain." "My parakeets have more sense than he does," she said. Myrtle is also very intolerant of fellow volunteers who cannot fulfill their duties as she sees them. "What's she good for?" she said of one woman. "All she can do is sit." Similarly, Myrtle refers to a female whom she knows through the club as a "bitch" and says that she "hates" this woman because, according to Myrtle, all she does is complain and she will not do anything for herself. The opposite also seems to hold, namely, that Myrtle is critical of people whom she perceives as flaunting their competence. On several occasions, Myrtle criticized people in leadership positions for wanting to "take over."

Myrtle's criticism of others often reflects her wish to reject others before they have the opportunity to reject her. When explaining why some people from the club for people with handicaps whom she had invited to her housewarming party did not show up, she dismissed them with a wave of her hand and said, "Forgit 'em." The same tendency underlies Myrtle's complaints about Lennie's family; because she feels rejected by them, she makes a point of also rejecting—and withdrawing.

Underlying all of Myrtle's personality, however, seems to be a sense of profound depression. One indicator of this is her preoccupation with death. The subject of death crops up frequently in Myrtle's conversation, as when she told me, perking up as she did so, that she had purchased three grave sites, one each for her "baby sister," Peter, and herself. On another occasion, she joked about restraining herself from asking, "You going to die soon?" when she saw an elderly aunt in the hospital where she volunteers. She also mentioned, somewhat wistfully, that she almost died four times in her life and joked, "They don't want me."

Myrtle revealed her thoughts about death more directly during an audiotaped interview. When speaking about one of her illnesses, Myrtle said, "I thought I was going to die. Talking about it, I wish I did." She also remarked that she wished she could "change places with my baby sister . . . to get rid of my misery." During the same interview, Myrtle also wished to "get well." When asked what she wants to be cured of, she replied, "Anything that is wrong with me. No, if I could go back like to school time again, I'd try to get better schooling." This last statement suggests that Myrtle thinks that something is wrong, something that could be "cured" by more schooling. This interview was a critical one, in that Myrtle revealed feelings that she had not mentioned before and did not mention again afterwards. Not only does she reveal a longing for death, but she implicitly recognizes that her life has not been all that it could be. Although Myrtle mentioned these very private feelings only once, the significance of these feelings for her present life should not be discounted.

CONCLUSION

Previous researchers described Myrtle as an extremely dependent and passive woman. The degree of her dependence on her first husband, Peter, was clearly highlighted in the *Cloak of Competence* study. Out of a total of 48 ex-patients ranked in order of relative independence, Myrtle ranked 46th—the third most dependent. The picture that emerges of Myrtle now, 25 years later, is considerably different. Although Myrtle still exhibits many of the characteristics attributed to her by previous researchers—notably deference or withdrawal in the presence of groups of people and dominant personalities—she also exhibits qualities unremarked upon in the past. Since Peter's death and her marriage to Lennie, Myrtle has shown herself to possess a degree of self-reliance, assertiveness, and self-confidence that could not have been predicted 25 years ago. Her marriage to Lennie undoubtedly has acted as a catalyst. His obstinacy, his refusal to protect her the way that Peter did, and, in the early days of their marriage, his drinking, probably all forced her into a more independent and assertive stance towards the world.

Given the social contact Myrtle has with Lennie's family, as well as through activities she has sought outside the home, Myrtle appears to have more social contacts now than she ever had in the past. Although this increased contact is positive, in that it provides her with emotional and instrumental support, it is also a source of stress for her personally and in her relationship with Lennie.

Myrtle's public face is that of a relatively competent and self-assured person, although there are indications of deep and pervasive self-doubt. Myrtle is rarely explicit about these self-doubts, however. Even when she jokes about her mistakes, the implication is always that other people make similar mistakes. Evidence of Myrtle's self-doubt can be gleaned indirectly from such characteristics as her tendency to withdraw, her sensitivity to rejection, and her comments about other peoples' competence. These feelings of dissatisfaction and self-doubt also seem to underlie her stated wish that she were dead and the implied feeling that her life has not been very successful.

Although both of Myrtle's marriages have been to men with forceful and domineering personalities, there are distinct differences between Peter and Lennie. Most significant perhaps is the fact that Peter had a visible physical disability that made him need Myrtle as much as she needed him. Peter was also fully aware of her history of hospitalization and clear about the fact that she was "handicapped." The situation with Lennie is considerably different. Not only is Lennie much less dependent and without a visible disability, but he also is not aware of the entire reason she was hospitalized at Pacific State Hospital. Apparently the only handicap that he is aware of is her epilepsy. This does not mean that Lennie does not perceive Myrtle as being a little "slow." His frequent irritation at her inability to grasp certain ideas and do certain things attests to that. In addition, several knowing winks at me plus the surreptitious comment, made just out of Myrtle's hearing, "She couldn't keep up with me if she were trying and I was asleep," all suggest that he does not think that Myrtle is very smart. Still, Lennie lives in a social milieu where many people just manage to graduate from high school, if that. He did not graduate from high school, and at least three of his four children did no more than that. In addition, one of Lennie's closest friends appears to be only semi-literate. In such an environment, Myrtle's inability to read and write well could be attributed to lack of education as easily as to lack of intelligence.

Aside from the fact that Peter was more dependent on her than Lennie, and thus needed her more, Peter's physical disability may have attracted Myrtle because it was something with which she could identify. Myrtle's concern for people and animals who are vulnerable and in need of protection suggests not only that she identifies with them but that she experiences an underlying sense of powerlessness. Part of Myrtle's struggle is to gain some sense of power or control over her life. The struggle for control, in fact, can be seen as underlying much of the conflict in her present marriage. Lennie maintains control over aspects of her life that Myrtle clearly considers important, including transportation and finances. That Myrtle seems to feel cheated or short-changed by this was illustrated when Myrtle made a point of not telling Lennie or anyone else about several hundred dollars she won gambling in Las Vegas and at bingo. The defensive hiding of this money appeared to be a response to the anger she felt when Lennie gave her only $200 for clothing, an amount that was sufficient for her needs but that she resented because it was only a small part of the money he actually had available. When I asked what she planned to do with the money she had hidden, she shrugged and said, "play bingo." Clearly, the satisfaction Myrtle felt in hiding the money from Lennie and his family came from the sense of control it gave her, not from what she planned to do with the money.

The struggle for control obviously involves more than just material goods; it also involves Myrtle's quest for self-respect. Myrtle's unsuccessful protest over Lennie's purchase of a new gun was an example of her desire to be taken seriously. Similarly, Myrtle was frustrated in her attempt to get Lennie to admit that she had forced him to quit drinking. When Myrtle contended that Lennie had quit drinking because she had given him an ultimatum—quit drinking or get a divorce—Lennie denied that Myrtle had had anything to do with his decision. Lennie, in fact, sometimes goes out of his way to prove Myrtle wrong. "When is the middle of the year?" he asked me one day. When I replied that it is between June and July, Lennie said to Myrtle, "See there?" as if being vindicated. He then told me somewhat condescendingly that Myrtle believes it is June 21. Myrtle did not respond to this attack other than to say that June 21 is the first day of summer. When Lennie went on to state authoritatively that the middle of the year is midnight on June 30, Myrtle withdrew and did not argue with him any further. As these examples illustrate, Myrtle is not always successful in getting Lennie to acknowledge her influence, competence, and worth as a person. This, in part at least, may account for Myrtle's diffuse anger and criticism of others.

It is important to note, however, that Lennie's interaction with Myr-

tle is more complex than it might first appear. Unlike Myrtle's first hus-\
band, Peter, whose own needs seem to have left him willing to control all
aspects of his life with Myrtle, Lennie refuses to do for Myrtle what he
thinks she is capable of doing for herself. Peter defined Myrtle as "handicapped," and therefore in many ways incompetent; Lennie does not.
However, if it becomes apparent that Myrtle cannot complete a task on
her own, or if Lennie knows that the task is something that Myrtle cannot
do, he will pitch in and complete it for her. The following incident, which
occurred while Lennie and Myrtle were refurnishing their house, is an
example of their multifaceted interaction. I had accompanied Myrtle on a
shopping trip for new furniture, and when she had found a bedroom set
she liked, she decided to call and ask Lennie to come and see it. When
Lennie arrived, they looked over the choices and Lennie told Myrtle his
preference, but he made it clear that the final choice did not really matter
to him—Myrtle could buy the bedroom set she wanted. After some de-
liberation, Myrtle decided to buy the set that Lennie preferred. In trans-
acting the business of the sale, Lennie pushed Myrtle to the fore. This was
sometimes done in a way that encouraged Myrtle to take responsibility;
at other times, Lennie seemed to be goading her. For instance, Lennie
made it perfectly clear who controlled the money by asking Myrtle in
front of the salesman where the money for the purchase was. Myrtle
acted slightly incensed and said, "You know I don't have any!" Only then
did Lennie pull out his wallet and give the salesman five $100 bills. The
three of them went on to discuss the best day to deliver the furniture, but
Lennie left the final decision up to Myrtle. When Myrtle mumbled something about new carpet, thus thoroughly confusing the salesman, Lennie
only half-successfully managed to get her to explain to the salesman that
the new carpet had to be installed first. Lennie finally pitched in and
made sure that the salesman understood. When it came time to fill out
the sales receipt, which required filling in their name and address at the
top and signing the receipt at the bottom, Lennie handed the receipt to
Myrtle. Although she balked, Lennie pushed her, saying that she knew
how to sign her name. Myrtle finally wrote out her signature, something
which, for reasons she cannot or will not explain, she is always extremely
reluctant to do. Myrtle then passed the receipt back to Lennie, and he
filled out the name and address section at the top. As difficult as Lennie
may sometimes be for Myrtle to live with, and as detrimental as he sometimes is to her self-esteem and feeling of control over her life, Lennie has
nevertheless encouraged Myrtle's independence by demanding that she
accept responsibility for those things she is capable of doing.

Although Myrtle's life has had its ups and downs, it has actually
been more stable than those of most of our other research subjects. She
suffered what turned out to be a temporary setback during the unhappy

period that encompassed the death of her first husband and the beginning of her second marriage. However, her life has improved in most areas since that time. Despite enduring tensions in her present marriage and indications of an underlying depression, Myrtle's life has stabilized, her level of independence has increased, and she appears to be coping relatively well with the demands of her everyday life.

5

"I Gotta Put My Foot Down."
RICHARD T. JARRETT, III

*by Robert B. Edgerton
and T. W. Ward*

A visitor to one of downtown Los Angeles's low-income neighborhoods might meet Richard Jarrett walking near the apartment where he has lived for almost 30 years. Now 68 years old, Richard is a tall fair-haired man with an enormous pot belly, a lumbering bow-legged gait, and a voice so resonant that it sounds loud to most people. At midday, he would ordinarily be eating at a nearby sidewalk hamburger stand, wearing one of his familiar cowboy shirts, blue jeans, and his black baseball cap with the Teamsters Union logo. There is nothing about Richard's appearance that would make him stand out from the people around him, and if the visitor were to talk with him, there would be nothing about their conversation that would seem out of place either. Despite his poor health—high blood pressure due to obesity—he appears to be happy and carefree, and he has reason to be. He retired in 1984 after spending 31 years on the same job as a truck loader and member of the Teamsters Union. For 31 years he made a good living, and today, his pension combined with his social security check give him a monthly income of more than $1,300. The monthly rent for his apartment is only $400, leaving Richard with considerable surplus income to spend on his favorite pastimes, "lending" money to his girlfriend and eating out. As a casual acquaintance, Richard T. Jarrett, III, would strike almost anyone as a quite ordinary, retired working man. Further acquaintance might suggest that Richard's memory is not always very good and that he seems slow to grasp some things, but there would still be no reason to doubt that he is anything other than a poorly educated, unskilled working man who is getting on in years.

In reality, Richard is a man with an IQ of 56 who spent 18 years of his life in a large state hospital for people with mental retardation. It is true that he has lived independently for almost 40 years, but his apartment is indescribably filthy, and he must pay other people to read documents and write letters on his behalf because he can neither read nor write. There is a woman in his life whom he refers to as his girlfriend, but like other "girlfriends" before her, she extracts large sums of money from him in return for very infrequent and very brief sexual encounters. He has no close friends and no concerned relatives. His singular appeal to others is his income, which they regularly exploit so ruthlessly that it is not uncommon for him to be penniless by the second week of the month. Richard is also in terrible physical condition. Despite warnings from his physician and the cook at the hamburger stand he frequents, Richard continues to eat enormous quantities of high cholesterol food every day. In spite of this unpleasant reality, it would be a mistake to conclude that Richard is unhappy. At 68 he is satisfied with his life, and he claims not to have a care in the world. He does not dislike himself, has no complaints about his present condition, and does not fear for his future.

EARLY YEARS

Although Richard was born in Fort Worth, Texas, in 1920, his parents brought him to Los Angeles in 1923. Richard's father was a railroad switchman with a third grade education; his mother apparently never attended school at all. The couple had two more sons in California, but their life together was troubled at best. While Mr. Jarrett was away at work, Mrs. Jarrett made a practice of seeking out what might be termed "gentlemen callers." When more conventional means of attracting men failed, she hit upon the idea of cutting the telephone wires to her house, a tactic that invariably brought a repairman. After several such "accidents," the telephone company filed a complaint with the police, although the repairmen themselves seem not to have objected. Mr. Jarrett took offense with his wife, and on one occasion, he chased her through the streets of Pasadena for 3 miles while brandishing a carving knife. This, too, led to criminal charges. Richard's father lost his leg when he fell under a train, and he was eventually hospitalized with syphilis.

Richard believes that he was sent to Pacific State Hospital at the age of 11 because he had been caught in sexual play with a neighbor girl. He recalls being beaten by both his mother and father as a result of this behavior, and he still claims that he was sent to the hospital for "bad sex." In 1960 he said, "Most of my life has been a sex life, but I've recovered from that," and he remains sexually active to this day. There were a number of minor sexual problems in Richard's childhood; for instance, he was accused of accosting female strangers on the street and embracing them.

However, the reason a court sent him to Pacific State Hospital was not that his sexual behavior was a danger to others, but that his parents could not provide him with a suitable home. When a court-ordered IQ test showed that Richard was mentally retarded, he was committed to a state hospital.

Richard's memories of Pacific State Hospital have changed over the years. When he was younger, he remembered his time there as pleasant. He attended school for a few months before he began to work on the hospital's farm. (The hospital was then a "colony" that attempted to grow much of its own food.) He was a strong young man who enjoyed working outdoors, and he remembered the hospital as providing many forms of recreation, ranging from trips to nearby fairs, picnics, and sports events to dances and games. But today Richard is more ambivalent about his stay at Pacific State. His memory has been influenced by one of his best friends at the hospital, Roberto (see Chapter 3), with whom, through the efforts of a fieldworker, he recently was reunited after 30 years. Today, Richard remembers the hospital much as Roberto does—a prison where he spent his time "being locked up." He recalls the fence that surrounded the colony and the bully named Rabbit who beat him up after visits by Richard's mother in order to steal the candy or money she had left him. Richard also tells of how his father, who was at that time without a job or a wife (Richard's parents were no longer living together), came to visit him at the hospital and took him on a trip. His father had visited before, to take Richard out for walks in a park in Pomona, but this time they hopped a train for Salt Lake City. He lived with his father there for 4 or 5 months before the police caught up with them. "They hand-cuffed both of us," Richard says, "and took me back to Pacific State Hospital."

In spite of this failed escape and his feeling of being locked up at Pacific, Richard still has some pleasant memories of the hospital. It was there that he learned how to ride horses (like any Texan should) and to farm. He loves to tell about the time that Payday, a large black mare that was pulling the plow, got loose. "When she got away I had to see-saw her down," he says. Richard was dragged by the horse for 100 feet before he managed to stop her by pulling the reins back and forth in a see-saw fashion. (Incidentally, it was Rabbit, the older bully who terrorized Richard most of the time, who had taught him how to "see-saw" a horse to the ground.) As a result of this incident, Richard had a bruised hip and was badly scraped on one side of his chest. "Every once and a while I feel a burn from it," he says.

Richard was released from the hospital when he was 18 years old and "paroled" to a job in a nearby sanitarium, where he worked in the kitchen washing dishes and cleaning up. After nearly a year outside the hospital, he was reinstitutionalized when he was accused of stealing a kewpie doll at a country fair. Richard insisted that he won the 6-inch doll, but the police were not convinced. He remained in the hospital for more than 10 years before he was considered ready for another try at life on the outside. Before he could be released, however, he had to agree to be surgically sterilized. After some reluctance, he underwent the operation and was paroled from Pacific State Hospital in 1950 at the age of 30.

ON HIS OWN

Richard's first job after his release was once again in a sanitarium where he did kitchen work for about a year. One day early in 1951 as he was walking not far from his small downtown Los Angeles apartment, he stopped to watch two men loading a large truck. He asked one of the men "how somebody got a job like that there," and was directed to the nearby employment office of what proved to be a large freight trucking company. When Richard was handed an application form, he said that he did not have time to fill it out just then but would return it the next day. For a small fee, a man at the sanitarium filled out the form for Richard. Richard did not reveal that he had been at Pacific State Hospital nor that he was then on vocational leave from that institution. "They wouldn't have hired me if they had known that," he said. He was hired and soon became a member of the Teamsters Union. According to Richard, he received his hospital discharge papers in 1958.

When our research with Richard began in 1960, he had 9 years of seniority in the trucking company, where he worked loading and unloading large trucks, earning $2.46 an hour (nearly $100 a week), a substantial salary at that time. His furnished apartment with kitchen and bathroom cost $62.50 per month. Richard was a thin, well-built six-footer, with blond crew-cut hair, wire-rim glasses, and piercing blue eyes. He usually wore khaki pants or Levis with checkered or western-style shirts. Although he was noticeably bowlegged, perhaps from riding horses at the colony, and walked with a rolling gait, Richard was an attractive man who looked younger than his age. He spoke more loudly than most people and was not always grammatical, but there was nothing about his speech or behavior that would immediately suggest mental retardation.

There was nothing unusual about his lifestyle either. He took care of all his needs, rode buses with no difficulty, and saved a little, although very little, money. His one-room apartment, although cluttered, was large enough to be comfortable. The furnishings were more than adequate, and Richard had added many personal touches, such as his pet parakeets and a collection of photographs, many of which he took himself with a new 35-millimeter camera he purchased. Some of Richard's color prints were nicely composed, and he also had a large collection of color slides that he liked to show with his new slide projector. He had also purchased a television set and radio, but his prize possession was a new 10-speed bicycle that cost $130. The bike was more than transportation; it was Richard's main recreation and his primary means of enhancing his self-esteem. Soon after Richard began to work at the trucking company, he began to rent bicycles at a nearby rental shop for weekend riding. The proprietor eventually convinced Richard to buy his own bike and to join a bicycle club. In all probability, Richard was the only person with mental retardation in this club, whose members included many professionals. Richard was soon biking as far as 200 miles in a single day, a distance that impressed his co-workers and gave him something exciting to talk about as he recounted his travels and adventures. Through the bicycle club he also joined the Sierra Club and went on hikes throughout Southern California.

Richard enjoyed his club activities, where he met what he called "outside people." When asked if he saw any of the people he had known in the hospital, he answered,

> Maybe it's just my way, um, maybe I don't associate with very few state hospital people, maybe I want to get out and associate with more of the outside people. Maybe you've noticed the different change in me since I've associated with the outside people. I more or less speak a little different than what the state hospital does.

Richard's determination to avoid "state hospital people" slipped once soon after his release, when he met and began dating Juanita, a lively, pretty, and charming Mexican-American woman he had known at the hospital. She was far more articulate than Richard and also had superior social and intellectual skills. She could read and write acceptably and was easily able to pass as a person of average intellect. She and Richard struck up a romance, and she moved into his apartment. Richard made enough money to support them both, so she stopped working as a part-time nurse's aide, and they were married. Richard loved the idea that his wife did not have to work, and Juanita obviously did not mind having the leisure time to pursue her own interests.

However, one of Juanita's interests was a better and more exciting life than Richard could offer her. Their life together was always tumultuous, and after 3 years, their fights took on epic proportions. Richard's wife moved out to live with Richard's best friend, a man she had met in the bike club and who had been the best man at their wedding. He was a chiropractor with a successful practice, and soon Juanita married him. It was a classic case, Richard said, "of the best man stealing

the bride." "What burned me up the most," he said, was that she wanted
to remain friends afterward and that she had a lot of nerve to run off
with his best friend and then wonder why he does not visit them. For a
while Richard was crushed, but with remarkable resilience he met another woman at the bike club and began to date her. It was this woman
who convinced Richard to buy a 10-speed bicycle. "For a while there, it
just tore me to pieces," Richard said of his divorce from Juanita, "So I had
to start gettin' out with this girlfriend, tryin' to forget her, and I finally did
and now I can mention her name to anybody, and it doesn't even bother
me no more." Richard took his new girlfriend, Julie, to dinner and to the
movies, usually riding in her Volkswagen, for which he would buy a tank
of gas. Julie was a pretty young woman who worked as a secretary and
loved to ride bikes. Apparently that shared pleasure is all she wanted
from Richard, because after dating him for a year she ended the relationship. Richard later admitted that he had never slept with Julie because he
did not want to "go too fast."

In December, 1960, Richard received the following letter from
Juanita:

> Dear Richie, we're writing you a few lines to say hello. We don't have
> too long before the divorce is final dear. The same time we're coming
> down Monday, December 4th, to sign the papers to make the divorce
> final. I hope we are friends. I've got a job now and I'm doing OK. We'll
> see you soon sometime. We don't know what day we're coming to L.A.
> We'll try to reach you between the week. We know who's the lucky girl
> and you won't give us a surprise when you tell us who she is. Juanita
> knows you for a book. It's a nice day today and why don't you drop by
> and see us sometime. We're home Sundays. What's the matter. Are you
> scared to see your ex-wife. Your ex-wife is not going to bite your head.
> When you marry again we'll send you a boquet [sic] of roses. Well,
> dear when we see you again we hope to see you happy. In case you
> come dear, why don't you come Saturday night or write us and let us
> know when you can come. Bruce works in Palm Springs so get off in
> Palm Springs and go to the Thrifty. He can bring you up after work.
> Why don't you come up in three weeks. And we can eat dinner to-
> gether, the three of us like we used to. By the way when is your birth-
> day. We forgot the date. When you come we'll take you back Sunday
> night dear. Close for love. Your ex-wife and best friend, Juanita Jarrett
> and Bruce.

Richard shrugged off the letter, which had been read to him by a
field researcher. He said that Juanita probably had asked him to come
down just because she wanted the $26 she had been trying, in his words,
"to get offa me" to pay for the divorce. All he could talk about were his
plans for the upcoming weekend, when he and his girlfriend Julie were
planning to use train passes to travel to Santa Barbara and back. "She'll
probably want to take all kinds of snapshots along the road there,"

Richard said happily. Julie did not show up for the expected train trip, and a few days later she sent word to Richard that she was, as he put it, "breakin' it up" with him.

Throughout this early period of Richard's adjustment to community living, he had little contact with his relatives. One of his brothers, who was apparently not mentally retarded, worked at a market in Pasadena, but Richard rarely heard from him. He saw his youngest brother more often, largely because his mother, who was 70 years old in 1960, repeatedly asked for Richard's help in coping with the brother's ill health. Shorter than Richard, this young man weighed well over 350 pounds and suffered from high blood pressure and other forms of cardiovascular disease. He soon died, apparently of a cerebral hemorrhage. Richard's mother then increased her reliance on Richard, whom, according to a friend who knew the situation well, she was "stealing blind." It is certain that she did "borrow" sizeable sums from him on a regular basis. Despite the fact that Richard supported his mother in her old age and paid the rent for her apartment, she did not give him moral support or encouragement. In fact, she often called him stupid and did not want him to see women at all, discouraging them from dating him by telling them that he would not make a good husband. What he remembers most vividly about his mother from his youth is the pepper-switch with which she used to beat him when he was naughty. Richard's mother died at the age of 75, from what Richard thinks were complications from constipation. "I kept telling my mother not to take milk of magnesium, 'cause that stuff is going to clog you up. And sure enough it did. She, uh, couldn't do number two or nothing like that atol." Richard was never close to his mother, and he blames her for his sterilization. "They done the operation because my mother said that, uh, I was fooling around with too many women. Now you grab ahold of that. Just ruined my life." When his mother died in 1963, Richard expressed little interest or grief.

THE MID-LIFE YEARS

In the years after 1960, Richard continued to live in the same apartment, work at the same job, and have the same kinds of problems with women. As a good-looking man with money to spend, he had little difficulty attracting women, but the relationships that followed continued to frustrate and confuse him. One of his longest relationships was with another Mexican-American woman, Ramona. Richard and Ramona dated and had sexual relations off and on for about 4 years, but they never lived together. According to Richard, Ramona did not enjoy bicycle riding or hiking. She wanted to "eat in them fancy restaurants" and go to movies. Most of all, it seems, she wanted to borrow money from Richard, who remembered her by saying with an unusual degree of annoyance that "all them women ever want from a man is money." She arranged for him to get a credit card at a large and expensive department store, where she encouraged him to buy her presents. Richard did so but neglected to pay his bills, so the card was invalidated. Later she borrowed over $1,000 from him, a sum she never attempted to repay.

In return for Richard's largesse, Ramona would occasionally allow him to have sexual intercourse with her, but again according to Richard, "She was always in a hurry, I don't know why." Their relationship was also troubled by the interference of Richard's sister-in-law (married to his brother, who worked in a market), who told Ramona that Richard had been in a state hospital. Richard says his sister-in-law also told Ramona "to forget me, you know, 'cause she'd have to treat me like a little boy and be a husband to me." (Richard apparently meant "mother" here.) Despite these dire warnings, Ramona continued to see Richard, although she found ways to avoid any lasting intimacy with him. Richard complains that she would never stay in his apartment or invite him to hers, and that when he made reservations at a "fancy beach-place the other side of Laguna Beach" (a prominent beach resort area), she took it upon herself to cancel the reservation. When he asked her why, Richard recalled, "I had her tongue twisted around in her mouth. Ramona didn't know what to say. I can't understand why she didn't want to go." Eventually, after Ramona was no longer willing to have sex with him, Richard refused to give her any more money, and she stopped seeing him. Even after 20 years, Richard thinks she's still mad because he "cut her off," and he is convinced that she engages someone to call him on the phone, or that she herself calls, only to remain silent and then hang up on him. Many times he has threatened to get a whistle to blow into the phone "to teach her a good one."

Through the years, Richard's activities and associates changed, and his apartment grew more frayed, grimy, and cluttered, but his job proved to be a bastion of security and predictability. The work was hard, lifting heavy boxes and crates in the hot sun, but there were union-enforced breaks and protection against exploitation. Richard recalls fondly how he sometimes reacted when the foreman accused him of loafing: "I'd say to that joker, I'm gonna go see Max Perez [the Teamsters Union shop steward] and he'd take off like a scare [sic] rabbit." He made friends, or more precisely acquaintances, at work with whom he would eat lunch and sometimes he would join them for a beer after work. Richard was twice injured on the job badly enough to require surgery; he developed a hernia from the strain of lifting an extra-heavy crate, and when another worker fell off a truck onto him, a nerve in his arm was so severely damaged that surgery was needed, leaving him with a scar from wrist to elbow, which he loves to show off.

Although Richard was never threatened with layoff and his salary rose over the years, his inability to read bills of lading on the job caused him endless torment. He often says that people have called him "dumb" because he is illiterate, and he admitted, "Practically all the fellows at work said that about me; even a couple of foremens [sic] said that about me." Sometimes pranks were played on him, and he responded angrily. For example, Richard says that a co-worker once replaced the hot water in his thermos with cold water just because he could not read or write.

> It made me so mad I felt like busting him right between the teeth. I did it to one fellow and he never fooled around with me again. And I told him, "If you fool around with my ass again, I'm gonna put your damn teeth right down your throat." Just because I couldn't read very good, they made fun of me.

A man who had worked with Richard for over 20 years admitted that some of the workers teased him, not only because he could not read but "because he would make stupid mistakes on the job and he was so dumb that it was easy to play tricks on him." However, he added that Richard was a "good-natured guy" whom some of the men protected against co-workers' tricks and jokes.

> Richie didn't mean no harm, you know. He was okay. He did his work and didn't bother nobody. He was strong as an ox, too, so's you had to be careful with him. One day he went after a guy who was teasing him and like to run him clean off the job.

As the years passed, Richard's job became more of a safe haven for him than a place where he was teased and tormented. It gave him stature as a union man, a man who retired after making "good money" with a comfortable pension. It left him with some painful memories about being called "dumb," but that problem was not confined to the work place. When she was angry with him, Richard's girlfriend, Carmen Flores, also called him "dumb."

AT THE AGE OF 68

At the age of 68, the most dramatic recent change in Richard's life was his retirement. Although he enjoys sleeping late, he obviously misses the sense of purpose that work gave him and the men he was with every working day. Richard recently referred to one of these men, Walker, as his best friend and said that he telephoned him every day about 5:00 P.M., but asked when he last saw Walker, he could not remember, saying vaguely that it was long ago. Furthermore, he does not know whether Walker is the man's first or last name. Since that time, Richard has lost contact with Walker, but his absence was filled by a woman he met in the supermarket, Gayle, whom he now calls frequently. Richard occasionally calls his former shop steward, and he faithfully attends Teamsters Union meetings whenever they are called. He often returns from these meetings disturbed that "business don't look too good."

He still lives a life of routine, arising before 8:00 A.M., going to the nearby sidewalk cafe for a roll and coffee, then meandering around the neighborhood and chatting with people until it is time for lunch. Sometimes he sits on a park bench or listens to country music on the blaring radio in his apartment. He usually has dinner in the same sidewalk cafe or at a nearby fried chicken fast-food stand before he ambles home to listen to more music and look at magazines. In the evenings, Richard uses the telephone to call acquaintances or friends. In addition to Gayle, Richard calls his friend Barbara to talk about the weather or complain about his girlfriend, Carmen. Barbara often scolds him for continuing to give Carmen money, even though she knows it will do no good. Every Saturday Richard calls his cousin Gene, a 65-year-old Baptist preacher in Fort Worth, Texas. Gene and his wife have established an audio-tape ministry with what they refer to as the "mountain people in the remote Ozark Mountains." Gene apparently chats with Richard about mundane matters, but he also tries to convince him to return to Fort Worth to be baptized and "born" again (something Richard has not yet done) and to send donations (something he has done). After talking on the phone, Richard takes a nightly ride on the bus to "see what's around." Should he spot a street lamp that is burned out, he takes it upon himself to call the Los Angeles Department of Water and Power to tell them to fix it: "I called last week and told 'em a light was out on 7th and Hoover and they still haven't fixed it. I guess I'm gonna hafta call 'em up again."

Richard's life has not changed much, but his appearance certainly has. After not seeing him for 30 years, Roberto (see Chapter 3), Richard's friend from the state hospital, did not recognize Richard recently. In fact, Roberto was so convinced that this large man before him was not his former friend that he refused to get out of the car to talk with him. Later, Roberto commented, "He sounds like Richie and he's still got that same smile, but I can't believe he changed so much. Richie didn't have that fat belly and he was damn good-looking . . . thin and blond and handsome." Once a clean, thin, good-looking young man, Richard is increasingly careless about hygiene, and he has steadily gained weight since his release from the hospital. His existing weight problem was most likely exacerbated by the decrease in his physical activity through the last few years. At one time, Richard rode long distances on his bicycle and worked a physically demanding job, but he gradually ceased to ride his bicycle for pleasure and then eventually retired from his job, leaving him with no regular form of strenuous exercise. Today, Richard weighs over 270 pounds, his clothing is grimy with dirt, and his body odor is offensive even at a distance (as some shopkeepers have told him when he enters). In lieu of bathing, Richard puts after-shave lotion under his arms. Holding up the bottle, he said:

> I bought some of this stuff, that generally in the summer time all my hairs up here [pointing to his armpits] will, uh, I sweat, you know, and it makes me smell, so I bought this here. Do you ever have trouble with your hairs smelling? My girlfriend tells me that sometimes I stink.

Richard practices no regular program of hygiene. Ordinarily he bathes and changes his clothing only after his body odor has become offensive and his clothes are filthy. He has three pairs of blue jeans, which he washes only after they are almost black with dirt. The pair he wears most often has a large hole in the seat of the pants, which reveals his sagging dirty-white briefs. Richard is proud of the fact that he has found a cheap laundromat where he can wash his jeans for 50 cents a load. He also saves 10 cents by taking the dripping wet pants home to his apartment to hang in his bathroom, instead of using the commercial drier.

Richard's physical appearance is mirrored by his apartment. His living quarters were always cluttered, but now they are a den for cockroaches. The floor is covered 3 inches deep with old newspapers (which Richard cannot read, but which he collects for the photographs), at least 200 empty soft drink cans, and a litter of dirty clothes. An old pull-down hide-away bed is left down, unmade with its single sheet and blanket bunched in the middle, exposing a thin grimy mattress. The single closet is jammed with clothes and a plastic Christmas tree covered with simulated snow. His dresser is covered with stacks of telephone books and pornographic magazines priced from $6 to $9 each. A worn and stained loveseat is positioned near the room's only window, which is always closed with the shade pulled down. Most of the small couch is covered with piles of newpapers and aluminum pans caked with food. Richard removed the door to his bathroom so that he could hang his clean shirts in the doorway. The bathroom itself appears never to have been cleaned; its stench takes one's breath away. The kitchen is worse. The refrigerator is a mass of mold and uneaten pizza, and the entire counter area plus much of the floor is covered with boxes of take-out chicken cartons (some still containing pieces of half-eaten stale chicken), greasy pans, and empty soft drink cans. The sink itself contains the same sort of debris, as well as some dirty silverware. Richard is reluctant to let anyone see his apartment; he apologizes for its condition and talks about hiring someone to clean it, but does nothing to clean it himself.

Richard's "Girlfriend"

Despite Richard's age, his deteriorating physical appearance, and poor health, as well as the almost unlivable condition of his apartment, his life still centers on his attempt to fashion a relationship with a woman. The current focus of his attention is a woman named Carmen Flores. She has been his "girlfriend" for 13 years or so, and, like her predecessors, she receives large amounts of money from Richard in return for an occasional sexual favor and virtually no affection or kindness. An old photograph shows Carmen (Richard always refers to her and addresses her as "Carmen Flores") as an attractive woman wearing a T-shirt with "Evil Woman" written across the front. However, today she is at least 50 pounds heavier, her hair is now dyed black, and she wears heavy makeup and flashy clothes with high-heeled shoes, even around her apartment. She speaks with a heavy Spanish accent, and her interactions with Richard seem to consist almost entirely of demands and reprimands delivered in a loud and querulous voice. Richard meekly complies, although when she has gone, he often says to the nearest ear that is listening, "I'm gonna hafta cut her off. You know, I'm gonna stop giving her money. I've gotta put my foot down."

In recent years, months have gone by without any sexual intimacy between Carmen and Richard, but he remains hopeful, if increasingly annoyed: "She don't treat me like a man. To tell you the truth, I don't know what's in that woman's head." One aspect of their relationship is constant—Carmen has an insatiable appetite for Richard's money. When Richard receives his pension check toward the end of the month, he takes it to a nearby jewelry store, where the proprietor cashes it, deducting the $200 monthly installment for a $3,200 gold watch that Richard bought for Carmen, and for which he still owes over $1,500. Richard receives his social security check on the first of the month, but he pays his rent with this and there is little left over, certainly not enough to interest Carmen. Richard's pension check, except for his $200 payments, is surplus income, and Carmen is punctual in arriving an hour or two after it does. In the past, they would infrequently have sex, but even on those occasions, Richard complained that Carmen was always in a hurry: "Sometimes she sure puzzles me." Whether Carmen was willing to have sex with Richard or not, she would always expect money from him, and she often got it by flattering him, saying that she wanted to have his baby, although rejecting his many proposals for marriage. Richard was puzzled by this too, pointing out that even when she would not have sex with him, she would talk about having a baby: "She knows I'm sterilized but I think she forgets." Carmen puts her request for money in terms of "helping her out," but Richard wonders about the inequity of their relationship. "I'll tell you the truth. She expects me to help her out but she don't try to help me out at all. It should be 50/50, shouldn't it?"

Despite his growing resentment, Richard always gives Carmen a large portion of his monthly income, usually $500, even though he is often left with no money of his own for most of the month. If Carmen needs money later in the month when Richard has no cash, she will "borrow" things of his and pawn them. Last month she went to the pawn shop with his wedding ring and the watch he was given for his retirement. She got $40 for the two items and gave $5 to Richard for his own use. Among other things, Carmen's car, a relatively new red Honda Accord, was purchased with the money Richard gave her.

Looking at the crass exploitation that so obviously characterizes their relationship today, one is tempted to suppose that once Richard and Carmen were more intimate. In fact, the relationship was always very much as it is today. Although they used to have sex more often than they do now, it was apparently never very frequent, and over the entire 13 years of their acquaintance, the only time they ever went out together in public was a single visit to Disneyland. Once when Richard was asked what Carmen liked to do, he said he did not know and would have to ask her the next time he saw her. When he was then asked what they did together, he answered,

> Nothing. I've been trying to get after her to, uh, maybe go set [sic] in the park or something, or go for a long drive somewhere in her car, you know. But I don't know what's the matter, she don't want to do it. I don't know why. I don't know what keeps her from doing it.

Although Richard knows where Carmen lives and has occasionally knocked on her door, she has never once let him in. She gets angry, shouts at Richard not to bother her, and says that she lives with a woman who works nights and does not like to be disturbed.

Richard often complains about Carmen's incessant need for money. She recently used his phone to call her parents in Ecuador, promising to repay Richard. The call cost $19.25, and although Richard says he doubts she will ever pay, he often says, "I'm gonna keep after her until she does." Richard also complains that Carmen won't give him any money, even when he has no money for food or medicine. "Carmen pulled a boo-boo on me. She messed me up too much. I just give her $60 and she won't give me nothin' back. I'm gonna hafta learn to say no to her." Richard also threatens to deal harshly with Carmen because she accuses him of being stupid, something she does whenever he does not "loan" her as much money as she requests. Recently Richard complained that Carmen had called him a "dumbbell." "I'm gonna ask her, 'Who ever told you that?' and I'm gonna make him eat those words. If she said it herself, I'm gonna make her eat those words." Although he builds up courage to confront her about this and her constant borrowing, he crumbles in the face of her domineering presence. Richard is unable to "put [his] foot down," but instead worries that she may find out that he was once in Pacific State Hospital and reject or humiliate him.

"Don't tell Carmen Flores that I have been in a state hospital. I don't want her to know. I don't know what she would . . . I don't know what she would think if I did tell her." Richard calls Carmen about once a week, but he rarely gets to talk to her.

> Now this sounds kinda crazy to me. I call over there to talk to Carmen Flores and you know these people are crazy enough—and they slam the phone down on my ear. And they don't wait 'til Carmen Flores comes and answers the phone. They hang it up. [Richard thinks Carmen told them to do it.] And then she tells me, "This phone is private." "They're all private," I said. "Don't give me no cotton-pickin' bull crap." I says, "All the phones are private."

Carmen does not visit him until the end of the month, when his second check, the one with liquid assets, arrives. Richard counts on her arrival like clockwork, "She'll be around before the twenty-sixth, you just mark my words." On one occasion after calling Richard and finding him not at home, Carmen left work to drive down to the jewelry store to give Richard a ride home and relieve him of $250 in cash. In between these visits, Carmen avoids Richard, refusing to allow him to visit her apartment. But because she lives only four blocks away from him, occasionally Richard sees her on the street. Last week, while sitting at the bus stop Richard saw her across the street and called out to her, but she intentionally ignored him. Asked if he thought she heard him, Richard said, "Yeah, she heard me. But she didn't want to talk."

Each time Richard gives Carmen money, he threatens to cut her off. Such threats quickly ring hollow, given his inability or unwillingness to say no to her. Though he has not stated it in so many words, Richard realizes that to cut off funds to Carmen would also cut off his sole source of affection, cold, infrequent, and impersonal though it may be. The importance of this affection to Richard can be measured not only in the large portion of his monthly check that he gives over to Carmen (up to $500 a month), but also in the threat to his own health this causes when he does not have enough money left to purchase medicine for his weak heart. He has asked Carmen to marry him several times, but "she kept giving me a lot of excuses." Before Carmen pawned it, Richard wore his wedding ring because he liked the idea of being married, and as he said,

"I wanted to see what would happen with Carmen and myself." He still holds romantic ideas about what could have been. Occasionally, Richard laments the fact that he cannot have a child. "If I had a son, he'd be Richard T. Jarrett, IV. Say like Carmen Flores. If I plant a baby in her womb I would name it Richard T. Jarrett, Jr. That's the way I'd do." Carmen had different intentions. She pawned his wedding ring, and when Richard went to claim it, it had been sold. He has invited her to the circus, the zoo, and to the park, but she will not go out with him. Richard ended up going to the circus by himself and watched them unload the tigers and elephants. Recently, Richard has been puzzled by Carmen's desire to have him placed in an "old folks' home," but he is determined not to go. "No way," he said. "They don't let you cook your own meals for you." He wants to stay where he is, explaining, "Because I can go places and have my meals fixed the way I want. There I wouldn't have my freedom at all."

Competence

Richard remains inordinately sensitive to any suggestion that he is incompetent. He frequently makes egregious errors, but he never admits that he is wrong. When someone confronts him with an obvious mistake, he ignores them and changes the subject without any apparent embarrassment. Many of his mistakes involve money because he cannot count money at all well and, in fact, does not even know how much money he receives every month. Once he showed his two checks to a field researcher and asked, "How much do I make?" When he was told that the checks totalled over $1,300, he looked surprised and said, "Whew, that's a lotta cabbage!" Once he showed the same fieldworker two $24 pawn tickets and said it would take $56 to redeem them. When he was told that the correct amount was $48, he simply said "huh" and changed the subject. On another occasion, Carmen told him that he was a fool to pay $56 for meal tickets that provided 14 meals at a sidewalk food stand. When he looked indignant, saying that he got a good deal, she pointed out that each of the meals he thought were a bargain cost $4 and that nothing he ate at the stand ever cost that much. Although it is true that Richard's favorite meal there, a double-decker hamburger, only costs $1.86, not $4, Richard merely stared at her and changed the subject. Small mistakes like this one are understandable, but often he seems to have no sense of the value of services. Because he is illiterate, he pays a woman in the neighborhood $10 to read any letter he receives, and when he asks her to write a letter for him, she charges as much as $50. Recently, she incorrectly addressed a letter that she had received $50 for writing, and Richard was neither concerned nor annoyed.

Notices that he receives in the mail often confuse Richard. Although he usually pays someone to read his mail, he often does not understand what is read to him. For example, he recently announced with genuine distress that he had just received a letter "from the Social Security" declaring that he was a "Nazi baby." What the notice (from a private group not affiliated with the Social Security Administration) actually said was that Richard was a "notch baby," someone born in the so-called notch between 1917 and 1921, and therefore affected by a change in the law determining how Social Security benefits are computed. Richard took the notice to a Teamsters Union lawyer who told him—as the notice did—that Congress was working on a remedy for this supposed inequity, but he still did not understand. The one thing Richard was sure of was that he wanted to clear his reputation and put to rest any accusations of being a "Nazi baby." He still threatens to get a lawyer and sue them for these false accusations. To be sure, the "notch baby" concept is a complex idea that could confuse many people, but Richard is confused about some quite simple matters too. In addition to money, which consistently baffles him, he is not sure about the relationship between sexual intercourse and pregnancy. He often asks, "How many times do you have to do it to get a baby started?" Also, although Richard brags about being a Texan and has made several trips through the state to Fort Worth, he still does not know what grits are, something that virtually every Texan knows.

Richard also lacks the kind of "street" knowledge that one would expect of someone who lives in a low-income area of a large central city. For example, although there are many prostitutes on the streets where he walks, Richard is completely naive about their activities (about which they are hardly subtle). One day recently, he excitedly said that he had heard "on the radio" about a woman who makes a date with a man and has sex with him "in the bushes" for $50. "Have you ever heard of such a thing?" he asked. Richard looked puzzled when told that such women are called prostitutes or "hookers." And although Richard's street is notorious for its drug dealers, he fails to understand why, when he sits on the sidewalk for hours, the police sometimes search him and tell him to leave.

> I don't know what in the heck I was doing to 'em, but I had two cops come up and search me for no reason at all. I never seen 'em after that, I guess they figured I was gonna get their numbers and turn 'em in.

Although Richard knows there are drug dealers on his street, he does not connect this with the police surveillance of the neighborhood. It is remarkable that, despite his innocence of the dangers on city streets through which he walks at night, no one has ever harmed him or, apparently, even seriously threatened him. It is possible that his large body and his naive self-confidence protect him. It is more probable however, that Richard is an unlikely target due to his slovenly appearance; he does not look like someone who would be carrying money or valuables worth stealing. His innocence may protect him in other ways as well. On three separate occasions he has attempted to shoplift items in drug stores or a market. (Twice he took bottles of vitamins, once he took a tube of Preparation H.) All three times he was caught in the act, yet he was never prosecuted. "I talked my way out of it," Richard said, explaining that when he was first apprehended he said to the security guard, "Ossifer [sic], I got money to pay for this [vitamins] and I don't want no trouble." The second time he told the market manager that he was "gettin' ready to retire and [he] didn't want nothin' bad on [his] record." Again he offered to pay for the item, and no charges were pressed. The same thing happened a third time, but by then Richard decided, as he said, that "three times was enough. No more."

Health

Richard seems oblivious to his deteriorating health. He continues to eat four meals of high-cholesterol food a day with snacks in between, but he does not think he is fat. Despite his family's history of obesity—both Richard's father and brother died from high blood pressure and his brother weighed 365 pounds at the time of his death—Richard does not think he suffers from such a condition. When asked if he got his large stomach from eating, Richard said, "No, it's natural. That's all." He holds this position even in the face of criticism from his girlfriend, Carmen. "Even Carmen Flores said that I have a big stomach." Richard justifies himself, saying, "They even took pictures of my stomach [in the hospital] and they didn't find anything wrong," and, "I've seen fellows bigger than I am." At times he takes the criticisms to heart and makes some gestures toward reform. "I may have to buy another [bicycle] to see if it will make any change in me or not." With the loss of his bicycle over 15 years ago, Richard lost his only form of exercise, but this did not diminish his appetite.

Despite the double portions of food he was given during a recent hospital stay, Richard thought it strange that his doctor "tried to starve [him] to death."

> Just because I asked for five eggs, and uh, the doctor said, "Nobody eats five eggs. Well, you know that eggs have cholesterol?" I says, "What makes you think that eggs is got cholesterol in 'em?" I says, "I've ate five eggs at home."

The owner of the hamburger stand where Richard eats also cautioned him, "If you eat too many eggs that's too much cholesterol. Believe it or not, but it's true." Richard laughed and said, "Huh. That's hard to believe. Give me a spoon, please. I can't believe that." Richard does not have a scale, and he is puzzled by the weight that was read by the nurse when he went to the hospital recently. "I don't know how I could weigh that much." Richard does not associate his obvious obesity with his high blood pressure. Nor does it concern him. "No, I don't worry about it. As long as the doctor is taking care of me, I don't worry about a thing. That's one thing that can make you sick, is worrying about it." His enormous weight gain has exacerbated his high blood pressure, which has begun to take its toll; Richard recently has been hospitalized five times in a period of 4 months.

It is ironic that, as a result of hospitalization, Richard's consumption of food actually increased. After his first trip to the hospital, he began receiving "Food-on-Wheels" meals, free food that he considers a supplement to his daily round. Before noon every day Richard receives a tray of hot food (including, for example, chicken breast, corn, peaches, a slice of bread, and a pint carton of milk) and a cold snack (sandwich, pudding, and orange juice), which he places on the kitchen counter before he leaves to go to his favorite hamburger stand for "breakfast." A typical breakfast for Richard is two fried eggs ("straight up, please"), three pancakes, and four or five pieces of rather greasy bacon. After his noon breakfast, Richard returns home to sit on the front step of his apartment building to watch passers-by, or to retire to his room for a nap, sitting up in his sagging love seat, listening to cowboy music. He returns at 5:00 P.M. to the hamburger stand for a double cheeseburger, fries, and a Diet Pepsi. (With no trace of irony, Richard said that regular soda has too much sugar, which is not good for him.) At 8:30 P.M., he eats his "Food-on-Wheels" meal, which has been sitting on the kitchen counter since before noon. Richard has a large collection of the cold meals wrapped in plastic bags, left over from previous deliveries, from which he snacks periodically between meals. After his 8:30 meal, he usually rides the bus for an hour to relax and talk to the bus driver. At 11:00 P.M., just before he goes to bed, Richard eats a 10-ounce steak or three pork chops, which he fries with a pat of butter in a large flat skillet.

"It sure flopped in my face," Richard says about his current health status. "I ended up in the hospital five times [because of] my heart and high blood pressure. [The doctor] took pictures of my heart," he said, "and I may have to have open heart surgery, but not right now. My heart is too weak for it." Amazingly, Richard attributes his weak heart and high blood pressure, he says, "to all my heavy drinking when I was a young fellow. And it all came right back at me. . . . It all bounced in my face." Later, he pointed to a drunk passed out in a parking lot and said, "Drinking will do that to you. It done it to me." This interpretation might not be so fanciful were it not for the fact that Richard only drank for 3 years (from the age of 30 to 33) and only on Saturdays (but not every Saturday), and his drinking consisted of one bottle ("almost a whole bottle," he said) of wine that he shared with his girlfriend and another friend. In order to give the impression that he is a real drinker, Richard often tells his "getting-drunk-and-throwing-up" story (a story he has repeated to one fieldworker on four separate occasions). Richard and his girlfriend Ramona had been drinking some wine before they went out to eat at what Richard calls "one of them fancy restaurants." He ordered some beer and proceeded to get drunk. Mixing beer and wine, he found, was not a good idea. "Boy, I'm telling you, that made me sick. I threw up all over the guy that played in the band. I had to pay $5 to get the guy's suit cleaned." To make matters worse, Richard said, "Ramona gave me hell; she bawled me out for that." He thought this was unjustified, and they parted with bad blood between them.

None of his five trips to the hospital (with an average stay of 10 days each) has worried Richard. His love of certain foods takes priority over his physical condition. Despite dire warnings from his doctor, he is still not concerned enough about his health to change his diet. As he said, "It's pretty hard to do that. Some things I like to eat. I can't stay away from it." Richard's panacea is the pills his doctor prescribed. He takes them religiously when he has enough money to buy the medicine, and he thinks that they will solve his health problems. Richard says he is not concerned about his health "as long as the doctor is taking care of me." His faith in the doctor's ability to cure him is unwavering, if unrealistic. But by displacing the responsibility for his health to his doctor, Richard can indulge in his favorite pastime without having to worry about the consequences.

Richard's breathing is so labored that he has trouble walking up one flight of stairs (20 steps) to his apartment without pausing once or twice to rest. Although he was breathing heavily on the upstairs landing, he denied that the stairs caused him any difficulties. "Oh no, it's no problem," he said. "Not since I got my medicine. It was worse before." With his shortness of breath, Richard is a painfully slow walker. Some of this can be attributed to his feet, which recently, for some reason he does not know, have become so swollen that he must wear loose-fitting rubber sandals instead of shoes. At his snail's pace, crossing the busy intersection at the corner of his block is hazardous, as there is neither a crosswalk nor traffic signal to help him. Richard has twice received a ticket for jaywalking, because he was blocking oncoming cars. When the researcher read him his ticket, which said "Approximate speed: 3 miles per hour," Richard laughed. "They put the craziest things on there. Three miles— me walking that fast!"

At 68, the only area of Richard's health that he considers noteworthy is his sex life. He said that he has asked his doctor to "give me something to uh, liven my sex life up, you know." Richard often complains that "Carmen Flores is not giving it to me like she should," and, "She's always in a hurry." He is puzzled about why this is the case, but once speculated that it might have something to do with his large size. "You know, my thing is this big," Richard said, indicating with both hands a circle with a diameter of 4 inches. "You don't believe me, but it is." Richard is also confused by Carmen's request that he wear a condom. "I don't sleep with anyone else and I don't have A," he said, meaning AIDS.

Finances

In the hope of gaining sexual favors, Richard continues to give most of his surplus income to Carmen. After she drains him of his cash, Richard complains that he does not have enough money for his own needs. He thus turns to Social Security, which he claims is not paying him enough. After little success talking to representatives at the local Social Security office, Richard asked a fieldworker to write the following letter to his senator in Washington, D.C. ("the one who takes care of all the Social Security money"):

> Dear Senator Cranston, Find out why is it such a rule that I like a lot of other people—that $605.80 can go a long ways. After I pay my rent all I have left is $180. I can't get by on that. I'd like to see you big shots get by on that. Food is expensive, meat and everything. I would like $11,000 or $12,000. [Richard said that he would like this amount, not annually, but each month.]

"They are cotton-pickin' dumbbells. I hate to say that. And they've had a high school education," Richard said, referring to the people at the credit bureau who informed him that he had a bad credit rating. Richard is determined to have a credit card. Although he has never said so in so many words, it seems obvious that for him possession of a credit card is a sign of normality. As he often discovers, not having a credit card can be a distinct disadvantage, especially when he runs out of cash thanks to Carmen. Yet he seems not to understand the necessity of making regular payments or that payments include interest. With assistance, he has applied three times for credit cards, only to be rejected because he still owed several hundred dollars from a previous debt. He paid his friend Gayle to write to the credit agency, enclosing $8 and asking that he now be given a credit card. When he learned by return mail that he would have to pay several hundred dollars before his credit rating would be restored, he then called the company only to be frustrated again:

> They are the most stupidest people I've ever run across. They haven't got no brains at all. I even told them, I says, "Can't you take that off of my, um, off my record and put a new record?" "No, we can't do that; we gotta have it written down on a piece of paper."

Richard thinks there is a 7-year statute of limitations, after which time "it's not supposed to be on your record." He says he will pursue the matter until they take it off his record so that he can get his long-sought credit card. "I'm trying to improve my credit, but I'm having a hard time doing it," he said. "I'm a Texan and I don't give up easy. I'll fight back."

Although he usually runs out of money before the end of the month, Richard thinks he has no problems handling his money. He likes to point out, however, that other people who are smarter than he is have financial difficulties. Recently, his friend Gayle was having difficulty paying an expensive long-distance phone bill as a result of calls to her parents. "You know that Gayle is twice as smart as I am, and she can't handle money," he said. "She calls San Francisco and talks for two hours." Furthermore, Richard thinks Gayle spends money needlessly. "She goes way out to Pasadena and pays $25 to get a shot of vitamins. I get vitamins for 90 cents, not $25 just for one shot." Richard met Gayle 4 years ago in a nearby supermarket where he buys meat. As a regular customer, Richard became friends with the butcher, who often borrowed money from him because, as Richard said, "He couldn't handle his money. He plays horses and loses everything." Gayle overheard a conversation between Richard and the butcher (whose name he does not know).

> He was borrowing money off of me. He said, "I'll pay you back when I get paid." And she said, "Why don't you pay him back now?!" And I told her, "Why don't you mind your own business?" She didn't know what to say.

Despite this rocky start, Gayle "befriended" Richard and soon began reading and writing letters for him in return for cash.

Social Life

Although he has a wealth of acquaintances like Gayle, Richard is fairly isolated. He has no one to whom he could turn in times of trouble, and there is no one from whom he could borrow money if he needed it. He recognizes that he is not close to any of the people he calls "friends." In a poignant moment of honesty, when asked by a fieldworker who his best friend was, Richard answered, "You. 'Cuz everything that I want to find out I ask you." It is indicative of his isolation that this researcher was the only person to visit Richard during any of his five stays at the hospital. Richard said that his only other friend is Barbara: "There's nobody else." That Richard would define the fieldworker, whom he has known for only 2 years, as his best friend, and Barbara, whom he sees only once a month when he accompanies her to cash her check at the supermarket, as his only other friend indicates a profound lack of social support. Asked about his cousin in Texas, Richard's only living relative, he said, "I've never asked him for nothing. I don't feel like I could ask him. He has problems enough."

If this lack of social support bothers Richard, one would never know it; there is no indication of it in his demeanor. He seems completely content with his network of acquaintances. Most often Richard refers to these people with whom he has daily contact as his "friends." For example, he addresses the cook/owner of the hamburger stand where he eats every day as "my friend," as in, "Two eggs up, my friend, straight up, please." Although he has been eating two meals a day there, 6 days a week (the stand is closed on Mondays) year-round for over 5 years, Richard still does not know the owner's name. Richard has been known to invent activities that he will do with one of his friends at some indefinite date. These fictitious trips are not spun from whole cloth, but are usually based on his misunderstanding of something an acquaintance has said to him, as was the case with the owner of a liquor store he frequents. Richard buys his milk and cream at this store (mixing a gallon of milk with a quart of half-and-half to drink with his meals) and often engages the owner in conversation. Richard once said that he needed to buy a new pair of tennis shoes to go hiking with this friend to a nude beach. ("Did I tell you that the men and women run naked down here? I think it's the other side of Redondo Beach." Asked why they run around naked, he offered, "Well, I guess it's just healthy for 'em, I guess.") Richard mistook a comment the owner made about this beach as an offer to visit it. Like most of Richard's "friends," he does not know this man's name.

The same is true for another of Richard's friends, the bus driver on the route he rides almost every night for entertainment. He has ridden with this driver for over 2 years, and their most frequent topic of conversation is "problems with women." Richard once referred to this man as a "wolf." "A wolf is someone who likes a lot of women—to have a lot of women," he explained. His friend the bus driver "likes 'em 14 to 16 years old. That's almost jail-bait," Richard said. "You wouldn't catch me fooling around like that! They can lock you up for that." When asked this driver's name, Richard said, "I never took the time out to ask his name." Although Richard is not someone these people would visit when not working, he is generally well-liked by them. He is friendly, has a good sense of humor, and is a good listener. Because he has nothing but time on his hands, Richard can afford to listen to acquaintances for as long as they wish to talk. He likes to engage people in small talk and says he talks to everyone in the neighborhood. This was borne out one day on his way to the bakery for his morning cup of coffee. Richard talked with, in succession: his mail carrier, a black woman approximately 30 years old (about when his regular carrier would return from her pregnancy leave); a neighbor, an Armenian man whom he had known for 2 weeks (about the man's unemployment check, which has yet to arrive); two elderly Anglo women (about the hot weather); a large Anglo policeman who was at the scene of a car accident (about what happened); and later a young Mexican drug dealer (Richard called out from across the street, "Hey, I've seen you all over town. You're keeping busy.").

CONCLUSION

Richard lacks many of the cognitive and interpersonal skills that are ordinarily associated with success in community adaptation. He is not street-wise, he neither understands money nor manages it well, he is easily exploited in various ways, and he has no friends or relatives who would support him in a time of crisis. Yet it would be a mistake not to recognize that Richard does have some important adaptive skills and assets. Perhaps the most important was his good fortune in finding a job that called for strength, endurance, and reliability, not literacy or quick wits, and that was partially protected by membership in the Teamsters Union. Although the union was strong and protective, the job itself was no sinecure. For 31 years, Richard got to work on time, carried out his duties well enough that the company did not attempt to fire him, and got along with his co-workers well enough that the union continued to support him. Although it could be said that finding such a job was purely fortuitous, holding it for 31 years would not have been possible were it not for Richard's willingness to work, his reliability, and his stability.

Richard illustrates the importance of attitudinal and personality factors in successful adaptation. He believes in hard work as a virtue, and for the most part, he does not believe that he has been wronged in life or that other people should solve life's problems for him. He will accept help when it is offered, but he is committed to self-reliance as a value. Although there is much that he does not understand about the world in which he lives, he is remarkably persistent in his pursuit of his goals. When he was troubled by something at work, he did not hesitate to speak to the shop steward or the union's legal representatives, and even today, despite his age, dishevelled appearance, and illiteracy, he will take on no less formidable a bureaucracy than the local Social Security office. He may well be treated rudely, but he does not back down. Recently, a put-out clerk brusquely asked him what he wanted, to which Richard answered forcefully, "I want to sit down right here and have you explain some things to me, please!" That he did not entirely understand what he was told is typical, but so is his determination to control his own destiny.

Although his memory is ordinarily not good, when what he sees as his vital interests are at stake, he can memorize phone numbers and addresses and remember the names of people to whom he has spoken.

He is never reluctant to be self-assertive about what he sees as his rights, and this attitude is combined with an innocent determination that assumes that if the wheel is squeaky long enough it will eventually get the grease. Richard credits this persistence to his being a Texan. Although he has not lived in Texas since he was 2 years old, Richard still considers himself a Texan. He is justified in this, he says, because he was born there, he is big (even if most of his bulk is at his waist), he is hard-working, and he is stubborn. He has regular contact with Texas in his weekly Saturday calls to his cousin, and he can always tell you what the weather is like in Fort Worth.

His stubbornness can be seen not only in his determination to get more money from Social Security, but also in his attempt to get them to spell his name right. He complained when letters from Social Security left out the initial "T" in his name. "Why do they avoid the 'T'?" he asked. "Because it's part of my name. The 'T' stands for 'Thomas.' I told the operator at Social Security board to put down 'Richard Thomas Jarrett, Jr.' so they can't mess up." Richard said that he would call them as many times as it takes to make the change. "I'm stubborn, I don't give up. That's 'cuz I'm a Texan," he said. When he was a young man, handsome and reasonably well dressed, this tactic probably paid off more often than it does now, but Richard persists nevertheless.

Another adaptive asset is Richard's stable temperament. He experiences few ups and downs of emotion, and in interaction with others, he is almost always reasonable, pleasant, and somehow appealing. Again, these winning aspects of his personality were more obvious when he was younger, but even now, as a badly overweight aging man, Richard is not repellent. He still projects an equable reasonableness that favorably impresses many people. Richard is friendly and open and nonthreatening. There is nothing strange or troubling about him, nothing that would suggest unpredictability or danger. Moreover, when people he knows complain about his behavior, he usually tries to change. For example, when a proprietor in a clothing store told him he smelled badly, he grumbled about it for a while, but he took her complaint to heart. "She said before you come in again, I wanta see you with different clothes on, so's I went and washed me 4 pairs of pants for 50 cents."

Another great asset for Richard is his consistently high self-esteem, which developed despite a lack of support from his parents. "They was always saying that I wouldn't make it on the outside of the world, by myself," he said. It is true that he tries to hide his early history at Pacific State Hospital and that he reacts angrily when he is accused of being stupid, but there is no evidence that Richard thinks of himself as being a stupid person or that he believes he ever deserved to be in a hospital for people with mental retardation. Richard freely acknowledges that he cannot read or write and that this failing handicaps him in life, but he appears to believe sincerely that his illiteracy is a result of his lack of formal schooling. He points out that his mother never went to school and was illiterate also. He is not at all reluctant to declare that he is illiterate, as when he was summoned for jury duty or when he attempts to vote. When he received his jury summons, Richard asked a fieldworker to fill out the form for him. When he went to vote, he asked for assistance from one of the attendants, and when the attendant refused, Richard said, "I just punched the holes where I thought it was all right." It is also likely that Richard's many years of successful employment solidified his self-confidence, but it should be kept in mind that he had the confidence to seek out the job in the first place, while hiding his illiteracy as a matter of practicality.

Just as Richard never admits that he is "slow" or "retarded," he rarely admits that he is wrong about anything. He even denies that he is overweight. It is tempting to conclude that Richard's denial of his inadequacy is a form of psychological defense, and it may be, but it is at least equally plausible that he is simply supremely self-assured. His extraordinary willingness to deal directly with almost any situation, from legal entanglements to credit ratings, exemplifies his confidence. Possibly because he does not understand the extent to which others see him as being incompetent, he is able to maintain his positive self-image. Richard uses denial and deflection. He is also able to point to others who are literate but have similiar or worse problems than himself. For example, Richard's friend, Barbara, whom he met at Pacific State Hospital, often criticizes him for giving away his money. Richard sees Barbara only once a month, when he accompanies her for protection when she cashes her check at the supermarket, but he calls her at least once a week on the phone. Richard's endless stories about his various girlfriends' demands for his money have convinced this illiterate woman with a borderline IQ that he is so incompetent that he should be placed on an allowance before predatory women reduce him to penury. Richard shrugs all this off, arguing that it is she, not he, who needs supervision because she continually puts off buying a bus pass, something Richard has done for years. She has been unable to make him understand that she rides the bus only two or three times a month and that it is less expensive to pay the fare than to buy a bus pass.

Part of Richard's self-confidence may have come from the positive reactions that his athletic good looks elicited from others when he was younger, but he is more than a masculine "dumb blond." Although it is undeniably true that he is limited in his ability to understand much that takes place in ordinary life, he has enough social and intellectual competence not only to cope successfully with the minimal demands of his environment, but also to enjoy his life and to perceive himself as an ordinary working man. Although his knowledge of the world is limited (he does not read the paper or listen to the news on the radio), Richard is able to carry on general conversation with neighbors, and he is remarkably successful at smoothing out the flow of conversation by glossing over his own ignorance of topics and by ignoring other peoples' corrections of his mistakes, as if being corrected were a normal feature of adult conversation.

Whatever the dynamics of his self-confidence, Richard has always had faith in himself. At every stage of his life, he has been optimistic, and even today he has no serious complaints about his life and no fears for the future. He is confident that he can cope with what comes, that he can deal with Carmen Flores, and that if new problems occur in his life, he will deal with them also. Although he knows that he has high blood pressure, that high blood pressure has killed other members of his family, and that he has been hospitalized five times recently because of it, Richard is not concerned for his health or his mortality. It is easy to dismiss Richard's "happy-go-lucky" approach to life as an inevitable consequence of his low intelligence, but others with comparable IQs are anything but self-confident, optimistic, and content. Richard's confident approach to life probably contributed to his successful adaptation, just as his relative success in life must have increased his self-assurance. The two cannot be separated.

Richard is an exploited man who is seen by most around him as slow and incompetent, yet he sees himself as a perfectly competent success in life. Although his insensitivity to his incompetence makes him vulnerable to exploitation, it also allows him to think well of himself and to face life with equanimity. When asked what he would change about his life, Richard could not think of anything. Although he has few friends, he said, "Well, I always run into more friends." And although he is terminally short of money, Richard said, "Well, we always have more money." Despite his constant complaints about his "girlfriend," Richard said he would not want to change that either. He has a remarkable ability to ignore what most would consider profound problems: the possibility that he will need open-heart surgery; the fact that he has no money and no possessions, only debts; the filthy conditions of his apartment and his own hygiene; and the fact that he has no one to care for him, only a "girlfriend" who exploits him to the best of her ability. Given these circumstances, one would expect Richard to be depressed, anxious, worried, or at the very least a little discouraged with his plight. He has little reason to be happy with the way things are, but nonetheless, he is happy with things exactly as they are.

Author's Postscript

Richard died on December 17, 1988 at the age of 68. His health had deteriorated severely, the inevitable result of his eating habits. I visited Richard the day before he died. He had made several trips to the hospital in the previous two months— so many, in fact, that the paramedics told him not to call them anymore, that he should call a private ambulance service instead, which he did twice. The morning I last saw him, Richard looked pale and was short of breath. He said he had an appointment to see his doctor that afternoon. With some pride, Richard said that he was following his doctor's orders, that he had cut from his diet the two chocolate bars he usually ate every day, and that he was taking his heart medication regularly. We started toward the nearby bakery, but Richard could walk only 15 yards before he needed to rest on a parked car. He waited there while I brought the coffee and doughnuts to him. The next day, he called an ambulance and was taken to the hospital, where he died of heart failure.

T. W. W.

"Keeping Hands and Mind Busy."

MARTHA MCDOWELL

by Marcia A. Gaston
and Dana M. Baldwin

Of all the original sample members from *The Cloak of Competence* study with whom we still have contact as they grow older, Martha McDowell is the most obviously haunted by her past institutionalization. While most other sample members have come to terms by one method or another with this period in their pasts, Martha has been far less successful in doing so. Other sample members have used strategies including outright denial, "rewriting" of the past through reformulating their personal histories, and sometimes simply refusing to think or talk about that period of their lives, in order to bring some perspective to the past that allows them to go on with the business of living today. Martha also indulges in some of these strategies, most notably by clinging to her claim that her institutionalization was a mistake and by insisting that there was nothing wrong with her and that she was committed to Pacific State Hospital simply because she had no family. She openly blames virtually all of her problems and personal inadequacies on the fact that she was institutionalized against her will and deprived of her freedom and schooling during many of the formative years of her life. Through the years as she has aged, some of the anguish and despair with which Martha presses her claims has lessened, but in Martha's own view, her institutionalization has remained one of two overwhelmingly significant factors in her life. The second factor, but one that is intimately bound in Martha's mind to her institutionalization, is her complete lack of any family.

THE PAST

Martha was born out of wedlock in 1921 to a 15-year-old schoolgirl from West Virginia who was sent to a Los Angeles home for unwed mothers to have her baby. After Martha was born, the mother put her up for adoption, returned to West Virginia, and was never heard from again. Martha was adopted at the age of 2, but she was literally abandoned by her new parents a few months later. Her life from then until her commitment to Pacific State Hospital at the age of 14 consisted of one foster home after another. Martha remembers finding warmth or a sense of family in only one of these homes, where she lived until she was approximately 6 years old. However, according to Martha, she and the other children were scattered to other foster homes to prevent too much attachment between the foster mother and the children. Martha says that the state had such a policy at that time, which has since been changed, and she states, "You feel like your life has been destroyed living like that. . . . It's like a scar inside you. It's the scar that stays with you, that it's hard to forget." During this period, as well as her years at Pacific, Martha describes desperate feelings of confusion because of her lack of identity. She knew nothing about her past until after her discharge from Pacific when she was in her 30s; one of her benefactors, a social worker, helped her by getting a copy of her birth records. According to Martha, until that time, "No one ever told me why I didn't have a mother or father like other people." Martha says that finding out even this tiny piece of information about her past "made me feel like a person."

Although Martha insists that there was nothing wrong with her and that she was committed to Pacific because she had no family to take care of her, there are indications in the records that she had become quite difficult at the foster home where she was living, because of extreme irritability, bedwetting, "open masturbation," and her temper. She had reached the fourth grade in school at the age of 14, but she was having difficulty there as well, both with her school performance and her inability to get along with her classmates. The immediate reason given for her commitment was several severe episodes of menorraghia (excessively prolonged menstruation), and she underwent a hysterectomy at the age of 15.

Martha was diagnosed at Pacific State Hospital as being mentally retarded, with her IQ being variously reported between 67 and 74. However, the possibility exists that the extreme deprivation she suffered as a young child may have caused so much emotional damage that it masked her innate intellectual ability and left her dysfunctional. Martha was hospitalized at Pacific State Hospital for more than 18 years without leave of any kind, the longest uninterrupted hospitalization of any of *The Cloak of Competence* sample members. She received no further schooling beyond the fourth-grade education she had when she arrived. She describes herself when she was released on leave at the age of 32 as nearly incapacitated with fear, both of dealing with the outside world and of the possibility that if she did not do well on the outside, she would be returned to the hospital. Even today, when asked what her greatest fear is, Martha replies, "That somebody's going to grab me and put me back in the hospital," although she admits that within the last few years the fear is no longer as immediate as it once was.

At the time of *The Cloak of Competence* study in the early 1960s, Martha was almost completely isolated, unable to find and hold a job, and almost totally dependent on the benefactors she had managed to accumulate. On a scale ranking the 48 sample members from most independent (1) to most dependent (48), Martha ranked number 40 out of the 48. Serious questions existed as to whether Martha could survive in the outside world without heavy dependence on her benefactors.

Through the years since that time, Martha has managed not only to survive, but to build an independent life for herself. Her level of competence and adaptation have slowly but steadily increased to the point where she handles her life and her day-to-day affairs entirely on her own. As her original benefactors have disappeared through death or by moving from the area, she has not replaced them, and today she has no direct benefactors in her life, no one who routinely helps her run her life or who makes decisions for her. Martha does have people on whom she could call if she needs help, including one woman whom she has known since her days at Pacific State Hospital, as well as a few with whom Martha is acquainted through her membership in a nearby Methodist church, but she only calls on these supports in real emergency situations because she does not like "to be a burden" to anyone.

With the exception of a job working as a stock clerk in a used clothing store run by a local sheltered workshop, which she held for approximately one year ending in 1963, Martha has never held a full-time job in the competitive workplace. Although Martha found and applied for this job on her own, she had trouble getting along with others, as she did even on part-time jobs, because of her irritability, occasional unpredictable outbursts of temper, and bossiness. She also had great difficulty when put under any kind of time pressure, and her anxiety when faced with criticism of any kind caused her to become nearly hysterical. Thus, her income for many years has come through disability benefits from the state, based on her past history of institutionalization. However, Martha does not view these payments as a handout. Because of her extreme feelings about what she views as the unjustness of her institutionalization and its effect on her life, Martha sees her disability payments in some general way as an indemnity paid to her by the state for the damage done to her life.

LIFE TODAY

However, Martha does not sit idle. For the past 10 years, she has volunteered 4 days a week, from 9:00 A.M. to 1:00 P.M., in the Senior Meals program that operates out of the basement of her church. In the more relaxed and tolerant atmosphere of volunteer work, Martha has managed to carve out a niche for herself. One of the "captains" under whom she works says that Martha is her best volunteer. Martha comes in earlier than the other volunteers and organizes and prepares the work for the others. She is very knowledgeable and organized, and her excellent memory for numbers is a great help. For instance, the captain mentioned above says that Martha can remember daily how many meals are served in the program and by whom, which is something even the captain has trouble remembering. Martha, in fact, does part of the work that the captain would ordinarily do, and the captain shows her gratitude by "just staying out of Martha's way" when Martha gets quite bossy and directive. However, there are some other volunteers who have difficulty tolerating Martha's behavior. Martha's captain is so appreciative of Martha's reliability and hard work that she has arranged the shift schedule so that Martha simply works on a different shift from those who have difficulty with her. Martha also volunteers regularly in the church office, doing whatever work needs to be done. The rest of her time is spent in completing any necessary errands or chores and keeping her apartment in immaculate condition.

All of this activity is very important to Martha. For many years, the idea of keeping her "hands and mind busy" has been a constant refrain with Martha because such activity has been her only defense against the anxiety and depression that have plagued her all of her life, what Martha refers to as her "fearful feelings." Also, as Martha herself says, "because otherwise you feel like you're not wanted, like you're useless."

> When you're doing something, you feel like you're going somewhere, you belong somewhere, like doing Senior Meals or something. When you're just sitting there and not having your hands and mind busy, oh, it's an awful feeling. You feel like there's nowhere you belong.

As she has since her discharge from Pacific State Hospital, Martha lives in a small city not far from the hospital. She does not drive, a fact that she attributes to her past institutionalization, but she has managed to arrange her life so that virtually all of her activity takes place within walking distance. She will occasionally take the bus, and on rare occasions throughout the year, someone will take her somewhere in a car.

Martha lives in a rather unattractive, boxlike older apartment building that, although in need of painting, appears to be otherwise well maintained. By living in such an old building, Martha is able to afford a spacious one-bedroom apartment. The size of her apartment, however, has meaning for Martha beyond the obvious issues of comfort. When complimented on how spacious her apartment is, echoes of her past are immediately apparent in her response: "It's important not to feel locked in." (Paradoxically, although Martha is obsessive about the issue of "feeling locked in," she is also quite security conscious; she not only locks her door diligently, but uses safety pins to keep all of her curtains closed tightly.) The apartment is sparsely furnished with furniture that Martha has either been given or has accumulated from thrift stores. Although her furniture is old and somewhat dingy, it is also fastidiously clean and neat. However, in spite of the fact that Martha has made obvious efforts to create a homelike atmosphere, there is something sadly impersonal about it all. She hangs pictures and exhibits knickknacks that are meant to make the place seem homey, but they actually have the opposite effect because they are someone else's former treasures, which Martha has picked up at rummage sales or thrift shops, and they have no real connection to Martha's own past. It is noteworthy that the only room in Martha's apartment that does not fit into the "tidy" image is her bedroom, the room most likely not to be seen by others. The bedroom furnishings consist of a worn, sagging bed, an old television, storage boxes piled on top of one another, and mops and brooms cast into the corner.

Martha's clothing, like her furniture and many of her other possessions, comes mainly from Goodwill Industries and other thrift stores, and although Martha is always clean, she often does not appear so because her clothing is worn and stained. This is particularly unfortunate because Martha is physically unattractive as well. She is of medium height and build, and her dyed reddish hair is poorly cut and frequently goes grey at the roots between trips to the beauty shop. She does look better at the times she has been able to have her hair done, but on her small, fixed income, this is a luxury she cannot afford on a frequent basis. Martha has deep brown discolored patches on her face, and she applies a heavy coat of dark makeup to help even out her coloring. However, this gives her an unusually dark complexion and a ruddy, blotchy cast to her face.

Martha's face also has a slight lopsidedness, which may have some connection to the periodically painful facial condition that Martha identifies as "neuritis." This is, in fact, Martha's only known major health problem. The painful attacks are excruciating, and Martha states, "I just want to bang my head against the wall" when they come. A doctor in the past tried giving her Dilantin for this condition, but Martha refused to continue taking the Dilantin because it made her drowsy, which reminded her of the medication she was given while at Pacific State Hospital. This memory is complicated by the fact that Martha perceived such medication as a punishment, given to patients designated as too "excited," "nervous," or "upset" by the staff and accompanied by being locked in a "side room." She now attempts to control the pain using Excedrin, and she keeps as many as ten large bottles on hand in her kitchen. Martha's eyes are crossed, and one eye "wanders." Coupled with her very poor vision, this causes her to squint and to peer with sometimes-unnerving intensity at people and objects that are right in front of her. Martha does own prescription glasses, but she finds them uncomfortable and rarely wears them. Martha's poor vision, together with a poor sense of balance, causes her to move very slowly with small steps, and she has been described as negotiating stairs "like an off-balance tightrope walker."

One problem that added to Martha's physical unattractiveness in the past has, fortunately, been alleviated. Her own teeth were yellow and protruded prominently, and she exacerbated the problem by trying to hide them from people with her tongue or her hand or simply by keeping her mouth tightly shut. Martha now has false teeth, which are more attractive than her original ones. However, she only wears the top plate because she was never able to become accustomed to the bottom plate. Although Martha insists that she does fine with this arrangement, it appears that she has a tendency to incompletely chew her food, which may have something to do with her periodic complaints of stomach trouble.

Relationships

Coupled with her physical appearance, Martha's demeanor, particularly when meeting someone new, is anxious and deferential to an extreme and sometimes off-putting degree. Her anxiety is often accompanied by nervous, fluttery, almost child-like gestures and exclamations. All in all, Martha is not a person to whom one is immediately drawn, although her childishness and apparent helplessness do elicit solicitous responses from others. Martha looks and acts emotionally disabled. One can only wonder at the extent to which Martha's entire life, including the terrible deprivation of her childhood and young adulthood, has been influenced by the fact that she is considered by others to have an extremely unattractive appearance. Through the years she has learned to exude an aura of nearly overwhelming need in order to attract people's attention.

To her credit, Martha has never been willing to see herself as simply the object of pity and goodwill in these interactions. Although her aura of need may initially draw people into interaction with her, those who have known her over time have learned that Martha insists on reciprocating as she can. Her oldest friend, Rose, whom Martha has known since her Pacific State Hospital days when Martha was a patient and Rose was a recreational therapist, pointed out that she has learned over the more than 30 years of their relationship that Martha wants to be seen as a "social friend," not as the recipient of goodwill. For instance, Martha would never accept gifts of money, even when she needed it. If Rose wanted to give money to Martha, it was necessary to give it in return for something, such as cleaning house or baby-sitting. Martha was then able to view the situation as one friend helping another.

Unfortunately, the true nature of her relationships is not as Martha would like to see them. When asked to name her friends, Martha puts Rose at the top of her list. Although they have known each other for more than 30 years, Rose does not consider Martha a close, intimate friend. She cares about Martha, keeps in touch by telephone, and sees her occasionally, although through the years this contact has dwindled to every Christmas Eve, some Thanksgivings, and perhaps one other contact during the year. Rose is aware of Martha's need to see herself as an equal friend, and she helps Martha to perpetuate this image, but it is clear that Rose's perception of their relationship is very different.

Martha's list of friends also includes two women with whom Martha corresponds sporadically, but rarely sees. One is Rose's sister, Hope, and the other is Eileen, who is now in her 90s and lives in a beach community many miles away. Eileen and her sister, who died a few years ago, were introduced to Martha by a fellow member of their Community Assistance League, who met Martha while accompanying a friend to visit her son at Pacific State Hospital when Martha was still a patient there. One of Martha's most consistently repeated stories, even today, is of this meeting. According to Martha, the woman had brought along some clothing to donate to the patients at Pacific. Martha worked in the clothing room, and the woman offered her a blouse. Martha tried the blouse on, but it was a little too small, so Martha suggested that perhaps someone else could use it. The woman remarked on Martha's generosity, praising her for it. When the woman discovered that Martha had no family and that no one ever visited her from the outside, she arranged for Martha to begin writing to Eileen and her sister, who were unmarried and childless. The extreme importance that Martha attaches to this story is not difficult to understand. Not only did the incident garner her rare and precious praise at the time, but it helped establish her first link to the outside world after many years at Pacific. Martha has met Eileen and her sister on rare occasions through the years, and she still corresponds with Eileen, although less frequently now because of Eileen's ill health. Martha also lists as friends and corresponds with: one of her two major benefactors from the past, the social worker who obtained Martha's birth records and who has since moved from the area; and two relatives of the second benefactor, who died a few years ago.

Toward the top of her list of friends, Martha also includes her pastor and the church secretary, Jeanette, for whom she volunteers in the church office. In fact, when Martha was asked in 1982 whom she felt closest to of all the people she knew, Martha named Jeanette. Although Martha often refers to these two people as friends and says that she can rely on them for help, Jeanette seems to know very little about Martha other than in the context of their work together at the church, and Martha's relationship with her pastor is purely in his professional capacity. Jeannette's contact with Martha outside of working together seems to be limited to taking Martha out to dinner on her birthday and perhaps getting together during holidays. For instance, last year Jeannette and her mother took Martha with them to a Christmas pageant.

The last person on Martha's list is Lily, an 86-year-old woman who is the only person with whom Martha visits regularly outside of those she sees in the context of church or her volunteer work. Due to her age, Lily has difficulty getting around, and Martha worries about her and helps her by bringing items that Lily needs so that she will not have to go out for them. Martha also describes Lily as lonely, as Martha herself is, and she visits Lily to provide company for her.

Like many people, Martha tends to notice when others are in need in ways with which she can identify, and even sometimes to project her feelings on to others. In some instances, she can be quite perceptive and generous. Martha's comments about interacting with Senior Meals recipients when she occasionally works the delivery route provide a good example:

> The people with Senior Meals, I talk to them and they say that we are the only ones that they see. A lot of them are always up and around, waiting for their dinner with a smile, and they says, "Oh, you people are so good to us, and we appreciate you people coming like this and helping us." On rainy days, they are so concerned about us, and on hot days. And I say, "Well, we help each other." I said, "People like you are the highlight of the day." And then they brighten up, and I say, "We help each other, you help us and we help you. You give us something to do and think about, and you people think about us and have something to do by looking forward to your dinner." So we help each other and there is a gleam in their eyes when I tell them that.

Martha herself is quite familiar with the need to feel useful and important, and she recognizes it among these elderly people. Martha also gets something from these interchanges. She has been able to console someone else who is at a disadvantage, and she can feel good about herself for being such a giving, unselfish, and good-hearted person.

Martha's lack of close interpersonal relationships has been created through the years by her great difficulty in relating to other people; she finds it difficult to initiate and sustain interaction with others. Although her generosity, as illustrated above, is often appreciated, it has only been a tolerant few who have been able to withstand the onslaught of her obsessive need.

Predictably, Martha has a poor self-image, even with her attempts to bolster it. For instance, she had been volunteering in the Senior Meals program for 5 years before she felt confident enough to join the church in whose basement she was working, even though she had received numerous invitations from other church members to do so. Martha says she feared that she was "not good enough" to join and that she might not be accepted. Another problem exists, especially among the older volunteers in the Senior Meals program. According to Martha, there is much discussion about families, past and present, and she frequently feels out of place because she has no family about which to talk.

Because Martha has difficulty directly initiating interaction, the typical pattern has been for someone to be drawn in by her helpless quality and her obvious need. When that person takes an interest in her and begins to do things for her, Martha reciprocates with extreme gratitude, including giving them small gifts or sending them cards. For instance, Martha presented one of her past fieldworkers with an indoor/outdoor thermometer on her second visit. At another time, Martha insisted on giving a different fieldworker a small datebook and some candy. Martha explained that sometimes these are things she has accumulated and kept for just such an opportunity. Both fieldworkers felt that Martha's gift-giving was especially notable because of her meager finances. Most people eventually get worn out or overwhelmed by the intensity of this interaction. When they attempt to establish some limits or, worse yet, to withdraw, Martha increases her subtle manipulation based on need and gratitude in an attempt to control the situation. The usual result is that people are pushed even further away. When Martha feels that the person is drawing away, she reverts to extreme irritability and outbursts of temper, sometimes refusing to be in the same room with the person. The result is that Martha is alone again. Such an incident was related by Jeanette, the church secretary. A woman, whom Jeanette describes as "very nice" and who had at one time "really cared about Martha," came into the church office while Martha was there working. Jeanette says that she heard a hissing noise and could not figure out what it was. The woman whispered that Martha had made the noise at her. Jeanette says that she was very surprised at Martha's behavior.

Although Martha tends to deny these episodes when they occur, or to blame other people by saying that they just do not understand her or that they are discriminating against her because of her hospital background, there is some indication that Martha is at least sometimes aware of her behavior. A rare example is provided by an incident that happened with a fieldworker on one of her last visits with Martha. However, two crucial pieces of background information are necessary to understanding Martha's behavior. First, during the previous visit, the fieldworker had told Martha that after the next visit, she would not be coming to see Martha as often as she had up to that point. This was an effort, probably easily identifiable to Martha, to begin the termination process. Second, during the coming week, Martha was facing a visit to the Social Security office to take care of some business there concerning her disability benefits. Martha does not like these visits to Social Security because of all the questions they ask. When the fieldworker arrived to see her, Martha was irritable and cross, and she tended to snap at the fieldworker when she tried to carry on a conversation with Martha. This behavior continued throughout nearly the entire visit. Finally, as the visit was drawing to a close, Martha apologized to the fieldworker for "acting funny sometimes," and explained, "Sometimes my mind doesn't act the way it should." Martha then attributed her behavior in this instance to the upcoming visit to the Social Security office.

One kind of relationship that has been completely lacking in Martha's life is any remotely romantic or sexual relationship with a man. She has never had a boyfriend or even displayed any desire to do so. She has indicated in the past that she is afraid of men, but she does not know of any reason for this except that she was cautioned when young to be wary of men. When asked about marriage, her standard refrain through the years has been, "I just don't think I'd work out in a marriage." When asked to elaborate, she has said that she thought she would find marriage "confusing."

> Seems like there's too much competition in marriage and a lot of pressure and stress with bills and things. [Do you wish you had gotten married?] I've been around so many . . . when I was at the motel working, after I got out of the hospital, there were more unhappy married people than single people and they were always fuming and a-fighting, married people with children and all, and I think that turned me off.

As the case study of Martha in *The Cloak of Competence* pointed out, it is as if this entire part of life simply does not exist for her.

Although she has done some baby-sitting in the past, Martha does not seem particularly interested in babies or young children, and her inability to have children of her own does not seem to bother her. Martha's lack of conflict in this area, besides possibly being the result of her own childhood, may have a basis in the unusual circumstances surrounding her sterilization at Pacific State Hospital. For most of the other sample members, sterilization was performed on an otherwise healthy and functioning reproductive system, simply as a result of their patient status. For

Martha, the menorrhagia that initially brought her to Pacific in the first place was painful and frightening. The hysterectomy she underwent was performed in the context of fixing something wrong with her body and may have produced a different set of feelings than the standard sterilization did for other patients.

Daily Life

Martha's day-to-day life is lonely, and she is socially isolated, although certainly not to the extent that she was in the past. However, she still spends long stretches of the day alone. Martha is very organized about her time, as she is about many things. She has, in fact, structured her week to correspond to typical daily working hours just as people with "regular" jobs do, including being able to enjoy "sleeping in" on the weekends. In fact, due to a mix-up in scheduling, a fieldworker surprised Martha by showing up unexpectedly early one morning to keep an appointment for a visit. Martha was in the middle of doing her laundry. When the fieldworker apologized and commented that Martha appeared to be busy, Martha snapped, "I'm busy just like other people, you know. I don't just sit here and stare at walls!"

Martha usually gets up at 6:30 A.M. on weekdays. She has coffee and an English muffin for breakfast and then does various household chores. Four days a week, she goes to the church at 9:00 A.M. for the Senior Meals Program. Martha arrives early, usually even before the captain, and gets everything organized for the work crew. She gets the cartons out, counts out the tin trays that hold the food, gets out the portable stoves that keep the food warm, plugs in all of the stoves, sets out the coolers for the people who go to get the food from the local hospital that prepares it, and engages in many other tasks. When she is done, she frequently stands at the curb to see that no one parks in the spaces used by the delivery people. When the other volunteers arrive, Martha sees that everyone on the assembly line who packs the food into individual containers has the utensils and materials needed to do the jobs. She then takes her place on the assembly line to perform her assigned task, such as dishing up vegetables. Unless she is riding with one of the delivery volunteers to help deliver food, Martha makes sure that everything is cleaned up and stowed away, and that any leftover food is divided into "care packages" to send home with the volunteers. Because most of the volunteers are elderly and on fixed incomes, these care packages are quite welcome.

On her free days or in the afternoon, if she is not volunteering in the church office, Martha shops, does errands, or perhaps goes to visit Lily. She will also do any additional household chores. For the last few years, Martha has eaten a meal provided by the Senior Meals program for her midday meal. Her limited income qualifies her for the program and makes it a necessity that she take advantage of the low-cost meal. Martha was initially upset by the fact that rising prices made it necessary for her to become a recipient of the program, but she has become accustomed to this routine and now refers to lunch as her "one balanced meal of the day." In the past, Martha used to enjoy going grocery shopping as part of her daily routine, but she says that she no longer likes going to the grocery stores because she does not like to see "how much everything costs." Any shopping that Martha does for pleasure revolves almost exclusively around thrift stores.

Martha is always home and safely locked in by dark. Unlike many older people, who do this for safety's sake because they are getting older and the elderly are perceived as easier targets for criminals, Martha has always done this. Martha has always seen the world as a threatening place, and she does not take her physical safety for granted. However, the one incident in which she faced personal violence occurred during the daytime. In 1970, when she was 49 years old, she was approached and physically threatened by two men wearing stocking caps who stole her purse, which contained about $15:

> I was at the Goodwill and I had a package, got a few things there, then I went to the drug store and got a few things, and I saw these funny-looking characters in the . . . I saw these funny guys with these funny hats and things on, and I got to the corner and before I got across the street . . . "Give us your purse and money or we shoot you" or something. Oh, and I got mad and I threw it and threw all the stuff I had in the street screaming. [It must have been frightening.] Oh, it was an awful feeling. But they had these hooded hats. For a long time, everytime I seen somebody with these caps on . . . And everytime I saw somebody walking towards me, I had fear for the longest time.

Dinner for Martha consists of a diet chosen from the vast assortment of prepared or instant foods available today. In the past, she used to cook meals for herself "from scratch," including a variety of fresh vegetables. However, she now says:

> They came out with so many instant foods . . . I like the easy way. Cooking fresh stuff takes too long, where frozen, you put it in the pan, and you have it in 10 minutes. Lots of times, I fix myself a grilled cheese sandwich and french fries. That's easy to cook—I like the easy things.

During the early evening, Martha frequently sleeps for about 3 hours and then gets up and watches television until about midnight before returning to bed. Martha likes sitcoms, such as *The Golden Girls, Facts of Life*, and reruns of *Three's Company*, as well as the nighttime version of *Wheel of Fortune*. (Martha never watches daytime television because "there's too much else to do.") She dislikes violent programs, and although she usually watches the news, she complains that it is always the same. One interesting observation that Martha makes about the news is that over and over through the years, people, including politicians, keep getting into trouble for their activities, but nothing much seems to happen to them, "while people like me get locked up and their freedom taken away from them, with locked doors and bars for windows."

Martha also occasionally watches educational television, and she particularly enjoys programs such as National Geographic specials or anything to do with animals:

> I watched a good program Sunday night. Called "The Elephant." It's an elephant you find all over Taiwan. And showed the children and all that they did. I think it was Taiwan, some foreign country, and this elephant went all over, from one place to another. Very fascinating it was . . . I'd like to see it again. . . . It was kind of fascinating. It showed boating and everything. Taiwan? [Could be. Thailand?] That's what it was. [Do you know where Thailand is?] In another country, clear across the country.

Martha, in fact, loves animals in general, and on her occasional shopping trips will include a nearby pet store as one of her stops. One restaurant in the area, where others have taken Martha to eat on occasion, is a particular favorite of Martha's because it has a pond nearby, complete with ducks she can feed. Martha slips into more childlike and enthusiastic behavior around animals, leading one fieldworker to theorize that perhaps it is because animals offer more direct and unqualified affection than do people.

Other than television, Martha does not have many evening activities. She has no hobbies, unless one considers her obsessive cleaning as such. She does read the newspaper, and an occasional "house" magazine such as *McCalls* or *Woman's Day*. In the past, Martha did have reading material'visible in her apartment, mostly books she had purchased at thrift stores, including a medical reference book in which she sometimes used to look up any problems she might have. However, these books have been packed away and are no longer visible. This may be due to the increasing failure of Martha's eyesight. It is difficult to evaluate how well Martha reads because her sight is so bad at present that she must hold reading matter almost against her nose to see it, and she therefore reads very slowly.

Martha says she has problems in the evening if there are no good television programs to keep her interest, and she can find nothing else to do. Because of her need "to keep hands and mind busy," and not to let her "fearful feelings" come to the surface, she will sometimes end up pacing her apartment on these occasions until she is tired enough to sleep.

Competence

Although Martha has difficulty with interpersonal relationships and loneliness, she is very competent in many other areas of her life. She handles all of her own money, and for many years has had a checking account. She takes care of all of her own bills and has had trouble only once. Several years ago, the telephone company billed her for numerous long-distance telephone calls that she did not make. She contacted the telephone company herself and successfully negotiated having the calls removed from her bill. She says that her telephone is very important to her because she lives alone, and she did not want to take any chances that it might be removed if she could not pay her bill. Martha is extremely frugal and knows how to make her money stretch as far as possible. She takes advantage of senior citizen discounts, thrift stores, special sales, and anything else that will help make her money last. One of Martha's benefactors started Martha on the habit of saving a little money for security when Martha first was released from Pacific, and Martha probably has some money saved for an emergency, but she refuses to discuss this with anyone. When Martha first applied for financial assistance years ago, she had about $1800 saved through the prompting of her benefactor, but she was told that she had too much to be considered for assistance. To Martha, this money represented some little security for her, but she had to dip into it before she could receive any sort of help. Today, she simply refuses to discuss the entire matter except to say that she has a little saved, but not enough to prevent her from receiving her disability payments.

Martha can also deal with "the system." She takes care of all business concerning her disability payments, and she knows which agencies to contact if she needs specific help. She usually does not discuss this with anyone else until after the fact. When Martha decided more than 10 years ago that she needed activity to keep her busy and to prevent her from becoming depressed, she started out by making informal contacts with people and trying to help them out in their homes. However, this became "confusing" according to Martha, because she was going different places all the time. She finally went to City Hall to inquire about more organized forms of volunteer work, and they sent her to Senior Meals. The success with which she handles her work there is another demonstration of her competence.

Martha also shows intelligence in many areas. She is keenly observant, as some of her statements quoted in this chapter prove. She has a good memory, especially for numbers and frequently for names as well. Martha shows a startling knowledge of the informal history of the area where she lives. She can frequently recount the history of buildings and sometimes whole blocks in terms of the businesses that have been located there. She also remembers the family histories of numerous people whom she has known throughout the years, including information about their children and grandchildren.

Martha reads a daily paper and can do a creditable job of discussing current events, although her interest runs toward the more sensational and "gossipy" news items. For instance, she was aware of the contretemps involving Gary Hart and Donna Rice that cost Hart his bid for the presidency, and she has followed the misfortunes of Jim and Tammy Bakker, but she was not knowledgeable about the Iran-Contra scandal, which was being covered by the media during the same general time period. Although she is interested in current events, some of them national in scope, Martha is not registered to vote. She maintains that her right to vote was denied her while she was institutionalized at Pacific State Hospital, and even though she understands that she is now eligible to register and vote, she stubbornly refuses to do so. Her attitude seems to be that if she was not allowed to do so then, she refuses to do so now.

Martha does tend to be suspicious of people. Although this may further interfere with her already difficult social skills, it has prevented people from taking advantage of her. She is also quite capable of speaking up for herself when she is pushed far enough.

> I just hold things in so long and then all of a sudden I burst out. When you keep all bottled up, then all of a sudden [you] say, "Why me? Because I'm by myself, why me?" and I feel like people are ripping me off and taking advantage of me. [Do you feel like people are taking advantage of you very often?] No, but when they are, I flare up at it. Because sometimes if you don't speak up, if you stay bottled and don't speak up, you never get nowhere. They just take you for granted.

There is only one known instance of someone taking advantage of Martha to the point that she was forced to ask for outside help. A few years ago, Martha made the decision to move to a new apartment when her rent was increased by $20 per month. In the process of hurriedly arranging a new apartment, Martha got mixed up with an unscrupulous landlord and agreed to take an apartment that she had only had a chance to see through the window on the door. The landlord refused to let her see the inside of the apartment until she had paid the first and last month's rent and a $300 security deposit. Among the papers that she signed was one that stated that everything in the apartment was accepted by her as in working order. When Martha finally took possession of the apartment, she found everything a filthy mess and discovered that the stove and refrigerator did not work. On top of everything else, she had spent all the money she had in order to make the move, and she did not have any money left for food. Martha was very upset, and she talked about the problem with some of the people at her church. When her pastor heard what had happened, he contacted the landlord and forced him to fix the broken appliances and see that everything in the apartment worked. Other people at the church helped Martha fix up her apartment and took her to a program that helped her with food so that she could make it through the month. However, this is the only incident of something like this happening to Martha. She is usually very careful about her business dealings. In her haste to move, she apparently made decisions with less care than she normally would have exercised. Martha carefully watched and waited for about 2 years, until she saw that her former apartment was again vacant and moved back into it.

It is interesting that Martha has lived in this same apartment, where she currently resides, three different times. She moved into it for the first time about 1972. Approximately 5 years later, at the suggestion of her friend Eileen, Martha moved into a security building organized for senior citizens, where she lived for about 3 years. Although at 56 years old Martha was still below the age limit for this facility, she qualified by her disability status. The reasons for Martha wanting to leave at the end of 3 years are not clear. Martha says that all the locks on doors and security features reminded her of the hospital, and they bothered her so much that she decided to leave. Others who lived and worked there say that Martha had difficulty getting along with some of the tenants and decided to move out. Whatever the reasons, Martha suddenly decided that she wanted to leave. She apparently did not discuss her intentions with any of the people she has named as those she could rely on for help, all of whom have stated that if they had known, they would have tried to talk her out of this plan. Their perception was that Martha was both safer in case of illness or accident and less isolated and lonely living in the center. By the time that Martha informed anyone of her decision to leave, she had already ascertained that her former apartment was again for rent, and she promptly moved back into it. Martha lived there for about 2 years until the incident discussed above involving the rent increase occurred. Her most recent tenure has lasted approximately 3 years, and Martha says she is glad to be back where she is and she does not intend to move again. Her repeated returns would indicate that, for whatever reasons (its size, the accessibility of the bus stop, its proximity to her church, the privacy it affords), this apartment is Martha's preferred home.

CONCLUSION

There are some areas of Martha's life that seem to have deteriorated slightly within the last 10 years. However, this deterioration seems to be happening for reasons having nothing to do with Martha's competence.

Her grooming was described 10 years ago as somewhat better than it is today, especially in terms of her hair and clothing, but with prices rising faster than her meager income, there is less money for anything other than necessities. Martha's diet was also somewhat better in the past, with more fresh fruits and vegetables, but her use of prepared and instant foods is probably typical of many Americans who have sacrificed freshness for convenience. The last area in Martha's life that shows a decline is the number of her long-term relationships that still exist. Many of these people are older than Martha, and at age 67, she is slowly losing them to death or as they move away when they retire. All of the things described above are typical of older Americans, and in these Martha is no different from others. In fact, Martha's "differentness" may be diminishing relative to others in her age group. It is, after all, not perceived as unusual for an elderly, eccentric woman to live alone.

Martha is also no different from many other elderly people in her fears for the future. Martha worries that age will bring on helplessness so that she cannot care for herself and that she may lose her hard-won freedom. In Martha's case, this fear is particularly poignant when seen in the light of what she says has always been her greatest fear: "that somebody's going to grab me and put me back in the hospital."

Although Martha's fear of becoming helpless as she ages is common among older people, it is exacerbated by her own personal experience. Most of the other volunteers with whom she works at the Senior Meals program are older than Martha, and many of them are ailing. Some have spouses who are in even worse condition, and there is considerable conversation concerning health and aging among the volunteers. Thus Martha is confronted on an almost daily basis with the meaning and consequences of advancing old age. Also, Martha spent considerable time helping and caring for one of her original benefactors, on whom Martha was extremely dependent when she was released from Pacific State Hospital. This woman had become old, helpless, and senile. She had lost much of her memory and was unable to do very much for herself. She was, however, apparently cognizant enough to realize that she was having difficulty, because for a long time she asked Martha not to tell anyone. Martha was caught in the middle. She thought that her friend should have more help, but her feelings of loyalty demanded that she honor the woman's wishes. The woman eventually died, which was quite difficult for Martha. Given her experiences, it is no wonder that Martha's reflections on her future are vague. When asked about her feelings and plans for the future, Martha replied, "I don't really think about it." She says that she does not make plans because she has learned that when she makes plans, she usually has to break them, so it is better not to make them in the first place. Martha deals with her feelings about the future by engaging in here-and-now activity through which she feels that she is making some sort of productive contribution to other people's lives.

The goal of being independent and productive has always been very important to Martha. When she was asked the hypothetical question, "If you could change anything you wanted about your life, what would you change?" Martha answered:

> That will never be. Just keep on wishing you had the chance, wishing I had the chance. And then trying to get a job, a paying job, everybody turned me away and made me feel like a ex-convict, not wanting to give me a chance. And I wish I had the chance of going to school and learning skills, so I could have had a job and not have to be taken care of.

Martha has worked very hard through the years to increase her competence and to build an independent life for herself. She has accomplished more than probably even she herself understands. Although Martha was initially very dependent on benefactors after her release from Pacific State Hospital, she openly acknowledges her extreme gratitude for the help they gave her. In perhaps the truest sense of reciprocity with her benefactors, Martha has gone on to develop an independent life in which she no longer needs someone to help her run it. She has truly made use of the help that was given to her.

Part II

$\mathbf{T}$he following chapters are about three developmentally disabled adults, Hilda, Elaine, and Sam, who are over the age of 50. They receive services as persons with mild mental retardation, although their IQ scores range from the mid-70s to the low 80s. Elaine and Hilda live together as roommates, and Sam lives in a "retirement hotel," a board-and-care facility for senior citizens, where he is the only resident with developmental disabilities. Sam visits Hilda and Elaine most Saturday afternoons, and, although Hilda is his "girlfriend," he enjoys the company of both women.

Hilda, Elaine, and Sam each began to live independently relatively late in life, after one or both parents died. Hilda and Elaine had previously lived at home with their families; Sam had lived most of his adult life in an institution for people with developmental disabilities while maintaining ties with his family, whom he visited periodically. All three blossomed late in life when they finally began to live on their own and work at TRM, a sheltered workshop for people with developmental disabilities. By their own accounts, their lives became richer, more interesting, and more satisfying, in spite of the traumatic circumstances that pushed them toward greater independence. Recently, however, all three have begun to experience mild problems in maintaining the routines they had come to enjoy. These problems are related to aging and to the changing policies of social service agencies that touch their lives. Nonetheless, these three people have so far adapted successfully to the new challenges they face, and they continue to look forward to the future with considerable optimism.

One important change that took place during this period concerned TRM, the central focus of Elaine, Hilda, and Sam's lives since they began to live independently. Recently, the workshop was moved from a site that was close to their homes to one much farther away, which requires several buses to reach. The public transportation system in the area is poor, and the change meant that these three people, each of whom has mild physical limitations, had to spend more time, energy, and money getting to and from work. At first, they handled the change with confidence and aplomb, being quite adept at taking city buses and proud of their ability to do so. However, daily transportation was increasingly taxing, and they accordingly reduced some of their other activities, especially as their various physical limitations, which have increased with advanced age, became more acute. Eventually, new arrangements were made for them. Hilda and Elaine were consigned to the workshop van for transport to and from work, something they had previously resisted because they enjoy taking buses. Sam, who is several years older, was retired from the workshop and assigned to a senior day-care center closer to his home.

The most serious change at the workshop in recent years concerns TRM's management of their employees with developmental disabilities. These changes were mandated at federal and state levels and are implemented with Regional Center cooperation. They are aimed at increasing worker productivity and, ultimately, at "mainstreaming," the current focus of "normalization" policy. It is hoped that the most productive workers can be phased out of the workshop and into competitive employment, initially under a "supported work" program. Correspondingly, the workshop has phased out most of the extra-curricular activities that used to make TRM seem a bit like a school: classes in art, dance, exercise, food preparation, hand calculator use, and current events, as well as occasional field trips. Hilda, Elaine, and Sam greatly enjoyed these activities and regret their cessation. Instead, the shop has become more like a genuine factory, with time clocks and time cards, alternating shifts, briefer breaks, more mechanized assembly lines, more performance pressure on workers, and deafening noise levels. Whereas the workshop clients used to suffer boredom during occasional "down time," when there was no contract work available, more recently, a major government job contract has brought an abundance of work and the pressures and health hazards that go with it, as well as increased pay rates and the presence of some co-workers who are not developmentally disabled.

Hilda, Elaine, and Sam each have mixed feelings about the increased industrialization of their workplace. They all appreciate less down time, which leaves them bored, restless, and even depressed. (The government contract did not do away with down time altogether, in spite of initial staff optimism.) They also appreciated the new jobs, especially those they perceived as challenging or prestigious, rather than the "busy work" requiring no skill whatsoever that they are given in slow periods. As has been noted among workshop employees elsewhere, they have a keen sense of the relative status of various tasks. Self-esteem is closely tied to job performance, and like anyone else, they feel best when they are confident that they are doing a good job and earn praise accordingly. Fatter paychecks have been an unquestionable boost to their morale as well.

On the negative side, Hilda, Elaine, and Sam are unanimous in their belief that their relations with staff became more brusque and impersonal and that their opportunities for socializing with staff and other clients at TRM became fewer. The increased work pressures made them more aware of and anxious about their limitations, especially physical ones such as lack of balance, coordination, and speed. Their negative perception of TRM as it is today and nostalgia about how it used to be are especially acute because they each began at TRM when previous policies and management were more caregiving-oriented and thus helpful in assisting them through a major, traumatic transition point in their lives.

These changes have posed special challenges to Elaine, Sam, and Hilda because of their advanced ages. TRM management policies are aimed primarily at a young workforce. When research began with Hilda, Elaine, and Sam in 1985, there were only 13 clients at the workshop over the age of 50. Since then, a few others have reached that age, but at least one person retired in addition to Sam, at least one woman died, and others left for various reasons. By May 1988, TRM reported having only 5 clients over the age of 55. Although new, and presumably younger, clients are recruited into TRM all the time, there are few precedents for dealing with aging employees.

One final aspect of TRM's influence on the lives of Hilda, Elaine, and Sam deserves mention. As Regional Center clients, they attend annual Individual Program Plan (IPP) meetings, where goals for improvement are discussed with counselors and family members. The meetings are held at TRM, so the client's TRM counselor presides and generally has the most extensive list of recommended goals and data on performance. (Since Sam retired from TRM, his IPP meetings have been held at his residence.) The client's Regional Center caseworker also attends, but this is one of the few times the caseworker has any contact with the client, thereby making the caseworker dependent on TRM for most relevant information. If the client has an independent living counselor (Hilda and Elaine do; Sam does not), that person also attends, since he or she is vendored through Regional Center and sometimes visits the client at TRM. Clients' family members may act as advocates at these meetings, but this role is balanced against the gratitude they feel for services received from TRM and Regional Center, services which considerably lighten their own burden of responsibility. For the most part, relatives use these meetings as opportunities to seek information from counselors, since this is one of the few occasions during the year that such contact is established and information exchanged.

Hilda, Elaine, and Sam look forward to their IPP meetings with positive anticipation, usually expecting a certain amount of praise, reassurance, and clearly stated direction. All three also see it as an opportunity to air certain concerns or complaints, which they do, though with considerable restraint, because they are mildly intimidated by the formal setting and authority figures who surround them there. In fact, their anticipation is always tinged with nervousness, almost as if it were a test. It is indeed a "rite of passage" each year, being held close to their birthdays, and they see the meeting as more or less certifying their competence for another year.

Hilda and Elaine come from relatively privileged backgrounds, and even Sam's family life and institutional experiences were relatively comfortable, so there has been some continuity throughout their transition to independent living, at least in terms of the standard of living they enjoy. The scale and pace of life in their community suits them. Their neighborhoods are reasonably safe, and the weather is mild, so they often go out in the evenings and on weekends. They live close to major bus lines and know the routes and schedules in great detail. There are plenty of malls and other shopping areas in close proximity, and they enjoy visiting these on a regular basis. They frequent nearby parks and social clubs, eat out regularly, and have even visitied libraries occasionally. (All three read and write.) All in all, they lead comfortable, active lives.

The relationship between Hilda, Elaine, and Sam is distinctly triadic, including some elements of a romantic triangle. At the workshop, they preferentially interacted more with each other than with the other clients during breaks. Of the clients over 50, these three are the most alike in alertness, social skills, and interests. They are intensely loyal to each other. Some TRM staff members even believed that they were becoming too dependent on each other's company and occasionally sought to separate them, but this never altered the basic strength of their relationship. Since leaving TRM, Sam's contact with Hilda and Elaine has been limited mostly to his visits on Saturdays and monthly dances at the local Salvation Army, but he continues to ask Hilda and Elaine for news about the workshop and staff, and the two women enthusiastically relay greetings back and forth between Sam and various people at TRM.

Each of these three persons exhibits a slightly different style of independence, attributable to differences in their disabilities and personal histories. It is important to keep in mind that they are still in the process of developing independent living skills, since none of them had the opportunity to live independently until late in life, within the last 10 years. As will be clear in the following chapters, the relative success of these three people in living independently has been based on their interdependence with each other and their liberal reliance on other people, mostly female, to help them in various ways. This is not the "rugged individualist" model of independence so often romanticized in American popular culture and in recent public policy debate, but it has been the key to a successful aging experience for them.

Hilda, Elaine, and Sam have achieved remarkable success at independent living in a relatively short period of time. Instead of a late-life crisis, they have experienced a renaissance. Indeed, their success so far, achieved so late in their lives, has given them a predominantly positive attitude towards aging. They all say that they anticipate the coming years will only bring more of the same satisfactions they enjoy now. They do not consider themselves old and barely recognized the category "retarded," seeing themselves instead as being selectively handicapped rather than generically different from the "normal" population.

Their optimism may not be completely realistic, considering the problems that could lie ahead in years to come, when their lives may once again become more constrained by increased physical disability and the social isolation often associated with aging in its later stages. However, their positive outlook may help them cope with present and future challenges. Their backgrounds have prepared them to actively and unself-consciously seek help from others in times of crisis, rather than withdrawing into loneliness and depression as many nonretarded seniors do when their faculties wane and their lives contract.

The chapters that follow describe how Elaine, Hilda, and Sam have achieved independence, the problems they face, and the satisfactions they enjoy. Particular attention is paid to their uniquely symbiotic relationship and the special benefits and strains this has contributed to their lives.

7

"We Were Lucky to Find Each Other."
ELAINE GOLD AND HILDA MUELLER

by Hilarie Kelly

As roommates, Hilda Mueller's and Elaine Gold's lives have become remarkably intertwined, in some ways resembling the close relationship of a married couple. Indeed, their success at "independent living" is largely based on interdependence and complimentarity. For this reason, their lives are described here in a single chapter.

Elaine is developmentally disabled, with an IQ in the high 70s, but this is not immediately apparent to the casual observer. She is a bright, articulate 58-year-old woman, energetic and sociable and still fairly youthful in her appearance and demeanor. Pictures of Elaine in her teens and twenties show a very pretty young woman, and she is still attractive. To someone meeting her on the street or in the supermarket, she would appear to be an average, casually dressed, middle-aged woman. Her recent decision to use a walking cane alters this image only slightly.

What is most notable about Elaine is that she loves to talk. Elaine is remarkably garrulous with her roommate Hilda, her mother (through daily phone calls), and assorted counselors, workshop staff, medical professionals, and people in the service industry, such as bus drivers and waiters. She occasionally strikes up conversations with strangers (most often women) just to pass the time of day while waiting at a bus stop, sitting in a doctor's office, or shopping at the mall. Once Elaine warms to a topic, however, she becomes preoccupied with long-winded narrations of her own experiences and begins to break many of the rules of good social conversation. Although Elaine is exceptionally articulate and has few problems with vocabulary, pronunciation, grammar, and syntax, there are some properties of Elaine's style of discourse, such as the amount and quality of detail, coherence, story structure, and narrative performance, which hint at mental impairment.

Elaine drones on in a conversation, often ignoring what others have to say and frequently interrupting with comments that are transparently designed to bring the conversation back to her. She sometimes shifts abruptly from topic to topic, taking for granted that her references to people, places, and events known to her are also understood by the listener. She ignores or is unaware of subtle cues that listeners may not understand or are losing interest, and she sometimes continues talking even as they walk away. The more intensely interested she is in a topic, the more convoluted and incoherent her conversation becomes, although it is clear that Elaine herself is keeping track of the point. The impression is not one of lack of mental integration, but rather a lack of ingrained social/conversational skills. It is by no means certain that Elaine fails to exercise these skills because of an organic, neurological malfunction related to her disability. It is just as likely that certain aspects of Elaine's socialization produced this behavior. A casual observer, then, might not conclude that Elaine's obsessive, voluble self-concern indicates mental retardation; it could as easily be interpreted as some other mental or emotional disturbance. But once the observer is clued in to Elaine's oddness, subtle physical details come into focus. Her facial structure is vaguely unusual, even slightly unnatural looking, as a consequence of childhood strabismus (problem with eye focusing, as in cross-eyes) and the surgery to correct it. Elaine says that she also had cosmetic surgery on her nose and cheeks. She has a very mild speech problem that derives from the unusual way she holds her mouth when she speaks. Her lips are slightly slack, and she moves them only a little while speaking, causing her to mumble. However, she can correct the mumbling when she is reminded to do so.

Elaine talks compulsively about her multiple medical problems, which she describes in alarming detail. Indeed, she makes her conditions sound so extreme or bizarre that this further reinforces the impression that there is something "different" about Elaine. Her complaints include some conditions that have been medically diagnosed, such as:

varicose veins
chronic nosebleeds
chronic earaches
chronic eyelid inflammations (blepharitis, sties, and chalazions)
thyroid deficiency (goiter)
high cholesterol count (mild)
minor vision impairment requiring glasses
penicillin and sulfa allergies (wears identification bracelets)
mild foot problems (e.g., toe webbing), surgically corrected
chronic dental problems requiring extractions and a bridge, dentures

Other complaints have been much harder to diagnose definitively, such as:

arthritis
bone injury in right arm (from blow by father in childhood)
failing eyesight (denied by doctors)
neuro-muscular condition (proximal dystonia—irregular walking, head twitch, hand shakes)
back spasms

The last three complaints have occurred recently, coincident with Elaine's attempts to protect and redefine her position at TRM. These and some of the other complaints will be discussed later in the context of how they appear in her life. Taken together, Elaine's conversational quirkiness, the obsessiveness and anxiety reflected in her narratives, and her numerous physical complaints, combine elements of mental retardation, mental illness, and physical disability.

Another conversational giveaway that Elaine is not entirely "normal" is her constant reference, without explanation, to the ephemeral "they" who direct her life. "They want me to be very careful," she has said, but she typically fails to state explicitly whether "they" refers to TRM staff, counselors, or doctors, or whether "they" includes her mother. The listener may have no idea what she is talking about because she has failed to precede her sentence with the necessary contextual background. Elaine's descriptions and explanations of what she does are often phrased and rationalized in terms of what others tell her to do or not do, even if such instructions were never, in fact, given. Elaine often infers the desires of authorities in her life to garner approval for her actions. Only occasionally does Elaine say that she did something purely on her own initiative, and then it is only when she feels certain that her independent actions would be approved *a priori* by others. The "others" who are most important to her (besides Hilda, with whom she is very close) are figures of authority in her life, such as workshop staff, her independent living counselor, her Regional Center case worker, various doctors, her mother, and even this researcher.

Elaine's unelaborated use of pronouns, especially "they," in conversation communicates something important about her learned social role as an adult with developmental disabilities. She sees herself as lacking primary control over her own life, at least in many important areas. Elaine is not convinced that she has the right to control her own life, nor does she unambiguously want to do so. She actively seeks the advice of others, even if she is selective about accepting it and highly manipulative in soliciting and citing such opinions. For example, Elaine frequently says "we," usually referring to herself and her roommate, Hilda, when explaining choices for which she does not want to take full responsibility.

> Elaine could not bear to give up the four-egg omelette loaded with cheese that she ate at the coffee shop every Sunday, in spite of the fact that her doctor had advised her not to eat more than two eggs per week because of her high cholesterol count. She was torn between immediate gratification (the omelette) and following the advice of authorities. She therefore asked Hilda, "What do you think, Hil? Do you think I could have it just once a week? Do you think it would hurt, Hil?" In her compliant but ambiguous fashion, Hilda answered, "I guess it wouldn't hurt. I don't know." Elaine ate the omelette, explaining later, "We thought it would be okay."

Elaine manufactures similar questionable endorsements from her mother, her counselors, her doctors, and me to add to her arsenal of rationalizations for things that she wants to do, but that she knows might draw criticism.

That it does not always occur to Elaine to specifically identify the people behind the pronouns is also an indication of how routine-oriented her life is. It does not seem to occur to her that her listener might not share in that same routine. Routine, in fact, is very important to Elaine. By her own admission, she becomes unduly "emotional," "nervous," and "anxious" when any kind of change, large or small, threatens her sense of security. Her most common response to a change in routine is to complain incessantly, often in tones of outrage disproportionate to the circumstances. Like many other people, retarded or not, who feel they have minimal control over their own lives, she is highly manipulative of others. Often, her manipulations are aimed at winning reassurance, security, and support. If thwarted, she sometimes has tantrums: she throws things, destroys them by deliberately "dropping" or tearing them, hides, stomps her feet, shouts, whines, sulks, and makes impulsive or even threatening gestures.

In summary, Elaine has a volatile and dependent personality. Her two most characteristic features are a need for constant attention and reassurance followed by profound anxiety if she does not get them. However, Elaine is also willful and rebellious, expressing her needs with a determination and persistence that under some circumstances can be admirable. Her greatest strengths are sociability, vivacity, articulateness, and a strong sense of identity. However, these strong points can also become her greatest weaknesses when they are expressed as cloying dependence, pushiness, querulousness, and self-centeredness. Her considerable intelligence is frequently dissipated in the interests of short-term manipulation rather than long-term problem-solving. Often, when Elaine is most intent on obtaining the attention and security she craves, she ends up alienating others and reinforcing her own anxiety. Fortunately, she is usually clever and sensitive enough to stop short of burning out her most important, instrumental relationships. In that sense, Elaine walks a tightrope.

In contrast, Hilda is quite different from Elaine. Her parents were immigrants from Germany. In her speech, Hilda often substitutes "w" for "v," reflecting the German language she spoke in her childhood and still understands to some small extent. Hilda often mentions her "strict" upbringing, and her high standards of proper behavior and good manners are indications of her family's strong sense of values. Hilda's conversation is littered with popular bromides referring to "correct" behavior, such as "It's better to give than receive," "It's better to be a good listener than a good talker," and "A penny saved is a penny earned." Although the use of these clichés may indicate a certain lack of original thought, they nonetheless accurately reflect the values that Hilda lives by and holds dear. To Hilda, proper behavior means not only following certain rules, but also showing great consideration for others. Following this principle is the linchpin of Hilda's self-esteem, which is quite high. If one word could describe Hilda's character, it would be integrity.

Hilda's physical appearance is not as "mainstream" as Elaine's. She has a flat, chinless face, tiny eyes, and a negligible nose. (She and Elaine, whose face was surgically modified, affectionately call each other "button-nose.") Some muscular slackness is evident in Hilda's facial expression, especially around her mouth. Her pale brown hair is wispy, and she prefers it worn very short in a "pixie" cut, giving her head a slightly pointed look. Unlike Elaine, whose short hair was dyed various shades of red for a number of years to hide the gray of aging, Hilda has firmly decided to let her hair gray naturally, and she refuses Elaine's suggestions that she dye it. Hilda is short, and as the years have passed, her occasions to exercise have diminished, so she has become rather rounded, especially through her midsection.

Her appearance, however, is not entirely unattractive. She has unusually dainty hands and feet, and she considers them to be her most attractive features; she is even slightly vain about them. The delicate and graceful way she holds her hands and her elegant way of sitting and crossing her legs contrasts with the coordination problems and tremors that she has had since birth and struggles to control. Hilda eats very slowly because her hands shake so much that it is sometimes awkward even to bring a cup of coffee to her lips without spilling a few drops. She worries about her sense of balance and is easily startled by any sudden movements around her, sometimes appearing to be in imminent danger of toppling over. Indeed, she has fallen several times, resulting in minor gashes about her head and, once, in a broken hip.

In spite of her handicaps, Hilda is notably alert and bright, although this is not always immediately evident to others. She attended public schools as a child and did reasonably well in special education classes, receiving certificates of completion at each graduation. Like Elaine, she remembers that she found math especially difficult. Hilda enjoyed reading, something she often does on her own even now. She has always had a fondness for homemaker magazines, her favorite being one her mother used to read. When Hilda and Elaine visit the library, Hilda ends up picking out many of the books for both of them, because Elaine constantly asks her opinions on which ones to get. Hilda picks well-written dramatic novels similar to ones she read in school and in her family home, rather than romances or action stories, which are Elaine's preferences. Although Elaine seems to have little patience for actually finishing a book and seems to begin them mainly to please others (such as a researcher who encouraged them to utilize the library more often), Hilda not only finishes hers, but is also able to give a coherent and lively précis of each.

Hilda's IQ is in the low 80s, compared to Elaine's score in the high 70s, and she even tested higher than Elaine on her verbal abilities. Given her facility for reading and writing this may not seem surprising, except that Hilda is not nearly as talkative as the garrulous Elaine. Elaine may talk a blue streak, but she clearly has difficulty maintaining her attention span in noninteractional settings. This may explain why her performance on IQ tests is lower than Hilda's, although her anxiety at being tested may also have been a factor.

Hilda was much better than Elaine at keeping a diary when I asked that they do so. Elaine kept hers for 5 months, but Hilda managed 9 months before they told me that the exercise had become boring and they would like to quit. Hilda continued with hers right up to the time she told me she wanted to stop; Elaine repeatedly said she was "working on it" to elicit my approval, but she evidently was not. Self-discipline and methodical dedication to a task is characteristic of Hilda. Her entries were much richer in detail and more varied than Elaine's, even though her writing contained more errors in spelling and grammar. The following two examples of entries for the same day, the first from Hilda's diary and the second from Elaine's, demonstrate this point:

> She [the researcher] came in our apartment to pick us up in her car. Then she drove over to Sam's Place to him up [sic] in her car. Then she took us out for dinner. We enjoyed it very much. Then she drove over to City Hall in her car. We took a walked with her. Then we took the Elevored up to the second floor to hear zoning committee. Then we left City Hall. We went to her car. She drove over to Seven-11 to get two containers of Ice Cream and cookies. Then she drove over to our apart-

ment. I unlocked the apartment door and we came to celebrate Sam's birthday. We had root beer, Ginger Snap, and Ice Cream. We enjoyed it very much. Then H. took Sam home in her car.

It was H. for dinner. Then we went to the City Hall of [she gives the name of the wrong city]. Then we had some of the favorite Ice Cream.

Hilda's entries in her diary are longer than most of her conversations. "I'm not a talker," she admits frankly. In fact, when pressed with direct questions, Hilda often replies with one-word answers, says, "I don't remember" while holding her hand up to her forehead to indicate mild distress, or complains, "I'm a little tired now." Taped interviews with Hilda alone reflect how excruciating such imposed, one-to-one conversations can be for both parties. In one interview, after a long stream of attempts to ask questions that would evoke some conversational response, with each question followed by the briefest and dullest of answers revealing little about what Hilda really thought, I asked Hilda if she was comfortable talking with me. She replied, "Yes. I'm just a little restless now. I was going to do some vacuuming." Hilda does not have the same insatiable need for conversation and attention that Elaine exhibits. In fact, Hilda has stated often that she likes to be alone at times, unlike Elaine, who has absolutely no desire to do so.

Hilda's sister Ada also reports having difficulties in brief, highly structured conversational encounters aimed at eliciting information from Hilda. This reticence may simply be Hilda's way of handling what she perceives as an asymmetrical and intrusive interchange. Elaine, by contrast, participates in interviews enthusiastically. Elaine typically appeals for attention and approval by sharing more detailed personal information than is requested, while Hilda is a much more intensely private person.

Basically, Hilda feels uncomfortable when put on the spot and does not enjoy being the focal point of attention. This is not really shyness on her part. Rather, she has a very strong sense of personal boundaries. This may even function to protect her self-esteem, given her awareness of her handicaps and her need for the help of other people. In informal and unstructured conversations, however, Hilda contributes regularly. This is especially true in Elaine's presence, whenever she can get a word in edgewise. In fact, her competitive instincts are often aroused by Elaine's single-minded domination of the floor, and she will bravely interrupt. Sometimes her comments are oddly mistimed, relating to a topic that had passed several minutes before, but this may be because of her difficulties in breaking into the conversation when Elaine is "on a roll." Hilda is also at something of a disadvantage because her voice is rather high and quavery, sounding like that of a much older woman. She speaks more haltingly than most people, with occasional breaks in odd parts of a sentence, suggesting that speech may not come fluidly to her. Nonetheless, Hilda can be quite persistent in making a point, and her voice carries better than Elaine's nasal mumbling, which dominates conversations primarily because it occurs in an unending stream.

Because of Elaine's unwillingness to leave Hilda's side, there was rarely an occasion to interview Hilda alone. Indeed, Hilda rarely converses with anyone without the mediating presence and active participation of Elaine, except when they are separated temporarily by their families, by doctors' appointments, or by their TRM jobs. Elaine still recalls with an exaggerated sense of outrage the time one of Hilda's independent living counselors locked Elaine out of the room while conducting business with Hilda. Elaine screamed, cried, pounded on the door, and called her mother to express her displeasure. Elaine sometimes so dominates conversations that she actually speaks *for* Hilda. For example, I once attempted to ask Hilda about her health, only to have Elaine immediately answer every question, in spite of the fact that I was directly addressing and maintaining eye contact with Hilda.

> Researcher (to Hilda):   What about your head?
> Elaine: Dr. P. has to do a follow-up on her.
> Researcher: What's that for, Hilda?
> Elaine: She had fallen up here at the step . . . And I didn't know what to do at first. I picked her up and brought her in and washed her, got something for her head and washed it down, but it didn't stop. . . .
> Hilda: It hit an artery.
> Researcher: So how is it now, Hilda?
> Elaine: Looks better.

It would be an overstatement, however, to say that Hilda necessarily dislikes Elaine's tendency to dominate a conversation. Although Hilda often advocates that people speak up for themselves, she herself may appreciate having the more voluble and articulate Elaine to keep the conversational ball rolling, thus allowing her to insert her own opinions occasionally while still maintaining her own sense of reserve. (The major exception is when Hilda is with Sam. She then prefers Elaine to keep out of the conversation and will compete furiously for Sam's attention by speaking more aggressively and through using body language, for example, by taking Sam's arm in hers.) Hilda and Elaine have become such adept conversational foils for each other that they sometimes complete each other's sentences:

> Researcher (to Hilda):   I like that outfit you have on now.
> Elaine: That's from . . .
> Hilda: Ada . . .
> Elaine: Ada.
> Hilda: . . . bought it.
> Researcher: Tell me what you need to buy again.

Elaine: She has to get this girl, Louise . . .
Hilda: . . . a present.

Hilda's long-term memory is not as good as Elaine's, but this does not prevent Elaine from constantly consulting Hilda to remind her who did what, when, and where. This can border on the ridiculous when Elaine asks Hilda about events having nothing to do with her or that took place outside her presence:

Researcher: When did you last see your doctor?
Elaine: I think it was . . . let's see, I think it was last Tuesday. Hil, when was it I saw Dr. P. last?
Hilda: Wednesday.
Elaine: Wednesday. We both had appointments that day.
Researcher: Dr. P.'s never told you what's wrong with your thyroid? Why do you have to take Synthroid?
Elaine: I don't think so. Wait, let me ask Hil. Hil, why did Dr. P. say I have to take Synthroid?
Hilda: I don't remember.
Elaine: You don't remember?!
Researcher: How would Hilda know?
Elaine: She was there.
Researcher: In the doctor's office with you? In the examining room?
Elaine: No. But I told her about it right after. I just don't remember.
Researcher: Why do you think she'd remember?
Elaine: She's my roommate. She's supposed to remember.

Elaine constantly uses Hilda as a kind of social secretary and memory bank, challenging Hilda's memory limitations, which are less serious in more recent time frames. Hilda often rises to the occasion, recalling the details requested or correcting Elaine:

Elaine: I got a card from the book store that says I'm a member of their book club, and I get 10- or 15-percent off on all books.
Researcher: Why didn't Hilda get one?
Elaine: I don't know. I think she didn't want one, she wasn't interested.
Hilda (interrupting in background): No. They didn't offer me one because I'm not a senior citizen.
Researcher: How old do you have to be to be a "senior citizen"?
Elaine: Oh, 58, 59. [This is her own age.] Hilda's 55.
Hilda: 54.
Elaine: Yah, so I got one but she didn't want one.
Hilda: No. They didn't offer me one.

Although Hilda sometimes becomes vexed at the constant questioning from Elaine, she also derives some satisfaction from being consulted and thus being able to demonstrate her knowledge. Hilda further functions as a kind of calendar keeper, dutifully reminding Elaine of upcoming events and obligations. Elaine often needs this service because she is so disorganized and scattered that she frequently does such things as make a doctor's appointment for the same day and hour that Rachel, their independent living counselor, routinely visits them every week.

Hilda's memory limitations should not be over-emphasized. When discussing events obliquely, rather than in response to direct questioning, Hilda can often remember significant details, even from the distant past. Hilda's occasional comments show that she is much more aware of current events and matters of practical relevance than Elaine, inspired in part by her television viewing and reading habits. For example, she correctly explained the word "consumer" to Elaine, as well as what a popular consumer advocacy television program is all about. Hilda is quite willing to talk at length under circumstances that are comfortable to her. When Hilda does speak, her conversation reveals more internal coherence and direction than Elaine's, which tends to ramble and go off on tangents.

LIVING ARRANGEMENTS

The modest apartment Hilda and Elaine live in is in an average but not inexpensive neighborhood. There are 12 units in the two-story building, and theirs is located on the bottom floor. It is a one-bedroom unit, with a living room that extends into a dining area next to a tiny kitchen. There is a small bathroom with a shower/tub and a sunny bedroom with a large closet. As one would expect with two people in a small apartment, the place is over-furnished and cluttered. This state is made worse by the fact that SSI regulations and Upward, the training program for independent living they both attended, encourage them each to acquire their own household effects, right down to the toilet paper, even if it means duplication. Hilda and Elaine are both competitive and imitative in this respect, something like siblings; if one buys a magazine, a sweatshirt, or a stuffed toy dog, then the other must too, often an exact duplicate. The resulting clutter is occasionally a cause for concern. Their empty suitcases (unused since they moved in) once came tumbling out of the top shelf of their over-stuffed closet and almost hit Hilda on the head. On another occasion, the clothing rod in the closet collapsed from the sheer weight of accumulated clothing, more than half of which belongs to Elaine, who is a more acquisitive and impulsive shopper than Hilda. The bathroom once became so clogged with duplicate toilet paper rolls, shampoos, conditioners, hairsprays, soaps, bubble bath, and lotions that for months neither woman would take her turn at cleaning this room.

The bedroom decor reveals a lot about Hilda and Elaine. There are twin beds, one against each of the side walls, each nestled into a corner of the room. The bed linens are a frilly, floral pink, purchased for them by Ada, Hilda's elder sister. Several stuffed animals are piled on each bed;

the women occasionally play with these dolls and always sleep with them. Each has pinned up, on the wall next to her bed, a varied assortment of birthday cards, pennants, certificates of accomplishment, and celebrity pictures. The decor is overwhelmingly adolescent. Elaine's presence dominates the room. On the small table next to her bed sits a lamp and a radio that she listens to in the morning and at night. At the other end of the room is her chest of drawers, covered with knickknacks, mail, and her television, which she is fond of watching from her bed. Hilda's smaller chest of drawers is squeezed in next to the closet, and it too is covered with Elaine's knickknacks.

Hilda presides over the living room, where she likes to stretch out on the couch and watch her own television, using a remote control device. The two women prefer different television programming; Elaine likes game shows, and Hilda prefers serial dramas and comedies. Hilda often dozes off in the living room and sometimes ensconces herself there in the middle of the night if she is having trouble sleeping, a frequent complaint that may partly reflect her desire for greater privacy. Next to the couch is a low, round table on which Hilda keeps her magazines and mail. At one end of the couch is Hilda's small, antique-style writing desk, covered with her knickknacks and correspondence. File boxes holding both women's financial records are stored under the desk.

The walls of the living room are decorated with original artworks, mostly donated by Elaine's relatives and, in one case, a mosaic made by Hilda. Across the room from the couch are two matched, upholstered chairs with a small telephone table, a lamp, and an ottoman in between. Whenever Elaine is in the living room she sits in one of these chairs, her feet propped up on the ottoman. She frequently uses the telephone, which is placed on the small table in between the chairs. On the wall behind one of the chairs is a tiny crucifix and a small card with a religious saying printed on it, put there by Hilda. Hilda is from a Lutheran background and Elaine is from a Jewish family, but neither is actively religious.

The kitchen is so small that there is barely enough room for two people at a time. The cupboard space is divided between them for their respective kitchen utensils, cutlery, and so forth, and for their separate grocery purchases. Hilda and Elaine keep the cupboard well-stocked with a good range of basic food items. Hilda does most of the cooking and cleaning for both of them, while Elaine's contribution is usually limited to setting the table. They always eat at the dining table. A list of rules for avoiding conflict, written by Elaine's former psychotherapist, is posted on the refrigerator, while a chart showing the proposed division of household chores is on the wall above the stove, and a letter showing the current rent, which they divide in half, is taped next to that.

The standard of cleanliness in their apartment is acceptable but sometimes problematic. An accumulation of dust and clutter frequently testifies to the low priority of housework in their lives. The kitchen especially suffers from such laxity. Dishes and utensils display a noticeable residue, and the women's tendency to leave food packages unsealed, produce and meat rotting in the refrigerator, and bags of trash waiting to be dumped sometimes aggravates a pre-existing cockroach problem. Poor ventilation further contributes to an occasional build-up of noxious smells. The two women notice these problems, but generally explain that they were "too tired" or "too busy" or unable due to minor physical complaints to keep up with the housework.

Housework is not a favorite activity for either woman, although Hilda is markedly more willing than Elaine. Housework figures prominently in Hilda's diary entries, in contrast to Elaine's, which almost never mention housework. Hilda's entries suggest not only that she does most of the housework, something that is verified through observation and interviews, but also that doing these tasks gives her a sense of satisfaction and competence. Perhaps this is why Hilda tolerates, if reluctantly, Elaine's routine avoidance of these chores. However, it should not be assumed that Hilda necessarily enjoys being solely responsible for the housework herself, or that she does it thoroughly. Some tasks remain undone for long periods, with both Hilda and Elaine stubbornly refusing to be the one to capitulate. There is a largely unspoken tug-of-war between them regarding who should be doing what chores on which day, leading one to neglect work if she feels the other might do it or if the other is not doing her share.

Hilda and Elaine do not appreciate criticism of their housework standards and tend to become defensive when the topic arises. They have each stated explicitly that, because they are now living independently, this should be their concern alone to work out between them. However, in 1988 they accepted an arrangement made by their independent living counselor to have a housecleaning service come every few months. Rachel, their independent living counselor, has recently devoted more attention to monitoring their household purchases to avoid clutter, and she has devised a check-off chart for housework, demanding they stay home on occasional Saturdays to complete their chores to her satisfaction.

FAMILY BACKGROUNDS

Elaine

Elaine was born in 1930 in New York of an upwardly mobile family. Her father was a dentist. Elaine's mother, Elizabeth—or Liz, as she prefers to be called—recalls that during the pregnancy, she and her husband were involved in a car accident, which she believes may account for Elaine's disability. It was her first pregnancy, and by her own account, she was terribly naive and inexperienced as a new mother. Her first concern about Elaine's development was that as a baby she was not eating well or gaining weight very rapidly. However, she had nothing to measure her child's development against, and the doctor made no specific diagnosis. It was not until Elaine entered school that Liz was told by a teacher that her child might need some special attention. Nonetheless, he admonished Liz to keep Elaine in regular schools. "Don't let anyone call your daughter retarded," she remembers him as saying. To this day, Liz does not use the word "retarded," preferring "disabled" or "handicapped."

Elaine was raised by a loving family that had encouragement from fairly enlightened authorities, and she attended regular schools, although she often had to take "remedial" classes and did poorly in some subjects, especially math. This "normal" yet supportive environment nurtured Elaine's verbal abilities and social skills, and prevented her from feeling segregated or stigmatized. (She claims she did not learn the meaning of "retarded" until middle age, when she enrolled in the Upward independent living skills program.) On the other hand, she was often indulged and sheltered by her family in ways that limited her independence. She was included in the lives of the nondisabled people around her, like her parents and their peers, but got used to receiving special, solicitous attention from those responsible for her. Her life was both secure and stimulating.

Elaine's family was well-off, sometimes had a maid, and often travelled, taking Elaine with them. Elaine recounts sampling sushi in Japan, where she admired Mt. Fuji; she recalls seeing Big Ben, the changing of the guard, and Westminster Abbey in London; and she still has pictures from a Caribbean cruise on her bedroom wall. "Where haven't I been?" she says with characteristic brashness and aplomb. Elaine accompanied her parents to restaurants and parties, a pretty girl with a good-looking, fashionable mother and a tall, handsome father. Those Camelot images still linger in her memory. Elaine was not left out of life's pleasures because of her disability—she was escorted through them instead.

The dynamics of Elaine's family were not without problems, however. Liz, somewhat dependent herself, was overwhelmed by the task of raising a child with Elaine's needs, and apart from occasional well-meaning advice and the accommodation of Elaine's educational needs by the public schools, the family did not receive any special assistance in coping with the stresses of raising a child with a handicap. She was frequently exasperated by Elaine's stubbornness and says, "She always knew how to get her way." Her husband, by contrast, demonstrated extraordinary patience with all children and was especially loving towards his daughter, who was the apple of his eye. With some relief, Liz deferred to him in raising Elaine.

The strength of the relationship that existed between Elaine and her father, idealized now in her memory, cannot be overestimated. He not only loved and indulged her, but he also taught her a great deal and clearly enjoyed her company. She returned his devotion by absorbing everything he said, even by imitating him outright. Elaine's vocabulary is surprisingly sophisticated, and she usually appears quite poised and self-confident. Her conversational references sound cosmopolitan and knowing. She is acutely aware of social expectations and social graces, even though she ignores them regularly when she is self-absorbed, anxious, or otherwise distracted by self-interest. When she feels secure and not too preoccupied with the need to seek more attention than she is getting, she can actually be an entertaining companion, a quality her father cultivated and enjoyed in her.

Elaine was very much "Daddy's girl," and this clearly caused some friction between her and her mother, who may have felt at times that she was competing with Elaine for her husband's loyalty and attention. Elaine learned how to appeal to her father whenever pressed by her mother, and probably even played them off against each other in much the same way she plays her counselors against each other today. This did not always work. Elaine has a lurid memory, which she repeats often to anyone who will listen, of an occasion in her childhood when her father hit her after Liz complained to her husband that Elaine had said a "bad" word to her. What seems to have stayed with Elaine through the years was the way in which this incident betrayed the benevolent image she had of her father, as well as the fact that he had sided with Liz against her. Elaine highly values consistency and loyalty.

In response to the special attention that Elaine's father gave her, Liz developed a closer relationship with Elaine's younger brother, Albert, than either one had with Elaine. Albert seldom appears in Elaine's reminiscences. (One researcher who repeatedly interviewed Elaine mistakenly thought she was an only child.) The siblings were never close, and Liz reports that Albert was always embarrassed by his sister's disabilities. Elaine does not verbalize any awareness of Albert's embarrassment. Albert and Elaine still live in the same city, but Elaine only sees her brother at occasional family functions, like Mother's Day or religious holidays, which she attends with the now-widowed Liz. Liz says Albert is not willing to assume any responsibility for Elaine when she (Liz) dies.

Elaine's family moved to California when she was still in high school. They lived well, residing in a wealthy area, and Elaine attended a renowned area high school. She sang well and belonged to a choir, even appearing on television with them. In the summer, she attended special camps, learning how to ride a horse so well that she earned a prize, which Liz still speaks of with pride. She began to attract the sexual attentions of men, something that frightened her permanently because of two traumatic experiences. In one, a camp counselor offered her a ride home and instead drove her into the hills where he threatened to assault her. It is not clear how far the attempted rape proceeded, but Elaine had the presence of mind to recognize the neighborhood, and she managed to get out of his car and run to a family friend's house for help. On another occasion, Liz arranged a date between Elaine and a young man from a "respectable, well-off" family of their acquaintance. Perhaps Liz hoped that Elaine could attract a suitable husband who would care for her in the future. Instead, the evening turned into a fiasco when the boy persuaded Elaine to take the key to her father's dental office, drove her there, and demanded that she "strip down" (in Elaine's words), beating her when she balked. Again, it is not clear from Elaine's account how far things went before her father arrived on the scene and rescued her.

Elaine once claimed that she had been sterilized, but later denied this. She may not entirely understand the procedure, but she does understand its purpose. "I didn't want kids," she explains, "They're too much trouble." Elaine recalls having undergone several gynecological operations (dilation and curettage), due to painful menorrhagia, and these ordeals further discouraged any positive interest in sex or reproduction.

After graduating from high school, Elaine went to work in her father's dental office as a receptionist. Her mother explains that she was given the minimum wage and limited responsibilities and that she performed very well most of the time. Elaine continued to work in her father's office for many years, earning enough wages to accrue Social Security income later in life. She "retired" from employment when her father became too ill to work any longer. The 20 years of Elaine's adult life between high school and recent years is a pleasant blur in her memory, except for the trips abroad. In recalling her life, she often telescopes the passage of time, making it seem as if she passed directly from adolescence to middle age, which in a social developmental sense she did.

The biggest tragedy of Elaine's life was her father's death in 1983. He had cancer, and his health had been failing for a few years. During that time, he retired, sold his home, moved his family into a spacious apartment, and enrolled Elaine in the TRM Workshop in 1978. He made arrangements for her to become a Regional Center client and to get Social Security and Supplemental Security Income (SSI), just as he had always seen to it that she had a network of trusted doctors to deal with her various medical problems. When he died, Elaine was absolutely bereft. Not only had she lost her father, benefactor, and best friend, but she also had to deal with a major and traumatic change in her lifestyle. Working in her father's office had been one thing, but working at TRM was a shock at first. Never before had she been surrounded by people with developmental disabilities. Far from being a "normalizing" experience, it seemed to her like a surreal step backwards into a raucous and disorderly school for strange and unpredictable "kids." (Elaine, perhaps taking a cue from her mother and from the school-like idiom that used to prevail at the workshop, habitually refers to the other clients at TRM as "the kids," even though most of them are adults.) With her father's death, Elaine's control over her childhood world crumbled, and she stood, somewhat unwillingly, on the threshhold of a much-delayed adult independence.

Hilda

Hilda was born in 1934 in California. Compared to Elaine, she does not remember a lot about her own childhood. Hilda thinks of her family life as having been very normal and ordinary. Her mother sometimes took her to visit her father at work, where he was an independent cabinetmaker. She remembers being especially close to her mother and spending most of her spare time with her. Hilda also remembers fighting on occasion with her two sisters: Ada, who is 4 years older, and a middle sister, Beth, who died in 1971. These fights seem to have been normal sibling encounters. Hilda recalls a rough-and-tumble argument with her now-deceased sister, insisting, "She started it, but I'm the one who got punished." Hilda then thinks a minute and laughs. "I could be a little stinker at times."

Ada reports that their family was very close. Schooling was strongly emphasized, but extracurricular activities were not. On hearing of Elaine's extensive travels with her family, Hilda wistfully comments, "I never went anywhere," and neither, apparently, did Hilda's family. Ada says that it was always understood that she would take over responsibility for Hilda when their parents died and that her daughters, Hilda's nieces, will assume that responsibility if Ada predeceases Hilda.

Like Elaine, Hilda claims not to have known that she was "retarded" until recently. Hilda knew that she was mildly physically handicapped by her tremor and coordination problems and that she was a "slow thinker." Otherwise, she says, she was not in any way segregated or made to feel different. Although Ada attended parochial school through the eighth grade, Hilda attended public schools, graduating from high school at age 20 in 1954.

After high school, the three sisters went different ways. Ada learned accounting and married in 1957, and then she and her husband established their own business. Beth became an airline stewardess and then went into business with their father until his death in 1967, followed by hers in 1971. Hilda was sent to a private boarding facility in Texas for high-functioning young adults with developmental disabilities. According to Ada, this was because in the late 1950s their mother "decided she'd just had enough" of raising three daughters, and at the suggestion of a doctor who was a family friend, she sent Hilda away.

Hilda is not sure if all of the other residents at the Texas facility were handicapped or "slow thinkers." She and Elaine both tend to perceive the term "handicapped" as referring primarily to physical problems; they regard themselves as being both handicapped and slow thinkers. Hilda saw the liberal and fairly expensive institution as a finishing school, teaching the students proper social behavior and thus reinforcing the kind of lessons Hilda had already learned at home. (Hilda and Ada always refer to it as a "school," and not as an "institution.") More practical independent living skills were apparently not included, however.

In comparing herself to others in the school, Hilda says that she felt she was among the better residents, because some of the others "didn't behave right" and "didn't know how to get along." Hilda also liked the mild regimentation of life at the school, as well as the sense of order and routine. She cannot remember anyone specific from that period of her life, but she says she had many friends there and got along well. The only thing she did not like was that "it was a bit noisy sometimes." Asked if she was ever homesick, she replied, "No. Sometimes. I went home on summer vacations and for Christmas. I'd been at home long enough."

Ada has the impression that Hilda had a problem with one or two of the other residents at the school and that she was unhappy there in the last years, leading to her return home in 1968 when she was 34 years old. As Hilda remembers it, her mother wanted her at home for company after the recent death of her husband, Hilda's father. Hilda's memory of her father's death was recorded by one researcher as follows:

> I was at boarding school at the time and when I came home after the term they told me. He had been dead for three weeks already. That really hurt a lot. More than if they had told me when it really happened. They [her mother and Ada] were trying to protect me, I know, but they were wrong. I've been overprotected. I think a little protection is good but I've been too protected all my life.[1]

Elaine is always moved by Hilda's painful recollection of missing her father's death and by Hilda's memory of later having been at her mother's deathbed. Elaine insists that she too was kept in ignorance of her father's imminent death and that she was not allowed to see him one last time before he died. She relates this with tears of indignation in her eyes, but

---

[1]From the fieldnotes of Dr. Steven Stumpf (1984), who did his doctoral dissertation on the Upward program.

her mother, Liz, insists just as ardently that Elaine was indeed present in the hospital at her father's death and was, in fact, called into his room especially to say "good-bye." Regardless of which version is correct, both Elaine's and Hilda's attitudes toward grieving are similarly focused on their desire to be included in such important family events, perhaps as an expression of control over their own lives.

By the time Hilda returned to her mother's home, her sister Ada was married and had three daughters. Although Hilda relates that she and Ada never got along well and fought fairly often as children, she still sees the relationship as being close, and she is especially delighted by Ada's children. Hilda saw them routinely and still writes to them periodically. They send her birthday and holiday cards, call her now and then, and write. Hilda is exceptionally proud of them, and their names come up routinely in her ordinary conversation. This is in contrast to Elaine, who rarely mentions or shows any interest in the children of her brother Albert. Asked if she ever wanted her own children, however, Hilda says, "No. They're too much work. They cry a lot and make a mess. But I love my nieces." Hilda says she was never sterilized. "My periods ended naturally when I got older, during the change."

This post-school period of her life is a blur in Hilda's memory, continuing for over 5 years until her mother passed away in 1973. When asked what she did during this time, Hilda says she helped her mother around the house. Her mother, age 75 when she died, needed assistance around the house and enjoyed the mature Hilda's company in her final years. The family was quite well-to-do, and Hilda's mother could have afforded to hire professional help around the home or even nursing help as her own health declined. But a maid came only occasionally to clean the house, and a live-in nurse was required only in the last stages of the mother's terminal illness. The true significance of Hilda's help around the house for those several years can be inferred from the fact that her mother stayed on and died in her own home, rather than in a nursing home or a convalescent hospital.

While at home, Hilda enjoyed a life of quiet gentility. She sometimes read with her mother and did mosaics, needlepoint, and embroidery, all crafts that her mother had taught her. She watched television, and although Hilda recalls going everywhere and doing everything with her mother, most of the time they stayed at home. Her mother continued to do most of the cooking, with Hilda helping rather than taking over the task herself. Ada recalls that the two of them ate a lot of "TV dinners," a habit Hilda dropped after going through Upward, which emphasized more nutritionally conscious cooking. When pressed about what kept her busy all that time, Hilda mentions cleaning house and gardening. The house had a lovely, large yard, and Hilda vividly remembers the flowers, which she enjoyed tending. Her mother taught her how to care for the garden, and Hilda recalls that she did this quite well in spite of her shaking.

Hilda remembers with satisfaction that she was "right there" for her mother's death, unlike the occasion of her father's passing. Although she reports that she cried a great deal, she also demonstrated amazing self-control and self-assertion. After her mother's death, she refused to move from the house and continued to live there alone for 5 years. Ada stopped by regularly, and her nieces often visited, but Hilda insisted on her independence. In recalling that period, Hilda says that she enjoyed living alone. Unfortunately, Hilda fell one day while gardening and broke her hip. After that, she lived briefly with Ada and her husband, but Hilda explains that by then she was too old to be ordered around by her sister, who—like Hilda—is soft-spoken but independent and strong-willed. Two of Ada's daughters were still living at home at the time, and Ada says theirs was already a full house. Hilda stayed with Ada's family less than a year.

While Hilda was in the hospital recuperating from her broken hip, a social worker suggested that Ada contact a Regional Center for people with developmental disabilities. Ada did this and was mildly surprised that they were not interested in talking to her but insisted on dealing directly with Hilda. Because of Hilda's relatively high IQ, there was some question about whether she was eligible for their services. A sympathetic TRM administrator, Joyce, lobbied on Hilda's behalf, and got her into the workshop as well. Because Hilda and Ada were having a hard time adjusting to living together, Joyce also suggested that Hilda move to a residential care facility that housed some people with developmental disabilities, although most of the residents were mentally ill.

Hilda hated the residential care facility. It was too restrictive for her tastes, and most of the other residents were too incapacitated, dependent, or quirky from her point of view. It was noisy, and many of the residents smoked or had other habits she did not like. In addition, it was regimented like the school she had attended in Texas, but without the stimulation or veneer of propriety. Cooking, cleaning, and the planning of social activities were all done for the residents. Elaine, whom Hilda had befriended at TRM, remembers visiting her there a few times and recalls that the facility was "fussy" about visitors. Hilda fell into a depression and complained to Ada. Ada recalls that she was not impressed with the facility either and had considered it only a temporary arrangement. After only a few months, Ada again sought Joyce's advice, and Hilda was enrolled in a special program at a nearby city college and subsequently in the Upward program while she continued to work at TRM. Elaine entered these programs at about the same time.

THE TRANSITION TO INDEPENDENT LIVING

After her husband's death, Liz soon decided that she could not care for Elaine by herself, so she enrolled her daughter in the Upward program, hoping that Elaine could learn to live independently. Liz herself was feeling the effects of age and infirmity by this time (she was nearing the age of 70), and she felt it was all she could do to get her own life in order after losing a husband who had made most of the decisions, including financial ones, throughout their married life. Elaine's introduction to the Upward program was a bit rocky. Liz eased the transition by calling frequently, having Elaine home on some weekends and holidays, and giving her familiar things from home with which to furnish her apartment. Elaine was also reassured somewhat by all the individualized attention she was getting from counselors in the program, and it may have helped that most of the participants were also clients at TRM. Nonetheless, Elaine had a number of adjustment problems. First, she had never before learned to cook, budget money, do housework, or share responsibilities with anyone. This, of course, was true of many of the participants, but Elaine was an extreme case. For example, while still living at home as a teenager, Elaine went for psychological counseling. Elaine says it was because she got "so emotional," crying and throwing tantrums when things did not go her way. She also admits that her mother was aggravated by her refusal to do any housework, including cleaning her own room. This was a real bone of contention between them that was not resolved by counseling and that contributed to Liz's decision to send Elaine to Upward.

Another example of Elaine's unpreparedness for independent living was her attitude towards money and budgeting. Independent living skills specialists tend to view financial management skills as essential to "normalization," although many nondisabled individuals have trouble in this area too. Elaine still recalls that her father frequently used to give her money so that she would always have some in her pocket. Thus, she still associates having an ample amount of unmonitored spending money in her possession with security and well-being. However, she does not have much restraint in spending it because she also associates the freedom to buy on impulse with well-being, self-esteem, and even independence. Conditioned by her father's largess, she still expects to have her spending money replenished whenever it is used, regardless of her budget.

A second and more serious problem that Elaine had at the Upward program was her excessive emotional need for security and attention. In spite of the fact that Elaine quickly learned the rules and practicalities of independent living and could recite them with such facility that the staff were impressed and gave her much sought-after approval, she did not seem to be able to put them into practice very well without reverting to a kind of learned helplessness reminscent of her mother's. A researcher recorded an instance when anxiety over grocery shopping by herself for the first time got the better of Elaine:

> The visit was fraught with instances of barely concealed fear, all stemming from having to captain her own shopping expedition. No sooner had we set off for the store in my car than she realized she forgot to make a shopping list. We returned to her apartment, whereupon she was immediately beset with catastrophes: her mail bore bad news; she lost her wallet while we sat there; finally she began to feel an intense and teary longing for Lisa, her [Upward program] counselor. Once her anxiety subsided, she found her wallet (in her purse). At ease, she retired to the bathroom but left the door ajar so she could maintain eye contact and conversation with me all the while.[2]

Grocery shopping has since become routinized for Elaine, but even years later, she finds it enormously difficult to go to the grocery store without Hilda there for moral support. She still neglects to make shopping lists, misplaces her wallet and other essential items in moments of stress, becomes overwhelmed by one problem after another until she "breaks down" (in her words) and cries, and keeps the door to the bathroom ajar while using the toilet so she can continue conversing with Hilda. (The more modest Hilda finds this amusing.) She requires continual, verbalized reassurance, which she elicits with an unending stream of questions, often under the guise of seeking information or opinions. An example follows:

Elaine: What do you think of this shirt, Hil? Do you think it's too cold out to wear this?
Hilda: I don't know. I haven't been outside yet.
Elaine: But do you think it's too cold? Should I wear a sweater? Hil?
Hilda: I don't know. That's for you to decide.
Elaine: Oh brother. So now it's up to me decide, is it? You're my roommate, Hil. Just tell me what I should wear.
Hilda: Don't wave that hairbrush at me.

Elaine's demands for reassurance proved to be too draining for most people, and she quickly wore out her welcome among the staff and participants at the Upward program, as she has at TRM. Still, she showed enough progress to avoid being thrown out of the program, although she took longer than anyone else to graduate from it. That it took her so long was due to the third obstacle she faced in the program, that of finding a roommate with whom she could live. The first two matches arranged by the program, both of whom were younger than Elaine, were unsuccess-

---

[2]From the fieldnotes of Dr. Steven Stumpf (1984).

ful. The first was a very independent and sexually active woman who resented Elaine's prudishness, tattling, and unwillingness to share the housework. The second was a more passive-aggressive woman who viewed Elaine as too stodgy and emotionally volatile. Both women found Elaine's emotional demands and self-centeredness unacceptable.

Finally, Elaine was matched with the "perfect" roommate, the secret of her subsequent success at independent living: Hilda. Here at last was someone of her own generation with a similarly sheltered background who seemed to complement Elaine's personality, someone who could tolerate Elaine's excesses. Most important, Hilda herself derives considerable satisfaction from the relationship, and so, after 7 years together, their relationship has proven to be quite stable, much to everyone's relief.

Elaine was in her early 50s and Hilda in her late 40s when they were matched. Elaine had had no previous experience at independent living, but Hilda had lived alone during the 5-year period following her mother's death. Hilda had also learned some social skills required of roommates in boarding school, but Elaine had never lived away from home and was considerably less accustomed to compromise or housework. They knew each other from TRM, and they hit it off remarkably well. The family members who take primary responsibility for them, Hilda's sister Ada and Elaine's mother Liz, are delighted at the apparent success and stability of this arrangement, and they have taken a number of steps to encourage it. For example, they contributed furnishings to the apartment, routinely take Hilda and Elaine shopping and out for meals, and make themselves available to both when problems or emergencies arise.

Hilda went to the Upward program with a very positive, determined attitude. Although the first two women she was matched with as roommates were inappropriate, due to differences in age and emotional maturity, Hilda did not reject altogether the idea of rooming with someone. In fact, Hilda recalls that she was the one who suggested that she and Elaine become roommates because they had already become friends through TRM. Hilda desired a mature roommate who, like herself, was something of a homebody, and Elaine fit the bill. Elaine and Hilda may well be the longest-lived, most successful same-sex roommate pairing to have emerged from the Upward program.[3]

Understandably, Hilda at first found the lifestyle at Upward somewhat confusing. There were skills she had never fully mastered at home because her mother had always treated her as a helper rather than an independent "doer." She had never had a checkbook or managed her own funds, for example, and had simply asked her mother for money

[3]Personal communication from Dr. Steven Stumpf.

when she needed to buy something. Furthermore, her mother always accompanied her to make the purchases. Reports from her early days in the Upward program show that she gamely tried her best, but she was often tripped up by small mistakes and oversights. When this happened, she simply excused herself by proclaiming, "I'm mixed up." This was not only an explanation for her lack of competence at the moment, but it was also an implicit plea that the counselor either explain things again or back off and exert less pressure on her.

Hilda's and Elaine's different styles of eliciting assistance are evident in an account of a session in which the Upward counselor attempted to explain routine financial calculations to Elaine and Hilda. Elaine pretended to understand until the last moment, when she at last made it clear that she did not understand, which then involved the counselor in an eleventh-hour remedial lesson that eventually netted her extravagant praise for finally "getting it." Elaine typically spends as much effort selectively demonstrating incompetence, especially in financial matters, in order to strengthen valued relationships, as she does demonstrating her competence. During the session on finances, Hilda indicated right away when she did not understand something. Hilda therefore received appropriate guidance at an earlier stage and required less assistance later on. This is a more efficient learning strategy, but it netted Hilda much less attention and praise. These days, one rarely hears Hilda say, "I'm mixed up." She exudes confidence in her ability to perform the independent living tasks required of her and rarely needs to seek remedial assistance. Elaine, on the other hand, is still demonstrating precisely the same problems, especially in finances, that she had 7 years ago. Hilda will sometimes decisively turn down help, even if that means turning down an opportunity to get attention. This is something Elaine would never do, because she routinely manufactures "problems" for herself as an excuse to ask for help and increase her interactional opportunities, especially with authority figures.

Adaptation to the Workshop

At TRM, Hilda was at first alarmed by the seeming chaos of the workshop environment, very much as Elaine was. However, the idea of systematically performing tasks with her hands appealed to her. Hilda has good powers of concentration and enjoys being left to do some task on her own in order to occupy her time and give her a sense of accomplishment. Unlike Elaine, she does not seek constant reinforcement or external verbal stimulation. This is reflected in their respective diary entries. While Elaine repeatedly wrote that she was praised at TRM, overtly or implicitly, Hilda never mentioned praise, but instead related what tasks she did, those with whom she socialized, and how she spent her breaks.

When she first came to TRM, Hilda compared herself carefully to the other workers and was pleased to note that her level of competence is quite acceptable, in spite of her slowness, and that her behavior is more mature than most.

Asked what she likes most about TRM, Hilda replies, "seeing friends and helping people." Most of her friends are of approximately the same functional level, but there are specific people, Sam included of course, whom she chooses to help in various ways, such as by carrying small items, holding an arm to steady someone, tying shoes and straightening clothes, sharing supplies, explaining instructions, and offering moral support. Why does Hilda help people? Hilda is straightforward in her answer:

> Because I like to. It makes me feel good about myself. People should help each other when they need it. Some people can't always help themselves. I can. "You should always help those less fortunate." My mother taught me that.

Hilda is comfortable interacting with friends with mental retardation at the shop, unlike Elaine, who finds the unpredictable social behavior of her co-workers to be a source of anxiety. While Hilda is able to spontaneously praise the performance of others in the shop, saying that someone is a "good little worker," Elaine is more inclined to complain about other clients, whose behavior often distracts her. Elaine attempts to cultivate friendships with staff; Hilda treats staff professionally, but not deferentially or as friends. Hilda easily accepts the shop hierarchy, which Elaine frequently chooses to ignore or transgress.

Hilda and Elaine are both seen by staff as "good workers," but Hilda's productivity levels have seldom matched Elaine's because of her greater physical disability. They are vividly reminded of this difference every time they receive their paychecks, as Hilda's check is usually considerably smaller than Elaine's. Thus, Hilda has not been seriously considered for supported work. Her physical appearance, less pleasingly "mainstream" than Elaine's, may also discourage outside placement. In fact, her Regional Center caseworker recently intimated that Hilda may want to retire from TRM, ostensibly because of the raucous noise level. Hilda firmly rejected the suggestion, surprised and a little alarmed that it had even been made.

Elaine has always been among the more productive workers at TRM, limited more by her emotional adjustment problems than by physical disabilities, although this is not always how she herself explains it. Elaine calls constant attention to a variety of physical complaints as a means of engaging other people in conversation and supportive relationships, as well as to avoid work assignments that are stressful or that separate her from her friends. Elaine dislikes the appellation "hypochondriac," understanding and resenting the implication that she "makes it all up." She complains that she has met with this charge, even from her parents, for most of her life.

Elaine freely admits that she gets "nervous" and "emotional" and that this sometimes prevents her from doing her job well. Elaine is considered a good candidate for supported work, but the possibility of leaving TRM disturbs her deeply. She suffers extraordinary anxiety whenever she senses that her control over familiar aspects of her life is threatened. TRM is the cornerstone of her life's routine and her primary source of satisfaction and self-esteem. More importantly, she shares this routine with Hilda, who is more than just a roommate; she is the closest, most intimate friend Elaine has ever had. Because Hilda is not a candidate for supported work, Elaine's enlistment in the program would mean a significant separation from Hilda.

In response to the perceived threat of being sent away from TRM, Elaine began to complain that she suffered from imminent blindness and a crippling condition in her legs, and she started to walk with a cane to reinforce her claims. This development was greeted with some disbelief and derision by TRM staff, although they did not attempt to check with Elaine's doctors. Indeed, her eyesight was not failing, according to her ophthalmologist and optometrist, who have tested her routinely and carefully. Her leg problems were more difficult to discount medically, however, because she did have a long-time habit of walking improperly, and she now began to claim that her "feet turned under" involuntarily as she walked. She demonstrated this for the TRM staff and her doctors, but careful observation revealed that this only happened when Elaine knew someone relevant was watching. Nonetheless, her doctors could not discount the possibility of some organic cause to her complaint, and she was referred to a neurologist. After repeated tests failed to reveal anything specific, the neurologist surmised proximal dystonia as the cause for Elaine's condition. A drug was prescribed, but Elaine quietly neglected to take it, fearing its possible side effects and not entirely trusting the neurologist. TRM staff were still skeptical.

Around this time, Hilda began to experience sporadic but excruciating pain in her lower back, diagnosed as a slipped disc and a pinched nerve, which eventually required that she wear a brace. Hilda's sister and Elaine's mother, concerned that the two women were becoming increasingly disabled, intervened and secured a doctor's request that Hilda and Elaine both be transported to and from work in the TRM van. Elaine returned to the neurologist, complaining further about her feet and legs, but refusing to take any more drugs. Eventually, she was sent to a specialist in prosthetic devices, who obligingly provided her with braces for both lower legs, which she now wears whenever she leaves the house. Her various doctors each reassured the persistent Elaine that she "could" use the cane and braces if this made her feel better, because there was nothing else any of them could offer to remedy her complaints. Elaine reinterpreted this for TRM staff, reporting that her doctors told her she "had to" use these items. She had successfully manipulated the medical system to gain the validation she wanted. For the time being, this has effectively tabled the idea of getting her into supported work outside of TRM.

At the beginning of this episode in 1987, Elaine's work productivity did not decline, in spite of her claims of physical debilitation. Indeed, she actively sought more prestigious and better-paying jobs in the shop, and her productivity rose. Although this made perfect sense in terms of her work satisfaction, rewards, and self-esteem, Elaine's high productivity could ultimately pose a much more serious threat to her security. The higher pay rates meant that Elaine's increased income level would soon jeopardize her SSI and Medi-Cal status. (This would also be likely in competitive employment.) Elaine's Regional Center caseworker pointed out that she could always reapply for SSI and Medi-Cal should she again become eligible through impoverishment. Understandably, neither Elaine nor her mother want matters to come to that.

Elaine, her mother, and her independent living counselor are trying to develop a strategy for handling this new challenge, monitoring Elaine's finances carefully and continually seeking advice from the Social Security Administration. TRM staff disclaims responsibility for monitoring or mitigating the situation, or for advising clients and their families of potential problems. Although TRM's parent organization has the reputation of being an advocacy and service-oriented agency, TRM itself has increasingly narrowed its focus to that of employer rather than benefactor. Elaine finally began to understand that the higher productivity and pay associated with the more challenging, prestigious jobs were jeopardizing her desired security. Elaine's response was to acquire a letter from her family doctor requesting that TRM not assign her to any job requiring her to stand, due to her recent complaint of back pain, which was very similar to Hilda's complaint of 6 months earlier. Elaine now works next to Hilda on a lower-productivity assembly line, earning far less than she was before.

The sad irony is that, although Elaine may exaggerate her ills, she unquestionably does suffer from a variety of physical complaints, some of which may worsen as she continues to age. At her age, if she had to forfeit SSI and Medi-Cal and depend entirely on a minimum wage at TRM or in competitive employment, she would face the future with virtually no financial or health care security at a time when her health status and productivity are more likely to decline than to improve. When she reaches age 65, she can apply for Medicare and additional Social Security benefits, and she could reapply for SSI on the basis of age, if nothing else. However, that is still several years in the future and offers her little security for the present.

Family Support

Elaine's and Hilda's transitions to independence have been assisted by Liz and Ada, whose styles of proferring help are quite different. Liz occasionally demonstrates a sharp intelligence when it comes to protecting what she perceives as Elaine's interests. Unfortunately, her own protected past has left her ill-prepared to deal with the myriad details of Elaine's legal and financial status, and she has found it difficult just to keep her own and Elaine's affairs in order. Albert willingly helps and advises his mother on her own affairs, but avoids getting involved in Elaine's.

Liz sporadically communicates with TRM and Elaine's independent living counselor to be sure that Elaine is being properly protected. However, she is not at all systematic about getting information concerning Elaine's status, nor does she routinely monitor Elaine's finances or medical care, leaving this to Elaine's various counselors and medical specialists. Dealing with faceless bureaucracies is simply beyond her experience and emotional capabilities. Her inclination is to locate alternative protectors who will assume the greater burden of care for Elaine.

Liz never assumed legal guardianship for Elaine, but she is the official "payee" on behalf of Elaine for receipt of her Social Security and SSI checks. This is a designation she will not abjure, even though she does not see or deal with these funds, as they are deposited directly into Elaine's account. Liz does not supervise Elaine's finances; that is Elaine's independent living counselor's job. Liz keeps Elaine's TRM pay records and all written communication from Social Security and Medicare, but she has some trouble organizing and retrieving this material, as well as understanding any changes that take place. Recently, both a Social Security advisor and Rachel have strongly advised that she allow Elaine to be her own payee, so that Rachel or someone else more competent than Liz could legally take responsibility for helping Elaine handle all the necessary bureaucratic details. Liz is considering the proposal, although she is somewhat reluctant to relinquish what she sees as a mother's natural prerogative and her only legal right to intervene in Elaine's affairs.

Liz was unaware of such issues as the advisability of MediGap insurance or a burial savings account to shelter some of Elaine's income. She was recently advised by Elaine's Regional Center caseworker to seek legal advice from his office on these and other matters, such as setting up a trust for handling whatever Elaine will inherit from her mother or other relatives.

Liz's major role in Elaine's life is that of mother: a natural advocate, the ultimate moral authority, and a source of moral and, occasionally, material support. Their relationship is close, but fraught with the difficulties one might expect between a mother who still sees her adult offspring as a child and an adult who is still ambivalent about independence from her mother. For example, Liz's attempts to direct Elaine's behavior tend to seem critical and patronizing. Liz is firm in her belief that, because of her disability, Elaine is still essentially a child. (She says of people with developmental disabilities in general, "I don't care what you say or do, they will always be children.") She frequently reprimands Elaine, even in public, usually generating an argument. Even so, Elaine loves her mother, but she admits to everyone that they never got along well. When they are together, Liz is impatient and deprecating, causing Elaine's anxiety level to rise and often leading her to revert to childish whining and displays of temper. They fight in private and in public, much to the consternation of Hilda or anyone else in their presence. They never seem at ease with each other.

It is not only Elaine's social behavior or intellectual functioning that evoke Liz's apparent displeasure, but also Elaine's physical appearance. Although Liz recalls that Elaine was a "gorgeous baby" and "cute as a button," she expresses frequent dissatisfaction with Elaine's looks. For example, although Liz is demurely vague about Elaine's facial operations, Elaine says outright that she had surgery to reform the bones in her face, including having her nose "clipped," as she put it, "just like Mom." More recently, Elaine had surgery on her legs to repair unsightly varicose veins, largely at her mother's urging. Elaine's hair is graying, but for years Liz insisted that she have it dyed regularly at the beauty parlor, a process that Elaine found tiresome but endured for vanity's sake. But what really causes friction between Elaine and her mother is Liz's tendency to criticize constantly and fuss over what Elaine is wearing or how she combs her hair. Elaine prefers casual clothes, mostly jeans and sweatshirts, and she likes to slick her short hair back, giving herself a somewhat masculine appearance that is sporty and not necessarily unattractive. Her mother prefers a more feminine appearance and often insists that Elaine change clothes or recomb her hair when they are going out together. All of this suggests that Liz does not really accept Elaine as she is and that she may even be embarrassed by Elaine, just as she claims Albert is. Although Elaine goes along with many of Liz's demands, she frequently rebels against Liz's more routine fussing. Elaine does look attractive when she puts on a fancy dress, hose, and heels and when she is carefully coiffed and made-up. (Such occasions are limited to the annual Christmas ball and rare family events.) But when she has to spend much time and energy getting ready for an outing, she invariably becomes impatient and anxious. As it is, she is so anxious getting dressed each morning that she demands that Hilda help her select and put on her clothes, something Hilda finds tedious.

Hilda has been assisted in her mid-life transformation to independence by having her sister Ada to help her and to serve as a role model. Ada is a very composed and organized woman who is virtually unflappable. Ada does not attempt to intervene much in Hilda's daily life, but she is always there on request when needed. Low key and ultrasensible, she talks through problems with Hilda, usually prefacing her suggestions with questions, for example, "Do you think . . ." or "Do you want . . ." that elicit Hilda's input. Although Ada still underestimates many of Hilda's capabilities, she does not do so in an obvious manner. She takes Hilda's basic competence and independence for granted, largely because Hilda herself has made it clear that she has earned that esteem and that Ada is her sister not her mother. Hilda's self-possessed calm, which she obviously learned from her family, is one major reason for the success of her relationship with Elaine.

Ada assumed conservatorship over a generous trust fund left to Hilda by her parents. Hilda knows little about the legal mechanics of the trust, beyond what amount she gets from the fund each month when Ada gives her a check to deposit in her bank account. Hilda has successfully managed a checking account since the Upward program, with some assistance from an independent living counselor. She recently opened a savings account for depositing the considerably larger checks she was beginning to receive from TRM. The amount Ada forwards from the trust each month, which is comparable to what Elaine receives as combined SSI and Social Security income, covers most of Hilda's basic expenses. Thus, Hilda is protected from the endless Social Security anxieties shared by Elaine and her mother. Ada has also arranged for insurance and other legal needs. She runs a business with her husband, and her education and experience has better prepared her for coping with Hilda's circumstances than was the case for Liz. Indeed, Liz occasionally consults Ada for advice, but she is loathe to lean too hard on a relationship that she simply cannot afford to burn out, for it looks as if Ada may be assuming considerable responsibility for Elaine when Liz dies, by default if nothing else, because none of Elaine's other relations are prepared to take Liz's place. Liz politely disclaims any intent to impose on Ada, but it is quite clear that this is a major reason why she is vitally interested in encouraging the stability of Elaine and Hilda's relationship.

Ada has proven to be an ideal facilitator of Hilda's independence, and she often takes pains to treat Elaine with nearly the same amount of consideration she treats Hilda. Purchasing them matching turquoise rings, sweaters, bed linens, and living room chairs are a few examples of Ada's even-handedness, which further nurtures Elaine and Hilda's close relationship. Liz has also given them identical gifts on occasion, but much more rarely, partly because she feels herself less financially capable, being a widow on Social Security, and partly because of her fear that SSI might deduct the value of any substantial gift from Elaine's checks. Thus, Elaine's standard of living can be both bolstered and to some extent protected from the vagaries of SSI regulations if she lives with someone financially better off who is *not* receiving SSI.

Ada and Liz divide some of the labor of providing practical assistance to "the girls," as they both refer to Hilda and Elaine. Liz takes them grocery shopping once a week and to the beauty parlor every few months, while Ada picks up and returns their laundry each week or so. Both Liz and Ada take them out for a meal once a week, and both are in phone contact with them at least once a day. It is understood that Ada is to be called for most emergencies, especially those occurring after dark or on rainy days, when the elderly and partially disabled Liz feels less secure about driving. Three examples of emergencies that arose demonstrate how they are handled.

On the first occasion, Hilda experienced a debilitating back spasm when she was out on a Saturday afternoon walking with Elaine and Sam. Hilda was momentarily unable to move. Elaine and Sam became alarmed and were unable to offer much physical help other than holding Hilda's arm while she stood stock still waiting for the pain to pass. Elaine instructed Sam to wait with Hilda while she went to phone Ada, who came to drive them home and subsequently arranged for Hilda to see a medical specialist.

On another occasion, the manager of Hilda and Elaine's apartment building decided to fumigate their unit for cockroaches, a continual problem. The entire building had been professionally fumigated the previous year, requiring Hilda and Elaine to spend two days away with Ada and Liz respectively, but this time the manager used canned bug "bombs" that she had purchased herself. The manager set the fumigation "bombs" off in their unit one night while Hilda and Elaine were there. None of them read the instructions, which clearly stated humans should not be inside when this is done. Hilda and Elaine became violently ill and called Ada. Unfortunately, Ada was not in that evening, so Rachel (their independent living counselor) came and drove them both to Liz's house and later took Hilda to Ada's house. This particular incident demonstrates the dual vulnerability of Hilda and Elaine, both as adults with developmental disabilities who have limited experience and judgment (at least in this instance) and as low-income renters who have limited negotiating power with landlords and apartment managers whose judgment may be questionable.

Although Ada sometimes complains about Elaine's repeated phone calls regarding every minor "crisis," real or imagined, real emergencies are not that frequent. Sometimes, Hilda and Elaine handle serious problems on their own. On a third occasion, when Hilda slipped and fell in front of the apartment, opening an artery in her temple, Elaine called 911 for assistance, only to be told they would not respond. Elaine then called Ada, who pointed out that it would take her too long to arrive, so Hilda and Elaine took a cab to the nearest hospital, where Hilda was treated while Elaine waited. (Similarly, Hilda accompanied Elaine to the hospital in a cab when a sudden nosebleed turned into a hemorrhage.)

Ada takes a keen interest in Hilda's health, sometimes accompanying her to medical appointments, where she conscientiously asks questions and makes suggestions to Hilda on how to improve her standard of self-care at home. For her part, Hilda obediently heeds the advice she has been given by her doctor and displays more conviction and self-discipline in independent self-care than either Elaine or Sam.

Hilda's weight gain became a concern when she developed spasms in her lower back, and Ada thought the problem might have been triggered by a too-rapid addition of extra pounds. This was remedied by a prescription for thyroid supplements, which helped Hilda bring her weight down again. The thyroid treatment was eventually discontinued when blood tests showed slightly elevated thyroid levels and after Ada had voiced concern to the doctor that Hilda's hand tremors, present since birth, were getting worse.

Hilda's weight gain is due primarily to lifestyle changes fairly common among seniors, including less exercise and deteriorating dietary habits. In Hilda's case, she has been walking less in recent years and getting rides more routinely, as well as eating more ice cream and other sweets. With encouragement from Ada and her counselors, Hilda has attempted to exercise more and eat fattening foods less often, with some limited success.

Unfortunately, Hilda's health has been more fragile lately. Most recently, she suffered from a sudden, post-menopausal hemorrhage. Elaine loyally accompanied her to the emergency room and reassured her by pointing out that Liz had been through a similar ordeal, and by commiserating when Hilda had dilation and curettage, a procedure Elaine had undergone several times herself. Hilda is frankly admiring of Elaine's generally robust health. "Elaine just goes on and on and on," she says, noting that even when Elaine is sick, she frequently goes to work at TRM anyway. Hilda is, of necessity, much more careful about her health.[4]

DAILY LIFE

Elaine and Hilda's relationship resembles a marriage in its stability, closeness, and comfortable routine. Their weekday begins at 5:00 A.M., when they awaken to enjoy the luxurious sensation of stretching in bed for an hour before rising to get ready for work. They alternate in the bathroom, then get dressed together, and share a "breakfast" of orange juice, vitamins, and prescribed medications. They leave the house between 7:00 and 7:30 A.M. When they were both taking the bus, this togetherness sometimes broke down if Elaine grew impatient with Hilda's slower pace and rushed off to the bus stop, leaving Hilda behind to lock up the apartment and catch a later bus. Elaine would never tolerate being left behind herself, but her work routine and the approval of TRM counselors were strong enough incentives to separate her temporarily from Hilda, something that in other circumstances would be unthinkable.

For her part, Hilda complains that Elaine always leaves her to wash the juice glasses, as well as having demanded Hilda's time to help her get dressed, and that this is why she, Hilda, is sometimes late. Hilda also complains that whenever they leave the apartment Elaine invariably expects Hilda to lock the front door, saying she does not want to look for her keys. Elaine's routine inconsideration reveals an important point about her sense of satisfaction in a secure relationship: to her, it is terribly important for others to do things for her, however small.

TRM's workday begins at 8:30 A.M., but both women like to arrive early enough to have time to greet their friends at the workshop. Although their relationships with their workmates pale in comparison to their relationship with each other and are rarely reinforced outside of the workshop, the daily ritual of greeting friends is a major means by which shop friendships are maintained. Job assignments change from time to time. Elaine is ambivalent about all the shifting. The uncertainty bothers

---

[4]After the dilation and curettage, tissue analysis showed Hilda had uterine cancer, and a complete hysterectomy was performed. Her recovery was rapid, and her attitude remains positive. "It could have happened to anyone," she said repeatedly. Although her prognosis is good, Hilda's doctors are still concerned that the cancer may have spread, and she is currently undergoing radiation therapy. This entire episode was a complete surprise to everyone, as Hilda had been seeing her doctor for twice-yearly checkups and was generally in good health. However, she had not had a Pap smear in many years and had never had a breast exam. This is surprising in view of the fact that her mother died of breast cancer, and her father died of cancer as well. This raises questions regarding the quality of medical care that both Hilda and Elaine receive, even though they are seen regularly by a team of doctors who work in a very reputable, middle class medical center.

her, and she often argues with staff about it, but both she and Hilda appreciate the variation in tasks that this affords. Once at their assignments, there is little opportunity for socializing until the morning break at 10:30 A.M. This is when Elaine and Hilda have their first solid food of the day. The shop has no food facilities other than machines with "junk food" and soda pop, but a catering truck comes during breaks and is swamped with eager customers. Elaine and Hilda used to get coffee and donuts or sweet rolls, but in recent years they have put on too much weight, so they often get yogurt instead. For lunch, they used to buy hot dogs or hamburgers, but recent health consciousness has encouraged them to choose yogurt, cottage cheese, and fruit juice at this break too. They both consider it too troublesome to prepare and bring a lunch.

Hilda and Elaine socialize with others during lunch break, especially since Sam is no longer there requiring their help. Their friends at the workshop tend to be among the higher-functioning employees, although of no particular age range. They do reveal a slight preference for older female colleagues and certainly for female rather than male staff. During break, Hilda is better at initiating conversations with other employees than Elaine, who, due to self-consciousness, is a bit reticent about approaching her co-workers. Elaine gravitates more to the staff, but when she does initiate conversation with a co-worker her style is a bit awkward and brusque, although she means it humorously. Being a vivacious person, however, she blossoms into conversation when others take the initiative first, and Elaine does have a few friends at the workshop who enjoy her company and with whom she feels comfortable socializing. Breaks are brief, however, which does not facilitate the development of very deep relationships.

A few employees socialize regularly outside the shop, but most do not. Those who do are, like Elaine and Hilda, higher functioning, and most live independently. Elaine and Hilda sometimes run into their co-workers at common haunts: the bank where many of them started accounts while in the Upward program, the monthly dance at the Salvation Army, the weekly meetings of a club for adults with mental retardation, a popular coffee shop, and a shopping mall near the beach. Rarely do either Elaine or Hilda talk to a co-worker on the telephone. Hilda is not fond of telephone conversations in general, but this seems odd for Elaine because she so heartily enjoys talking on the telephone with her mother, her counselors, and me. Yet it is understandable in terms of Elaine's self-centered conversational habits, which are probably tolerated less over the telephone than face to face, at least by those who do not feel obliged to listen to her.

The staff at TRM interpret Elaine's preference for their company over that of her co-workers as inappropriate dependency. They recommend that Elaine socialize more with other employee/clients who are assumed to be more appropriate peers. (This is in some ways a questionable, paternalistic, and discriminatory assumption.) However, Elaine is easily distracted and upset by the erratic behavior of some of the more poorly adjusted workers, and at times she herself is ostracized by co-workers because of occasional tantrums. She finds staff behavior to be far more predictable than the behavior of other clients, as well as more instrumental in terms of her own specific concerns. Elaine cultivates peer relationships with staff (and with the researcher and her independent living counselor) by continually engaging them in conversation unrelated to work, even extracting an amazing range of details from them about their personal lives. Unfortunately, she regularly sabotages any hope of having symmetrical peer relations with staff by periodically succumbing to anxiety and aggressively acting out her more childish dependency needs.

When asked what she enjoys about her experiences at TRM, Elaine mentions the following:

> The work is interesting.
> She learns a lot.
> She has a chance to see her friends, including favorite staff.
> Many people (staff) "help" her so she can do better.
> She takes pride in doing a good job.
> The staff take pride in her.

This last point is of exceptional importance to her, and she frequently makes reference to whatever praise she receives at the workshop. Praise from staff was frequently mentioned in Elaine's diary entries, but not in Hilda's. Elaine is delighted to be occasionally assigned limited responsibility for supervising her co-workers. Elaine is always proud of her paychecks, even when they average no more than $25 every two weeks. She proudly announces her earnings to her mother, counselors, and the researcher, and gleefully compares the amount to the wages of the usually less-productive and lower-paid Hilda. Elaine's diary entries were almost entirely about her routine at TRM, and they eventually became so formalized and repetitive (presumably as she lost interest in the diary) that workday entries were exact duplicates of each other. Yet her actual experiences during that time were not especially boring, her days not so featureless and unmemorable. She left out all the problems, crises, arguments, and excitement that make her real life interesting and contribute to her volubility. Elaine did not mention any co-workers other than Hilda and Sam, while Hilda mentioned several. Rarely did Elaine write of any problems at TRM, although these came up frequently in daily conversation. Instead of being a real record of what she did or thought each day, Elaine's diary represented an occasion to produce a repetitious paean to her life at the workshop.

Elaine and Hilda sometimes have doctor's appointments during the day that cause them to miss time at TRM. They have the same general practitioner, podiatrist, dentist, and ear, nose, and throat specialist. (Only the last one is not seen on a regular basis.) In addition, Hilda has an orthopedist who sees her for back and hip problems and a gynecologist; Elaine has an optometrist, opthalmologist, and recently a neurologist. In the past Elaine has also seen a psychotherapist, a physical therapist, a gynecologist, and a cosmetic surgeon. Often Elaine and Hilda have their appointments on the same day, but even when only one had an appointment, it was their common practice to take time off together to "keep each other company." TRM tolerated this when work was still slack, but more recently forbade them both to leave if both did not have appointments.

Elaine and Hilda used to volunteer twice a week at a local Senior Meals Program, where they helped to package and deliver hot lunches to elderly people whose infirmities prevent them from leaving their homes. This was arranged by TRM when there was a lot of "down time" and their counselors wished to expand the two women's work repertoire and social experience. Elaine especially enjoyed this job, taking pride in mastering yet another interesting job and revelling in having a set of non-disabled, kindly, mature women as peers. Unfortunately, when a new director took over at Senior Meals, Elaine and Hilda were told they were no longer needed. "We were fired," was Elaine and Hilda's interpretation, and they were both deeply hurt by what they saw as blatant rejection. When asked if they would ever like to do such a job again, they both demur, explaining, "It really hurt our feelings. We don't want to risk it again." They also cite this as one reason why they are both wary about the idea of working outside TRM. The unintended lesson that they learned from the Senior Meals experience was that jobs outside TRM are minefields for their self-esteem. This occasion is one of two in their lives when they recall feeling discriminated against because of their handicaps. The other occasion was when they were apartment-hunting after leaving the Upward program and were explicitly turned down because of their disability by the landlord of an apartment they sought, even though all parties knew this to be illegal.

On leaving the workshop each day at 3:30 P.M., Elaine and Hilda follow a familiar routine. On Monday through Thursday, they formerly took the bus home, but since the beginning of 1988, they have taken the TRM van. After arriving home, they sometimes go shopping at a neighborhood drug store, where they fill their prescriptions and purchase various necessities, magazines, and items that appeal to them. On Monday nights, they go out to eat, usually at their favorite coffee shop, where Elaine has cultivated first-name relationships with several of the waiters and waitresses. Alternatively, they sometimes go to a burger or pizza place "to change off." Until recently, the coffee shop was their un-disputed favorite, however, and they cite its unrushed atmosphere, com-fortable booths, varied menu, generous portions, and reasonable prices as the reasons. Normally when they go out, each pays her own check, but occasionally one will treat the other. More frequently, it is Hilda who treats Elaine.

In mid-1988, Elaine was robbed by a "street person" as she stood at the entrance of the coffee shop. She was putting her change away, but unwisely had in her hand her entire cache of approximately $70, which the thief boldly seized. (Elaine takes pleasure in counting all her money, on this occasion an unusually large amount given her budget.) Restau-rant staff called the police, and the badly shaken Elaine gave a statement, but the man was never caught. She and Hilda stopped eating there tem-porarily, fearful that this could happen again because the number of ap-parently homeless persons loitering in the vicinity had increased.

Tuesday, they eat at home. Hilda usually does the cooking. When asked why she does not cook more often, Elaine explains that she is wait-ing for her independent living counselor to give her more lessons. How-ever, Elaine and Hilda both had cooking lessons at the Upward program, both have several cookbooks, and they both buy "women's" magazines for the recipes. Elaine's explanation reflects her typical unwillingness to take the initiative herself, as well as her tendency to manipulate informa-tion to make her failings seem like someone else's responsibility. In fact, Rachel, her counselor, *has* given Elaine several cooking lessons. Further-more, the dishes they commonly prepare are not very complicated or varied. Typical meals, for example, include boiled hot dogs and canned beans, baked chicken or fish and frozen vegetables, tuna and cheese sandwiches, or hamburgers. Other excuses Elaine gives for not cooking or cleaning pertain to her many physical complaints or even the mun-dane and frequent excuse of "I'm too tired." The truth is that Elaine sim-ply enjoys having Hilda cook for her. Most of the time, Hilda complies. When Elaine does cook, she so persistently badgers Hilda with questions ("What should I cook?" "What do I do now?" "Should I add more sea-soning?" "Do you think it's done?") that it ends up being a joint project.

On Wednesday nights, they sometimes eat at home, but at other times Ada takes them out to a coffee shop. On Thursday evening, Rachel comes by the house to monitor their budgets and check on how they are doing. According to a schedule worked out with Rachel, they are sup-posed to eat at home on Thursday night, but as on other nights when they are supposed to cook for themselves, they sometimes go out instead. On average, they go out to eat more nights than they cook. For example, in a typical 4-week period, they ate out 16 of the 28 nights, or 57 percent of the time.

On Thursdays, they used to attend a club for adults with mental retardation at a nearby park. They took the bus there and rode home with staff or parents of other club members. Recently, this club was disbanded because of poor organization. The club had parties, barbeques, and movie and restaurant outings that Elaine and Hilda enjoyed. However, Elaine had one painful, humiliating experience with this club in early 1988, when the club had really reached its nadir.

> Park Club usually celebrates the birthdays of its members, but this year is especially significant because Elaine's birthday actually falls on a Thursday. According to their printed agenda, they were going to Elaine and Hilda's favorite coffee shop tonight, and Elaine anticipated that they would have a cake in her honor, thus sharing the occasion not only with club members, but also her friends who work there. She called last week just to confirm the plan and was told by the club's director that they could meet the others at the coffee shop. Today, Elaine was so beside herself with anticipation that she called again to confirm. The line was always busy, so she called the operator, only to be told that the line must be off the hook. Finally, she got through to a park staff member, who confirmed that she was to meet the group at the coffee shop. She and Hilda went to the restaurant and waited in vain for one hour before finally giving up and ordering for themselves. By that time, the coffee shop staff had learned that it was Elaine's birthday, and they were kind enough to bring her a donut with a candle in it and a birthday card. This eased the pain somewhat, but Elaine called the park again the next day to demand an explanation. The assistant director told her that he had taken the group to a different restaurant altogether, one that had not been listed on the agenda. He had assumed Elaine and Hilda were not coming because they did not show up at the park for a ride as the others had. (The park is in one direction from their house, the coffee shop in another.) He lectured her that, "You know it has always been our policy to meet at the park first. You should have followed directions." When Elaine explained that she had called twice and had been told to go directly to the coffee shop, he countered by saying she had not talked to the "right" person or called at the "right" time, thus resorting to bureaucratic doublespeak and again shifting the blame to her. In effect, Elaine had been punished for her intelligence, foresight, and independence. That was the last time she or Hilda attended the club.

Friday is a hectic day for Elaine and Hilda. After work, they go to the bank to make deposits and to withdraw their weekly spending money. Until recently, they continued to go to the local bank they started with through the Upward program. However, Elaine has always complained bitterly that the bank's posting policies meant that their balance and hers never matched, making her very nervous because she never really knew how much money she had. The tellers also made frequent errors, and they did not use a computerized record system, making information retrieval a lengthy proce:s. Elaine had demanded a change of bank for years, and Rachel had agreed, but Liz opposed the idea. Liz was intimidated by the lengthy (4-month) bureaucratic process required to have Elaine's Social Security and SSI checks sent to a different bank, fearing that the money would be tied up and unavailable for Elaine's living expenses. Finally, when TRM moved to another part of town and Elaine and Hilda began taking the van instead of the bus, it became clear that they would both have to change to a bank closer to home. Liz still resisted, but finally agreed after being assured by Social Security personnel that the change was not as complicated as she imagined. Elaine is delighted with the new bank, which is much closer to home, and she has already cultivated first-name relationships with several of the staff, whose business cards she keeps in her wallet, along with many others.

On Friday evenings, Elaine and Hilda again eat out. Once a month, they may attend a dance at the local Salvation Army headquarters. The dance is organized by an enthusiastic young couple who take a personal interest in many of the participants. Many parents show up as well, and some even join in the dancing, although most stand together in the back of the room and talk. There are "regulars," mostly from the workshop, but other programs for adults with mental retardation also bring their members. The music is often rock-and-roll cassette tapes, but occasionally High Hopes, a musical group composed of "gifted" members with disabilities, performs more traditional tunes, which Elaine, Hilda, and Sam prefer. During the evening, the directing couple also lead some standard party games (like musical chairs), which Elaine, Hilda, and Sam avoid because they see them as too physically taxing or boisterous. Elaine, Hilda, and Sam usually like to sit surrounded by friends, watching some of the younger, more active participants put on a real dance show. Later, punch and cake are served, which they all enjoy with relish.

Weekends are more relaxed, but not much less active. Elaine and Hilda sleep late in the mornings, enjoying a late breakfast or brunch. On Saturdays, Sam comes by at exactly 1:15 P.M. They sit for a while, offer Sam refreshments, and then usually all three go out somewhere together. Sam always leaves them at 3:30 P.M. to get home in time for supper at Exeter, the convalescent home where he lives. Occasionally, Elaine sabotages this routine by staying in her pajamas until well past Sam's arrival, delaying their departure and yet refusing to allow them to go without her. Elaine simply will not allow Hilda to go anywhere without her, unless it is with Ada, and even then Elaine is usually included. Hilda is less frequently invited to Elaine's family events, perhaps because of their frequently religious character, but Elaine's family's ambivalence and even embarrassment about retardation may also be a factor.

Hilda has pleaded with Elaine to let her go alone with Sam sometimes, but Elaine invariably throws a tantrum and threatens to lock her out if she leaves. Elaine's counselors and I have tried to reason with Elaine to no avail. The only strategy that works is if Elaine's mother, her counselor, or I take her out at the same time that Hilda is going elsewhere, as this represents an acceptable trade-off to Elaine. Elaine's obsession is not just with Hilda's company, but involves a more fundamental aversion to being left alone or left out. No amount of arguing about Hilda's right to privacy and time on her own will convince Elaine, who always argues back: "I don't think it's right. We're roomates, and roommates are supposed to be there, with each other, at all times." It does not help that Liz supports her daughter on this issue, blithely ignoring Hilda and Sam's stated desires, with the argument that, after all, Hilda and Sam are not married so why should Elaine not accompany them? Her position may be less an indication of thoughtlessness regarding Hilda and Sam than an example of her instrumental desire to strengthen the bond between Elaine and Hilda so that it will still be there for Elaine to rely on when Liz is deceased. That bond is also very convenient for Liz now because it takes care of most of Elaine's emotional needs, needs that Liz herself is plainly unprepared to fulfill. Clearly, in Elaine's mind, her relationship with Hilda is the equivalent of a parental or marital bond.

On occasional Saturdays Elaine and Hilda go to a beauty parlor to have their hair done, escorted by Liz, who often supervises the work being done on her daughter. This always makes Elaine uncomfortable, although for the most part she enjoys the care lavished upon her in these outings. On rarer Saturdays, Elaine and Hilda elect to stay home and do housework, usually at the urging of Rachel. They generally stay home Saturday evenings.

Sunday mornings Liz takes the two of them out for brunch at a coffee shop. In many of her Sunday diary entries, Elaine appreciatively mentions their favorite order, the Cheddar Scrambler (the notorious four-egg omelette mentioned earlier). Food has special meaning to Elaine: familiar food, comfort food, indulgent food. It is also important to her when others make it or buy it for her. She often mentions in her diary that Hilda has prepared a meal or that her mother has "taken care of" the brunch. Following brunch, Liz takes them to a nearby grocery store to do their weekly food shopping, while she waits in the car. As with the beauty shop bill, Hilda and Elaine pay their own grocery bills.

The fact that Liz takes them grocery shopping is a bit surprising, because the market is only six blocks from their home and they could conceivably take the bus there and back. However, this pattern of assistance became firmly established while they were still in the Upward program, living in another apartment some distance from a market. Upward had recommended the use of fold-up shopping carts for carrying their purchases along city sidewalks, but these were really too cumbersome to get onto the two buses they had to take each way. For a while, Hilda and Elaine took taxis at a fare reduced for seniors and disabled persons, but this proved to be expensive and unreliable in a city not known for good taxi service. A possible solution would have been to limit their purchases, small in number anyway, to what they could carry without using the cumbersome shopping carts. But they were still concerned about occasional bad weather, Hilda's fear of losing her balance while carrying packages, and the infrequency of buses on Sundays, so Liz accepted the responsibility of driving them as her weekly contribution. This persisted even after they moved closer to a market. On the rare occasions when Liz cannot make it, Elaine and Hilda manage to get to and from the market on foot or by bus.

On Sunday afternoons, Elaine and Hilda used to walk with their laundry to a nearby laundromat, using the fold-up carts. However, when Hilda's back problem developed in mid-1987 and Elaine began walking with a cane, Ada agreed to pick up their laundry once a week to have it done professionally. They reimburse her for the cost, an acceptable expense since their TRM earnings rose.

This is their basic, weekly routine. It is highlighted by other small details as well. Some evenings, Elaine and Hilda go to the corner liquor store to buy diet soda and ice cream. Liz calls Elaine every evening if Elaine has not called her first. Their conversations are brief, usually affectionate, but sometimes full of tension. Elaine frequently gets calls from Laura, a former Upward client who has kept in touch with her. Elaine is not terribly appreciative of Laura's calls, however, and complains that she calls incessantly. When I pointed out to Elaine that she tends to do the same thing to her counselors and to me, she replied, "Yah, but I'm not Laura's counselor." Indeed, Elaine was stating a fundamental truth in her worldview: Counselors are supposed to listen patiently to their client's calls. But she realizes that more equal friends cannot be expected to put up with it.

Elaine and Hilda have developed a few other interests to keep them busy in their spare time besides television and radio. For example, Elaine did some embroidery in the past, while Hilda has done needlepoint, although they both seem to have abandoned these activities in recent years. They enjoy word puzzles and buy books of them. Elaine prefers word puzzles of a graphic sort, while Hilda likes crossword puzzles. They used to play board games, but have not played recently. On learning that they had not been to a public library in some time, although they had gone in the past, I helped them get new library cards, and for a while they were reading novels. When the library closed temporarily for renovations, they lacked the initiative to go to another nearby branch as an alternative and so fell out of the habit. More commonly, they read magazines and an occasional newspaper. Elaine's attention span tends to be shorter than Hilda's, and she more often craves easy stimulation and quick gratification. Surprisingly, she rarely goes to movies, which would seem to be an ideal entertainment. She enjoys movies on the rare occasions when someone else takes her to one, but shows no initiative in going with Hilda or Sam. The reason she gives is that going to movies at night would keep them out too late. When asked why she does not go to weekend matinees, she concedes that this is a good idea, but claims not to know of any good movies. When asked to choose a movie from those advertised in the newspaper, she tends to select those few aimed at children and "family" audiences, explaining that she was taught by her parents to select those with a "parental guidance" rating.

RECIPROCITY

Elaine's relationship with Hilda is not entirely asymmetrical and exploitative, although it may seem so at times. In some ways their relationship is more reciprocal than has been described so far. Hilda derives considerable satisfaction from exercising her own competence in the course of dealing with Elaine's needs, and Elaine is on occasion a helpful, inspiring, and entertaining roommate. When one of the roommates is sick, the other will generally cook or get take-out food. When an emergency occurs while they are together, one seeks help for the other in distress. When one is distressed, ill, or upset, the other will do little favors and try to cheer her up. On many such occasions, Elaine has proved capable of being the giver of help when the circumstances demand it. When she comes through for Hilda, she is quick to tell others of her contributions, which she relates with some pride, expecting due praise.

Although many among the two women's counselors and family look upon Elaine and Hilda's relationship as ideal because it seems to have solved an immediate problem, others view Elaine's emotional dependency and manipulation of Hilda as an obstacle to her development of "genuine" independence. Turning around one researcher's contention that Elaine's relative success living independently can be attributed to her good luck at finding Hilda as a roommate, the question becomes, "What would Elaine do if something deprived her of Hilda?" That event could be as traumatic to her as the death of her father.

Hilda's special field of competence is not her verbal abilities or her ability to direct others to do things for her. Her productivity at TRM, although acceptable, is fairly low, so her work abilities also are not an area where Hilda shines. Hilda's special skill is in identifying other people's needs and then determining which of her own abilities could be used to help them. This is why she prefers friends who are retarded to staff friends. Hilda has found in Elaine a perfect foil for her own greatest strengths. She is placid and calming where Elaine is anxiety-ridden, nurturing where Elaine is demanding, thoughtful where Elaine is selfish, and cautious where Elaine is impetuous. Hilda is organized where Elaine is scattered. She remembers social obligations and events, while Elaine is sometimes forgetful. Hilda is dutiful and mindful of rules, while Elaine is rebellious and neglectful. And, to a point, Hilda is prepared to generously overlook Elaine's exploitative behavior. Superficially, Hilda may look like she can be pushed around, but Elaine's emotional dependency on her is a weapon that Hilda knows she can use in a pinch.

An example of Hilda's potential power over Elaine has arisen recently, as Hilda has begun to rebel against Elaine's more oppressive demands, which have increased along with Elaine's growing boredom. First, some background would be useful. The good-natured Hilda has had only one enemy at TRM, Shirley. Shirley was another middle-aged woman with mild developmental handicaps who was very articulate like Elaine, and for this reason TRM had tried early on to encourage the two to become friends. This had not worked out well because Shirley was very independent and looked disdainfully on Elaine's emotional dependency. Shirley nonetheless asked Elaine to be roommates, before Elaine paired up with Hilda. Elaine was not comfortable with Shirley's tendency to demand that Elaine do things for her, something Elaine found especially outrageous. (Hilda commented, "I think she [Shirley] wanted a maid.") Liz had also taken a strong dislike to this very outspoken and independent woman; Shirley, it was apparent, had not been charmed by Liz either. When Elaine became roommates with Hilda, Shirley turned her ire on Hilda, saying unkind things about Hilda to others at the workshop. What infuriated Hilda most were Shirley's attempts to sabotage her relationship with Sam. Not only did Shirley tell Sam outright to stay away from Hilda, but she also deployed some members of her high-functioning clique, from which Hilda and Elaine were often ostracized at her behest, to give Sam the same message.

Hilda became obsessed with Shirley's machinations and began to blame her negative influence for all manner of things, including Elaine's problems with attracting and keeping boyfriends at the shop. Shirley had become Hilda's nemesis. The mere mention of her name sent Hilda into lengthy denunciations of Shirley's misdeeds. Hilda's counselors, disturbed by the vehemence and persistence of her obsession but unable to alter the situation, repeatedly advised her to ignore Shirley and to not speak of her again. To this day, whenever Shirley's name arises in conversation, Hilda will apologetically say, "I'm sorry to mention her name, but. . . ."

Late in 1987, when Hilda and Elaine were going through an especially rough period, particularly over the issue of Elaine's tagging along on Saturday outings with Sam, Hilda suggested to Elaine that maybe she should consider moving in with Shirley. Elaine was devastated. The fact that Hilda could not only suggest an end to their being roommates but also propose that Elaine join forces with Hilda's own arch-enemy sent a clear message to Elaine regarding the depth of Hilda's displeasure and the extent to which she might go to rebel against Elaine's manipulation. Elaine was so outraged that she reported this gross breach of loyalty to her counselors, only to be told that Hilda could choose to stop being roommates if she so desired. Whenever Hilda made the suggestion, Elaine threatened to call her mother and call Ada, so Hilda softened her tone and said she had not really meant that Elaine should leave, just that Elaine should stop, according to Hilda, "bothering me all the time." When asked by the researcher what this meant, Hilda explicitly mentioned not only Elaine's incessant demands for attention, but also mild physical abuse, something which had long gone on in the relationship, but recently had escalated. This included grabbing, squeezing, twisting, and pinching Hilda's arms, hitting her with a hairbrush, and occasionally "tapping" her with a cane. Elaine also frequently makes threatening gestures, although this often seems more like a game in her attention-getting repertoire than a real attempt to do bodily harm.

The argument raged on for months and still crops up periodically when Hilda gets upset. When this happens, Elaine complains vociferously to her mother and counselors, and Hilda reassures Elaine that she did not really mean it; nonetheless, Hilda continues to raise this issue in an attempt to modify some of Elaine's excesses. In fact, it was Hilda who deliberately brought this issue to my attention, expecting me to be sympathetic to her and disapproving of Elaine's more abusive behavior. This was an effective strategy because Elaine does actively seek my approval, and yet an appeal to me to mediate a dispute has fewer negative repercussions than an appeal to a counselor or a family member. The now-deceased Shirley is herself no longer the issue, but Hilda still occasionally suggests that Elaine get another roommate. After all, she will remind Elaine, she, Hilda, does not mind living alone. Although Hilda too stands to lose a good thing if they separate, she could be serious in her implied threat to terminate this long-standing relationship.

THE TRIANGLE: HILDA, SAM, AND ELAINE

The relationship between Sam and Hilda was originally engineered in 1984 by Joyce, a former administrator at TRM. Hilda's calm, nurturing qualities were thought to make her a good match for Sam, who shows a definite preference for such women. They had not gotten together outside of TRM earlier because Hilda has never been aggressive in pursuing relations with men (she was raised very strictly, she says), and Sam had always been drawn more to solicitous, nonretarded women, especially staff. The counselors thought that Sam should be encouraged to interact more with people other than staff, the unchallenged assumption being that other clients with mental retardation were his true "peers" and therefore more appropriate friends with whom to socialize. The staff also felt that Hilda and Elaine should be weaned a bit from each other. Another questionable assumption was that a girlfriend/boyfriend idiom would be a more powerful motivating factor than a same-sex friendship. In fact, Hilda says she had never had a boyfriend before, and Sam claims he had never had a girlfriend. Sam was slightly embarrassed at first at the idea of having a girlfriend, and he still blushes when others tease him about it. However, part of him is clearly pleased. To accomodate his reticence, Hilda tells people, "We're just good friends," but in reality she is slightly proprietary.

Joyce suggested that Hilda meet Sam at the beach so that they could both get some exercise. This did not work out well, however, because Elaine resented being left out. Elaine also wanted a boyfriend. Unfortunately, the man she had been paired with by her psychotherapist had not seemed appropriate to her. He was also a TRM client, but he did not live independently and was so emotionally dependent on his elderly parents that the relationship with Elaine went nowhere. Subsequently, Elaine had a much higher-functioning boyfriend who was, in contrast to the first one, socially and sexually advanced beyond Elaine. Their relationship rarely extended beyond the workshop and eventually ended when he left the workshop to engage in supported work. Elaine herself helped sabotage both relationships, being nervously hesitant about acting out the usual girlfriend/boyfriend behaviors.

More to the point, however, Elaine did not want anything to come between her and Hilda. Elaine convinced Sam and Hilda that he should visit them in their apartment and be entertained there first, before going out. Then, if Sam and Hilda wanted to go out, usually for ice cream, Elaine always tagged along. They tolerated this most of the time because of Hilda's loyalty to Elaine and her real enjoyment of Elaine's company and because Sam found Elaine to be at least as stimulating as Hilda. Sam also expressed some fear of being alone with Hilda in case she fell down, something that happens on occasion. Problems arose, however, whenever Hilda began to resent the way Elaine dominated Sam's attention and when Elaine annoyed Sam by petulantly insisting they all go when and where she wanted to go, regardless of his desires, causing him to get upset and go off by himself.

At this point it should be mentioned that all three appear to be almost entirely without interest in sex. Hilda claims never to have had any interest, citing her strict family upbringing. Sam and Elaine each had at least one traumatic, coerced sexual encounter when they were young, and understandably they both express some negative attitudes about sex based on these experiences, in spite of having undergone psychotherapy later in life. Hilda and Elaine disclaim any interest in masturbation, and their touching of each other, while affectionate, is quite limited. They are not entirely ignorant of sexual matters, however. Hilda and Elaine had sex education classes at a local college while they were in the Upward program. Sam says he had no sex education, although he used to talk to his father, he says, "about anything I wanted to," and this may have included some sexual concerns. He becomes intensely embarrassed talking about sex, unlike Hilda and Elaine, who are matter-of-fact about it.

The triangular relationship between Hilda, Elaine, and Sam is not about sex, then. It is about companionship, social role-playing, and perceptions of "normalcy" and competence. When Sam comes by on a Saturday, Hilda often presents him with cookies or other "goodies" that she has baked for his benefit. Elaine occasionally does the same, taking her cue from Hilda, in spite of the fact that she otherwise has much less interest in cooking. (More recently, Elaine has occasionally baked things for their TRM van driver, a woman with whom she is attempting to develop a personal relationship.) Sam, who has a definite sweet tooth, is very appreciative. Hilda abides by some very conventional ideas about sex roles. "They say the way to a man's heart is through his stomach," she tells Elaine. She also extolls the virtues of being a "good listener," something Sam is always seeking. Hilda obviously was raised to be very considerate of others, and the little favors she does for Sam are not lost on him. (For example, Hilda attentively serves him the cookies she bakes.) When they go out, Hilda links her arm possessively with Sam's, ostensibly to "help him," but it is clear she has in mind the image of a steady couple, which is indeed what they look like. Although Elaine often manages to deliberately interpose herself between them, she otherwise shies away from physical intimacies with Sam, except occasionally to help him on with his coat. When the three attend monthly dances hosted by the Salvation Army, they stick close together. Hilda and Sam occasionally dance together, while Elaine rarely dances with anyone. The three spend most of the time sitting and listening to the music, chatting with each other and with friends who stop by to greet them.

Elaine's relationship with Sam is far less important to her than her relationship with Hilda. At times, Hilda plays the mother to Elaine's teenage daughter, quite willingly acting out the kind of relationship Elaine misses with her own mother. For example, Hilda tucks Elaine into bed each night and kisses her goodnight on the forehead. At other times, Hilda performs many of the functions of a traditional wife, such as cooking, cleaning, and providing moral support, while Elaine assumes the role of a traditional husband, such as being waited on at home and mailing out paid bills. In the past, Hilda was very close to her mother, while Elaine was much closer to her father, so their quasi-marital relationship may represent their complementary attempts to imitate beloved departed parents. By sharing an interest in Sam, Elaine is reinforcing her relationship with Hilda, not intentionally competing with her. Shortly after she started to see Sam, Hilda named one of her stuffed toy dogs "Sammy." Elaine immediately named her identical toy dog "Sammy Two." The two women sometimes play with their toy dogs together, heaping sentimental words on Sammy and Sammy Two while amiably discussing their joint plans for the coming Saturday.

Hilda has not successfully resolved the problem of Elaine's intrusion into her relationship with Sam. She complained in a diary entry about Elaine's behavior when she and Sam wish to go out alone.

> Sam and I can't get out Because Elaine keeping us waiting. She always wants going along. I don't it all time because might surprize her sometime. We can't get out Because she wants to go along all the time. It's embarassing the away she acts around a friend. She started kicking at me, I didn't like it, because was in front Sam. Try push her hand out the way. She said "no, no, no to me. I said to her "Don't tell what do." Sam started leave the apartment. Sam and I want go alone somewhere. Elaine went along seven weeks. Elaine always like to tag along with us. Then we took Sam to his Bus and went home. Elaine sometimes acts like Big baby. When someone is around I would let her go out alone with a friend. She should a little consedertion for Sam and me on Saturdays.

This situation is unlikely to be resolved as long as Elaine and Hilda remain roommates. Although Hilda nurses her resentment about this, and Sam complains as well, neither has had the strength to openly defy Elaine. Elaine's self-centered behavior has proved remarkably resistant to modification, even by professionals, perhaps because it is so integral to her worldview and experiences. In spite of their irritation, Hilda and Sam are drawn to Elaine precisely because she does have such a strong personality and because she does seek so ardently to engage them.

Hilda's relationship with Sam is something of a refuge from the intensity of her relationship with Elaine. By identifying Sam as her boyfriend, Hilda attempts to deflect some of Elaine's possessiveness and demands on her attention. On Elaine's part, she seeks to enjoy Sam through and with Hilda, as a kind of vicarious steady boyfriend, having been unable to keep one of her own; she leaves the job of managing and sustaining the relationship to Hilda. Sam enjoys the doting attention of both women and vacillates somewhat in his loyalties. He fears Hilda's physical vulnerabilities and possible possessiveness, but he also fears Elaine's erratic emotionalism and resents her demands. Their triangular relationship is not just problematic, but also dynamic, having its own dialectic, and it may persist for some time despite all its tensions.

Hilda's relationship with Sam is of great importance to her self-esteem. By helping Sam and being his companion, she is proving her ability to fulfill two socially valued roles—helpmate and girlfriend. Hilda was raised with a strong sense of convention and propriety, and she is acutely sensitive to social norms and models, including what she sees on television or in the homemaker magazines she reads. Hilda's mother was her most important role model early in life. Her sister Ada, a proper, gracious, well-spoken, and well-dressed married woman, is now her most important role model, and she has a definite impact on reinforcing Hilda's values. Hilda projects a much more traditionally feminine image than Elaine; she dresses more carefully and with a decidedly more feminine flair, she routinely applies lipstick and lotion, and she shows greater interest in housework, especially cooking. Hilda's somewhat stylized behavior with Sam, such as taking his arm while they are walking, baking and/or serving him sweets when he visits, and exhibiting jealousy, are also consistent with her feminine role playing.

Elaine's major role model was her father, only secondarily her mother. Her quasi-masculine role playing, self-absorption, dependence on authority figures, and sexual fears have all hindered Elaine's ability to develop a lasting relationship with a boyfriend. Yet, she too recognizes the normative social desirability of having one. Thus, this triangle—her relationship with Sam via Hilda—is for her an ideal solution to her problem.

ATTITUDES TOWARD BEING HANDICAPPED

Hilda's conventional femininity, it could be suggested, is not just the product of her upbringing. It is also an important part of her attempt to overcome and compensate for her handicap. Although she claims to have been unaware of the category "retarded" until she joined the Upward program, Hilda is intelligent and sensitive enough to have realized for most of her life that she is perceived as being different from most people in a decidedly negative way; her physical characteristics and tremors made this fairly obvious. Although Hilda could never pass for non-disabled in the way that Elaine often does, she has not allowed labels to hinder her development into a mature, responsible woman. Unlike individuals with mental retardation living in the community who deny their handicaps, hide their lack of competence, and attempt to prove their "normality," Hilda does not deny her handicap. She frankly acknowledges her impairments and lack of experience in certain areas, but says, "That doesn't mean I can't live a normal life like everyone else." Like many individuals, Hilda has lived her "normal" life in stages over time. It just so happens that her adolescence lasted a bit longer than usual, overlapping with a kind of spinsterhood while she lived with her mother after leaving the boarding school. It was not until she reached her 50s that she assumed a spousal role in her relationships with Elaine and Sam.

In contrast to Hilda, Elaine embraces her handicaps and even manufactures new ones in an effort to hold on to center stage. Her childhood experiences taught her that to be handicapped was not to be stigmatized, but to be rewarded. This was the unintended consequence of her father's loving attentions. She learned to use her intelligence and social skills to attach herself firmly to adults or authority figures and thereby enjoy stimulating but eminently safe relationships and experiences.

Three episodes in Elaine and Hilda's recent life demonstrate more about their own ideas concerning independence and being mentally retarded. The first was Elaine's insistence that she was going "blind" and "crippled," a claim apparently precipitated by her fears regarding supported work. In repeated discussions, Elaine made it clear that she recognized that being retarded is no longer regarded as sufficient reason to remain at TRM indefinitely. For that reason, she began to emphatically insist that she was actually "physically handicapped," even to the point of denying that she was retarded, just to be sure there was no confusion. When Elaine was asked how she could continue to work at TRM if she indeed was becoming "blind" and "crippled," she pointed out all the clients in the shop who suffer from severe disabilities: "And they're good workers." From Elaine's point of view, being physically handicapped is not any more demeaning or limiting than being mentally handicapped, and neither, in her experience, is particularly unpleasant.

Of course, this rosy view of physical disability is entirely unrealistic, but that did not matter because Elaine knew she really was not going blind or becoming physically disabled anyway. The point is that her perceptions of her place in the world had reversed themselves in less than a decade. Before coming to TRM, she had never participated in a setting devoted exclusively to people with handicaps, and the idea was an alarming novelty. Now Elaine cannot imagine herself existing happily without TRM, where she has found a strong sense of belonging, even if that means redefining her own handicap as entirely and drastically physical.

A second episode concerns Elaine and Hilda's personal hygiene, but more deeply, their right to privacy and their right to ignore the hygienic standards of others should they choose to do so. When Rachel drew up a hygiene chart to ensure that Elaine and Hilda bathed regularly, something they had fallen out of the habit of doing, Hilda complied but Elaine chafed at this bit of regimentation. Because it was not a priority to her, being a solitary activity, Elaine continued skipping baths, coming up with her usual excuses of being "too tired," "recovering from a cold," and so forth. Such reasoning had been routinely accepted from both women in the past, but when it became apparent that Hilda was bathing and Elaine was not, Rachel grew impatient and insisted one evening that Elaine get into the tub immediately. Rachel followed her into the bathroom, dousing Elaine's head with water and helping her wash her hair. She supervised the entire process.

Elaine was outraged at this violation of her privacy, but not by having her physical nudity exposed to the other woman. Specifically, Elaine was offended that she was being treated like a "little girl."

> I thought we were supposed to be adults. Wash ourselves, clothe ourselves, feed ourselves. What's the point of having a hygiene chart if she's going to come charging in here, throws me in the tub, and then dumps water all over me? I can bathe myself. For five years nobody's said anything about this, so why now, all of a sudden?

Elaine makes it quite clear that, to her understanding, being an independent adult means having the discretion to *not* follow the rules, and yet not be humiliated as a consequence. She argues convincingly that cleanliness has little to do intrinsically with independence or adulthood. Nonetheless, Rachel is motivated to change Elaine's behavior by health considerations and by a conviction that normalization and independence require meeting minimum standards of social acceptability, such as not repelling others with body odor. Rachel finally devised the strategy of fining Elaine and Hilda $5 of their budgeted weekly allowance if a bath or other personal hygiene task was skipped. However, this works only slightly better than hustling Elaine bodily into the tub because it requires that Elaine be scrupulously honest when filling in the details of her chart.

A final episode demonstrating Elaine's and Hilda's views on independence concerns their standard of housekeeping, which is similar in principle to the personal hygiene issue. As mentioned earlier, Elaine and Hilda were so lax in their housekeeping by late 1987 that Rachel suggested they bring in a maid service. This made sense because clearly their hearts were not in the task; they had both been complaining of physical problems that made it difficult for them to do housework; and they had both been earning so much money at TRM that they could more than afford to pay for the service. Hilda objected only mildly, in her usual laconic fashion, "I don't like it much. I'm used to doing my own things." But she ultimately agreed to the intrusion, perhaps because she had always done most of the housework anyway. Elaine, however, was livid. "I don't want them in here. We can do it ourselves. We aren't babies. We know how to do it. I don't see why strangers should come in here and clean. Aren't we supposed to be adults?" Elaine shirked housework at every opportunity, yet she was deeply insulted at the implication that they were not competent to do the job. That they never actually did housework with any thoroughness was irrelevant. When Rachel pointed out their poor housecleaning performance, however, Elaine countered with an even more powerful argument: "We work hard all week. Aren't we entitled to a little time off on the weekend? Isn't it supposed to be our time, to do with as we please?" Elaine's point may not have won the day, as the maid service now visits periodically, but it was a clear and reasonable defense of her own competence and self-esteem.

COUNSELORS

Hilda is not the only parent-substitute in Elaine's life. Since entering TRM, and especially since her father's death and her departure from her mother's home, Elaine's life has been dominated by counselors of various sorts. These tend to be young, usually female, figures who wield considerable authority in her life by virtue of their control over her participation in TRM, over her independent living situation with Hilda, and over her financial security as mediators in her relationship with Regional Center and Social Security. To some extent, these counselors even mediate her relationship with her mother. However, Elaine is not intimidated by the power her counselors have over her life. Rather, she expends considerable energy in cultivating her relationships with them, successfully manipulates them in various ways, and revels in the fact that these individuals are professionally obliged to regularly spend time listening to her, helping her, reassuring her, and directing her. Elaine recognizes the fundamental power asymmetry between herself as "client" and her assorted counselors, and she simply seeks to turn this situation to her advantage. Elaine's dependency is thus reinforced, even as her counselors attempt to ease her transition from a dependent adult child living at home to an ostensibly "independent" employee and roommate.

The impersonal, bureaucratic functioning of social services, the multiplicity of counselors with authority over her, the high turnover rate in some counseling positions, and the large case loads that limit counselors' interaction with clients all contribute to Elaine's sense that ultimately she does not have much power over her life, except by manipulating various authorities. She does not always regret this lack of power, seeing quite clearly that dependency is often her strongest tool for getting what she wants, which is security and attention. Independence for its own sake has no evident value for Elaine, nor, given her experience, should it. Some of her counselors have come to the conclusion that at her age this is unlikely to change. She simply does not have lengthy experience, which starts for most nondisabled persons in late adolescence, to build on.

Elaine's class background and relatively sheltered existence have given her a particular worldview and set of values, to which she ardently adheres. Elaine expressed this quite clearly when she commented on a documentary film about an aging man with mental retardation who lives in an impoverished inner-city neighborhood, but who, in many respects, leads a much more independent existence than she does. Her reaction differed from that of researchers, who frankly admired the man's achievements. Elaine too admired his "spunk," and even identified elements of his life as being similar to her own, but she also felt sorry for him because "he's kind of like a homeless person." Elaine was reacting both to the evident squalor of his life and to the lack in his life of a support network that is familiar to her. ("Rachel would never, never let us get our apartment as messy as his," she commented with disapproval.) From Elaine's point of view, her own life is more normal and successful than his. For example, she was quite surprised that he could not read or write and that he consequently experienced trouble grocery shopping for a neighbor. The idea that he had never learned to read and that this had become a lifelong obstacle to him was incomprehensible to her, as it is to many literate people who take this skill for granted. She commented:

> Even Sammy can read, and his eyes are bad! And he goes to the grocery for Amy [a nurse at Exeter] all the time. He doesn't even need a list. *We* don't use a list. We don't write one, it's in our heads. Couldn't he [the man in the film] remember?

That the man in the film had greater independence in terms of his lack of institutional and authority supports seemed, to her, beside the point, even tragic.

Although Elaine spends a great deal of time and effort in cultivating what look like dependent relationships, she nonetheless sees herself as being fairly independent and takes pride in this. She even chafes at "help" from her mother and counselors when this intrudes unduly on her self-image or personal inclinations. In Elaine's mind, having a broad support system of mother, roommate, roommate's sister, independent living counselor, TRM, Regional Center, doctors, and so on, to use at her own discretion is part of being independent and living a "normal" life.

Elaine and Hilda have three major types of counselors. Elaine's Regional Center caseworker has been with her several years now and is very pleasant and encouraging. He has been so impressed by Elaine's progress at TRM that he is the primary proponent of putting her into a supported work program. However, he sees her only for about an hour once or twice a year at her IPP meetings. She has his business card and calls him occasionally to ask about her IPP. Since he suggested supported work, she has also taken pains to remind him several times on the phone that she does not want to leave TRM. Her mother has also called him occasionally to register her concern about this issue. The counselor reassures them that Elaine will not be forced to do anything she does not want to do but continually urges them to think about it some more, and the recommendation continues to appear on her IPP reports. "He's trying to wear me down," Elaine astutely observes.

Hilda's long-time Regional Center caseworker met her first when he was director of the residential care facility she stayed in briefly before entering the Upward program. Hilda felt as if she could always call him for assistance or information, if need be, although she very rarely did. Recently, he was replaced by a young woman who knows little about Hilda and whose only opportunities to find out more will be at yearly IPP meetings. "I feel like I'm starting all over again," complained Hilda, who went on to say that she will miss her original caseworker. She felt helpless to do anything about the change, however. "It's not up to me. Sometimes you just have to accept these things." While Elaine usually has a mid-year IPP meeting as well as her annual one, Hilda has only the annual meeting at which to see her caseworker face-to-face. This is because Hilda's productivity is expected to remain relatively stable and because her record of compliance with what is expected of her is so reliable. Elaine, on the other hand, has many more behavioral problems for IPP goals to address, and she herself demands these extra meetings, enjoying the extra attention. Hilda is not bothered by having fewer IPP meetings than Elaine. "I prefer it. I get nervous at meetings. I just try to do a good job and mind my own business."

Like all other clients at the workshop, Elaine and Hilda each also have a TRM counselor. In the hierarchy of TRM staff, counselors are above instructors (who change frequently) and below the director. Counselors are not paid especially well for what is a stressful job, and most of them eventually move on to other jobs, often at Regional Centers. Those who have stayed longest all "burned out" on Elaine some time ago, so Elaine is continually being reassigned to newer counseling staff.

Counselors and instructors are often frustrated by how disruptive Elaine's behavior can be to the work routine and to relations *among* staff. For example, Elaine sometimes abandons her workpost to get the attention of staff members or sits stock-still as if in a trance until someone pays attention to her. Sometimes she cries or destroys her working materials while in this trance state, later disclaiming any awareness or intent. If she is anxious about something, she seeks support from any and all staff members she feels might be sympathetic, instead of going to the most appropriate one. She is critical of how other employees on her line are working, even interrupting the flow of production to register her disapproval. She is easily distracted by the misbehavior of other employees. Elaine's disruptive behaviors have been brought under some control in recent years by making their eradication part of Elaine's IPP goals. She receives praise at each meeting for the degree to which she complies with this goal.

Elaine is very adept at playing staff members off against each other by telling them discrepant information. Elaine is an expert at manipulating information as well as people. She feigns innocence, forgetfulness, or misunderstanding when "called on the carpet." One of her most commonly used ruses, both in and out of TRM, is to claim that some person in authority has made a sudden, unreasonable demand on her, completely without explanation. This is almost invariably rebutted by the person in question, who usually claims to have explained matters quite painstakingly to Elaine. Of course, what Elaine is really saying is that, in spite of the explanation, she really does not want to do what is being required of her. Just as surely and stubbornly, the authorities in her life generally insist that she do it anyway, whether "for her own good" or for the convenience of others. In this kind of situation, Elaine is actually seeking a kind of independence on her own terms, although within the context of her structurally dependent relationship with authority. Unfortunately, this strategy reinforces her reputation for being errant and willful and consequently reinforces the paternalism of authorities.

Eventually, authority figures realize that more time and energy is being spent trying to untangle the web of Elaine's complaints and deceits than is spent in encouraging her more socially acceptable abilities. Unfortunately, some authority figures become antagonistic toward Elaine, expressing a sense of smugness when they can catch her in her own game and reprimand her accordingly. This becomes tedious after a while, especially because it does not deter Elaine. In fact, several people have noticed that Elaine often seems to want to be caught and reprimanded, perhaps because she feels that negative attention is better than no attention at all.

In contrast, Hilda is completely convinced of the desirability of a low profile: "I don't like to call attention to myself at TRM. I stay out of trouble that way." Hilda has had the same TRM counselor, Deana, for many years. Deana praises Hilda for her consistently compliant behavior. However, Hilda never approaches this counselor to discuss any of her concerns, complaints, or criticisms. "Deana doesn't talk to me much. I can take her or leave her." Hilda's main concern is simply to avoid provoking her disapproval.

Elaine has also "burned out" several independent living counselors, all of whom were vendored through Regional Center. She finally was assigned to Rachel, a very energetic and determined counselor who believes that her success with Elaine is due to a firm, consistent approach and judicious use of behavior modification techniques. Rachel has worked with Elaine for several years and has succeeded where many others failed, forming a lasting partnership with Elaine and persuading her to gradually change some of her more irritating and problematic habits. Rachel is now the primary facilitator of Elaine's independent lifestyle. This relationship is not without its problems, including the ones described above, but like Elaine and Hilda's relationship, Elaine and Rachel's has proved to be stable, even mutually reinforcing, and a source of satisfaction to them both.

Elaine's mother is somewhat ambivalent about Elaine and Rachel's relationship. Although she appreciates that Rachel assumes most of the burden of monitoring Elaine's mundane concerns, she expresses mild jealousy at times over the usurpation of affection and authority. Another adult's managerial and behavioral success with Elaine only highlights Liz's own relative lack of success in this area. For example, Liz regretfully but readily admits that Rachel and I seem to know more about Elaine's present life than she does, and to make matters worse, she feels Elaine is more willing to "listen" to us than to her. Liz complains that Rachel does not keep her sufficiently informed or return her phone calls promptly. That may be partly true, but a more fundamental reality is that Liz herself is resistant to involving herself any more than she already does in her daughter's life.

Liz is the model and catalyst for much of Elaine's dependent and emotional behavior. Not only does Elaine react to her mother with nervousness and anxiety, but she also imitates her mother's similar behaviors, just as surely as she imitates her father in other respects. As Hilda astutely observed to Elaine, regarding her admitted "emotionalism:" "I think you get a little of it from your mother." To which Elaine replied: "Two emotional people don't go good together." Elaine further describes her relationship with her mother as follows:

> I have to be careful when I go to see Mom, because Mom is a very excitable, highly emotional individual. Smart too. You didn't notice? You don't know that Mom and I don't get along too well. That's the

reason they put me in the program [Upward program.] We never got along. She'd yell at me and I'd argue back or something. . . .

Elaine learned helplessness from her mother and exhibits it in much the same areas, for example, budgeting. Liz comments, "She takes after me in that." Thus, in trying to deal with Elaine's most serious deficiencies, Rachel is having to attack qualities that Elaine learned from her mother and that her mother continues to reinforce to some extent.

Some of Elaine's problems have endured despite Rachel's best efforts. Two examples are Elaine's poor record of taking care of her belongings, including expensive ones, and her handling of money. In both cases, Elaine's problems are much less by-products of her mental retardation than they are the result of anxieties and learned helplessness. Furthermore, Elaine's resistance to changing her behavior may be partially motivated by her awareness that, if she cleans up her act too well, Rachel may no longer have a reason to be so closely involved in her life.

When Elaine's anxieties get the better of her, she has a tendency to destroy things, although she insists that this is never her intent. Sometimes this occurs in the context of a full-fledged tantrum, but at other times, it is the result of mild irritation, carelessness, or a tendency to fidget. When she went through three pairs of prescription glasses in less than a year, MediCal would not pay for another replacement pair, and Rachel brought the issue up at Elaine's IPP meeting. Rachel may have hoped that such a formal, public discussion of the problem would force Elaine to take it more seriously and avoid fidgeting with her glasses in the future. Elaine, who ordinarily expects praise at these meetings, was indeed embarrassed by this open disclosure of her misbehavior, but so was Liz, who quickly came to Elaine's defense. Liz argued with Rachel over various details and then scornfully announced that if MediCal would not pay for new glasses, she would. This, of course, undercut what Rachel was trying to accomplish. As Elaine herself later revealed, her parents had always dealt with her destructiveness by replacing the ruined item. Liz expects destructive behavior of Elaine by virtue of her disability and feels that replacement is practical and not a problem as long as she can afford to do so. Thus, when Elaine is destructive, she is fulfilling what she thinks is expected of her, and she has learned to expect no enduring negative consequences. This has had a significant impact on Elaine's understanding of what it means to be handicapped.

Another example of Elaine's destructiveness is the rate at which she has demolished transistor radios. As mentioned before, Elaine likes listening to the radio. Employees at TRM are allowed to bring radios with headphones to the workshop on the assumption that it may help them concentrate on their work and be less distracted by each other. In recent years, such radios have become quite the fad, and Elaine yearned to have one. She argued that a radio would help her control her emotions better while on the job, and Rachel agreed, including this purchase in Elaine's budget. (Such radios are not cheap, ranging in price from about $20 to $70.) Elaine bought a low-priced radio and proudly took it everywhere, but within a week it malfunctioned, and Rachel suggested she take it back and exchange it for a model that was better made. Sensing a criticism of her own judgment in this, Elaine next opted for the most expensive model at the local drug store. A month later she dropped it in frustration when the batteries ran out.

Within the space of 2 years, Elaine proceeded to go through approximately a dozen radios in similar mishaps, sometimes purchasing cheap models on the sly with money her mother slipped her or with weekly allowance money she had surreptitiously saved, in order to avoid Rachel's displeasure. Eventually, even Liz insisted that she should have no more radios until she learned how to take better care of them. Elaine went without a radio for a few months and then persuaded Rachel she was ready to try again. That time, she made the mistake of loaning her new radio, even against her own better judgment, to a workmate who tore the volume dial off. Rachel decided she did not want to hear one more word about Elaine's radios ever again, perhaps hoping that if Elaine's destructiveness received no more attention, it would cure itself. Elaine again purchased a cheap replacement on her own, arguing, "It's my money." But because Rachel's primary responsibility is monitoring Elaine's finances, customarily down to the last penny, it has proven almost impossible to ignore the continual outflow of cash for Elaine's ill-fated radios.

In late 1988, Rachel abandoned the precise monitoring of Elaine and Hilda's spending habits, although she still limited their weekly spending money allowance, reasoning that their higher incomes made scrutiny less necessary and that they had more or less learned as much as they were going to about this matter. Elaine's apparently destructive tendencies did not cease (e.g., her new dental bridge broke "while it was in my hand, for no reason"), but it is now left up to her to deal with the consequences. Rachel's dilemma has been to decide at what point intervention actually reinforces the very dependency and other negative behaviors she is trying to eradicate.

Elaine's most enduring and possibly serious behavioral "problem" is her handling of money. She often deliberately mismanages money and claims incompetence in budgeting in order to evoke both the attention and the continued commitment to intervention of her counselor. It is important to make clear that Elaine's budgetary problems have little to do with a deficiency in math or any conceptual incompetence on her part. In fact, Elaine seldom makes mathematical mistakes in her computations, being quite adept at using a hand calculator. Unlike her mother, who never reconciles her own checkbook, Elaine has always been intensely interested in precisely how much money is in her accounts, exactly when her Social Security and SSI checks come in, and how much money she is budgeted for her weekly spending needs. Rather, there are certain rules that Elaine simply chooses to ignore. For the most part, these have to do with limitations on her weekly allotment of spending money, as determined by a budget worked out between her and Rachel.

In principle, Elaine accepts the idea of a budget, but she does not wish to accept limits on her weekly withdrawal of cash, even if she does not necessarily spend every cent by the end of the week. As explained previously, this attitude is partly due to her late father's largess, but there are other, more important reasons for its persistence. Elaine knows that she can get money from her mother if her bank account temporarily runs low. She also fears losing her SSI and even has nightmares about that possibility when her recertification comes up each year. The rules of the SSI system make Elaine aware that saving money is not the solution. She knows about the upper limits on how much money she is allowed to have in her accounts and still receive SSI, so accumulating large amounts of money in the bank has never been a goal for her. Furthermore, a major pleasure in her life is spending money. Finally, Elaine feels very strongly that the money in her bank accounts is hers, and she actually desires more independence in handling it, although she does not wish to give up Rachel's help as this might threaten their relationship.

In balancing her need for approval against her desire to do things her own way, Elaine sometimes resorts to subterfuge. She will deliberately botch her financial recordkeeping to mask the fact that she is making her own decisions about spending against the advice of counselors. She was so persistent in this that shortly after leaving the Upward program she was deprived of a checking account and forced to make withdrawals from a savings account only, which were duly recorded by bank personnel in her bank book. Elaine paid bills by taking out money orders. In the long run, this proved to be awkward; the bank kept making mistakes, and in 1988, Elaine's income rose to a point where it made sense to give her more freedom to try a checking account again, because she had accumulated a reasonable buffer of financial security. This was in spite of the fact that Elaine had continued to make "mistakes" and devise excuses to withdraw more cash than Rachel had authorized for her weekly budget. She was invariably caught and scolded, and she would argue again with Rachel about the principles involved. Moreover, Elaine augmented her weekly allowance by borrowing outright from Hilda or persuading Hilda to pay for her in many instances. Both Hilda and Ada objected to the fact that Elaine neglected to pay back her loans from Hilda, and borrowing was henceforth forbidden, although it continues to take place on occasion. Hilda's "treating" of Elaine and her payment of the larger part of grocery bills is harder to deal with because Rachel notices it less often.

Accompanying them several times on their grocery shopping trips, I noticed that Elaine consistently managed to choose groceries that cost less than those paid for by Hilda. (They pay separately for approximately 8 to 10 items each, even though most of these items are destined to be shared by both.) Hilda was aware of this discrepancy because they systematically compared tabs on the way home. She began to monitor her own purchases more carefully. Liz, whose perspective is understandably different on this matter, recently complained that Hilda refuses to put certain items in her cart because she deems them "too expensive." Elaine then puts those same items in her own cart, thus driving up her own bill. Liz said that she did not object to Hilda's frugality, only to Elaine's "Lady Bountiful" response. She asked Rachel and me to help correct this problem, arguing that she could not persuade Elaine on her own.

While Rachel was pursuing her goal of independence for Elaine through fiscal restraint, Elaine had quite a different vision. Her strategies, like using Hilda's resources, to achieve control of more discretionary spending money may superficially appear to be dependent. But one could just as easily argue that Elaine was *independently* pursuing her own agenda and resisting the authoritarian directives of others, although at some cost to Hilda.

When Elaine got her new checking account, she employed another strategy to get more cash than her budget allowed. This time, Elaine was annoyed that Hilda had been allotted slightly more in her weekly allowance than she had, while her requests to Rachel for more spending money were being ignored. When they went to the bank together, Elaine asked Hilda to write an additional withdrawal check for $20 and to give the cash to her "for emergencies." Hilda agreed. Eventually, Rachel, who is also Hilda's counselor, uncovered this and firmly reprimanded Elaine. Elaine argued about her limited spending money, then appeared contrite and promised not to do it again, as usual. But her artful manipulation of Hilda's money had only been a testing of the waters, because shortly thereafter Elaine began to write her own checks for excess cash withdrawals. Why is Elaine so persistent? One could just as well ask why Rachel does not increase her allowance, since her bank balances have begun moving close to the limit for SSI. Elaine's budget has become a test of wills between her and Rachel.

There is a pattern to the timing of Elaine's financial schemes. They invariably happen when Elaine knows that Rachel will not be seeing her the following week. This may seem futile, because Rachel eventually catches up with her, but Elaine undoubtedly wants to get caught, since

she usually tells others what she has done, though still feigning innocence. Her timing contains the real message here: Elaine has become
increasingly angry at Rachel for cutting back on the number of her visits.
Elaine is especially galled that, although Rachel has praised her for her
improvements, she still has not increased the spending money limit and
now appears to be withdrawing from the relationship somewhat. Elaine's
schemes are her attempt to remedy the situation by drawing Rachel back
into the relationship, even if for negative reasons.

Rachel and Elaine's relationship seems to have reached a critical
juncture. Rachel is also explicitly trying to reduce Elaine's emotional dependency on her by withdrawing her presence but not her underlying
guidance. Recently, Rachel made arrangements for another counselor to
alternate with her in visiting Elaine. Rachel acknowledges that Elaine
will probably always need her services, but she says that Elaine's development in some areas has reached a kind of stasis. Stasis, of course, is
what Elaine wants in a relationship, but Rachel (like counselors at TRM
and Regional Center) is professionally committed to a more dynamic
goal of measurable progress towards what is currently defined as "independence." To Elaine, however, her personal relationship with Rachel is
far more important than the skills she learns by being counseled. She
finds Rachel stimulating, entertaining, compassionate, and challenging
in ways that no other friends are.

Hilda used to have her own independent living counselor who saw
her only once every two weeks, compared to Rachel's once a week with
Elaine. Hilda's sole expectation is to receive assistance with her budgeting
and checkbook, in contrast to Elaine, who expects cooking lessons,
shopping expeditions, and generalized trouble-shooting. Since Rachel
took on Hilda as a client as well, Hilda has been seeing her once a week
and is also subject to Rachel's hygiene regimen, household chore schedule, and shopping list suggestions. In such small ways, her independence
may have been slightly compromised, but the presumed payoff is the assistance she receives in improving her standard of self-care. Rachel also
plays a role in mediating her relationship difficulties with Elaine, such as
monitoring and curbing Elaine's habit of "borrowing" money from
Hilda. However, Elaine tends to get more counselor time than Hilda.

It is interesting that, in spite of her family's relative wealth and her
limited experience with budgeting, Hilda is quite frugal. Hilda's penny-
pinching does not mean a lack of good taste, however, for she displays
careful judgment in shopping. For example, when discussing what she
intended to buy Elaine as a birthday gift, Hilda said she intended to take
into consideration the kinds of things Elaine likes, as well as the cost. I
asked what Elaine liked. Hilda replied, "Oh, Jean Naté or something. It's
nice and not too expensive. Elaine likes it." What makes Hilda's judg-

ment and thoughtfulness all the more impressive in this instance is that Elaine had not given her a birthday present that year. (Hilda's birthday is a few weeks before Elaine's.) However, as Hilda patiently explained to me, Liz had given her some perfume, so that had essentially covered Elaine's obligation as well. Characteristically, Hilda prefers to handle her obligations herself.

CONCLUSION

There are two important aspects to aging that have strongly affected Elaine's life. First, her relationship with her mother inevitably began to change after her father's death. They became emotionally closer, in spite of—or maybe because of—living apart. The role reversal that often occurs between adult children and their aging parents is beginning to appear in their relationship. Elaine is very concerned about her mother's health and expresses this in a very mature fashion in her conversations. She speaks as if she wishes to shelter her mother from any undue difficulties or inconveniences. Although Elaine is loathe to spend a night away from Hilda, for example, she agrees to spend the night at her mother's when they attend a family function together so that Liz will not have to drive home alone in the dark. She enjoys displaying solicitous concern for her mother, even though they still quarrel nearly every time they are together. Her emotional and physical distance from her mother has allowed her to be far less dependent on Liz than she was on her father and even less dependent than she is on Hilda or Rachel. Elaine dreads her mother's eventual death and gets anxious and teary-eyed even mentioning it, but the event probably will not precipitate a traumatic change in her current lifestyle. Although Liz is worried about what will happen to Elaine when she dies and was very distressed when the intended alternate caregiver (a cousin of Liz's) died last year, she underestimates Elaine's independence and overestimates her own instrumental importance. Liz will be missed emotionally, but she has not been a very effective facilitator for Elaine's independence during her adult life. Liz has, however, functioned importantly as an advocate of last resort in dealing with the social service bureaucracy, and it is doubtful that anyone else will perform this role with such commitment when she is gone.

The second aspect of aging that is affecting both Elaine and Hilda is the contraction of their physical activities and daily/weekly routine that has occurred gradually over the last 2 years. TRM's move to a new site further from their home has reduced their casual activities in their own neighborhood, where TRM was previously located. Leaving Senior Meals was also a major shift. The club for adults with mental retardation disbanded. Taking the van instead of the bus cut down on their daily exercise and social interaction. Elaine stopped seeing her psychotherapist, who used to be a major figure in her life. Most recently, Rachel and I have begun to withdraw somewhat from earlier levels of intense involvement. The net result is that Elaine is bored. Her demands on Hilda have increased accordingly, putting a definite strain on that relationship, which just might prove to be the last straw for Hilda's patience.

Elaine has had some notable successes in recent years. She has earned praise in her IPP meetings for achieving most of the goals set for her, including the modification of some of her more difficult behaviors. The consensus is that she has matured greatly and has made appropriate strides towards greater independence, occasional regressions notwithstanding. Elaine's counselors are beginning to mute their criticisms of her behavior; her desire to pursue her own vision of "normalization" and "independence" is being given some respect, if for no other reason than that Elaine is smart and persistent enough to continually evade the more onerous demands of others. She may prove to be just as capable of determining what is best for her as anyone else, as the interaction below indicates:

> I asked Elaine to think of some low cholesterol foods. "What about liver?" she asked. I didn't know the cholesterol content of liver, and suggested she look it up in one of her cookbooks. She did, and eventually found some information about cholesterol in meats, but liver was not included. Stumped, I had to admit "That was a very good question, Elaine." "Not 'good'—*intelligent*," she replied with dignity.

Hilda's transition toward independence has been easier than Elaine's. Her trust fund will probably be sufficient to support her for the rest of her life, and she can always depend on Ada or her nieces to handle her affairs. She has always been more sheltered than Elaine from the harsher realities of familial discord and nonfamily rejection or abuse. She has taken far fewer risks than Elaine in interacting with people who are not mentally retarded outside of her own family. Hilda's strict adherence to propriety and rules entails fewer risks too. Elaine's flagrant rule-breaking and rule-testing (e.g., her financial manipulations) do not always constitute dependence. Her manipulations can also be seen as an attempt to define independence in her own terms, however self-limiting this is in the long run. Hilda, on the other hand, prefers a conventional, if dated and limited, model of independence.

Given Hilda's financial and familial security, perhaps it is easier for her to appear more independent than Elaine, at least on an emotional and interpersonal level. Perhaps her challenges have not been as great. But ultimately, it may be Elaine who faces the greatest challenge in the future, that of being without familial support and cast financially and legally adrift in a bureaucratic social service sea.

The relationship between Hilda and Elaine appears to be stable and successful. There are four possible threats to its continuation. The most obvious weak point is Elaine's need for attention and preferential treatment. Her demands on Hilda are very taxing, and Hilda increasingly complains about this. Emotionally, Elaine is more dependent on Hilda than the reverse, and Hilda could conceivably rebel by refusing to be her roommate any longer. Given the emotional and practical symbiosis between them, however, this seems unlikely, at least for the moment.

Another possibility is that a substantial change in financial status or a change in social service policies could deprive one or both of that critical margin of support that currently allows them to succeed independently as roommates. This would most likely occur if Elaine lost her SSI and Medicare, assuming that Liz could not support her independent living arrangement (which she says is the case) and assuming that Hilda and Ada were unable to cover at least part of Elaine's rent and food costs.

Third, they could at some point face eviction from their present quarters or an unmanageable increase in rent. The difficulties in finding alternative affordable housing could temporarily force them to live with their respective families or in more restrictive environments, possibly even separating them to different ends of the city. The "gentrification" of the community has already taken a toll on the numbers of low-income seniors and people with developmental disabilities who can afford to live there. In anticipation of this possibility, Rachel has already begun investigating the possibility of having Hilda and Elaine move to an independent housing project run by parents of adults with developmental disabilities. This would be a more secure living situation, both financially and in terms of supervision, but it would also be more restrictive, because the other tenants already residing there are far less independent than Elaine and Hilda and because there is a resident supervisor with considerable authority to monitor tenants' lives.

A fourth threat, physical debilitation associated with aging, is the factor most likely to compromise the two women's ability to live together independently. This, of course, is a possibility faced by all seniors in our society. Hilda's health appears to be the more fragile, and it may continue to decline quite gradually or a major health crisis may occur some time in the future. Either way, her productivity at TRM will decline to the point where retirement will be inevitable. If Elaine is still working at the time, that will be the first challenge to their continued relationship. But at some point Ada is likely to intervene and persuade Hilda to opt for a more protected, supervised environment with medical help readily at hand.[5] The question then is, will Elaine be willing or able to give up her hard-won independence and move with Hilda? If not, Elaine would suffer a terrible sense of loss, because Hilda is without doubt the most important person in Elaine's present life.

---

[5]After the diagnosis of Hilda's cancer and her subsequent hysterectomy, Ada advocated placing Hilda in a board-and-care facility. Both Hilda and Elaine resisted this suggestion and anxiously raised the issue with me and with Rachel. We discussed the possible ramifications of such a move with them, including not only the likely limits this would place on their independence, but also the fact that no longer living independently would mean an end to their relationship with Rachel or anyone else vendored by Regional Center who might help them retain a measure of their former independence. Rachel suggested that they instead arrange for in-home services to help with housework, shopping, and laundry, while she and her partner would check on them twice a week for shorter visits, just to be sure that all is well. This would alleviate some of the problems that may have motivated Ada's suggestion, and yet still allow them to continue living independently. Regarding Ada's evident anxiety about Hilda's health and welfare, Hilda astutely commented, "She's afraid it might happen to her."

8

"Am I Doin' All Right?"
SAM WISE

*by Hilarie Kelly*_____

Sam was born in New York City on May 31, 1917, and if you ask, he will even tell you exactly what day of the month that was, or what day of the month it falls on for any year you choose. Sam is more than just good at dates, he is a "savant,"[1] able to connect any calendar date to its proper day of the week in any year, even leap years. He was one of several savants consulted by Dustin Hoffman, who played such a character in the feature film *Rain Man*. (This did not greatly impress Sam, although he enjoyed the movie.) Sam loves to perform this calendrical feat and brightens visibly whenever anyone asks him to do it. He will even initiate a problem to solve himself, for example, by asking people when their birthdays are or when major events occurred in their lives. "It makes me feel good," he says, sounding very much like similarly gifted people with mental retardation described by Oliver Sacks in *The Man Who Mistook His Wife for a Hat*.[2]

Sam's IQ is in the low 70s, slightly less than those of Elaine and Hilda. Like them, he can read and write, but his vision is much poorer, making these tasks more difficult, and his penmanship is poor. He is less articulate, largely because of a stuttering problem that makes it hard for him to keep pace in a conversation in spite of a clear, well-projected voice. Sam frequently just sits and listens to others until he becomes bored, at which point he begins to hum softly and rock back and forth to amuse himself. He sometimes even dozes off under these circumstances. Sam often complains of boredom, and a lack of sufficient stimulation has often hindered him. Although he can read reasonably well, he is not

---

[1]The term *savant*, meaning a wise or learned person in French, is now used to refer to people whose conventional intelligence is extremely low—usually persons with autism or mental retardation—but who are nevertheless capable of extraordinary feats of calendrical or mathematical calculation, or in other instances musical or artistic achievement.

[2]Sacks, O. (1970). *The man who mistook his wife for a hat and other clinical tales*. New York: Harper & Row.

nearly as proficient as Hilda and Elaine, possibly because he was never exposed to the same wide range of reading materials due to differences in his educational and residential background. Similarly, his sheltered existence in an institution for 30 years resulted in his being far less worldly than either Elaine or Hilda.

Sam's psychotherapist, Marge, who specializes in treating people with developmental disabilities, is of the opinion that he is *not* retarded, but that his intellectual functioning may have declined over the years and was certainly stunted by institutionalization. Other specialists and observers might disagree, because Sam exhibits some physical and behavioral cues that set him apart. In fact, two researchers for this project independently spotted Sam walking in his neighborhood and recognized him as developmentally disabled before he was identified and contacted through TRM, the sheltered workshop where he worked at the time. However, Marge's point is well taken because Sam's intellectual functioning, like that of Hilda and Elaine, is acute enough to raise questions about the utility of the label "retarded." Like Hilda and Elaine, Sam was socialized to be dependent. Since leaving the institution, he has made remarkable strides toward greater independence, a process that continues.

At the age of 70, Sam is still a reasonably attractive man, and he possesses some endearing qualities that draw people, especially women, to him. He is not very tall and has put on weight in recent years, most of it evident in a protruding stomach, so he has a generally "cuddly" appearance. His preference for being outside in the warm California sun has given his skin a healthy glow, and the combination of luxuriant silver-gray hair with thick, black eyebrows is quite handsome. When not suffering from some specific anxiety, Sam is engagingly friendly. For several years, his eyesight was dimmed by cataracts, which were surgically removed in May, 1988, and he still squints a great deal. One eye has poorer vision than the other, so he often cocks his head to one side while trying to focus. As he concentrates on something in this position, he pulls his lips back into what looks like a large grin. The overall effect of his facial expression is that he looks impishly happy much of the time. His sense of humor, when piqued, matches his jaunty look. If something pleases him, Sam emits a hearty laugh, usually evoking laughter or smiles in those around him. People who like Sam, some of whom help him in various ways, often comment that his sunny disposition makes *them* happy. Sam also displays an acute awareness of certain social graces, and he is routinely polite and considerate of others.

Sam suffers from right-side hemiparesis (muscular weakness) in his upper and lower extremities, which is related to cerebral palsy. This condition, for which he has only infrequently received physical or occupational therapy, has always been one of his biggest obstacles in life. Marge laments that by the time the Regional Center had arranged for an occupational therapist to teach him such things as tying his shoes, he already had a long-established attitude of: "I can't do it." By his 60s, many tasks had become more difficult for him. Sam holds his weak right forearm close to his body with the hand hanging limply at the wrist. The muscles have very little tone, but he can move the forearm and hand slightly, and he is able to grip things between his right thumb and palm. His right leg is markedly less agile than his left, but he walks fairly well anyway, with only a minor rocking motion, not even a limp. He does have mild coordination problems, however, and he greatly fears falling. For this reason, he often likes to have someone take his hand or arm when he is walking. He has some trouble sitting and getting up, especially in cars or low-slung sofas and chairs, a problem now exacerbated by his increased weight. When Sam needs help or special consideration because of these problems, he generally asks for it, something that some of the staff at TRM disapproved of, apparently based on rather rigid notions of what constitutes acceptably independent behavior. This became a major point of frustration for Sam.

Nonretarded people with physical disabilities have been struggling for decades for the right to say *for themselves* when and if they need assistance, rather than having others make that decision for them. Sam feels deeply hurt when he is not given the same consideration. Sam is obviously less handicapped than many others at the workshop who suffer more serious disabilities, especially those who are not ambulatory, but it upsets Sam that he, in effect, is penalized for being better off. Some of the TRM staff apparently assumed that Sam was not making the proper judgments as to when he did or did not need help, and they tried to alter his behavior by discouraging him from asking for assistance at all.

There is some disagreement among the various people who care for Sam as to exactly what he can do by himself. Sam sometimes asks for trivial kinds of help doing things he probably could do himself, although with extra effort, either because the extra effort is a nuisance or because he uses such a request to express the closeness he feels towards someone. An example is when he asks me to help him take some change out of his coin purse, something he does for himself every time he takes a bus. However, some workshop staff also underestimated how difficult Sam's paralysis really makes certain tasks. An example is handling food. Sam tried both bringing a packed lunch to the workshop and purchasing food from the catering truck. He found it very difficult during the lunch break to unwrap and open things, cut certain foods into manageable portions, or juggle items while walking from the catering truck. As it was, breaks were brief and chaotic, and Sam was often delayed getting a space at the table or a place in line at the truck. Because he is ambulatory and nonspastic, he did not merit special assistance from staff, as workers with more severe physical disabilities do. So he asked for help from Elaine, Hilda, and even some staff members. He was sometimes scolded by particular staff persons for this "dependency" on his friends and urged repeatedly to "Do it yourself!" At one point, the workshop's director suggested he obtain a tool called a "rocking knife" that might help him do these things for himself, but this was never followed up. Lunch breaks became such an ordeal for him that he eventually ceased eating lunch at all, something the staff failed to notice.

However, on other occasions, Sam was instructed by counselors to seek assistance from staff or others. As recently as his 1987 Individual Program Plan (IPP) meeting, the issue of when and whom Sam should ask for help at TRM was still being thrashed out, as these fieldnotes make clear:

> Sam has long complained that he has trouble opening beverage cans and bottles, yet he is reluctant to ask others to do this for him, unless they are friends (like Elaine and Hilda) or authority figures he perceives as being responsible for his welfare. He is loathe to bother people he sees are "too busy," and is easily hurt by refusals. When the issue arose once again today, Marge, his psychotherapist, commented: "Sam grew up in the old days when they opened bottles for you, and when machines had bottle openers in the front that you only needed one hand to use." Joyce [former acting director of TRM, more recently Sam's Regional Center caseworker] once tried to persuade the owner of his residential hotel to teach Sam how to open containers for himself, but the owner declined, arguing that he didn't need that particular skill at Exeter because all beverages are served in glasses or cups. Marge pointed out that Sam is usually put off by the TRM staff whenever he asks for any help from them, so it was suggested he be encouraged to ask the catering truck personnel to open beverage containers for him. It was unclear how receptive the catering truck staff would be to such a request, with other employees crowded around clamoring for service during the brief breaks. No one acknowledged that Elaine and Hilda often help him at lunch break or suggested this as a remedy, although with the changed lunch schedule this year, they are not always on the same lunch shift as Sam anyway.

> Another example of Sam's dilemma regarding whom and when to ask for help arose, this time concerning what happens on the assembly line when Sam runs out of materials. His TRM counselor reminded him today to ask specially designated client-monitors for new materials when this happens, rather than wait until a staff person notices he's not working. Marge noted that TRM used to allow Sam and the other employees to replenish materials on their own and surmised that Sam may have trouble recognizing and approaching his fellow employees as authority figures (especially since they are usually appointed only temporarily), and that he may feel stigmatized having to ask them for assistance when some of the other employees continue to help them-

selves. No discussion of these possibilities followed, and the TRM counselor continued to instruct Sam to ask for more supplies from the monitors.

In past IPP meetings, Sam was always advised to talk to his counselor whenever he was confused or upset because otherwise he tended to brood and subsequently "act out" his accumulated rage by yelling and slapping himself. Sam has exhibited such rages, periodically, for most of his life. For many years he has been taking Mellaril (thioridazine), ostensibly to help control these rages. Mellaril is an antipsychotic drug that can produce side effects, including confusion, short-term memory problems, disorientation, and impaired attention. In other words, the drug exacerbates behaviors that lead others to label Sam "retarded." He has also been seeing Marge for several years to help him deal with feelings of frustration and anxiety stemming not only from his present life but also from his past.

Sam is often unduly worried about "saying the wrong thing," and sometimes even cuts himself off in mid-sentence with the comment, "I'd better not say." In so doing, he seeks to avoid the anger of others. "She [or he] might get mad," he says, or, "I like to keep things to myself. It's better that way." Sam has stated that he first developed this attitude in response to his mother's critical behavior towards him during childhood and that his attitude was reinforced throughout his life in various institutional settings. By suppressing his own opinions and feelings, Sam only temporarily delays self-expression. He has a strong personality, with definite likes and dislikes, and he is easily agitated (or as Sam puts it, "excited"), so it is not surprising that his emotions occasionally burst forth as anger or tears. In Sam's 1987 IPP meeting, it was noted that these acting-out episodes were no longer occurring at the shop, but, ironically, by that time his retirement was already a foregone conclusion.

Sam feels it is very important to have someone with whom to discuss his feelings, and in the last few years, he has continually bemoaned the fact that his various counselors spend less time talking with him than in the past. Although he sees his psychotherapist for only 15 minutes every two weeks, these visits are very important to him and have a salutary effect, like "recharging his batteries," Marge says. Having trusted confidants is a central concern in Sam's life, even if they are not intimately involved in his life on a day-to-day basis. His desire is based on a very special relationship he had with his father.

SAM'S BACKGROUND

Sam adored New York, and would like nothing better than to visit there again, something he sadly acknowledges probably will not happen because, he says, "Nobody will take me." Sam's love for New York is partly tied to fond memories of his childhood there and the associated memories of his father, whom he also adored. "He was *all right!*" says the 70-year-old but still-very-boyish Sam. Sam is also passionate about life in New York because he found it exciting. The hustle and bustle of street traffic, the skyscrapers, the massive landmarks—he loved them all and, by comparison, finds his current West Coast environment sadly lacking. If he sees cosmopolitan images in a movie, on television, or in a magazine that remind him of New York, he immediately exclaims with pleasure, "New York!" even if it is really Chicago or Tokyo. Sam's father used to take him to Rockefeller Center and Radio City Music Hall, and very little in his experiences in California can compare to those thrills of youth, now enshrined in his memory.

Sam does not remember much about his family life because he spent most of his life first in a boarding school for children with mental retardation based in the state of New York, and then at Maplewood, an institution for people with mental retardation in Pennsylvania. The boarding school changed venue to Florida every winter, from November to May. Sam remembers with glee the train trips back and forth, and how wonderful the Florida beaches were. (He swam as a youth, "but no more," he admits wistfully.) From the school, he went home on holidays for a week during Christmas, on his birthday, and once every 3 months for a break. Sam took the train by himself to and from Grand Central Station, another beloved landmark that he often recognizes on film and in pictures. The high points of his life were when he saw his father, who took him to the places in New York that he remembers with such excitement, especially the "shows" at Radio City Music Hall. Sam has always loved music, and to this day, he remembers an impressive array of songs and tunes from that period of his life, many of which are included in his large record collection, his most cherished possession.

Sam's parents came to see him occasionally at the school as well, as did two other favorites, his Uncle Otto and Aunt Francis, who visited once a month. "They were very nice to me," he recalls with obvious pleasure at the memory. His family phoned him about once a month. This pattern of family contact continued when he was at Maplewood, except that his aunt and uncle came less frequently, until they both passed away. Sam's sister and brother never visited, and Sam and his siblings never had a chance to develop a close relationship until he left Maplewood, much later in life.

Sam remembers his father as loving, gentle, and very compassionate. "He told me I could always talk things over with him. I could say anything I want, and not to be afraid. Anything. I could talk to him. It made me feel better." "Talking things over" with someone has always been extremely important to Sam, because he tends to be overly sensitive (or exhibits "frank paranoia," according to his psychotherapist's reports) and is often fearful of expressing himself until he finally begins to "act out" his frustrations. According to a 1981 report, taken from early records of his residency at Maplewood, "He was diagnosed as having a passive dependent personality disorder and was known to have rapid mood swings, changing from laughter to tears within a matter of seconds." Sam is very eager to please others, especially authority figures, or at least to avoid their censure. When out with me for a social occasion, he frequently seeks reassurance by asking, "Am I doing okay?" or, "Did I do the right thing?" I have heard him ask Hilda and Elaine these questions as well, and they always respond by fondly and enthusiastically praising him. If he goes out to eat with someone, he always either insists on paying for himself, explaining, "I feel better that way," or he asks if it is expected that he pay for himself. When others pay for him, he says, "At least I'm willing to do it myself. At least I asked."

Sam has a tendency to focus on compassionate yet distant figures whom he remembers as having talked especially kindly to him and who let him talk in return about his concerns. Although many people like Sam and show him compassion, these more distant figures hold special importance for him, perhaps because they were not with him consistently enough to display boredom, impatience, or criticism. His father is one such figure, and another is the first researcher in this project who interviewed him. Although she only saw him three times in 1985, she made an indelible impression on him. When suffering anxiety, Sam may suddenly ask, "Where's Mary? I want to see Mary. May I see her some time?," or "Have you seen Mary? How is Mary? Will you tell her I was asking for her?" The inquiry functions as a kind of personal mantra to calm him down. In explaining why he is so fond of the woman, Sam explains, "She talked to me just like my father." There are several other people in Sam's life who spend much more time talking with him, people whom he loves to be with. But few seem to reach the heights occupied by his father and Mary in Sam's esteem.

Sam does not express a high regard for his mother, whose temper contrasted sharply with his father's patience. "She was always fighting," he recalls. Sam saw his father as an empathetic ally against this apparently quite intimidating woman. This is demonstrated in a comment Sam once made in the context of a conversation about Elaine. When discussing Elaine's insistence on tagging along with Sam and Hilda on their Saturday dates and her annoying habit of never being ready to leave the house when Sam and Hilda wish to, I suggested that Sam simply take

Hilda's hand and walk out the door with her, leaving Elaine behind. Sam was doubtful that this would work, but he laughed at the idea and recalled with glee:

> My father did that once. My mother was fighting and yelling, and my father just took my hand and walked out. That's what he did. Oh boy. We just left her there and went by ourselves. My father was *all right!*

Sam's sister Ann corroborates his opinion of their mother: "She was very difficult, arrogant. Sam was scared of her." Ann also noted that their mother was the major reason for Sam's long estrangement from his siblings. "My mother was very embarrassed about Sam. She could afford to put him in an institution, so that's what she did. Most of our friends never knew we had a brother." Like Elaine, Sam was the firstborn, and Ann astutely observes that there was little counseling available at the time he was born for parents of children with mental retardation to help them deal with feelings of shame, guilt, frustration, and inadequacy. Sam was 3 or 4 years old before his disabililty was diagnosed, and Ann recalls that there was some uncertainty about what had caused it. "There were so many stories; I don't think they ever really told the truth." She remembers one story in particular that had the delivering doctor injuring Sam with forceps, and so she assumes that a birth accident probably caused his disability. She said that Sam's startling rages, which began when he was young, precipitated his being sent away to school and then to Maplewood.

Before Sam entered Maplewood, he had a traumatic sexual encounter (designated a "homosexual rape" in his records) at the age of 17. This happened in New York City, while he was on his way home alone one afternoon. Sam used to take the subway by himself, and he remembers such independence with joy. (Perhaps that is how he developed his exceptional sense of direction.) He was approached by a male stranger who forcefully convinced Sam to go home with him. It is not clear if Sam had any idea what the man intended, but once they arrived, the man beat Sam about the face sufficiently to leave swollen bruises and cuts. Sam is not specific about the mechanics of what happened, and he becomes very agitated and nervous in talking about it in any detail, except to say that the man "did dirty things" and detained him until 8:00 P.M. "You won't tell anyone at the shop, will you?" he pleads, when he discusses this incident. Sam claims that he had no further encounters "like that" ever again. If there were any sexual shenanigans at Maplewood, Sam is not saying. He giggles embarrassedly at the mere thought.

Like Elaine, Sam will repeat his rape story more than once to the same person, on different occasions, with little variation, and without necessarily being asked. This behavior may be an artifact of their cumulative experiences with numerous counselors, all of whom have socialized them to relate such painfully intimate details with minimal reticence. Perhaps that has been cathartic and has helped in their psychological healing. However, both Elaine and Sam were permanently scarred by the experiences in two ways. First, whatever interest they might have had in sex is now associated with coercion and the shocked reactions of their families, who of course treated these experiences as a crisis, and second, Sam and Elaine are both afraid of men. Sam's marked preference for associating with kindly, solicitous women masks a darker aversion to interacting with adult men, especially those who are aggressive. When Sam refers to someone as "the man," without using any name or pronoun, this is usually an indication that he fears or dislikes that particular man, especially if he feels that man has treated him unkindly or unfairly. There are some men Sam does like, such as a former director of TRM who was widely regarded as saint-like in his devotion to the clients. Sam also likes the young man who supervises the Salvation Army dances, who always greets Sam enthusiastically, brings him extra refreshments, and gives him a ride home. However, these men have clearly been extraordinary in their solicitousness towards Sam.

Sam's fear of men may have affected him at Maplewood, where he was housed in an all-male section. When asked whether he had friends there, Sam replied, "No. They were all the same to me." This fear of men probably also affected his roommate relationships at Exeter, the retirement hotel where he now lives. Sam's only male friend at Exeter is Al, with whom he has never been roommates. They sometimes sit in the lounge together to watch sporting events on television, or sit outside in the patio to enjoy the fresh air. Al is jovial and very nonjudgmental, and he takes the time to chat amiably with Sam. Unlike Sam, Al does not get out much because of ill health, so keeping company with Sam is an important source of entertainment for him. (Sadly, Al was recently hospitalized, and upon his return to Exeter was still quite weak. "He doesn't talk much anymore," Sam regretfully noted.) Sam has not yet made any male friends at OPTIMA, his senior day-care center, where the only male alert enough to converse with him has an abrasive style and instead torments Sam with unkind "jokes."

Sam entered Maplewood in 1946 at age 29, and left in 1977—more than 30 years later. His memories of the place are not very detailed or elaborate. He worked as a mailman there, a job he loved and was apparently good at. The job allowed him to ramble about the place greeting people, something he has always loved to do, with his mannered and courtly salutations. In spite of his fear of men, Sam was popular at Maplewood, at least among staff. Sam hates having nothing to do, and boredom makes him terribly depressed, so he actively seeks out people, even crowds in which he just sits on the sidelines. Asked what he liked best about life at Maplewood, he unhesitatingly replied, "The movies." Films were shown twice a week. He also remembers that residents sometimes put on performances, singing and dancing. He claims he has never performed, but he admitted that he could sing when a woman friend at Exeter lavishly praised his ability. When requested to give a demonstration, Sam chose to sing "My Country 'Tis of Thee," which he rendered in a clear and steady voice, much in contrast to the stuttering that marks his ordinary speech. He later repeated this performance in front of a large audience for a talent contest at a Salvation Army dance, where he won a prize for his effort.

It is amazing that 30 years of a man's life could have passed so uneventfully, but even so, Sam says he liked Maplewood "all right." Curiously, Joyce (former TRM administrator and later Sam's Regional Center caseworker) suggested that Sam might have been better off if he had stayed at Maplewood because of its purportedly rich social environment. Perhaps by comparison, Exeter looks bleak and uninspired to others, but Sam has made it abundantly clear that what he values about his life now is the freedom to go wherever he wants and not to be confined to a residence. He does not regret leaving Maplewood one bit. His sister, Ann, who eventually became his conservator and arranged to have him taken out of Maplewood, argues that Sam's development was stunted by living there because "absolutely everything was done for him." Mary, Sam's favorite researcher, recorded in her notes:

> Ann says it's frustrating because she knows if Sam had been born today that a lot more could have (and would have) been done to help him be independent. She definitely believes that he is capable of being a lot more independent.

Ann has repeated this to everyone she knows with an interest in Sam, suggesting that she wants to distance herself from the original decision to institutionalize Sam, but she also lets it be known that, as a consequence of institutionalization, her burden in caring for Sam later in his life has been made more difficult. Like many other family caregivers, she welcomes any assistance that will help Sam avoid complete dependence on her.

Sam's mother died in 1976, and Sam's father, who was very ill himself, moved to California to be close to his daughter, Ann, who resides there with her husband. Sam's father lived in Exeter. When his condition went into a steep decline, Ann and Daniel, Sam's brother, decided the time was right to bring Sam out to California. It was getting to be too expensive to keep him at Maplewood anyway, on the small trust his grandparents had set up. Besides, Pennsylvania was too far away to be sure he was receiving proper care. Sam arrived just as his father slipped into a coma, so there was no real final reunion. Still, Sam is glad that he was able to be there when his father died. Like Elaine and Hilda, he wanted to face squarely the death of his beloved parent, not be shielded from it. It was a turning point in his life.

BECOMING INDEPENDENT

After their father's death, Sam's brother and sister became responsible for him. Sam fondly remembers his younger brother, Daniel, with whom he was reunited from 1977, when Sam left Maplewood, to 1980, when Daniel died. "He was very good to me. He took me for rides." Although Ann is currently Sam's conservator, he only sees her once a month (at most) for a home-cooked meal or an occasional shopping trip. She does not attend his annual IPP meetings, unlike Hilda's sister, Ada, and Elaine's mother, Liz. Ann is concerned but somewhat distant, saying, "I'm not terribly good with him yet. I'm not patient. My husband is much better. But he works weekends, so he doesn't have much time for Sam." Ann, an articulate and intelligent woman, praises Sam for his "remarkable memory" and ability with figures, and she notes with some pride that most people who meet Sam like him. She does feel satisfied with the progress that Sam has made since leaving Maplewood, and she likes to think that her no-nonsense approach might have contributed. "I treat him just like another adult. And he tries, he really does. He often says, 'Daddy would be proud of me.' "

Ann and Daniel decided that it would be most convenient to keep Sam at Exeter, where he had been staying since his move to California. Exeter offered Sam a much less restricted environment than he had had in years, and he was already enjoying the proximity to the beach and the freedom to come and go as he liked. The facility is small (no more than 15 units), slightly cramped, and quite old, but well maintained. It is located in a fairly up-scale neighborhood, only a few blocks from the beach. Sam adores the beach and the bustling yet relaxed atmosphere of nearby parks and shopping areas. He spends most of his free time away from Exeter, taking bus rides to his favorite haunts and to visit Hilda and Elaine. He does not like to stay at home much, he states emphatically. This is partly because he simply enjoys going out, but there are also some more negative reasons. The supervision of some staff members, especially those whose impatience he perceives and takes personally, makes him very self-conscious. (One staff member, however, is a special friend whose company he enjoys greatly.) Additionally, he is not entirely comfortable with roommates, of which he has had several. One died, one was transferred to a convalescent hospital, and two or three harshly criticized him for petty things like snoring, watching television or listening to music too late or too early, and turning on the bathroom light late at night, until he was moved to other rooms. Sam is actually unassuming, considerate of others, and easily intimidated. Exeter staff placed the blame for these problems on the roommates, difficult men who were themselves having trouble adjusting to life in a board-and-care facility. They had been placed with Sam precisely because of his mild character, but he suffered from it. In 1988, Sam was finally given a private room, much to his delight, even though it was on the second floor and this meant negotiating the stairs. Sam's right-side paralysis makes this difficult, but he has so far managed successfully.

Sam's room at Exeter came furnished with a bed and a low table. All rooms have a private bath. He has his own chest of drawers, in which he hides his most personal possessions. These include pictures of his family and friends at TRM and OPTIMA and a diary. His most prized possession, however, is his large record collection of big band music. When he is at home, he enjoys listening to music on his record player. So as not to disturb others in the residence, he uses headphones. He also has a television on which he watches the news. He sometimes joins other residents in the common television room, especially for sporting events like baseball games. Compared to Hilda and Elaine's abode, Sam's room appears spartan and much cleaner. Of course, the housework is done by Exeter staff.

Ann, who is perhaps mildly defensive about Exeter's seediness and lack of stimulating activities, remarks that not many other places would accept Sam as a resident, not only because of his mental retardation but also because of his difficulties with roommates. She ascribes these difficulties to Sam's "faults," for example, his habit of having the television and phonograph on "late" at night (up to 10 or 11 P.M.) and early in the morning (6 to 8 A.M.), although she later acknowledged that Sam routinely uses headphones out of consideration for other residents. Ann also comments, "If you're a normal human being, you can't have much of a conversation with Sam," apparently unaware that Sam's roommates have been far less articulate or conversationally inclined than he.

Although Sam was happy to stay at Exeter, he was bored without the routines and job he had had at Maplewood, so Ann sought out the assistance of Regional Center, which she had heard about through friends who had relatives with developmental disabilities, and she subsequently enrolled him in TRM. To Sam, the workshop seemed a much more familiar environment than it did to Elaine or Hilda. It was reminiscent of Maplewood, except that both men and women attended. It is interesting to speculate that Sam's late-life blossoming may be especially gratifying to him because, for the first time in 30 years, he at last has had the opportunity to freely enjoy the company of women of his own choice.

Although Sam's boyish innocence is not the least bit suggestive of burgeoning sexual interest, he certainly expresses robust delight in the company of a wide range of special women friends. These include not only Elaine and Hilda, but also favorites from OPTIMA and a senior recreation center he visits on Sundays, as well as Joyce, an instructor at TRM, the woman in charge of the Salvation Army dance, and a nurse and a fellow resident at Exeter. The diversity of his female friends may have been a major reason why he felt some concern initially at Hilda's largely symbolic possessiveness, at least until she wisely reassured him that she did not mind his friendships with other women at all.

Sam is not comfortable with all women, however. He deeply distrusts those who are distinctly not warm and solicitous of his welfare. Two examples are a former counselor at TRM and one of the other nurses at Exeter. The former counselor, Deana, is a very attractive and fashionable woman of a basically pleasant disposition. She is proper, professional, and well mannered, but undoubtedly overworked as well, and the result is that she had less and less time to spend listening to Sam's concerns. Before leaving TRM, Sam said, "I don't like Deana like I used to. She's changed. She doesn't talk to me too much anymore."

Charged with the task of acclimating him and many other workers to the many new changes at the workshop, Deana's patience was often stretched, and it sometimes showed. Beseiged, she felt it was all she could do just to get clients to comply, even if that meant issuing strident commands and brooking no requests for reassurance. This was cause for considerable complaint among dependent personalities like Sam and Elaine, who was also one of her charges. Deana took Sam and Elaine's complaints as further evidence of inappropriate dependency, and she became increasingly distant and abrupt with them. Sam ended up being thoroughly intimidated and discouraged by the new workshop routine. This was a major reason he was willing to leave the workshop for OPTIMA. He had as much given up hope at TRM as TRM staff had given up trying to retain a place for him there.

Sam's feelings about Deana were also affected by the fact that she is black. He has somehow developed a mildly suspicious attitude toward black people. "Black people don't listen much," he says. He also complained repeatedly about two of the black male instructors at TRM, whom he felt were unduly harsh with him to the point of persecution. Both instructors were especially adamant about Sam doing things for himself, but, like Deana, they seemed to like Sam nonetheless. Perhaps Sam felt a bit threatened by the hearty, "can-do" style of these instructors. During this period, staff were themselves pressured to implement new policies regarding productivity and "normalization" that discouraged the kind of catering to clients' personal needs that had previously been allowed. Sam is, in effect, comparing the behavior of Deana and the two black instructors to his nostalgic memory of the less industrialized "old TRM," when Joyce and the former director presided over a more school-like workshop and had the time to extend more caring, personalized attention to clients. There has been an increase in the number of black staff persons working at TRM since the workshop moved to its new location and became more industrialized, possibly strengthening Sam's tendency to associate black staff with his growing sense of malaise there.

A second example of Sam's problems with women who do not respond well to his dependent personality is highlighted by the differences in his relationships with the two night nurses at Exeter, Grace and Amy. Grace is on duty the nights that Amy, Sam's favorite nurse, is not. Amy is warm and motherly, and she enthusiastically interacts with Sam not just as a client, but as a friend. Sam helps Amy by going to the store for her on small errands, and he plays board games with her to keep her company on slow nights. They meet and chat on the bus sometimes, and she has shared information with Sam about her life away from the job. They even quarrelled once, when Sam refused to abide by Amy's professional orders as a nurse, but this incident actually strengthened their relationship because Sam is convinced of her fundamental concern for his welfare. Sam only has access to such a relationship because of his physical disabilities and the kind of residential care facility in which he lives, where he is able to see Amy 8 hours a day, 4 days a week. Sam's special relationship with Amy is largely a personal friendship, but its friendly, personal character is not intrinsic to the nurse's job, as Grace, the alternate nurse, has made abundantly clear.

Grace is Amy's opposite. She is brusque, uncommunicative unless critical or giving orders, uninterested in Sam as a person, and even resentful of his presence. She apparently sees him as nothing more than extra work, and not simply because of his dependency needs. She even becomes annoyed at him when he demonstrates independence. For example, if he goes out and does not come back until after dark, he knows he will be locked out if Grace is on duty. This is because she likes to lock the building early and retire upstairs, unlike Amy, who leaves the front door open much later. When Grace does have to open the door for Sam at night, she is decidedly surly. She ridicules him when he is upset about something, accusing him of being a "baby," and crudely pokes fun at him for getting fat, something he is extremely sensitive about. It is absolutely clear that this woman simply does not like Sam and does not care who knows it. Sam observes, "Grace doesn't know how to act. Sometimes I see her on the bus and I say 'Hello, Grace,' but she never says anything. She always sits way in the back then. She makes me feel sad." Yet Sam is so determined to avoid confrontation with her that he will deliberately arrange his schedule so that he is home on the nights that Grace is on duty, in order not to come into conflict over a locked door. He then keeps to his room as much as possible to avoid her. Conversely, he will elect to go out occasionally on those nights when his favorite nurse Amy is there, even if it means missing her good company, simply because he can be sure there will not be trouble when he returns. Sam has said many times that, apart from his past roommate problems, Grace is the main thing he does not like about life at Exeter. Because he values his life in this community, however, he deliberately avoids antagonizing her as much as possible, and he is unfailingly cordial and polite to her. Considering this difficult situation, Sam has shown considerable diplomatic skill.

Sam once agreed to try living in another board-and-care home in another city, one which offered more services and activities than Exeter. Joyce had thought perhaps he would be more busily occupied there than at Exeter or TRM, where it was always difficult to find appropriate tasks for him to do. However, she had underestimated the importance to Sam of the total environment surrounding Exeter, which he dearly loves moving around in on his own initiative. She also underestimated the importance of a job to his self-esteem. Sam hated the placement in the home, which was very restrictive, and he soon moved back to TRM and Exeter. He was so upset by this experience that he usually refuses to talk about it. Joyce, gracefully recognizing her mistake, assured Sam that he would never be forced to move again. And when it came time to phase him out of TRM and into OPTIMA, she was very careful to discuss this thoroughly and to engineer a gradual transition.

There is a woman resident at Exeter, Patrice, with whom Sam has a very delicate relationship. Patrice came to Exeter because she had seizures. She seems slightly frail and eccentric, but she still plays the pretty coquette, and she has taken a liking to Sam. Patrice often sits in the evenings with Sam and Amy, and Sam agreed to walk with her every night to the nearby Catholic church. She flatters him and makes a special effort to converse with him about things she knows are of interest to him. Sam finds her appealing and her company enjoyable, but he is a bit bewildered by her vulnerability, which she seems to overplay in the manner of a southern belle. It seems doubtful he would respond sexually to any of her friendly, feminine overtures. When asked if he has ever had any girlfriends, Sam replied, "No, they might get you into trouble." When asked what kind of trouble, Sam said, "People get murdered on television." To Sam, sex, even with women, is fraught with danger. His attitude may derive in part from the sexual trauma he suffered as a boy, but it is likely that his fears of heterosexual sex have also been affected by television and film, as his comment suggests, and by the rules at Maplewood and at TRM against overt, flirtatious behavior toward members of the opposite sex.

In TRM reports on Sam and in reports from his psychotherapist, repeated mention is made of the fact that Sam prefers to socialize with staff (at whatever institutional setting he is in) rather than with "peers," and recommendations were often given to change this. The major positive incentive, as far as Sam was concerned, to leave TRM entirely and attend OPTIMA 5 days a week was the fact that at OPTIMA he was not discouraged from interacting with staff. Sam's preference for OPTIMA staff, and theirs for him, is understandable in light of the low functional capabilities of most of the other, nonretarded seniors who attend.

It is important not to assume uncritically that the most appropriate "peers" for a person with mental retardation are invariably other people with mental retardation or other disabilities, or that seeking social contact with staff or other authority figures necessarily translates into dependency. Sam's patterns of sociability often call these assumptions into question. Sam's friends include other people with mental retardation, like Elaine and Hilda, as well as various counselors and other nondisabled people who take a special interest in him, like Amy and the couple who supervise the Salvation Army dances, and nondisabled seniors, like Patrice and a woman he met at Boardwalk Senior Center, a popular senior center at the beach. The variability of his friendships has enriched Sam's life, as he has enriched the lives of others. As with Elaine, the process of transforming counselors, staff, and other nondisabled people who help or notice him into friends is part of Sam's idea of "normalization."

Even when he chooses authority figures as friends, Sam is less concerned about status than with their sensitivity and capacity to genuinely like him and with their inclination to take time to listen to him. It is not surprising that higher functioning people with mental retardation such as Sam and Elaine might find relations with those who take a professional interest in them more stimulating than relations with most other people with mental retardation, who may have their own preoccupations. It is because, in many respects, Sam and Elaine *want* to be considered "normal" and independent that they choose as their friends people who *are* "normal" and independent. Hilda fits less into this mold because she is more emotionally independent and reserved than either Sam or Elaine, having fewer close friendships of any kind.

Sam clearly appreciates the instrumental aspects of his friendships with authority figures and other nondisabled people who facilitate his independence, but he is far less manipulative than Elaine in this respect. Sam is not above asking for favors, however, or even engaging in some mild manipulation himself. For example, while eating ice cream at my house one evening, Sam asked, "Do you have a phone?" He knew the answer was yes, but because he never initiates phone calls himself (not having his own phone at Exeter), he clearly was not intending to use it on his own. Then he commented, almost offhandedly, "Elaine and Hilda are home tonight. They haven't gone to bed yet; it's still early." This was a clear hint that he hoped I would call the two women and arrange to take Sam to visit them. When I did not immediately respond, Sam straightforwardly and unabashedly said, "I'd like to visit them tonight, just for a while. Okay?" Such requests have become more common since his retirement from TRM because his opportunities for seeing the two women are fewer.

Yet Sam does not wheedle, whine, prevaricate, invent crises, or throw tantrums like Elaine, and thus appears to be much less emotionally dependent on others than she is. His friendships with authority figures and other facilitators seem less deliberately asymmetrical than Elaine's. For example, even in IPP meetings, Sam was far more animated and took part in the discussions more independently than do either Elaine or Hilda, who behave more submissively. Sam sometimes refers to himself as a "student" at TRM, OPTIMA, and even Exeter (where he also refers to other residents as "students"), while Elaine consistently refers to TRM employees, herself included, as "kids." This is more than a semantic difference. While Elaine, at 58, still often behaves in a decidedly childish fashion when confronted with authority, Sam approaches authority figures as potential mentors, confidants, obstacles, judges, and dispensers of favors, but without sacrificing his integrity as an independent adult.

THE TRIANGLE REVISITED

Sam likes both Hilda and Elaine. Elaine is certainly the more stimulating of the two women, and Sam often responds to this. Sam and Elaine also have several things in common. They are both originally from New York, and both like to reminisce about their childhoods there. Sam and Elaine were apparently encouraged to appreciate music while young, and they each still use music to calm their emotions. When old songs are played, both Sam and Elaine frequently sing along. At one time, Elaine was also seeing Marge, Sam's psychotherapist, so the two would sometimes compare notes on Marge's services. Both Sam and Elaine are from Jewish backgrounds, but this seems to mean little to them. In spite of the commonalities between Sam and Elaine, in the long run Hilda's calm, nurturing qualities put Sam more at ease, and he has gradually come to regard her as his girlfriend and to feel more loyalty toward her than toward Elaine.

Partly because he knew it would upset Hilda, Sam says, he did not engage in special friendships with any of the other workers at TRM. In truth, though, none of the other female workers there showed any inclination to be as supportive and genuinely helpful as Hilda. Her wisdom about "the way to a man's heart" has been correct; no one else bakes brownies and cookies or buys packages of his favorite fig newtons especially for Sam.

Elaine rarely mentioned Sam in her diary, but Hilda's entries were replete with his name. A typical one from 1987 reads, "I met Sam on the bus this morning. We talked together. He told me won a prize at Bingo. Sam and I talk together at break, lunch and break. We enjoyed talking together during the day."

Although Hilda and Elaine's relationship is in some ways like a marriage and is of primary importance to both of them, it is also true that Hilda and Sam's relationship is getting stronger. Since Sam retired from TRM, his weekend visits to see Hilda have become the only opportunities they have to see each other regularly. This has made Hilda even more sensitive to Elaine's overbearing intrusiveness, described in the previous chapter. Sam too is becoming increasingly upset at Elaine, even to the point of tears. Elaine herself seems to be forcing the issue by persisting in her old trick of staying in her pajamas until well after Sam has arrived, thus delaying their outing but refusing to let them go without her. Although Sam likes Elaine, he complains about her bossiness and her insistence that the three of them do what she wants to do, rather than what Hilda and Sam prefer. For example, Elaine often insists that, instead of taking a walk, Sam and Hilda must accompany her on clothes shopping expeditions, one of her favorite activities, but one that the more budget-conscious Hilda and Sam find less pleasurable. Sam comments:

> I'd like to go with Hilda alone. Every time I want to go to Briarwood [a neighborhood where he likes to walk around with Hilda, get some ice cream, take in the sights], Elaine thinks she's the boss. Elaine always tells Hilda what to do. She always wants to get clothes. Sometimes she's not even ready. She always wants her own way. Not me. I'm not that way, am I?

Sam is sometimes moved to tears by Elaine's obstinacy, and he occasionally goes home early in a huff, but he and Hilda have not had any luck walking out on Elaine, as they are both easily intimidated by her threats and histrionics. Sam recalls, "I tried that once [leaving without Elaine.] It didn't work. She said, 'You're *not* going.' I don't know. She might holler. She might tell her mother."

OPTIMA

Sam was shifted gradually to the senior day-care center and into retirement from TRM. He was convinced in April 1987 to attend OPTIMA two times a week, just to see if he liked it there. He did like it because, in contrast to TRM, he was given much more attention by the women volunteers who worked at the center. Not only was Sam's natural charm an attraction, but, as mentioned previously, many of the other clients are far less interesting or responsive than Sam.

OPTIMA is located in a park within easy busing distance from Sam's home. He is pleased that the center is located in the same park where Elaine and Hilda used to attend their Thursday-night club meetings and that it is in a familiar neighborhood near their home. Sam had never cared to attend the club meetings, and they were indeed a bit juvenile for his particular tastes. He used to excuse himself by saying that he did not like going out at night by himself, but this was not entirely true because on summer nights when there are free concerts at the mall or the pier, Sam always attends. The real reason for his reticence is probably that no favorite authority figure ever personally escorted him to his first club meeting, to help him get acquainted and to familiarize him with the bus route and the club routine. (Sam has shown similar reticence about joining social activities planned by Rachel, Elaine and Hilda's independent living counselor.) In spite of Sam's disinterest in the club, he feels his attendance at OPTIMA in the same park gives him one more thing in common with Hilda and Elaine, and the park is another topic of conversation that excites their mutual interest.

By August 1987, Sam had agreed to attend OPTIMA full time. As mentioned earlier, his departure from TRM was something of a relief to him by that time, even though he still misses certain individuals. Sam's ties to TRM were not broken completely, however, because Elaine and Hilda continue to carry messages to and from Sam and his friends at the shop, and because Sam sometimes runs into his favorite TRM staff person, Audrey, at the beach on weekends. Sam also took two women staff members from OPTIMA to TRM to show them around. One of the women is his favorite counselor at OPTIMA, and she seems to have taken a special interest in him. She had heard him talk so much about the workshop that she thoughtfully suggested the trip. The other woman has a son of her own with developmental disabilities and was interested in the possibility of putting him in TRM once Sam told her about it. She even persuaded Sam to go with her a second time, together with her husband, so that they could make a final decision. Thus, Sam had the joy of visiting the shop once again, returning victorious, so to speak, with his new friends at the same time that he was performing a kind of service. To his great delight, he was greeted enthusiastically at TRM on these occasions by both staff and former co-workers. He even introduced the visitors to Hilda, whom he bravely identified as his girlfriend, to her everlasting satisfaction. Sam's transition seems to be complete, perhaps because he can feel that he always has a "place" at TRM, even if he is not physically there.

Sam arrives at OPTIMA every day at 10:00 A.M., much later than he had to be at the workshop. He leaves at 3:00 P.M., approximately the same time he used to leave TRM. Asked what he does with his extra time in the mornings, he happily reports that he now has more time to watch the news on television and to listen to his records. "I like to take some walks sometimes too." It is clear that Sam's move to OPTIMA has not left him depressed, as might be likely for some individuals who retire from a job to attend a senior day-care center. But then Sam is not self-conscious about the external trappings of success that could influence another man's self-esteem in the event of retirement; rather, Sam is more concerned simply about how he feels, and that is largely contingent upon having varied opportunities, especially for companionship with caring people.

Not all the activities at OPTIMA appeal to Sam, but he sits patiently, enjoying just being there, until something does interest him or someone on the staff offers to play dominoes, cards, or another game with him. He especially likes it when someone plays a record that he recognizes, at which point he exclaims with real pleasure, "I know that!" and starts to sing or hum along. His fondness for chatting with the staff is not discouraged, both because there is a very high staff-to-client ratio and because Sam is such an engaging attraction himself. Because the attention spans of many of the other clients are so truncated, activities are changed frequently, meaning that Sam has more activities from which to chose, and he does not have to sit for long periods doing nothing. However, in spite of the fact that Sam is not yet bored with this and does get lots of individual attention, he is definitely being under-challenged, and many of the skills he does have from his experience at TRM (and even from Maplewood) are being under-utilized. Perhaps in time, he might seek additional activities outside of OPTIMA.

INDEPENDENT LIFE

Sam does many things with his free time when he is not at TRM, OPTIMA, or Exeter. He adores taking bus rides around the city, and on holidays he will sometimes plan jaunts to distant locations just for the challenge and fun of the bus trip. He spends his evenings walking along the palisade above the Pacific Ocean, enjoying the exercise and hoping to run into someone he knows, which frequently happens. He regularly prowls the neighborhood mall, shopping for records to add to his collection, getting himself a haircut at his favorite barbershop, going for ice cream at his favorite coffee shop (where they are especially generous with the portions, he says), and just enjoying being in the crowd. On some Saturdays, if he does not visit Hilda and Elaine, he walks to the shuffleboard courts at a nearby beach-side park or takes long bus rides. On other Saturdays, he may visit his sister Ann and her husband at their home. Although he appreciates the visits and the meals Ann always prepares for him there, he complains, "She never takes me anywhere." He is most pleased with her when she takes him for a drive somewhere. On Sundays, Sam takes the bus to the Boardwalk Senior Center at the beach. He gayly greets his friends there, especially those who have made the effort to get to know him. Sam listens to the musical entertainment they provide and then joins them for lunch, usually bagels and cream cheese, which he loves. Afterwards, he sits out on a boardwalk bench in the sun and watches the crowds of roller skaters, surfers, tourists, and inner-city toughs walk by. His special delight on such days is to run into his various nonretarded friends down on the boardwalk. He remembers such casual meetings long afterward, reassured that their interest in him goes beyond the structured settings and relationships in which they met.

Since coming to Exeter, Sam has kept a daily diary in which he records what he does each day. He says he likes to go back and read it from time to time, to remind himself of all the things he has done. "Remembering" is one of Sam's favorite activities. He keeps his diary secret, hidden in his bureau along with his small cash reserve. Sam also keeps a small box of photographs of his family and various friends in his bureau, along with his electric shaver, which he is proud of being able to use himself. Fortunately, in spite of the unlocked doors on the rooms, Sam has had only one item stolen in all his years at Exeter—a watch that had belonged to his father, and its loss seemed to have caused him only momentary distress. (He has two others, one to wear and one as a back-up in case the other breaks.) The issue of lockable doors at senior residences is a controversial one. Sam cherishes his privacy, but like many other seniors in similar residences, he is not entirely capable or inclined to do his own cleaning or bedsheet changing, so staff members need to have access. Furthermore, the medical assistance required by many residents makes easy access by nursing staff necessary and is another reason given for not locking doors in some facilities. Owners usually claim that it is too much trouble to provide duplicate keys for each resident's door to all the necessary personnel. Nonetheless, Sam has said that he would prefer to have a lockable door, even though he never had one in boarding school or at Maplewood.

Sam is a somewhat secretive person, a quality that seems important to his sense of personal control and integrity. His sister gives him a small amount of spending money every month (he says $20–$40; she says $50), which Sam manages entirely on his own. The small amount makes banking it impractical, so he hides it in his room. (Sam used to use the bank only for cashing his TRM paychecks; now he has no need for banks at all.) Sam is usually able to save money from month to month, and he enjoys planning some especially desirable purchase. He adds to his record collection regularly from this meager budget, but he is a careful buyer. "I don't spend my money right away. I hide it. I put it in an envelope in one of my diaries and put another book on top of it." However, unlike Elaine and Hilda, who until recently had to relate their spending habits in elaborate detail to their independent living counselor, Sam does not report back to Ann how he spends his money or if he has any left over. "The less said about it, the better," he says resolutely. Ann is aware enough of his habits to comment, "God knows he has plenty [of money]. He seems to be very wise about money, though neither of his parents were." Once, when Sam's electric shaver broke the same week he planned to get a haircut, Sam was mildly distressed at the resulting cashflow problem, but he refused offers of a loan from Elaine, Hilda, and me and successfully juggled finances entirely on his own. Although he no longer receives TRM paychecks, these were never very large, and the fact that he is given a "free" lunch and snacks each day at OPTIMA allows him to save money that used to be spent at the TRM catering truck.

Another example of Sam's secrecy is that when he shares his feelings with me or Elaine and Hilda, he frequently asks, "You won't tell anybody, will you?" or he will mention someone specifically whom he does not want told. His secretiveness may have been cultivated while in residence at the boarding school and at Maplewood, where privacy was at a premium.

> I have to watch myself. I keep my problems to myself. Once I told Mrs. S. [the owner of Exeter], and she told Grace. Grace told everybody I'm a crybaby 'cause I worry. I'm better off if I keep problems to myself.

And yet, Sam often does want to share his problems with selected others. "When I feel sad, it brings tears to my eyes. I say to myself, I wish I could talk to somebody."

In terms of self-care, health, and aging, Sam has somewhat less control than he might be capable of or would like. A nurse at Exeter gives him a bath each Saturday, and he has to have help tying his shoes because he cannot bend that far or use both hands to do it himself. (This is one task some caregivers think he could do himself, but no one yet has been able to have him do it.) He sometimes has help dressing. To Sam, a grocery store is like a foreign country, because meals are always prepared for him. He only shops for clothes on the rare occasions when his sister takes him to augment his spare wardrobe, and he sometimes complains that she overrules his preferences. Sam always attempts to look well groomed, but his clothes are sometimes worn, spotted, and poorly laundered. He is supremely proud when sporting a new haircut or new clothes, makes sure he is always well shaven and as clean as he can manage, and likes to wear men's cologne. He was absolutely delighted when a woman who was visiting another resident generously splashed some expensive and heady cologne on him before an evening out with Hilda, Elaine, and me. Besides his watch, the only other jewelry he wears is equally functional—a military-style "dog tag" with his name, address, phone number, sister's name, and her phone number on it. Several years ago, Joyce arranged for some TRM clients to get these in case they got lost, injured, disoriented, or into trouble. (Elaine and Hilda do not wear tags, but Elaine wears a medical bracelet warning of her allergy to penicillin and sulfa.) Sam wears his tag constantly, and he does not seem to think it demeaning or a reflection on his competence.

Unfortunately, Sam has two minor hygiene problems. The first is related to his history of prostate trouble, which cause him to frequently experience an urgent need to urinate. (He plans outings with a mind to having access to bathrooms.) In the urgency of the moment, his physical limitations in dressing himself sometimes result in a urine residue on his clothes, which in turn can cause an unpleasant odor. The second hygiene problem concerns his teeth, which are worn down to stubs because of bruxism, his habit of grinding them while both asleep and awake. Although he has not yet required any special treatment for this condition (he sees a dentist every 6 months), his mouth often emits an unpleasant odor. Sam insists he brushes his teeth regularly, but his teeth and gums may be sensitive from grinding, so it is likely that his brushing is less than thorough. Sam does not appear to be conscious of these hygiene problems.

Medical and dental care is arranged through Sam's sister and Regional Center with the cooperation of Exeter staff. Although Sam used to have a number of health problems and had four hernias and a prostate operation, as well as cataract surgery, he is now in remarkably good shape for a man of his age. He shows little interest in and generally avoids thinking or talking about his past medical problems, which were, at the time each occurred, a major source of anxiety to him. Hilda and Elaine gave Sam considerable moral support when he nervously faced the prospect of cataract surgery. They reassured him by pointing out that Elaine's mother had recently had the operation herself and had "come through it with flying colors," as did Sam. His major health concerns at present are high blood pressure, for which he takes medication, and a weight problem. Much to Sam's dismay, his doctor nags him about losing weight and has enlisted the support of Ann, Exeter, and Joyce. Marge, his psychotherapist, disagrees, arguing that the psychic trauma is not worth it. "What's it going to get him? One more year of life? Come on, leave him alone. Give the guy some pleasure." Sam is an enthusiastic eater, always exclaiming "Oh boy, this is good!" whenever taken out or given special treats.

Sam does take some responsibility for watching his weight. For example, he always uses a sugar substitute in his coffee, has cut down to one purchase of ice cream or frozen yogurt a week, and genuinely tries to eat more healthy foods. However, the intervention of others rankles him. It pains him to be reminded of his weight problem and especially to be told not to eat something when he is so inclined. He became quite upset when Grace loudly reprimanded him one evening in the communal dining room for having four sandwiches on his plate and then proceeded to take away two. On the weekends, Exeter serves a hot dinner at noon, and a light supper of sandwiches in the evening. Knowing Sam had only had bagels and cream cheese for lunch, on this occasion the cook had sympathetically given him four sandwiches. Sam insists that he was only intending to eat three, and he was thoroughly humiliated by Grace's behavior. Sam is also displeased with his sister for no longer sending him sweets, such as his favorite fig newtons. To get around this, he has encouraged Hilda and Elaine to buy these for him, but he only eats them when he visits at their apartment. Just as Elaine regards food as an important form of self-indulgence that reaffirms her self-worth, Sam regards food as an important source of comfort, entertainment, and well-being.

In spite of his age, Sam appears to be quite robust, and he reports that he feels fine physically. Indeed, he is rarely ill, not even suffering from colds as frequently as Hilda and Elaine. However, he has a tendency to deny illness or any other debilitation beyond his paralysis. For example, when cataracts bothered him to the point that he could barely read a newspaper or even do much work at TRM, he played this down and resisted the idea of an operation for some time. Like Elaine and Hilda, he appears not to think much about aging, physical decline, or death, and all three individuals have said explicitly that they do not like to talk about these things. Sam sometimes gives the impression of being confused or vague about certain details, which may momentarily suggest senility. He has exhibited this same behavior for years and may have always done so, but for the most part he displays a good mind for detail. (As noted above, the Mellaril that Sam takes may be partly responsible for these lapses.) For example, on looking at a photograph of Elaine, he did not recognize her at first. We were alone, and a few seconds later he anxiously asked "Where's Elaine?" as if urgently expecting me to materialize her or take him to her. He gave the impression of being vaguely disoriented. Yet, a few moments later, he recognized a picture of himself and made the acute observation that in the slide, which was projected backwards, his left arm appeared to be paralyzed, when, in fact, it is his right arm that is disabled.

Although Sam reads the newspaper and watches news on television, he has a limited awareness of current events unless they involve something he is particularly interested in, like the 100th birthday of Irving Berlin or who won the Dodgers game. Ann believes he "doesn't really" read the paper or watch television. He is, however, merely very selective about what he pays attention to. He is vague and naive about some things. For example, he always refers to TRM simply as "the shop," never uses the term *IPP* but always refers generally to "meetings," and has asked at the beginning of these meetings what words like "goals" mean. On the other hand, Sam was always proud of his ability to get to and from TRM every day on the bus by himself, was keenly sensitive about his own role there, and participated constructively in his own IPP meetings even if he did not use the official jargon.

Sam's attentiveness is further demonstrated by his obsession with time. He is always punctual, makes sure to ask more than once when events are scheduled or his presence is required, and frequently looks at his watch and checks his time against other people's watches. (His precision regarding time may be related to his calendrical feats.) There is no clear evidence that Sam is deteriorating either mentally or physically.

However, it is reasonable to be concerned about what will become of Sam 5, 10, or 15 years in the future. As he heads towards his 80s and 90s, his health will have to be monitored more closely, and this task will fall to those who spend considerable time with him on a daily basis, such as the OPTIMA staff and the Exeter nurses. It is apparent how important Sam's relationships with these people are to his future, which is another reason not to assume he is cultivating an inappropriate dependency. Marge fears that Sam's most serious problem as he ages is likely to be boredom and depression, conditions common among the elderly. She hopes this can be alleviated by continued social stimulation and entertainment.

It will be interesting to see if Sam's relationship with his sister deepens at all in the coming years. She is a few years younger than he and thus will probably continue as his conservator until the end of his life, barring unforseen circumstances. She has thought about the issue and feels her adult son or daughter could assume the responsibility if necessary. Ann says she expects Sam to live a long time, as his father did. Will she feel excessively burdened by his aging, and might this take a negative toll on their relationship? Like Elaine's mother and Hilda's sister, Ann has only infrequent and perfunctory contact with Sam's battery of counselors and others who figure prominently in his life. As Sam ages, if more of the burden of caring for him shifts to Ann, who can she turn to for experienced advice, moral and logistal support, or any other kind of assistance? She may find such burdens difficult, and this may limit her willingness to become further involved in Sam's life than is absolutely necessary.

The trust fund that supports Sam was established by his grandparents before 1925, when it seemed adequate, but its value has been subsequently eroded by inflation. Ann is therefore acutely cost-conscious. She is reluctant to increase her burden of arranging benefits for Sam beyond what is fundamentally necessary. She feels at a disadvantage in negotiating with the bank trustee in New York, as she is not a parent but a younger sibling and one who had little experience in managing Sam's affairs until recently. The bank sends her money for him each month, some of which she passes on to Sam as allowance, while the rest is used for his pharmaceuticals (amounting to about $100 per month) and clothes. Apart from that, any expense to be drawn from the trust must be cleared with the trustee. For example, when Sam was finally moved from a shared room at Exeter to his own room, this had to be cleared with the bank because it involved a substantial increase (67%) in cost per month. This was offset by Sam's retirement from TRM, which had been billing the trust, albeit at a discounted rate due to Joyce's recommendation. Joyce also arranged a waiver of fees for Sam's attendance at OPTIMA because of his limited finances.

However, Ann's economizing is not just a practical issue, but also relates to how Ann copes with her perceived responsibilities towards Sam as a relative. Four examples will be given here. First, in commenting on Sam's love of new clothes, Ann recalls that their father used to take Sam to Saks Fifth Avenue to buy clothes, including suits, when the family still lived in New York. After their father died and Ann became responsible for taking Sam clothes shopping, she wanted to take him to less expensive stores and to buy him cheaper, more casual clothing, insisting that he did not need such fancy attire on the West Coast. It was a major struggle, she admits, but at last he agreed. He now dresses up only on special occasions, such as the Snowflake Ball, when he manages to look positively elegant. (Sadly, he did not attend last year because he was reluctant to ask Ann for the money.) It is tempting to speculate on whether Ann's recollection of their father's doting generosity towards Sam did not spark some remnants of sibling jealousy, a common problem in families with members with handicaps.

On another occasion, Marge suggested that Ann enroll Sam in a travel program for adults with mental retardation that would have allowed him to visit New York for a very reasonable price, but Ann declined. Undoubtedly aware of Marge's disapproval of her decision, Ann insists that, financially, "the trip was out of the question," and defensively claims that she discussed this with Sam, who subsequently said he did not care. Sam's response to the situation is typical of his desire to avoid conflict with someone who is so instrumental to his survival and continued independence. However, he still frequently mentions the issue of a trip to New York, reviewing over and over his sister's arguments that he no longer knows anyone there and his own reluctant acquiescence to her decision.

For some time, Marge has suggested to Ann that Sam be given a videocassette player to be paid for by the trust or as a gift, because he loves movies so much and this would be more economical in the long run than regular visits to a movie theater. Ann has not done this, arguing that he never really pays attention to films or television anyway and usually just falls asleep. Instead, she purchased an audiocassette player for him and gave him many of her old music cassettes. This seemed like a good idea, but Sam stated flatly that he did not want the cassette player and refused to take it home. He explained that he already has a record player, which he likes just fine. Sam's attitude is typical of his resistance to something new, but such mild technophobia is not uncommon even in the non-disabled population. A patient and gradual introduction of Sam to the mysteries of audiocassette players would probably win him over.

Ann underestimates the joy that Sam derives from film and television. Even if he does doze off on occasion, there are bits and pieces to which he responds intensely. Similarly, Ann says, "Sam is not interested in reading anymore." Yet he does read brief bits now and then, even out loud, and his joy in doing this has certainly increased since his eye operation, suggesting that he only lacks appropriate materials. Ann further mentioned that she had once given Sam a typewriter with which he had written them letters, but that, like the reading, "he let all that go." Yet she seems unaware that he daily writes in his diary, laboriously and by hand. Ann is inclined to adopt an all-or-nothing view of Sam's capabilities and inclinations, perhaps because communication between the two of them is infrequent and, according to both, sometimes tense.

These first three examples of Ann's style as conservator also reveal another interesting point—the potential for disagreement between kin and non-kin caregivers, an issue that has also arisen between Elaine's mother and Rachel, her independent living counselor. A fourth example of Ann's behavior, however, reveals an entirely different dynamic. At birthdays and on holidays, Ann arranges for Sam to give gifts to people who have helped him, like Marge, Joyce, Amy, and even Grace. She also arranges for small money gifts in the form of bonds from his trust to be sent to his nieces and nephews. Ann says that Sam has the final say and veto power over these gifts and that if he does not want to give to a particular person, she follows his wishes. More to the point, though, Sam is delighted at being a gift-giver, and he delivers them to the recipients himself, even though he is not the one who selects or arranges for the items. This accomplishes two very important things for Sam. First, it partially balances out his relationships with those who have helped him throughout the year, thus bolstering his sense of dignity; and second, it strengthens his relations with the younger generation in his family network, who might some day be in a position to help him if Ann no longer can. Thus, although Ann recognizes that she herself may have difficulties relating to Sam, she clearly understands the importance of nurturing his relations with others who facilitate his independence. In this sense, she is very much like Elaine's mother, Liz.

As with Elaine and Hilda, Sam has been sheltered his entire life from the necessity of controlling his own finances (beyond minor personal budgeting), and this continues to limit his independence, and theirs, as it is defined in "normal" adult society. It is ironic that, in practical terms, Sam's relationship with his sister is more dependent and yet more socially distant than either Hilda's or Elaine's relationship with sister and mother respectively.

CONCLUSION

The question then remains, "Is Sam independent?" He certainly thinks he is, and in comparison to his lifestyle in his youth, he unquestionably is. Although Exeter provides him with certain support, including prepared meals, house cleaning, laundry, and assistance in bathing and dressing, it could be argued that under Sam's particular circumstances, considering his physical disability, these services are the equivalent of the kind of assistance Hilda and Elaine receive from Rachel, their independent living counselor. These services may facilitate rather than detract from Sam's independence. Sam potentially could be taught how to perform some of these tasks for himself, but that possibility raises other, difficult issues. Marge and Joyce argue that there is little to be gained from insisting that, at age 70, Sam learn to perform menial tasks he would always have some trouble with anyway. Regarding his residence in a relatively protected environment like Exeter, his financial constraints mean that he would have trouble finding adequate, completely independent housing in his price range, and he almost certainly would have to have a roommate, something very difficult for most elderly men to accept. As mentioned previously, Sam has had a number of problems with past roommates at Exeter, based on their difficulties adjusting to the living arrangements and on his own fear of men.

Unlike Hilda and Elaine, Sam was never assigned an independent living counselor, who presumably would be the appropriate person to teach him basic housekeeping tasks and monitor his performance. This was partly because his residence at Exeter made an independent living counselor seem superfluous. However, there are many other aspects of independence that Sam can and does enjoy that a counselor could help him with, whether he lives at Exeter or elsewhere. An example would be introducing him to new and more stimulating social activities. Sam himself has stated on more than one occasion that he is jealous of Hilda and Elaine because they have Rachel and he has no similar person to discuss his problems with and to help him work through the routine challenges of his life. (Marge, his psychotherapist, deals more with emotional than practical issues and sees him only in her office.) Unfortunately, the decision not to provide Sam with an independent living counselor seems to have been based on the erroneous assumption that Sam is not capable of independence. Without the encouragement of such a counselor, this assumption has become self-fulfilling in certain respects, but by no means all.

Sam feels he is a success, in spite of various setbacks and limitations. Those authorities who facilitate his independence are no doubt important, but how truly critical any one of these are to his success is open to question. For example, Sam continues to see his psychotherapist, Marge, two times a month, as he has since moving to California, to help him deal with his emotions. Marge also used to see Elaine regularly, but unlike Sam, Elaine tried to further enmesh Marge in her life through incessant phone calls and manipulative behavior, strategies she employs with several other important figures in her life, including me. Marge resisted and Elaine eventually precipitated a break with Marge, full of angry fireworks over her unmet emotional demands, but in reality, this event was a declaration of independence by Elaine, indicating that she was going to start facing her life with one less authority on whom to depend. Marge regarded this as a victory and so did Elaine. Sam has shown no sign of making such a break and may never do so. But one should keep in mind that there are a lot of lawyers, stockbrokers, and entrepreneurs who see psychotherapists without calling their independence into question. Sam's case demonstrates that it is not the presence or absence of authorities or other facilitators that makes or compromises independence. Rather, it is the net effect on an individual's opportunities to make choices for himself or herself. Sam has made it clear that he makes his own choices.

Sam's story should be a reminder that achieving and maintaining independence is a life-long process, complete with ups and downs, setbacks and giant leaps forward. At any given point in Sam's life, we might attempt to measure the level of independence he has achieved, but that point-in-time judgment of his "success" would not be nearly as interesting or important as the total picture, in all its ambiguous and fluid complexity. It is encouraging to think that, at age 70, Sam still has the potential to enrich his life further.

Conclusion

by Robert B. Edgerton——————————————————

The most important conclusion we can draw is a seemingly banal one, which in reality is quite important. It is fitting that the most lasting impression these vignettes of older people leave with readers is the individuality of these men and women, not their commonalities. The lives of these older persons with mental retardation are highly varied, and if we are to understand them as people, we must recognize that in many ways each one of them is quite different from every other. It is important to recognize that neither they nor the lives they have led should be reduced to generalities about "older mentally retarded persons." No single set of services, no simple drafting of policies can begin to serve the needs of these many individuals, either now or in the future. Unless we take this message to heart, we are in danger of formulating solutions for aging people with mental retardation that will create more problems than they resolve. This cautionary note aside, most of these people and their lives do have some things in common, and in these closing remarks we shall comment on what they share with one another and perhaps with other older people with mental retardation.

Even our brief descriptions of nine such complex yet different people could easily generate scores of topics for more general discussion, and some readers may find it useful to pursue some of these many leads, but in these brief comments, we want to stress four particularly widespread and important findings: 1) Despite everything, these men and women have learned to live rewarding lives. 2) Although they have needed the support of others, they have contributed much to others in return. 3) The greatest danger they must face is growing ill health and the lack of adequate medical care. 4) The idea of these men and women zealously searching for independence is more illusion than reality. What they search for is well-being, and that may sometimes mean surrendering autonomy to gain security.

Like older Americans in general, these older people with mental retardation usually express satisfaction with themselves and their lives. Often they say that they are happier than they were when they were younger, and they are optimistic about what the future will bring. They live under all sorts of conditions, have many kinds of personal relationships, and enjoy different things. Some have worked for a living all their lives, some have worked only occasionally, and some have never held a job at all. Some are remarkably cheerful while others are anxious or depressed. Some have quite limiting intellectual handicaps while others appear to have nearly normal intelligence. Some are physically attractive and robust; others are unattractive or physically handicapped. But whatever they are like as individuals and whatever the conditions of their lives, they share this fundamental accomplishment: They have found ways to live rewarding lives. In doing so, they have repeatedly shown courage, strength, and a zest for living. This we saw time and again; even the morose Martha finds life worth living. They have also shown concern for others. In many ways, all of these people have given their time, energy, and resources to other people. The extent to which people with mental retardation contribute to the well-being of others has not been adequately documented. In reality, they not only often help to support relatives, friends, or acquaintances, but they highly value the opportunity to do so, and many would welcome the opportunity to do more. The ways in which these older people contribute to the happiness of others deserve emphasis. Older people with mental retardation may be exploited, but they are often a part of the support systems of other people, mentally retarded and nonretarded alike.

Although these older people are not simply passive recipients of help from others, it cannot be denied that they do receive help and that such help can be vital. Most of the individuals described in this book, like many other older persons whose lives we have studied, came from broken or very troubled families whose surviving members have been unable or unwilling to provide much support. They have had to find support elsewhere. When SSI or Social Security benefits are available, these are of enormous value to older people with mental retardation, but the income they supply cannot provide encouragement, reassurance, or good advice, nor can it solve the difficult interpersonal problems that sometimes arise. For help with solving life's emergent problems, friends or relatives may be necessary, and as people with mental retardation grow older, so do the people who support them. When these people become incapacitated or die, the loss of their support can create severe problems.

It would be a mistake to undervalue the strengths and accomplishments of older people with mental retardation—they are real and admirable—but it would be foolish to deny that as they grow still older, clear danger signs emerge. The greatest of these dangers is ill health. If serious illness or growing physical infirmity cannot be prevented, the nearly inevitable outcome will be the loss of independence. Without major improvements in the continuum of available care options, most older persons who experience serious illness or physical debility will find themselves in nursing homes or similarly restrictive residential facilities. For individuals who have struggled for so long to live primarily on their own resources, such an outcome would be terribly dispiriting.

Ill health and physical infirmity cannot be prevented altogether among the elderly; that is self-evident. But at least for those older persons whose lives we have discussed in this volume, the likelihood of serious illness and resulting physical debility is unnecessarily increased by the difficulties that many of these people have in obtaining effective medical care. Regular health care that might prevent the occurrence of serious illness is uncommon. For one thing, unless the older person is eligible for Medicare or Medi-Cal (California's Medicaid plan), regular visits to a physician are likely to be prohibitively expensive. And even when a person does have Medi-Cal benefits, it is increasingly difficult to find a doctor who will accept Medi-Cal patients because of reductions in the payments Medi-Cal will approve, as well as restrictions on forms of treatment and the length of hospital stays. And those physicians who will accept Medi-Cal patients may be inaccessible unless the older person has a friend with a car who is willing to drive them to a distant clinic.

As a result, preventive medical care is available to relatively few older persons with mental retardation. Indeed, some persons may not recognize the need for regular visits to a doctor. As we have seen, some people with potentially life-threatening symptoms may not seek medical care because they simply do not understand that they are in danger.

Even when older people with mental retardation do visit a physician, they often benefit little from the care provided. Some cannot effectively communicate their concerns to the doctor, some cannot fully understand the doctor's instructions, and some who can communicate well and understand what they are being told nevertheless receive perfunctory care from disinterested doctors. Some doctors routinely overmedicate older patients, as was the case with Elaine, Hilda, and Sam. Others fail to perform routine diagnostic procedures, as for example, when Hilda's doctor neglected to order a Pap smear for a period of 10 years. Some doctors make few efforts to monitor patient compliance with their prescriptions; in addition, those patients who cannot read have great difficulty complying with doctors' orders for taking prescription medications because most pharmacists continue to label medications as if all patients were literate.

Because the issue of aging and ill health is so important, an example from the life of Ted Barrett may be useful. Although we have not included a chapter about Ted in this volume, we know more about him than anyone else we have studied (e.g., Whittemore, 1986[1]); he is the subject of a film that examines the problems of aging mentally retarded people, (Marlow, 1988[2]), and a book (Langness, 1990[3]). Now age 61, he has an IQ in the low 50s; as this would suggest, he has significant intellectual limitations, including an inability to read or make use of elementary arithmetic. Yet he has great charm, resilience, and perseverance. Since leaving Pacific State Hospital over 30 years ago, he has lived on his own, often holding several jobs at once to make ends meet. As the years passed, we have chosen to describe his life as a model of adaptive success by a person of limited intellectual ability. Street-wise, tough, blustery, yet kind, gentle, and loveable, he is a paradoxical example of a man who has managed to cope with a complex central city environment despite his obvious limitations. To be sure, people have helped Ted along the way, but he has also helped many others, so many in fact that he is the center of a circle of friends who depend on him for kindness, joviality, and, most of all, money, which Ted liberally doles out no matter how little he can afford it. As a result, he appears to many to be a tower of strength, a man who has made it "outside," as he puts it, a man who is loved, admired, and respected.

This image, like most of its kind, is only partly accurate. Ted has many self-doubts, some having to do with his intelligence, others with his declining masculine powers. Although he never married, Ted has long boasted about his sexual prowess, and there have in reality been many women in his life. In recent years, these women have been prostitutes, and with growing distress, Ted has complained about sexual impotence. He is eligible for Medi-Cal, but the only available physician in his neighborhood was an Asian woman who, out of embarrassment, refused to listen to his sexual complaints while otherwise attending to his physical condition in an obviously perfunctory manner. Admittedly, complaints of sexual dysfunction are not assured of an attentive hearing by doctors who deal with aging poverty patients, but Ted's complaints about serious pain in various parts of his body have not always received serious attention either.

Even when Ted has seen other doctors who have carried out appro-

[1]Whittemore, R.D. (1986). Theodore V. Barrett: An account of adaptive competence. In L.L. Langeness & H.G. Levine (Eds.) *Culture and retardation: Life histories of mildly mentally retarded persons in American society* (pp. 155–189). Dordrecht, The Netherlands: D. Reidel Publishing Company.

[2]Marlow, F. (Director). (1988). *Manatic* [Film]. University of California, Los Angeles, CA: Socio-Behavioral Group.

[3]Langness, L.L. (1990). [Theodore V. Barrett]. Unpublished manuscript.

priate diagnostic procedures, he has often not complied with their treatment advice because he has not understood what they told him to do. For example, just as Richard Jarrett did not understand the relationship between his obesity and heart disease, Ted does not understand why rapid weight gain may worsen the pain in his arthritic knees. Also, despite several protracted attempts to explain the dangers of AIDS to Ted, he still does not understand why he should avoid sexual relations with prostitutes who use drugs intravenously. Even when Ted has understood doctor's orders, he has often not been able to comply because he cannot read the instructions on the medications he is given.

Declining health threatens the lives of some and the independence of many. In these respects, aging people with mental retardation do not differ from the rest of us, but because they lack access to quality medical care and stable sources of social support, they are in even greater jeopardy than the general population. If ill health leads to the loss of independence, many will bitterly resent their new dependence, but we should not conclude from this that independence is the highest goal for aging mentally retarded people. Independence means different things to the people in this book, but for most it is but one consideration among many in their pursuit of happiness. Many are more than willing to sacrifice some of their independence in return for greater security. In the preceding chapters, we saw various degrees of insistence on independence and many ways that people accept or even seek dependency in the search for greater security.

Unlike the people we wrote about in the first six chapters—those who had been living on their own for such a long time—those in the last three chapters (Sam, Hilda, and Elaine) were new to the experience of relative independence. For them, independence was something to ease into, as it is for so many younger people with mental retardation who find themselves newly introduced to a world that pretends to offer independence. For most of these people, young as well as old, independence is not the critical issue. What matters most is the quality of life they can enjoy. Independence is a concept much discussed by professionals and parents. They worry, and rightly so, about the relative ability of their clients or children to live without professional or parental support. Persons with mental retardation may come to value independence, even overvalue it, and when they do, the result can be cruel disappointment because independence is so seldom attained. The lives of persons with mental retardation may indeed be judged as more or less independent by certain objective criteria such as residence or employment, but all lives are interdependent, and as we have seen in the lives of the older persons described in this book, independence as such is rarely a central topic of discussion. Indeed, independence is not a term they use very often, and when they do use it, it can mean various things.

What these people care most about is making the best they can out of their lives, and that means acquiring access to desired resources, primarily in the form of helpful persons, without surrendering their right to do as they please with their lives. Money is important, so are living conditions, friends, and many other specifiable things, but most important, seemingly, is each person's determination to maintain his or her freedom of choice. Each person described in this book realizes that it is sometimes, even often, necessary to seek help from others, and although these people may provide badly needed assistance, with that assistance may come unwanted advice, restrictions, or interference. When this happens, the person with mental retardation must decide, like the rest of us must, whether we need someone's help badly enough to surrender some of our autonomy. What is central in the lives of these older people is the search for well-being, and that search involves an ever-shifting calculus that attempts to balance freedom of choice against the need for the help of others. We may choose to gloss this calculus as a dialectic between freedom and security; if so, security and freedom are inevitably in tension with one another. It may be more accurate to construe the central dynamic in the lives of these people as a search for happiness in which each individual sometimes surrenders some freedom of choice in order to deal with a vexing problem or circumstance. Depending on one's life circumstances, some individuals must yield more of their freedom than others, but we all must surrender many freedoms, and we must all learn to live with this inescapable reality. No matter how many freedoms we must surrender, we cherish those that we retain, and older mentally retarded people, no less than the rest of us, place great value on some aspects of their lives. It is these things that give their lives value, and it is these things that they strive to protect.

Those of us who are concerned about the well-being of older people with mental retardation should recognize that what they value in their lives has an intrinsic worth and do what we can to protect their freedom to choose or maintain what they value. Older people, who are so likely to have their freedoms taken away when they fall ill or seem to falter, should be helped to maintain for as long as possible the quality of life they have chosen. As much as possible, every one of us should have the opportunity to choose his or her own way of life. For the aging people with mental retardation among us, that will require changes in the availability of health care, housing, and recreational activities, as well as changes in the way we think about aging people in general. If these changes can be made, they will benefit not only people with mental retardation, but the rest of us as well. The key is to acknowledge their right to choose and to resist our temptation to decide for them.

Index